All Stories Are True

All Stories Are True

HISTORY, MYTH, AND TRAUMA IN THE
WORK OF JOHN EDGAR WIDEMAN

TRACIE CHURCH GUZZIO

UNIVERSITY PRESS OF MISSISSIPPI / JACKSON

*Margaret Walker Alexander Series
in African American Studies*

Publication of this book was made possible, in part,
by a grant from the State University of New York
and the Plattsburgh College Foundation.

www.upress.state.ms.us

The University Press of Mississippi is a member of
the Association of American University Presses.

Copyright © 2011 by University Press of Mississippi
All rights reserved
Manufactured in the United States of America

First printing 2011
∞
Library of Congress Cataloging-in-Publication Data

Guzzio, Tracie Church.
All stories are true : history, myth, and trauma in the
work of John Edgar Wideman / Tracie Church Guzzio.
  p. cm. — (Margaret Walker Alexander series in
     African American studies)
Includes bibliographical references and index.
ISBN 978-1-61703-004-8 (cloth) — ISBN 978-1-61703-
005-5 (ebook) 1. Wideman, John Edgar—Criticism and
interpretation. 2. African Americans in literature. I.
Title.
     PS3573.I26Z68 2010
813'.54—dc22   2010044961

British Library Cataloging-in-Publication Data available

Contents

vii	ACKNOWLEDGMENTS
3	INTRODUCTION
15	CHAPTER ONE "ALL STORIES ARE TRUE": PALIMPSESTIC STORYTELLING
48	CHAPTER TWO DECONSTRUCTING HISTORY: TRAUMA AND THE ALIENATION NARRATIVES
97	CHAPTER THREE THE RETURN HOME: MYTHIC NARRATIVES AND FAMILY HISTORY
144	CHAPTER FOUR THE JOURNEY BACK (AGAIN): THE POST-TRAUMATIC NARRATIVES
190	CHAPTER FIVE TRUTH AND RECONCILIATION: THE BLUES AND THE HEROIC ROMANCE
241	CONCLUSION
249	NOTES
295	BIBLIOGRAPHY
311	INDEX

Acknowledgments

I must begin by thanking E. Ethelbert Miller, poet and teacher, currently at Howard University, for introducing me to African American literary scholarship and nurturing my love of African American literature. He was my first reader on my work on John Edgar Wideman, and his continued mentorship, enthusiasm, and support are immeasurable. He has been the inspiration for what I do in the classroom and in my academic work.

Enormous credit must also be given to Robert DeMott, at Ohio University, who provided me with so many opportunities for growth as a scholar and teacher. He is a teacher's teacher and an honest critic, and his endless supply of energy and devotion to his students' research is miraculous. He unreservedly dove into this project from the very beginning to its completion and beyond. He always encouraged me to turn this into something more.

My work on John Edgar Wideman was fostered by Wilfred Samuels at the University of Utah, former president of the African American Literature and Culture Society (AALCS). His invitation to join the organization gave me a community and a confidence I had never known before. I still remember the afternoon that he, Keith Byerman, Karen Jahn, and several others suggested that we form the John Edgar Wideman Society. That group of charter members continues to motivate my responses to Wideman's work. Several of my former conference presentations for the Wideman Society and AALCS were nascent versions of this study. Further thanks are extended to Keith Byerman, currently serving as president of the Wideman Society. His dedication to scholarship on Wideman evokes my best efforts. As well, his and Bonnie TuSmith's collection, *Critical Essays on John Edgar Wideman*, opened the door for innovative and important work on Wideman's writings. Bonnie, especially, was helpful in focusing my ideas.

I would like to thank the University of Tennessee Press for permission to reprint a version of my essay "All My Father's Texts: John Edgar Wideman's Historical Vision in *Philadelphia Fire*, *The Cattle Killing*, and *Fatheralong*" for the TuSmith and Byerman collection, *Critical Essays on John Edgar Wideman*, here. Likewise, I thank Palgrave Macmillan for the permission to reprint a version of my essay "Courtside: Race and Basketball in the Works of John Edgar Wideman" from *In the Game*. I am also grateful to the editor of that collection, Amy Bass, for letting a literary critic into the mix of historians and cultural studies scholars.

This project is the result of Seetha Srinivasan's perseverance while at the University Press of Mississippi. She never gave up on the idea of this book and passed the torch on to Walter Biggins when she retired from active duty. Walter's equally steadfast and patient pursuit made this a viable manuscript. Additional thanks to the staff at the University Press of Mississippi for all of their hard work seeing this to fruition. I also am eternally grateful to the anonymous readers of the manuscript. Their insights and suggestions were clear, helpful, and generous and seriously improved this work. I would also like to thank Karen Johnson for her work on this project.

I would also like to thank my colleagues in the English Department—my home—and in the History Department. Their guidance and friendship have been invaluable in completing this book. The semester that I was able to lock myself away and do further research was the result of being awarded the Dr. Nuala McGann Drescher Leave. I am also grateful to the United University Professionals of New York and their stewardship of this program. I am also indebted to Dr. Thomas Moran and the fellows at the Institute for Ethics in Public Life. The lively and thoughtful discussions while I was in residence offered me a wider, interdisciplinary context to formulate the ideas in this study. I would also like to thank the staff of the office of the Dean of Arts and Sciences at SUNY Plattsburgh for their support.

Finally, I owe the greatest and most humble thanks to my friends and family for their support, especially during the years spent on this book. I am grateful as well to them for helping me weather all the ups and downs during the last few years. I have been absolutely dependent on my "council"—both old and new members alike—who listen to my stories and, thankfully, share their own. Their humor and concern got me through some tempestuous times. I also must include my thanks for my continued friendship with Tom Guzzio and his support over the years. He read versions of this work countless times, always with great care and encouragement.

Thank you to my mother, Lynn, for her unconditional love, for making me a lifelong reader, and for her help in keeping my household going when I need to write. And thanks to Gary Kroll, who provided expert and much-needed advice, especially during the final weeks of the project. He should be especially commended for how well he balances the roles of colleague, best friend, and partner in our lives. It's not easy to wear so many hats at once, but he is the only man I know who could have handled it as effectively and as gracefully as he has. And, finally, thanks to my daughter and little storyteller, Mirren, for sharing me with this project, which stole me away from her childhood pleasures more times than I would have ever wanted. The long nights at the laptop were less lonely and less stressful with her cuddled up against me asleep, dreaming of her stories.

All Stories Are True

Introduction

All stories are true, as Achebe tells us the Igbo say. Reliable and unverifiable as dreams.
—JOHN EDGAR WIDEMAN, "Malcolm X: The Art of Autobiography"

I remember the first moment that I was introduced to the work of John Edgar Wideman. At the time, I worked as a bookstore clerk. While shelving books—a task I usually enjoyed because it afforded me the chance to read in the back of the store—I grabbed a book that did not belong in the same corner of the store as the rest of the stack in my hands. I looked at its cover—the photograph of a shadowy figure in a jail cell. Reading the blurbs on the back, I was struck by the paradox stated in the book's summary: one brother was a writer and a professor; the other brother was in jail for life. Why this fascinated me I don't think I realized at the time. Perhaps I gravitated toward the book because of some need to investigate my own close but problematic relationship with a stepbrother often in trouble. Whatever the reason, I couldn't leave the book alone. I returned to it over a period of several weeks, stealing time to read passages. It became a touchstone for me, though I couldn't have articulated why at the time; it wasn't until a few years later, when I experienced the loss of my own stepbrother, John, that I finally addressed some of the issues that led me to that book. It took me much longer to comprehend how the book had moved me as a parable on the haves and have-nots, as an exegesis on race and culture, as a portrait of the dichotomous strands of the American dream—all woven through the fabric of this family and their traumas and triumphs.

It was some time before I picked up another work by Wideman. I had rediscovered his work in an African American literature class. The professor,

E. Ethelbert Miller, encouraged my growing interest in autobiography; and for the first time, nearly ten years after first encountering *Brothers and Keepers*, I began an earnest exploration of Wideman's work, reading everything available by him and about him. However, at the time, I found very little criticism on any of Wideman's novels or his autobiographical narratives. Even now, more than twenty years after I first stole company time to read *Brothers and Keepers*, there continues to be a paucity of scholarship on Wideman.

While there has been tremendous growth in African American literary scholarship during this same time—especially on writers like Toni Morrison, Zora Neale Hurston, Alice Walker, and Ralph Ellison—Wideman has been, by comparison, largely neglected. In the introduction to *Critical Essays on John Edgar Wideman*, Keith Byerman, one of the collection's editors, suggests that Wideman's work does not "fit conventional notions of the African-American writer" and that the labels of "difficult" and "postmodernist" usually applied to Wideman's writing have helped to push him to the margins of readership and scholarship alike.[1] Byerman also argues that the rise of female African American writers during the 1980s further obscured Wideman's work.

I agree that these reasons have contributed to the lack of attention given to Wideman. I would add that the marketing of Wideman and his work over the years has also been challenging. Early on, publishers tried to sell him as a modernist and as a writer in the tradition of Faulkner. Then later, even after numerous accolades and awards, he was characterized as the "angry" writer, bolstered by a photograph of him—displayed on countless occasions—with his arms crossed, dressed in a leather jacket, staring scornfully at the camera. His image seemed to scream "stay away." The aura of this now iconic photograph of Wideman is echoed by novelist Ishmael Reed in his analysis of *Philadelphia Fire*: "Reading this book was like attending a Miles Davis concert, where the artist turns his back on the audience. I felt that Wideman had turned his back on me. The book is reader-unfriendly, but look who's talking."[2] Being a "reader-unfriendly" writer usually will not get you a gig as the selection for Oprah Winfrey's book of the month. Wideman's work seems to require the most intrepid of readers.

Wideman has been most often illustrated as the writer whose works reflect the tragedies that he has personally suffered. With the publication of *Brothers and Keepers* in 1984 and the books of the Homewood trilogy in 1981 and 1983, reviewers and publishers alike drew attention to Wideman's background and family traumas. This, too, may be a cause of the lack of attention afforded Wideman—his subjects and plots are dark and haunting. Of course, Wideman purposefully chooses to write about these events himself, as, I would argue, a means to deconstruct American history. However, much of the early commentary on Wideman's work was more concerned with connections to his biography than with a critical and serious consideration of his writing. Many critics and reviewers focused on Wideman's own "story" and personal trauma as a means by which to evaluate his fiction. More recent scholarship has largely left behind these earlier considerations, opting to examine Wideman's writing through a theoretical lens rather than a biographical one. Nonetheless, scholars still occasionally bring Wideman's family troubles and losses into discussions of his novels. And while it is true that Wideman draws his stories from his family, from his personal life, and from his community, it is necessary for readers to look beyond direct correspondences between the man's art and the man's life. It is also time to consider Wideman's canon more holistically and to analyze the ways, throughout all his works, that he addresses historical trauma within the context of family stories.

One of the consequences of the current trend in the poststructuralist readings of Wideman's work, however, has been the continued neglect (or dismissal) of his first three novels: *A Glance Away, Hurry Home,* and *The Lynchers* (published in 1967, 1970, and 1973, respectively). Another result of this new direction has been the decrease in scholarly conversation on the works of the Homewood trilogy (*Damballah, Hiding Place,* and *Sent for You Yesterday*), once the platform for most of the biographical criticism of Wideman's writing. Though these books helped to launch most of the first scholarly examinations of the novels of Wideman, in recent years there has been little reconsideration of them or their place in the continuum of Wideman's work. Since these early studies of Wideman's writing, scholars have isolated the first three novels from the rest of Wideman's work in a manner that separates them stylistically and thematically from the rest, and the novels of the Homewood trilogy and *Reuben* now have begun to suffer a similar fate. Despite new trends in Wideman scholarship, many of the old habits of classifying Wideman remain the same. This separation of Wideman's catalogue may also be partly to blame for the scarcity of scholarship. The reading and "meaning" of much of his work seems to be fixed into categories, perhaps dissuading some scholars from discussing his literature since they believe there is little that is new to be said. It is also possible that another reason for the lack of criticism on Wideman is the sense that a reader needs to consider more than a single volume of his work when approaching his literature.

If we consider the two book-length studies of Wideman's novels and memoirs,[3] we see the paradigmatic division evolving. The first book of criticism considering Wideman's work, James Coleman's *Blackness and Modernism: The Literary Career of John Edgar Wideman* (1989), lays much of the foundation for scholarship to come. The study is a thorough examination of Wideman's canon up until the novel *Reuben*, yet the early chapters call attention to the first three novels as works that don't fulfill Wideman's potential as an author. Calling *A Glance Away* "artistically" the least successful of Wideman's novels, Coleman argues that the book is "curbed" by its attempt to echo the style of such modernists as T. S. Eliot.[4] While Wideman "improvised somewhat" on Eliot's themes, "his close approximation on Eliot's pattern limited the extent to which he might explore the black experience and various artistic and creative possibilities."[5] Coleman sees the first three books as the least valuable in Wideman's writing: "The early books certainly exhibit differences, but most evident at this point in Wideman's career is his depiction of the black intellectual's isolation from the black community. Wideman was influenced both by the modernist literary treatment of such alienation and, as the circumstances of his life indicate, by his own doubts about the black community and his relationships to it."[6]

Coleman further argues that it is not until *Hiding Place*, which he considers the first book in the Homewood trilogy, that "Wideman finally brings together the mainstream modernist tradition and the black cultural tradition in such a way to achieve a black voicing of problems common to the traditions."[7] This study of Wideman develops in a chronological fashion, and Coleman contends "that John Edgar Wideman during his career as a novelist has moved from an uncritical acceptance of the forms and themes of mainstream modernism as practiced by white literary masters to a black voicing of modernism and postmodernism that is consistent with Afro-American perspectives and reflects a commitment to the needs of the black community."[8] Coleman also argues that it is not until after *The Lynchers* that Wideman clearly establishes an African American modernist voice, despite the work's concern with the African American community.[9] And it is not until *Sent for You Yesterday* that Coleman concludes that Wideman is nearing a postmodernist voice, and his development culminates in *Reuben*, where Coleman believes Wideman fully reaches his "postmodern potential."

Coleman's distinctions are echoed by Bernard Bell as well in the brief consideration of Wideman in his study, *The Afro-American Novel and Its Tradition*. Bell focuses most of his attention on the work after the first three novels. He believes that "the Homewood trilogy marks the culmination of Wideman's move from a Eurocentric to a fundamentally Afrocentric tradition, his coming home as it were, in the form and style of an extended meditation on history: oral and literary, personal, and social."[10] While Coleman acknowledges only the seeds of postmodernism in the Homewood trilogy, Bell considers these books examples of the "black postmodernist's double vision."[11]

The second book-length study of Wideman's work is Dorothea Mbalia's *John Edgar Wideman: Reclaiming the African Personality*. Like Coleman, she asserts that Wideman's early work lacked an African American perspective. Where Coleman suggests that Wideman's early works were necessary steps in the evolution of his writing, Mbalia argues that the early novels "record the history of an author who has been taught to hate his culture, taught to hate himself, and all those who look like him."[12] Of all the critics of Wideman's work, Mbalia most rigorously applies biographical criticism to the novels. She refers to Littleman, a character in the novel *The Lynchers*, as Wideman; and later, in her discussion of *Philadelphia Fire*, she proclaims that "the reader feels comfortable accepting Cudjoe's experiences, thoughts, and words as those of Wideman."[13] Her criticism of Wideman's work reaches even into his personal life, his marriage, and his family.[14] *Philadelphia Fire* illustrates Wideman's "new thinking." This "new thinking," Mbalia argues, is a reflection of Wideman's "newfound Africanness." She does not call Wideman's later work postmodern, but, interestingly, she does refer to Eliot, one of the influences on Wideman's first novel, as "post-modernist."[15]

Mbalia also contends that the novels before *Philadelphia Fire* are not as clearly representative of the African personality. She asserts that it is not until *Philadelphia Fire* that we find Wideman using free indirect discourse, thus creating "a speakerly text." Mbalia theorizes that Wideman's use of the three-part structure in *Philadelphia Fire* is one of the most clear indications that his writing is a response to his "new found Africanness": "By quilting together these narrators in a single text, Wideman creates a triple-voiced narrative structure. But, even more important, he recaptures the collective voice, the collective worldview, of traditional Africa that was lost during the African slave-making process."[16] Coleman, however, establishes that this structure occurs in Wideman's first novel. Here "the overall presentation of the story through *Glance*'s three-part structure demonstrates Wideman's adherence to mainstream modernism."[17] Most theoreticians would consider the triple-voiced structure as typically postmodernist or even modernist (this will be discussed in more detail in the next chapter).

I have detailed these descriptions to illustrate the early characterizations of Wideman's work, and the energy that has been spent on how to label him as a writer. This desire to categorize Wideman is to be expected when you are first approaching a new writer, but the emphasis on typifying his writing and personalizing the analysis belies a consideration of a grander vision of the art. Even now, many other critical studies echo these characterizations—to the extent that they represent the standard reading of work published by Wideman before 1989. Most scholars seem to accept that the first three books are not as successful as the later work because they adhere to a European modernist model and that they are thematically discontinuous from Wideman's later work. Since the publication of Coleman's and Mbalia's studies, attention has moved away from the Homewood trilogy to Wideman's later novels and memoirs, especially to *Philadelphia Fire*, *The Cattle Killing*, and *Fatheralong*. Yet even these new critics have distinguished Wideman's work before the publication of *Philadelphia Fire* and the short-story collection *Fever* as inherently different from that which has come after.[18]

One of the epochal moments in Wideman scholarship is Wideman's own assertion that it was not until after the first three books, and the death of his grandmother in 1973, that he regained "his Homewood ear."[19] This "story" has taken on apocryphal significance in Wideman criticism and is largely responsible for the amount and type of attention given to his work between 1989 (when Coleman's study was published) and 1999. The invocation of the "Homewood ear," its loss and subsequent recovery of family and voice, becomes a metaphor for most critics of Wideman's alienation from his family and community and, ultimately, his race and himself. Because Wideman regains his "Homewood ear" after his return home for his grandmother's funeral, which happened the same year as the publication of *The Lynchers*, critics evaluated the first three works as disparate and distinct from the "typical" African American experience.[20]

In the preface to *The Homewood Trilogy*, Wideman notes that the experience of his grandmother's funeral reminded him of his family's ability to alleviate their pain and sorrow—to survive their shared trauma—through the sharing of stories. Wideman realizes that the exchange of these blues-like stories that find acceptance and even joy and humor, within this suffering is how his family and his race have always survived their often traumatic condition in America. Following his visit home, Wideman understands more than ever before the need to keep traditions and stories alive, stating in the preface to *The Homewood Trilogy*, "Such rituals, such gatherings must survive if we as a people are to survive."[21] It is evident that Wideman is altered by the experience of "going home," and it rededicates him to writing after 1973, emphasizing more clearly and more emphatically his family. The death of his grandmother, one of the primary storytellers of the Wideman family, signaled the loss of these stories to Wideman. It is not that Wideman forgot his roots or the need for stories—his grief made the need to share and remember stories more urgent.

I am uncomfortable with the assessments of both Coleman and Mbalia, however, when they suggest that Wideman did not know these traditions. It is clear that he had been surrounded by them his entire life and that his family was inhabited by vociferous and expert storytellers. Coleman's assertion that Wideman was "not knowledgeable enough about the workings of black tradition to achieve his full, mature black voice" negates other comments about his own work as well as the body of his writing.[22] Mbalia's criticism of Wideman's lack of cultural knowledge is even more severe, suggesting that he turned his back on traditions by "aping" the modernists.[23] Whether consciously or not, Wideman's work, even since the first novel, acknowledges the importance of "story" in the lives of individuals and communities and the need to be able to tell your own story. It is, after all, Eddie Lawson's inability to remember family stories in *A Glance Away* that condemns him to further suffering. He cannot heal himself or his family because he cannot share stories of his past. Each of the main characters in the first novels are tragic because they have forgotten the songs sung to them as children and the stories that sustained them through pain and trauma; they have forgotten their "fictions," which are weapons against the fictions that others have constructed about them. Their imaginations are as traumatized as their lives. Characters like this do not go away in later works by Wideman.

In the past few years, criticism and scholarship on Wideman's novels, short stories, and memoirs have slowly grown, as evidenced by the appearance of the aforementioned collection of critical essays as well as several conferences and seminars devoted to Wideman scholarship; however, few critics since the studies of Coleman and Mbalia have discussed the works as a whole—nor as a testament of Wideman's panoramic vision of African American literature and history. Nor have critics suggested that Wideman's canon—as opposed to specific individual works—is a counterhegemonic epic, recovering, revising, and re-imagining the African American narrative.

Therefore, one objective of this study is to consider Wideman's work in its entirety. This is neither an exhaustive nor even a comprehensive effort; rather, I argue that to best understand Wideman's artistic project, his philosophy of writing, his preoccupation with history and trauma, and even his broader themes regarding race, family, and identity, we need to read his published works as a continuous, multilayered or palimpsestic counternarrative to mainstream or popular American history.

I would like to turn to another early consideration of Wideman's novels in order to begin this project. This one presents a very different reading of Wideman. A year before James Coleman's book appeared, novelist Charles Johnson reflected on Wideman's contributions to African American writings. Johnson classifies Wideman with other contemporary African American authors and suggests that "much of black writing in the last decade or so is a meditation on remembrance. Praisesongs from writers who feel themselves to be keepers—or transmitters—of the past for the sake, as with Wideman, of future generations." Johnson continues by addressing an early criticism of Wideman's first books that dismissed his novels, arguing that these works were unnecessarily difficult because of his stream-of-consciousness style. Speaking in support of those same first three books, Johnson praises Wideman as a writer who uncovers the past "as an archaeologist might."[24]

Throughout Wideman criticism there are references to Wideman's recovery of family history, but only scant attention has been given to Wideman's interest in history beyond the family. Nor has there been a scholarly examination of the connection between family history and institutional or recorded history, and little has been said about Wideman's response to literary history and tradition—except to sometimes suggest that he was unaware of the African American traditions. Johnson's declaration about Wideman's historical undertaking not only pertains to the Homewood books, but also regards the first three novels (and those that have been written since Johnson's assessment as well). Johnson opened a door to reading Wideman that few have gone through. It was not until the later novels, such as *Philadelphia Fire* and *The Cattle Killing*—those illustrating a specific historical event—that critics fully explored this characteristic of Wideman's work.[25]

One of my goals here is to reclaim the first three novels of Wideman's career as essential to his theories of storytelling and criticisms of historiography. In neglecting or limiting these works, most critics have not emphasized many of the recurring themes found throughout Wideman's canon. And studies of his later works neglect to see the connections between the first three novels and his most recent writing, thus failing to recognize the interrelationship or intertextuality—and even interdependency—between his numerous published works. Dialogic discourses, three-voiced structures, images of circles and doubles, repeated characters or stories, lost children, and scenes of sharing stories or songs appear in each work. These recurring images, as we will see in the course of this study, reflect Wideman's meditation on history and on the traumatic past of African Americans and his own family. The aesthetic of Wideman's writing that I will propose in these pages purposefully de-emphasizes or refutes mere biographical considerations of Wideman's work.

Wideman has cautioned against such biographical readings in an interview with James Coleman that appears in the appendix to *Blackness and Modernism*: "Anybody who would try to make one-to-one correspondences, or think that the stories reflect the biographies of the people who hold the names, would just get in a mire."[26] Over ten years later Wideman reiterates in another interview: "Just because I write about some aspect of my personal life from my point of view, that doesn't mean it's open season for anybody else to say whatever they want about the same business."[27] Clearly, Wideman believes that intensely biographical considerations of his fiction miss the point of his work. He has even gone so far as repudiating the reception of his nonfiction work, *Brothers and Keepers*. Wideman states in a 1995 interview:

> You know, once upon a time in my life, I remember being fascinated to find that W.E.B. DuBois had written more than one autobiography, that there was a writing and rewriting of his life story as that life continued and the author changed. I think in *Brothers and Keepers* I oversold the idea of running away. I don't think I ever ran away from the black world in a kind of blind acceptance of something else. I made too much of a dichotomy between the white world and the black world—running from one, running toward the other. It's too simple. It's never that way. It was really more like a back and forth. Periods of immersion in one, then immersion in another.[28]

Wideman goes on to say, in yet another interview, that the "motif of running was also rhetorical."[29] It is clear that the early work, if read through the lens of the autobiographical/biographical *Brothers and Keepers*, is seen as further evidence of Wideman turning his back on his African American culture. Characters who run away in the first three books are portrayed by critics as representatives of Wideman's own flight from his community. Yet Wideman states that the image created in *Brothers and Keepers* is a fiction itself, a metaphor for African American history. It is a trope that he revisits and rewrites not only in *Brothers and Keepers*, but also in the early books. Wideman is already revising history, returning to images embedded in the consciousness of American culture and in the African American literary tradition.

Instead of the "alienated intellectual" or the story of "recovering" his Homewood ear as origin sites for developing an aesthetic of reading Wideman, I would emphasize Johnson's analysis and Wideman's adoption of the phrase "all stories are true." The phrase "all stories are true" represents Wideman's philosophy and his response to history. Wideman doesn't vocalize this statement until 1988, even though the idea that the phrase suggests can be found in all of his work. He repeats the phrase in several interviews.[30] It appears in an essay on Malcolm X. A collection of short stories bears the title *All Stories Are True*,[31] and we are reminded again of the phrase in *Fatheralong*.[32] In *The Cattle Killing*, Wideman's narrator, searching for the "correct" version of a mysterious African girl's life and death, decides, finally, "'I believed each story. My way of reckoning learned from the old African people, who said all stories are true.'"[33]

Despite the appearance of this phrase later in Wideman's career, his work has from the beginning reflected this statement in both form and content. Yet critical discussion of Wideman's art does not fully investigate the urgent philosophy behind the words "all stories are true." And very little criticism examines how the phrase "all stories are true" has affected the style and structure of Wideman's writing. Wideman's work seeks to dismantle the popular or mainstream positivistic view of history that has perpetuated the limited story of African Americans in this country. By challenging a monolithic view of history; by presenting other stories (those known and unknown); by repeating images of circles and circular narrative; by echoing characters and narratives throughout the spectrum of his work; by allowing past, present, and future time to remain fluid in the narratives; by permitting multiple voices and narrators to construct the story, Wideman embraces postmodern theories of historiography and relativism, but also reconnects to an African past, one that rejects singular, universal, determined "truth" in favor of "all stories." When asked to comment on the phrase's meaning in his work, Wideman responds:

> It refers to a kind of relativity—that each person's voice has weight and force and a corner of the truth. In that sense it's profoundly democratic ... when you get right down to it, knowing the fact that all stories are true is as much a place to begin as a conclusion, because it doesn't remove the necessity for sorting through the evidence—of working through the stories. What I like about it in particular is that it decentralizes the truth—it fragments the truth. It puts truth in the light of multiplicity, of voices as a kind of construct that you can't arrive at unless you do have a mosaic of voices.[34]

In understanding that the body of Wideman's work embraces the maxim that "all stories are true" and creates counterhegemonic narratives to confront the limited, and usually negative, portrayals of African American men and women in the American historical consciousness, readers can better appreciate Wideman's vision. Wideman speaks even more directly to these moments in his own writing:

> Both plots and themes of the fictions I write, and the fictions themselves, are an attempt to subvert one notion of reality with others, to show that there is not simply one way of seeing things but many ways of seeing things. And as people and as individuals if we don't jump into the breach, if we don't fight the battle of defining reality in our own terms, then someone else will always come along and do it for us.[35]

His work illustrates that the trauma suffered by African Americans in the period of slavery in America is re-lived and re-experienced in the continuing racism confronting African Americans in their daily lives as well as in the images projected by history, literature, and popular culture.

The first chapter, "'All Stories Are True': Palimpsestic Storytelling," places Wideman within a theoretical framework that considers his work in a poststructuralist context, highlighting Linda Hutcheon's "historiographic metafiction" as well as the "dialogic novel" formulated by Mikhail Bakhtin; it also situates Wideman within theories of the African American literary tradition. Much of the framework will illustrate that Wideman's work expresses qualities of "trauma literature" that situate individual pain within the historical context of a group that has survived shared traumatic events. Wideman's personal tragedies, his family background, and the legacy of slavery and racism that haunts his work, I argue, all interact to expose and to attempt to heal the violent and brutal history of African Americans.

The chapter titled "Deconstructing History: Trauma and the Alienation Narratives" primarily considers his first three novels, *A Glance Away, Hurry Home*, and *The Lynchers*. These are the works most often neglected by literary critics, but for my analysis they are essential to understanding the "history" —both literally and figuratively—that Wideman's characters are trying to escape. These works are also argued by some critics to be the most emotionally desolate of his works. But I would add that they are the most burdened by history. This despair and weight isolates and nearly destroys the primary characters in these works. Unable to re-imagine the legacy of the historical narrative written by others, these characters are crushed. The chapter also looks at the continuing portraits of the "alienated" intellectual and trauma narratives in Wideman's novels that still must struggle to endure these legacies.

In the third chapter, I analyze Wideman's "Homewood" stories and family narratives. These include *Damballah, Hiding Place, Sent for You Yesterday, Brothers* and *Keepers*, and *Reuben*. This chapter, titled "The Return Home: Mythic Narratives and Family History," examines Wideman's characters returning to stories forgotten or lost, the myths or "healing" stories of their family and their race. These stories act as a ritual to address the wounds of the past. Though the characters and these narratives are never able to overcome the trauma of the history, they create spaces where new stories and new histories *can* be told, thus disrupting the historical narrative that Wideman is attempting to counter. While most of the analysis concerns the works of the "middle period," I also discuss the continuing significance of family stories within the context of Wideman's canon. Wideman has said, "All of my books are about my family, family relationships, and reordering and transformation of family."[36]

The works *Fatheralong, Philadelphia Fire, The Cattle Killing*, and *The Lynchers* are discussed in the fourth chapter, "The Journey Back (Again): The Posttraumatic Narratives." Of all of Wideman's works, these three deal most significantly with a historic event or with historiography; they also each follow a writer or storyteller on a physical and figurative journey. Each of these works also directly confronts stories of profound loss, disease, and even the end of the world. This feeling of loss projects onto the page as disjointed structure, silence, irresolution, and dysfunction. Wideman suggests in these works that the present ills of society can only be understood (and perhaps not eased) by returning to our past—the root of the disease, the plague, the fire, and the violence that threatens African American life today. It is also clear that Wideman believes that if we do not understand how the historical narrative impacts the individual lives of African Americans, the damaging effects of racism will continue. The chapter also observes how Wideman configures the relationship between history and literature in his novels and nonfiction, not only in the later works but in the early works as well.

The final chapter, "Truth and Reconciliation: The Blues and the Heroic Romance," primarily focuses on *Two Cities, Hoop Roots, The Island: Martinque, God's Gym*, and *Fanon*. Wideman has stated that his most recent works are about "love." Wideman's later work presents men as failed, beaten down, neglected, diseased—but they somehow manage to find human connection through art, basketball, social justice, love, and redemption. While loss, regret, and trauma have marked the lives of the characters in these works, their suffering has brought them to a heretofore unknown level of spiritual and human understanding. While they cannot leave history behind (as they often say in these works), they have found a way to use their suffering to understand the past.

The boundaries between chapters are not completely discrete. It is difficult to write about one Wideman story without discussing another; therefore, the novels mentioned above may also appear in earlier or later sections, much like a Wideman story or character re-appearing in another novel. Thus, these chapter descriptions are a guide to where the primary focus is on the works listed. Moreover, this exploration of Wideman's work may not maintain a continuous chronological timeline by publication dates. These ways of reading Wideman's work shift between the chapters, across time, revealing the necessity of sharing and reading stories in Wideman's creative project. He reminds us of this necessity: to tell stories on your own terms, to tell stories to each other, to connect to the past and to the future, to escape the burden of history, to embrace it, to survive. Wideman cautions in *Fatheralong* that Promised Land, South Carolina, cannot be found on most maps because "Promised Land lies where it does to teach us the inadequacy of maps we don't make ourselves, teach us the necessity of making new maps, teach us how to create them, reimagine connections others have forgotten or hidden."[37] Wideman revises the stories and images that have been written about African American history, culture, and life, even those from his own tradition, so that he can clear a space for other stories to be told.

CHAPTER ONE

"All Stories Are True"

PALIMPSESTIC STORYTELLING

> Suddenly, the mist cleared. Below the people, the earth had changed. It had grown into the shape of the stories they'd told, a shape wondrous and new and real as the words they'd spoken. But a world also unfinished because all the stories had not been told.
>
> —JOHN EDGAR WIDEMAN, *Fatheralong*

Much of what informs the reading of Wideman's work in this study has its roots in the discussions of history and historiography in the postmodern era. Since Wideman responds in his writing to the traumatic history of African Americans, an understanding of the relationship between history, postmodern thought and practice, and literary trauma theory would be a fruitful place to begin the examination of the course of Wideman's philosophy and work. However, it serves little purpose to simply impose a theory of any kind on Wideman's work; there is clearly evidence in the novels, nonfiction, and Wideman's own literary criticism that allows an analysis to begin inductively—from Wideman's own words.

The use and illustration of the Ibo saying "all stories are true" postulate a way of reading Wideman's chronicle of his family and the history of the community and the race. The statement and its appearance in his canon direct readers to a meditation on history itself, the nature of storytelling, and the dialogue between cultural discourses. The phrase also directly confronts the "master narratives." If "all stories are true," then the privileging of discourses and histories (stories) of the Western tradition or in American culture is challenged.

We can also extend this to a consideration of Wideman's style and how it reflects his content. Multiple perspectives, narrators, versions of stories, and discourse modes interact intratextually and intertextually—Wideman's "palimpsestic" storytelling.[1] The imbrications or layers of these narratives allow stories and discourses to interact and speak to one another. This characteristic accounts for the relationship between works such as *Damballah* and *Brothers and Keepers* and the remarkable number of doubles found throughout Wideman's canon. It allows Wideman to engage both the European and African traditions in his narratives as dialogic and contrapuntal texts.[2] It also represents Wideman's historical vision, since palimpsestic narratives act as places where the "past influences the present."[3] Wideman writes his stories over the historical record to provide a "truer" and balanced view of African American life.[4]

Mr. Mallory, one of Wideman's artists (there are numerous ones), describes his photography as palimpsestic vision in his letters to sculptor Alberto Giacometti: "I want people to see my pictures from various angles, see the image I offer as many images, one among countless ways of seeing, so the more they look, the more there is to see. A density of appearance my goal, Mr. Giacometti. So I snap, snap, snap. Pile in layer after layer. A hundred doses of light without moving the film. No single, special, secret view sought or revealed. One in many. Many in one."[5] "Density of appearance" could easily describe Wideman's layering of texts in his own work; the many pictures in one illustrate the many voices that inhabit Wideman's writing. The desire to see things "from various angles" also reverberates in the phrase "all stories are true." Mallory also thanks Giacometti for "remembering what has been lost."[6]

Wideman acknowledges his multivocality and hybridity when he reveals the origins of his aesthetic:

> Story is a primal structure device in both people's individual identities and group identities, national identities, etc. One of my first insights into this was when I began to read French linguistic criticism—as much as I was able to understand of it anyway—and then the American followers. When I began to read this stuff in the late 60s, it became clear to me that much of what I was reading was also comprised in, and articulated by, the folklore conventions that I was also working with and trying to figure out—that is to say, a blues singer or a preacher in the African American tradition interrogated many of the same matters as these French estheticians and narratologists.[7]

Wideman goes on to say in the same interview, just moments later, that it is natural to internalize the conventions of story and then to play with them "in the same way that the jazz musician interrogates traditional, conventional music."[8] There is a purposeful linkage here between jazz, postmodernist thought, the African American literary tradition, and the beginning of Wideman's writing career. Wideman argues that he drew discourses from both of his worlds (the white university and the black culture) in his work. His ability to do this, Ishmael Reed speculates, is one of his enduring characteristics. Reed calls Wideman a "mulatto writer, neither black nor white. His double consciousness has always been his chief asset."[9] And Wideman notes elsewhere that literature in this country has always been cross-cultural: "You can't separate the strands out very easily. And what's incumbent upon critics and writers and all of us is to understand the interpenetration that's always existed from the very beginning."[10]

Much has been made in past criticism about Wideman's use of European models and writers (i.e., T. S. Eliot) in his fiction, particularly in his early works. But this type of analysis denies the hybridity that characterizes the work of many African American writers, including Toni Morrison, and even African American cultural forms such as jazz. Jazz and the blues are considered to have developed as a result of the interplay of European and African forms.[11] The influence runs in the counter-direction as well. Writing that exhibits jazz-like characteristics and/or hybridity is also often considered postmodern. The notion of discourses or cultures that are intertextual or exhibit this "interplay" or dialogue are also described as postmodern.[12] Even before the postmodern era, Mikhail Bakhtin theorized that the form of the novel is a result of "hybridization," the interplay or "mixture of two social languages within the limits of a single utterance."[13] And Bernard Bell suggests that one of the marks of postmodernist African American writers is their commitment to the use of "hybrid narrative forms."[14]

Wideman consistently weaves multiple narratives and discourses within his texts, sometimes even on a single page. He describes the cross-cultural or hybrid nature of his writing in several interviews, perhaps as a response to critics that have seen segments of his work as "wholly" Eurocentric in one period or Afrocentric in another. In Wideman's earliest interview he discusses the influence of eighteenth-century novels, particularly *Tristram Shandy*, and of modernists like Eliot on his writing.[15] He goes on to outline the influence of the classical Greeks, Ralph Ellison, the blues, slave narratives, and James Joyce on his work:

> What I think I have been able to do is look at these influences in terms other than race, so that I still am responsive to Faulkner's attempts to

capture the oral cadences of southern speech—and often southern black speech—in those long, flowing sentences, in that kind of crazy mix of vocabularies which comes from the King James Bible and from proverbs and illiteracies and all the rest. Joyce's improvisations and spontaneity, inventiveness with language are very, very important, still part and parcel of what I am doing ... so I don't want to make it seem that I exchanged one set of masters for another, because I hope that what I am doing is internalizing many different influences and shuffling among those and picking and choosing ... the black influences were never *not* there. Nobody had ever pointed out to me how they were there.[16]

To chronicle this idea fully in Wideman's writing, we will need to consider that his work is a cross-cultural response that borrows and blends ideas and artistic expressions found in African and African American literature and culture (including jazz and oral storytelling modes) and postmodern theories of literature and history. Wideman addresses these voices in his work simultaneously, layering them within and between texts. He also layers, or imbricates, stories, discourses, and texts within each work, blurring the boundaries between the categories of genre. Each of these characteristics in Wideman's writing resonates with the voicing of "all stories are true."

A discussion of Wideman's responses to history must also consider an examination of the current theories of historiography and the relationship of such theories to African American literature. This necessarily requires a cross-cultural dialogue that converses with both the European American and the African American tradition. Cross-cultural dialogue and interplay are characteristic of studies such as Henry Louis Gates Jr.'s *The Signifying Monkey*, Craig Werner's *Playing the Changes*, and Madelon Jablon's *Black Metafiction*, to name a few. Each of these studies could be characterized as a "polyrhythmic approach to literature." This approach is not unlike Mark Anthony Neal's definition of the "post-soul aesthetic" that uses "postmodern insights to illuminate the presentation of black life and culture."[17] A hybrid study is also the reflection of the cross-cultural tenor of Wideman's own writing throughout his career. Therefore, Wideman's palimpsestic storytelling demands an examination that layers and weaves multiple traditions and theories to contextualize his revision of history implicated in the phrasing "all stories are true." Such a study also requires a recursive analysis of Wideman's writing.

African American writers for the past several decades have found a place to address and dismantle the portraits of African American life in the mainstream. The popular acceptance of postmodernism as a theory and practice, even outside of the academic world, created a space for writers at the margins to practice their revisionary art.

Changing critical attitudes to the nature and construction of history in the wake of postmodernism gave birth to the prevailing notion that it is impossible, indeed, even undesirable, to reach an absolute and final truth, that knowledge or ways of knowing are not a scientific process, but a cultural one.[18] The consequences to historiography reverberated in the work of those artists concerned with representations of the past. Certainly, if Michel Foucault could suggest that as a historian he had "never written anything but fictions," then the once fundamental border between fiction and history can be blurred, even rejected. The acknowledgment by academic historians that "all is fiction" occurred alongside the recovery of alternative histories of silenced groups.[19] For many such writers, any novel of history or historical consciousness became an overtly or covertly political tool designed to question and critique the values of American society. The implication for writers who are marginalized either by their race, religion, or gender is a profound reworking of story. These ideas also enable the power of the imagination to recreate historical narratives or to address the gaps within the dominant historical consciousness. Thus, postmodernist practices not only undermine the legitimacy of history written by a dominant discourse, but also suggest that if one story can be "true," then all stories could be.

At the same time that artists looked to changes in historiography as the basis for new trends in their own work, historians began to look at the novel as a "way of coming to terms with problems in modern history itself."[20] The contemporary novel of history could resist the "satisfying" closure of the traditional historical narrative and reconceptualize, in the present culture, a historical period as well as historiography itself. Such a novel "throws the reader back upon the need to come to terms with the unresolved problems the novel helps to disclose."[21] The project of this art is inherently political, removing the reader from a stable historical consciousness that permits him or her to question the power that the past has over the present through constructed narratives that conduct national, societal, and individual perceptions. This writing allows the reader to engage with the past in order to "confront creatively the problems of the present."[22]

The genre of historical fiction is also transformed by such revisionary thinking. Postmodern theorists such as Brian McHale, Linda Hutcheon, and David Cowart suggest that the conventions of the historical novel are expanding in the wake of the postmodern theories about the essence and construction of history. Cowart redefines historical fiction in the postmodern era as a genre "in which the past figures in some prominence. Such fiction does not require historical personages or events . . . nor does it have to be set at some specified remove in time. Thus I count as historical fiction any novel in which a historical consciousness manifests itself strongly in either the characters or the action. Many a novel set in the present satisfies the proposed criterion because of its author's attention to the historical background of current reality."[23] Cowart's definition has import for African American writers, such as Wideman, attempting to understand or redress current racial attitudes, yet he does not devote significant space in his study to African American authors. McHale's study also spends little time with African American authors, with the notable exception of Ishmael Reed. Toni Morrison does receive some attention in Hutcheon's work, *The Poetics of Postmodernism*, but the description of "historiographic metafiction" outlined in her study clearly illustrates Wideman's response to history as well as his "all stories are true" aesthetic.[24]

Hutcheon's definition of historiographic metafiction is a form that "incorporates three areas of concern": fiction, theory, and history. This form, she argues, subverts genre conventions to question the validity of historical knowledge and brings to light the limited and subjective voice that belongs to history. Its self-awareness of the nature of historical writing allows it to rethink and rework the form and content of the past.[25] Historiographic metafiction is by its nature intertextual and fragmented, espousing plurality by presenting multiple points of view from its vast array of discourses. Its antecedent is the eighteenth-century novel that often mixed fact and fiction, an era and genre with which Wideman was well acquainted during his studies at Oxford, where he wrote his thesis on *Tristram Shandy*.[26] Wideman's work certainly exhibits the style and purpose of historiographic metafiction as defined by Hutcheon.

Wideman himself has suggested that there is no difference between fiction, "reportage," and autobiography. The removal of the boundaries between these discourses allows equal power in constructing "truth." Historiographic metafiction argues that "there are only *truths* in the plural, and never one Truth; and there is rarely falseness per se, just others' truths. Fiction and history are narratives distinguished by their frames."[27] Wideman's *The Cattle Killing* illustrates that fiction and history are equal narrative frames. The novel frames its "story" with the voices of a fiction writer and a historian. The two discourses "speak" and "write" to one another in the work—exemplifying the dialogic novel. The double-voicing of the frame in *The Cattle Killing* further characterizes Wideman's work as polyphonic.

The phrase "all stories are true" describes the polyphonic style of a work like *The Cattle Killing* as well as other Wideman novels and nonfiction. The opening pages of that novel condense Wideman's aesthetic and aptly categorize his work as historiographic metafiction. We are presented with a metafictional voice discussing writing the book that he will give to his father (and later share with his son, the historian). Within a few pages, Wideman balances this fictive voice with other writing "voices" or perspectives. The introduction opens with a quote from "The Book of Ezekiel." Wideman's allusion to a literary/historical/mythic figure replays again a few lines later when the writer's voice tells us that his friends nicknamed him "Eye" (a shortened reference to Ezekiel). When he hears someone saying his name, he can't distinguish if they mean "Eye" or "I."[28] The multiple meanings of seeing (through the allusion to the seer, Ezekiel) and the positions from which we see (and by extension, the way we speak from that point of view), as an "I" and an "eye," bring together the strands and voices that Wideman addresses in his fiction. We see the literary tradition (Ezekiel), autobiographical and family history (the "I"), and the ethnographer/recorder/historian (the "eye") voiced simultaneously in these pages. Wideman has taken the position of both "eye" and "I" in almost all of his writing (and often in ways that contribute to the complications that arise being both). As the literary artist, he also balances the fictional voice within these other discourses of autobiography and history (or ethnography). In Wideman's work, all of these voices and stories are necessary to approach the "truth" of his and his family's experiences as African Americans.

Hutcheon draws connections between her study and the work of Bakhtin in her description of the heteroglossia and collective discourse as a component of historiographic metafiction. The multiple worlds in these novels, created by the polyphonic nature of the work, offer other realities and possibilities, rejecting the limits of self and knowledge supported by the epistemology of modernism.[29] As an African American writer marginalized by the American literary tradition and as a black man often defined by the American popular imagination in negative terms, Wideman's polyphonic discourse serves as a way to disrupt and question historical "reality." Wideman's inclusion of different narrative communities occurring simultaneously in his work—the sermon, the picaresque, autobiographical writing, fiction, jazz, slave narratives, the European and American poetic and novelistic tradition, the tropes of African American literature, drama, auto-ethnography, genealogy, literary theory, African and African American folklore and history—fulfills Bakhtin's assertion of the novelization of the genres. Bakhtin suggests, "What are the salient features of this novelization of other genres suggested by us above? They become more free and flexible, their language renews itself by incorporating extraliterary heteroglossia and the 'novelistic' layers of literary language, they become dialogized, permeated with laughter, irony, humor, elements of self-parody and finally—this is the most important thing—the novel inserts into these other genres an indeterminacy, a certain semantic open-endedness, a living contact with unfinished, still-evolving contemporary reality."[30]

Other African American writers and scholars of the African American tradition have found in Bakhtin's description of the dialogic novels and heteroglossia a critical relationship. Even the form and characterizations of jazz music have been linked to Bakhtin. The language and vocabulary of jazz, with its simultaneous notes and chords, its antiphonal and contrapuntal structure, and its polyrhythmic sound, reverberates in Bakhtin's theories. Madelyn Jablon specifically links jazz to Bakhtin in her assessment that the theory of dialogism "has its correlative in African-American aesthetics. It exists in black music as synchrony and counterpoint."[31] Jazz is defined by its "dialogic substances."[32] And Gates uses jazz vocabulary and the theories of Bakhtin to describe the "double-voiced discourse" of the African American literary tradition.[33] Bernard Bell goes even further, extending Gates's reading of Bakhtin in light of African American literature, to suggest that double consciousness and double vision, primary tropes of African American life, are analogous to Bakhtin's theory of double-voiced or dialogic texts.[34] And Houston Baker characterizes the language of the blues and the blues novel as multivocal or polyvalent, speaking in a variety of voices.[35]

Wideman's self-defined literary style of "the academy and the street" reverberates in Bakhtin's description of polyphonic or "carnival" texts where different social discourses (what he calls "high and low") are in dialogue with one another.[36] The juxtaposition of "legitimate" discourse with the language of the folk challenges the authority and the viewpoint of dominant culture. Such works are necessarily double-voiced or hybrid.[37] Bakhtin notes this characteristic of the novel when he portrays the genre as an instance of two speech acts occurring at once.[38] Sounding very much like Bakhtin, Wideman maintains that the African American writer has always spoken in two voices. African American literature, even the early slave narratives, is a place where "dual messages are transmitted in a single speech act. The speaker acknowledges to himself and announces to his audience that he's not taking the language of the slave master altogether seriously."[39]

The characteristic polyphony in Wideman's work, then, is not only a reflection of his postmodernism. It is also an example of his voicing of African American culture. Hutcheon asserts that postmodern writers address fragmentation and bifurcation in their work by their "pluralizing recourse to the discourses" of history, science, philosophy, and such. "These genres are 'played off against each other.'" All of the discourses that Hutcheon outlines here are the privileged modes, yet her theory clearly reflects some connections to, and acknowledgments of, the work of past and present African American artists.[40]

Even the phrase "played off against each other" echoes the act of signifying, call and response, and jazz. The work of the jazz artist is to move between solo flights and communal interplay, using the group or the tradition to "play off against." Wideman goes even further to play genres off one another. History, fiction, and autobiography all commune with one another; the imposed borders are more fluid, less distinctive.

This too is characteristic of much of African American literature. The slave narratives "occupy the territory between history and art, biography and fiction, memory and imagination."[41] Even a work like *Black Boy* mixes fiction and fact. Our usual genre signifiers are used to disrupt the perceptions of what is fact and what is fiction. In modern African American autobiography there is "difficulty in distinguishing fact from fiction," and "black fiction is often so close to black autobiography in plot and theme that a study of the latter almost calls the former into question."[42] There is such an abundance of this in African American literature that Albert Stone has suggested that black writers have been partners with postmodernism in a lowering of "barriers separating self and society, history and fiction."[43]

The postmodern concerns with history echo the African American artists' critique of history in their work. Wideman's practices coincide with many of the concerns of other contemporary African American artists, such as Charles Johnson, Toni Morrison, August Wilson, Shirley Anne Williams, Ishmael Reed, and Ernest Gaines, to name a few. Michael Cooke notes that for several of these authors, and others in the last thirty years, history is the impetus for much of the writing, a site of immersion or reimmersion.[44] One of Cooke's examples of such a text that is immersed in history is Wideman's *Damballah*. In this context, any African American imaginative recreation of the past is necessarily "recursive, a fiction that begins and ends with history."[45] This direction in art is not just an example of historical reportage, however. This is an imaginative recreation of the traumatic past, a past that has often silenced or excluded the recorded history of African Americans.

As Darwin Turner pointed out in 1972, until the late 1960s and early 1970s, African American novelists had "virtually ignored the possibilities of transcending the past by reinterpreting it artistically."[46] The decades following Turner's pronouncement have seen a wide proliferation of artistic works devoted to history. Some of these have reached back as far as the mythic and historic African past and others to early twentieth-century American cities. Some of the most critically acclaimed literature have been the novels of slavery or "neo-slave narratives."[47] Certainly, the influence of Malcolm X profoundly affected young intellectuals and artists. His autobiography served, like other black autobiographies before it, as a potential weapon, a way to transcend the limitations of American society. It is also significant that Malcolm X stressed the importance of "knowing your history" and marked his own transformation, intellectually and spiritually, by his reading of history books during his confinement in prison.[48] For Wideman, specifically, Malcolm X continued the story of other black autobiographers but expanded the African American story into new horizons of identity. Malcolm X's story is "the struggle of the formerly enslaved, the colonized, the outcast, the dispossessed to seize responsibility, to forge personal identity and communal consciousness that will reverse centuries of subjugation, self-hate; a consciousness capable of opening doors through which healing, healthy people might walk unbowed."[49]

The birth and development of the Black Arts Movement of the 1960s also furthered the importance of understanding and transcending the burden of African American history, both politically and artistically, while reconnecting to the African heritage. Even if writers weren't specifically involved with the Black Arts Movement, it generated an atmosphere of change and possibility. During the height of the Black Arts Movement, Wideman returned from Oxford, England, where he was a Rhodes scholar and thus was not officially connected with these artists or their aesthetic.[50] However, Wideman later did announce the connections between his writing and some of the tenets of the Black Arts Movement's aesthetic, ones that mirror his own art's concerns to this day:

> The notion that black people had to tell their own stories, that black people needed to investigate the language, that black people are on the edge of a kind of precipice and that, as a people, we might very well disappear if we didn't start to, number one, demand equality in the political sense, if we didn't begin to investigate our past, if we didn't begin to see ourselves as part of a world, a Third World—all these ideological and philosophical breakthroughs were crucial to reorienting us, and they still provide a basis for much of the thinking and the writing that is significant today.[51]

By the end of the years of the Black Arts Movement, African American writers continued to be engaged by the possibilities of historical revisionism. As the critic Joe Weixlmann noted by the late 1970s, "much of our best fiction, white (and Chicano and Asian-American and Native American), as well as Black, especially in recent years, is about history, obsessed with it and obsessed with rewriting it."[52] The 1960s and 1970s were also the era of postmodernism's rise as a philosophical phenomena, ushering a general critical examination of history and historiography by writers and scholars.

For some artistic inheritors of the European tradition, a consciousness of historical subjectivity or "metahistory" did not redress the historical record.

Instead, such awareness produced disillusionment. These novels were nostalgic for a world lost, but for the marginalized writer, like Wideman, it became a chance to recreate the world anew. Novels that were engaged with the past became social and political tools, a way for many marginal voices to at last join the conversation of culture on a grand scale.[53] Wideman drew the same conclusions: "Minority writers hold certain, peculiar advantages in circumstances of cultural breakdown, reorientation, transition. We've accumulated centuries of experience dealing with problems of marginality, problems that are suddenly center stage for the whole of society."[54] This distinguishes his purpose for writing about the past from the modernists such as T. S. Eliot, the writer most early critics of Wideman cited as an overly prominent influence.[55] Wideman is not interested in recovering the loss of a stable history; he realizes, even in the early novels, that the past must be interrogated in ways much more in accordance with the postmodern project.[56]

Cornel West has suggested that the black artist and intellectual must adapt the Foucaultian model of history to "disrupt and dismantle the prevailing regimes of truth." West contends that the way that postmodern African American artists can dismantle such "regimes of truth" is by remembering and extending the practices used by the African American culture in its art and in its everyday life. These customs are "permeated by the kinetic orality and emotional physicality, the rhythmic syncopation, the protean improvisation, and the religious, rhetorical, and antiphonal elements of Afro-American life."[57] These traditions have been weapons of cultural resistance since the Middle Passage.

But as West's words imply, one of the differing characteristics between the goals of postmodernist thought and black writers in the postmodern era lies in the political and spiritual goals of the latter. African American postmodernism "maintains a grounding in moral values" necessary to rewriting and redressing the negative picture of African American life in history.[58] It is not enough to dismantle historical consciousness; something must be created (or regenerated) to serve in its place—a new story or, more accurately, many new stories. The fragmentation and the multiplicity associated with postmodernist thought, and the intrinsic multiple narratives that this implies, directly argue against essentialist notions of race in this country. Bernard Bell, in the spirit of West's characterization of African American culture and postmodernism, maintains that the African American postmodernist artist differs from his or her "white contemporaries" on some of these same points. African American postmodernists do not merely reject "the arrogance and anachronism of Western forms and conventions," they also rediscover and reaffirm "African-American ways of seeing, knowing and expressing reality."[59]

Such characterizations would suggest, at least for the purposes of this study, that African American cultural and literary theory and postmodernism share a reflexive or a dialogic relationship. Indeed, the fragmentation, pluralism, marginality, difference, play, emphasis on popular culture, circularity, and the polyphonic voice associated with postmodernism could easily be used to describe the history and culture of the African American tradition.[60] As such, some critics "believe that there is no such thing as African-American postmodernism, that the term itself is an oxymoron."[61] Rather than argue who shaped whom, or if even such a debate is necessary, its seems most practical for the purpose of a study of Wideman's work to consider that this cross-cultural relationship between postmodernism and African American culture resonates in Wideman's "all stories are true" aesthetic and storytelling method. His palimpsestic narratives vibrate with all of these influences.[62] This is a feasible conclusion given Wideman's continuing assertions that the "tension of multiple traditions, European and Afro-American, the Academy and the Street, animates" his writing.[63]

Wideman further suggests that he is conscious of his polyvocality and the simultaneous play of multiple discourses in his texts. He confesses, "I never know if I am writing fiction or non-fiction."[64] What we see in Wideman's work is a revisioning of the term, the form, and the genre of history and its claims to objectivity itself. Not only does Wideman sense that his own writing blurs distinctions of genre, he questions whether there is any difference at all between autobiography, fiction, or reportage.[65] He also muses, "I like to take chances, and one chance that I have been taking lately, and continue to take, is a chance with the texture of narrative—letters, hymns, poems, song lyrics, thoughts, speech, time present, time past, future time, philosophic discourse, scatting, etc., etc.... A kind of collage ... you find in somebody like an Eliot, but that you also find in traditional African art."[66] We can perceive this texture, the weaving or imbrications, of discourses, voices, and stories even in Wideman's earliest novel, *A Glance Away*, where he balances modernist stream-of-consciousness, scatting, French, and song lyrics. Wideman's interest in the modernist Eliot is perhaps a recognition of the ways that Eliot and other modernists borrowed from African American culture.[67] One of Wideman's primary imbricated discourses is music. It appears in some form or another (as content, theme, or style) in all of his work. Many African American postmodern writers "reproduce the techniques of jazz in their writing"; Wideman's writing has been declared jazz-like by critics not only because of its hybrid nature, but also because of its call-and-response patterns and its improvisational, "riffing" quality—riffing specifically through the multiple discourses that make up his palimpsestic narratives.[68]

While Wideman has never written specifically on jazz or the blues, he has reviewed Albert Murray's study of African American music. He notes that Murray's study highlights jazz and blues as metaphors for African American culture and literature and that there exists between African American literature and music essential links. Some links include those already noted above—improvisation, riffs, and call-and-response—as well as "breaks, parody, and stylized quotation of a variety of sources."[69] Wideman includes in his description here the same quality already portrayed above in his own writing—the cross-cultural influences and borrowings that also converse in a call-and-response structure. The relationship between jazz and Wideman's work is pertinent to note as further evidence that he is layering multiple stories, traditions, voices, and tropes in his work. Musicians are expected to know the vocabulary of jazz or the tradition that has gone before them; it is then a measure of their talent and their own voice how they take a familiar song or chord structure and rephrase it.[70] Jazz and its relationship to African American literature is self-evident. Henry Louis Gates Jr. argues that jazz music is a history of repetition and revision—a "signifyin(g)" internal structure—and connects the essence of jazz improvisation to African American literary intertextuality.[71]

Wideman's repetitions and rephrasings within his own canon and discourse modes of family stories, slave narratives, African American novels, European modernists, historical records, songs, and such can also be described as "riffs." Even one of his short stories exhibits this jazz technique. "Everybody Knew Bubba Riff" riffs on the life of Bubba Riff in one continuous, fluid sentence that plays with words and letters like a jazz artist would with notes. The story also riffs on the names of Homewood streets where Bubba lives and on Bubba's various names:

> I wish for voices hear empty porches hear my own feet on the pavement hear a car pass at the intersection of Braddock half a block away the oldest Homewood streets Albion Tioga Finance these streets where Bubba's known where they say his names Junior June Juney Junebug JB J Bub Bub Bubby Bubba all the silent names hidden behind curtains.[72]

The riffs of names and identities are metaphors for all the possibilities of self that resonate in the phrase "all stories are true." Wideman's repetition of characters' names and stories throughout his canon also recalls the repeated voicing intrinsic to riffing in jazz. But the riff also is a sign of repetition and multivocality and "serves as an especially appropriate synonym for troping and for revision."[73] Wideman's riffing *and* rhythmic style can be found in works as early as *A Glance Away* and *Hurry Home* (though here this same technique is most referred to by critics as modernist stream-of-consciousness).[74]

As Wideman observed in his review of Murray's study, the "break" is another intrinsic characteristic in jazz music. The break is described as a bridge or interlude in a cadence. In a break the "normal or established flow of the rhythm and the melody stop, much the same as a sentence seems to halt but only pauses at a colon. Then the gap, usually of not more than four bars is filled most often but not always by a solo instrument, whose statement is usually impromptu or improvised even when it is a quotation or variation from some well-known melody."[75] The break is "seen as an opportunity for the musician to make a personal statement."[76] Wideman seems very interested in these breaks (or pauses or gaps), drawing attention to them in his own writing (and by extension in the historical and literary expressions of African Americans). In one of his earlier works, *The Lynchers*, a character reflects on a Thelonious Monk piece: "It seemed you could count to ten between each note Monk chose to touch."[77] Wideman revisits this moment of silence and speech in his short story "The Silence of Thelonious Monk" and in his essay "In Praise of Silence."

Breaks, or spaces between notes, also figure prominently in a description of Albert Wilkes's piano playing: "Somebody had named the notes, but nobody had named the silence between the notes. The emptiness, the space waiting for him that night seven years ago. Nobody ever would name it because it was emptiness and silence and the notes they named."[78] The silences here suggest two meanings. Gaps or spaces are those fissures in history and literature where stories have not yet been told.[79] The sense is that this is also the measure of the call-and-response relationship between the artist and the community.

The silence between the notes is not a failure of Wilkes as a voice for Homewood; rather, this is a description of the call-and-response techniques of the jazz artist or storyteller who has left a space for other voices to join in. It is also the work of the jazz soloist who in a set must "fill in the musical blanks" left by the rest of the group, a space for his version of a story to be told—the call to the response.[80] The artist is within the community but is also defined by his or her separate identity. As Ralph Ellison famously insisted, "true jazz is an art of individual assertion within and against the group. Each true jazz moment (as distinct from the uninspired commercial performance) springs from a contest in which each artist challenges all the rest; each solo flight, or improvisation, represents (like the successive canvases of a painter) a definition of his identity; as individual, as member of the collectivity and as a link in the chain of the tradition."[81]

The influence of African American music on Wideman's writing cannot be stated often enough. He clearly sees it as a sustaining force in his life, as a dialogue with the traditions of his African American past, and as a metaphor of his style.[82] He believes that both in African American literature and in his own writing that music is a powerful means of expression and survival:

> Black music is a moveable feast, fluid in time, space, modality, exhibiting in theme and variations multiple relationships with the politically, socially, aesthetically dominant order, the fullest possible range of relationships including the power and independence, to change places, reverse the hierarchy, be the dominant order.[83]

These silent places or gaps in Wideman's work may also refer to blanks on the page, inviting the reader to make meaning; this is also the relationship the writer has with his or her own writing. The blank page set before the writer is a "place like the Australian aborigine's 'Dreamtime' where everything happens at once, everything connects, where the function of dream is story and the function of story to create the world."[84] Breaks, fissures, and gaps occur so frequently in Wideman's work that these Monk-like pauses often bedevil some readers who approach his writing and frighten off many but the most intrepid readers (especially in a work such as *Philadelphia Fire* or *Fanon*). *Philadelphia Fire*'s narrative structure ultimately fractures from the gaps, to the extent that it seems to have alienated many critics as well as readers.[85] The result is not only a text that is structured by many narrative voices, but also one that allows multiple conversations between text and reader and history. Wideman creates spaces where all stories can be told and heard. This is not only the nature of jazz and the relationship between the solo artist and the group; it is also a significant act in redressing the silences of marginal writers and voices in history. Gaps, call-and-response, multiple narrators, all "summon a silent subject who, otherwise, will not speak. The summoning requires a ritual involving what Robert Bellah calls community of memory. Often it is a rite of reclamation and, simultaneously, a rite of disengagement that we witness and may engage. Upon the enactment of the rite, a silent history becomes a resonant myth (memory)."[86] These gaps appear throughout contemporary African American fiction, but they can be found in autobiography as well (even in the early slave narratives). In the imaginative act, absences in American history as a whole can be filled with African American presence.[87]

Repetition and improvisation around a note or a theme is another prominent feature of jazz and the blues that echoes in Wideman's work. Wideman uses this repetition and variation to explore the possibilities of self, of vision, of stories. It is emblemized in blues music and mythology as the "X" of the crossroads, an intersection that "signals the multidirectionality of the juncture and is simply a single instance in a boundless network that redoubles and circles."[88] The blues or jazz musician, or the writer, is a trickster figure using art to subvert authority. Wideman's own work has a sense of play and trickery.[89] The image of play and trickery is marked at the crossroads by the trickster's ability to speak in doubles or play with the possibilities of the doubles, which occur "precisely on the axes, or the threshold or at Esu's crossroads, where black and white semantic fields collide."[90]

Doubles and images of the crossroads and circles appear throughout Wideman's work (in *Damballah*, *The Cattle Killing*, and *Fatheralong*). The crossroads is a site where time and space are dislocated in order to observe the past's connection to the present and the future, yet it exists outside of history; it inhabits the world of myth and religion. Time is fluid here, disrupting the linear model of progressive history that denies revisiting the past. At the crossroads, in circular time, the past can be revisited and re-imagined. The god Damballah is also often associated with the crossroads.[91] Wideman evokes this connection to Damballah implicitly in the short story "Damballah" and explicitly in *Fatheralong*. Describing Chinua Achebe's *Things Fall Apart*, Wideman calls the novel an "intersection like the one drawn with chalk on an earthen floor to summon Loa, like the crossroads sacred to Damballah where the living and the dead pass one another, like the X Malcolm chose to signify being lost and found, a symbol of transfiguration, one identity dying into new hope, new life, a new name yet to be spoken."[92] Or a new story yet to be told. Achebe is one of the sources of Wideman's phrase "all stories are true"; and through the representation of the crossroads, Achebe, Damballah, and Malcolm X simultaneously, Wideman reconnects Africa and the "new world" gods and inhabitants ("gathering them up," as Damballah is often called upon to do). As well, he marks the "X" of the crossroads as a site of possibility, through Malcolm X's rewriting of his historical and personal identity. Damballah, a Haitian deity, is the god of history and family and figures prominently as a symbol in the short-story collection of the same name. The figure embodies Wideman's dual purposes throughout his own work.

The image of Damballah is a twin serpent, and the notion of twins or doubles is present in nearly every work written by Wideman. Persons in the autobiographical work have fictional doubles that have still other doubles in other works of Wideman's fiction. Indeed, the "double" is such a significant repetition in Wideman's work that we should consider it a trope (even Wideman has multiple doubles, including Doot, Cudjoe, Doc, John Lawson, Paul in *The Island*, Thomas in *Fanon*, and the numerous nicknames given to him by his grandmother in the short story "Backseat"). Two characters are named Cudjoe: one is the writer in *Philadelphia Fire* and the other is the son of Kwansa in *Reuben*.

Wideman intimates that the double naming is "a conscious thing; they could be related. In a new novel I connect those two characters."[93] Though I am not certain what novel Wideman is referring to, it seems likely that it is *The Cattle Killing* (which he was working on at the time the interview took place). If it is, we can never really be certain; neither the main character, the novelist, nor the historian are named. In any event, the possibility of these characters returning again offers us another version of "Cudjoe."

Doubles in Wideman's canon echo the image of double-consciousness in African American literature, and they represent what Wideman has noted as the relationship of Africans and Europeans in modern history that continues even today: "We've always served as 'body doubles' for our fellow countrymen in scenes in which they either do not want to be exposed or in which there is great risk; our bodies are substituted for theirs in the psyche, in the imagination, and sometimes in the real world."[94] Wideman revises the negative image of the body double or double-consciousness to evoke other possible lives, beyond what others define for you. It could be a life missed or lost, but it is also, possibly, another "truer" life. In postmodern autobiography, authors often take on double or multiple voices or selves "to challenge dominant hegemonic ideologies."[95] Wideman simultaneously injects yet another meaning of the double as the doppelganger, in trauma narratives a symbol of the post-traumatic experience.[96] In Wideman's work all of these possible readings of the double allow for the multiplicity of voices and texts while questioning the need and desire for the figure of the double in the postmodern world.[97]

Two versions of a story, as well as characters, appear frequently in Wideman's work. The story of Freeda's scar appears in several places throughout Wideman's canon. He also admits to writing the Homewood books simultaneously.[98] One section of *Hiding Place* is repeated verbatim in *Damballah*. And various stories in *Damballah* are repeated and revised in *Sent for You Yesterday*. This doesn't occur only within the framework of the trilogy. Character names in *A Glance Away* repeat in the trilogy. Brother is a character both in *A Glance Away* and in *Sent for You Yesterday*. They may not be exactly the same character, but in the context and course of Wideman's work we have to admit both portraits of Brother are "true." John Africa appears as a character in *Philadelphia Fire* and in *Two Cities*. "Across the Wide Missouri" appears in *Damballah* as a story, and another version replays in *Fatheralong*. Thomas in *Fanon* "must imagine a second self, a made-up self like Thomas makes up, outside Thomas."[99] Even in the nonfictional work *Brothers and Keepers*, Wideman suggests that Robby is his double.[100] Cecil Braithwaite imagines that he is a "double agent." In *Two Cities*, Mallory's photography is characterized by his use of "double" exposure.

The work that most deeply deals with the idea of the double is *Reuben*. Every character has a double. *Reuben* has either a real or imaginary twin. The novel's premise is that doubles or other stories of the self must be possible: "If you killed your own sure enough double you'd be alone. Alone forever. With a double you had more than one chance."[101] There are either doubles between Wideman's texts or within them. Every major character in Wideman's work has either a physical or a named double, or the character reappears in another work (at *least* one other time). And this is not even an exhaustive list of all of Wideman's doubles throughout his oeuvre.[102]

The use of doubles, addressed throughout this study, connects Wideman to postmodern thought, to jazz (multiple versions and recordings of a standard), and to African American literature in the image of double-consciousness, but also in the double-voiced discourse outlined by Gates (and Bakhtin) and in the figure of the two-faced representation of Esu-Elegbra.[103] *Ashe* is the ability "to multiply," to embody different realities and selves. The deity that first exhibited this ability was Esu-Elegbra, who shares a relationship with Damballah as the guardian of the crossroads and is represented by a "double face," a Janus figure who can occupy two roles at the same time.[104] This echoes the character of the spirit, the "ogbanje," who takes several forms in *The Cattle Killing*. The double is also a figure of the Freudian (and by extension the Lacanian) "uncanny"—a doppelganger or ghost, the appearance of which signifies the "form of the symptomatic return of trauma."[105] The double represents the post-traumatic narrative (the ur-trauma repeated over and again), but it also resists powerlessness. The double in the postmodern era defies limited or constricted or even unified identity. It "raises questions about fixed categories" or histories; the doubles here also resonate as imagined possibilities beyond the limits of African American traumatic history.[106]

In his review of *Brothers and Keepers*, Ishmael Reed suggests that the work and its writer have revised "double-consciousness" into "triple consciousness."[107] Wideman agrees that the metaphor of double-consciousness needs to be seen anew: "DuBois talked about double vision, African-Americans having this double vision. I think that was a very suggestive and telling metaphor, only now it's time to revise it. I think having two sides—you are lucky if you only have two sides . . . most of us are many, many in one."[108] Wideman reflects this notion in his narrative arrangements. Multiple narrators operate in most of his works. Three, especially, is a magic number. *A Glance Away* is structured in three sections and the voices of the three main characters interweave with one another at the end of the final section; *Hurry Home* has a three-act movement: from home to Europe, then to Africa, and finally the return home. *The Lynchers* is also structured in three sections; there are three books in the

Homewood trilogy, which exhibit three types of writing: the blues, letters, and stories.[109] The lives of three generations and three timelines are interwoven in the *Damballah* stories; there are three narrators in *Hiding Place* and three sections/narrators and timelines in *Sent for You Yesterday*; *Brothers and Keepers* is structured in three sections and has three storytellers, Wideman, Robby, and their mother. There are three narrators in *Reuben*; in *Philadelphia Fire* there are three narrators (Cudjoe, Wideman the writer/character, and Wideman the narrator) as well as three voices (first, second, and third person) and three timelines; three generations of Wideman men are the subject of *Fatheralong*; there are three storytellers in *The Cattle Killing*: the fiction writer, the historian, and the unnamed narrator (a former slave). There are three narrators/characters in *Two Cities*, and there are three story strands in *Fanon* (the story of Thomas, Fanon, and Wideman's mother).[110] Wideman seems to be experimenting with the number four in *The Island*; nonetheless, there are doubles in that work as well.[111]

There are tripartite structures of some form in all of Wideman's works. It is not a characteristic of only the early or the later works. In fact, Wideman's repetition of three-voiced forms connects him again to the postmodernist argument against bifurcation and the hierarchy implicit in binary structures.[112] While there is some debate as to whether or not three-voiced narratives represent a modernist or postmodernist sensibility, Wideman's use of multiple narrators suggests a simultaneity of voices and discourses, reflecting the maxim "all stories are true." The tripartite structure of Wideman's work, even in the first novel (illustrated by the blending of three voices in a circle around a hobo camp), emphasizes plural stories and a nonlinear construction of history. While modernists view history as a stable "repository of cultural standards," Wideman's work reflects a vision of history as stable only in the consciousness of the hegemony.[113]

If doubles abound in Wideman's texts, they are only outnumbered by the number of circles (and, by extension, circular narratives). This, too, argues against hierarchy and Manichean bifurcation. Nonlinear time or circular or interwoven narratives occur in most of Wideman's writing, even as early as *A Glance Away* (again, for example, in the interwoven narrative of voices created by the speakers at the end of the novel in a circle around the fire). There are circular journeys, circular narratives, repetitive descriptions of Freeda's circular soap bubble, the image of a snake swallowing its tail, the circular plan of West African villages, West African beads in *Hoop Roots*; even the roundness of the basketball is reflected upon. The accumulation of these figures in the course of Wideman's writing questions and deconstructs the image of progressive, linear history and the certainty that this epistemological structure implies.

Repetitive circles also represent Wideman's presentation of time and space; time is fractured and fluid within all of the writing in some form or another.[114] Such a presentation of the interplay of the past, present, and future is a postmodern rendering of realistic time.[115] Wideman also believes that circular narrative, including its disruption of linear time, has its roots in an African tradition: "It's the West that has fractured time, has kind of tamed it and made it linear."[116] The circle is also a manifestation of relativism. No point on the circle is a progression. The circle in Wideman's work is reminiscent of the ring shout (whose antecedent is West African ring rituals), where all the voices standing around the ring "testify" or participate in the song—all the stories are heard in this chorus of voices.[117] And Wideman and his stories stand in this circle of voices or "inside of a weave of voices," as he writes in *Sent for You Yesterday*. The image of circles also implies the connection between voices and selves, between individuals and communities, between the past, present, and future. These images, as well as those of the double, direct us always to Wideman's historical vision and the need to redress the wounds of the past through the imaginative act. Wideman's recursive style here is also reminiscent of Toni Morrison's description of "re-memory" as a post-traumatic figuration of the past that loops back on itself.[118]

Wideman reminds us that "any voice we accomplish [as a writer] is really many voices, and the most powerful voices are always steeped in unutterable silences."[119] The silences of those African Americans whose stories are lost to the historical record haunt Wideman's writing. Contemporary African American writers seem especially interested in recovering a sustaining mythology from the African American tradition, but as Wideman's work illustrates, in order to accomplish this the writer must travel back to the sites of shared traumatic history. The rise of autobiography (or testimony) and the postmodern historical novel coincides with a cultural obsession with loss, dislocation, the fear of losing memory, and trauma.[120] When Wideman returns home for his grandmother's funeral, her death signals a loss of culture and family history that could vanish from memory, become silent, if another storyteller did not pick up the mantle.

African American storytellers have always combated the effects of the traumatic past through their imaginative art. The blues is an artifact of post-trauma, a sign of the traumatic past haunting the present. Even though the form appears in the era after the end of slavery, its content and its styling is purposefully reminiscent of slave songs and spirituals. At the same time, the blues criticizes America's "second slavery."[121] Scholars have for some time been interested in the blues as a means of creative resistance to white oppression, and playing the blues as an expression of emotional suffering and a confessional anodyne. This "post-traumatic narrative" continues as an imaginative response to the continued racism endured by African Americans. Not only must African Americans endure a traumatic history, they must also deal with "cultural shame and trauma as they are designated as the racially inferior and stigmatized other."[122]

But historical trauma is not the sole property of African Americans. Numerous scholars contend that we are in the grip of a traumatic or post-traumatic cultural obsession. They argue that we live in a post-traumatic world and point out a growing concern among psychotherapists about the number of patients reporting symptoms of post-traumatic stress disorder, once believed to affect only select groups such as returning combat soldiers and rape and incest victims. But in the past decade, psychologists have recorded seeing patients who are suffering from a variety of post-traumatic disorders including "post 9-11 syndrome." Many of the sufferers in question were not on the scene, some did not even live in the city, nor had they lost family members in the attack, yet they appear to have been traumatized by the experience. Psychologists have also been tracing for many years victims of post-traumatic stress whose parents had survived Nazi concentration camps, but who had themselves never even lived in Europe. Thus, even when we do not directly experience traumatic events ourselves, we represent a society that has, according to historian Dominick LaCapra, "an almost obsessive preoccupation with loss, dispossession, and deferred meaning."[123]

Without spending too much time on the psychological cases emerging, it is important to note that rather than a clinical diagnosis, this study is interested in the cultural implications of the relationship between history and trauma, postmodernism and the African American experience. I do not want to put Wideman on the psychiatrist's couch. I would argue that for over thirty years Wideman has called attention to a culture in chaos, to the relationship between personal, individual traumas and cultural traumas of the twentieth century.[124]

Historians and critics such as Shoshana Felman, Cathy Carruth, Dominick LaCapra, Leigh Gilmore, James Berger, and Kirby Farrell have all explicated, defined, and outlined the theories behind their definitions of trauma literature and post-traumatic culture, but only two of them pay attention to African American literature within their studies. Farrell only mentions that he considers slavery one of the "prosthetic" relationships which allowed for the abuse of another human being—while he is explaining domestic violence and child abuse—but he does not develop his remarks about slavery much beyond this. Gilmore, however, devotes a chapter to the work of Jamaica Kinkaid, arguing that racial violence and sexualized violence often are coexistent with each other in such works, but Gilmore does not link these associations with the history of slavery. Berger develops a more detailed account of the relationship between traumatic history and the work of Toni Morrison.

Currently, most scholars of post-traumatic culture describe it as a post-Holocaust phenomena, developing when historians began to sit down and sift through the records and personal testimonies of witnesses. The impact on the culture of writing and hearing these stories changed the way many thought about the very nature of historiography as well as philosophical truth. It is no coincidence, most argue, that postmodernism as a cultural trend and philosophy is situated in the same frame as these events. The postmodern became a "veil thrown over a set of traumatic social relations."[125] Indeed, in discussing the Holocaust, which Felman and Dori Laub describe as the "trauma" that is the "watershed of our times," they suggest the Holocaust will not be viewed as an "event encapsulated in the past, but as a history which is essentially *not over*, a history whose repercussions are not simply omnipresent (whether consciously or not) in all our cultural activities, but whose traumatic consequences are still *evolving* in today's political, historical, cultural, and artistic scene."[126] Unquestionably, they are correct in recording the Holocaust as the trauma of the twentieth-century, but what about the trauma of the eighteenth and nineteenth centuries—slavery—America's original wound?

Thus, slavery, and the white notions of supremacy that lie behind it, for the contemporary novelist, is the phylogenetic trauma, the original wound both to the American mythic narrative and to the African American body: it is the source of racism, Jim Crow, white supremacy, and black nihilism. In these different incarnations and repetitions, American culture and history exhibit typical characteristics of the post-traumatic. Cultural trauma and post-trauma are not "symptoms of the unconscious but of history."[127]

Kirby Farrell argues that trauma is a trope for a "strategic fiction that a complex, stressful society is using to account for a world that seems threateningly out of control."[128] This description of the world has been indicative of the African American experience since the Middle Passage. It is only now that the rest of American society has experienced a world seemingly out of control that trauma and the resulting post-traumatic narratives have taken center stage.[129] In a world where memory is clearly political, the novelist and the historian both must consciously see their work within the relationship between the past and present. But when a great deal of the eyewitness account has been lost, subverted, destroyed, or never recorded at all, writers like Wideman have responded by making certain that silence does not prevail.

Though the work is not necessarily an eyewitness account (this is true for even Wideman's more clearly autobiographical work), it is also no longer "the story of the individual in relation to the events of his own past, but the story of the way in which one's own trauma is tied up with the trauma of another."[130] In Wideman's case, especially in his family stories, his more overtly personal narratives connect across time to the stories of his ancestors—connecting his pain to theirs. Even if this discourse is problematized because it slips between history, fiction, and memoir, it presents a symbolic attempt at trying to process traumatic information through a cultural and fictional, as well as a personal, narrative.

Scholars of literary trauma have noted the characteristics of the genre in ways that are remarkably similar to postmodern narratives and to Wideman's works. The post-traumatic patient is afflicted with repetitive behaviors, "time-slipping," poor chronological awareness, memory lapses, illogical interruptions, and fragmented recollections. In literary trauma these elements are echoed in the structure of the narrative and are often accompanied by "textual gaps . . . breaks in linear time, [and] shifting view points."[131]

The description, as shown above, illustrates the structure and style of Wideman's narratives—both fictional and autobiographical. As well, Wideman's work appears to be caught in a post-traumatic loop, repeating and revising the past precisely because language inevitably fails when recording the trauma. There is no logical or ordered way to describe the original traumatic events because the memory is wounded, chaotic, dysfunctional—an emotional and psychological amputee. Wideman's style reflects the unspeakable and unrepresentable in the traumatic past. This is yet another reason why Wideman layers multiple voices and discourses in his writing. Not only does it suggest the chaos of the post-traumatic, it also reveals the desire to reach for anything that may attempt to capture the "truth," in much the same manner as Mallory's overexposed and layered photographs attempt to do.

This is perhaps most clearly stated in Wideman's preface to *Fatheralong*:

> We are in the midst of a second middle passage. To understand the scale of dislocation, violence, loss of life afflicting black communities in America today one needs a parallel as stark and comprehensive as the Middle Passage. Separated from traditional cultures, deprived of the love, nurturing, sense of value and identity these cultures provided, enslaved Africans in the New World found it necessary to reinvent themselves; if they were to survive as whole human beings in an alien, hostile, chaotically violent and threatening environment. Those are the precise conditions, the awesome tasks confronting young African Americans again. A configuration of devastatingly traumatic forces has severed a generation from its predecessors.[132]

The necessity to "reinvent oneself" can be seen in the earliest works. Cecil Braithwaite's dreaming of other lives and identities in *Hurry Home* is one of the first examples of this desire. But even Eddie Lawson in *A Glance Away* wants to alter the direction of his life. However, there is much less layering in the first novels, but Wideman had less of his own material from which to draw. So while history, literary texts, and family stories do weave through the early works in a multivocal structure, and Wideman does revise the tropes and images from these narratives, he does not begin his characteristic repetition of his own works until later. As Wideman's opus grew in size and scope, his layering technique evolved accordingly.

One of the difficulties in pursuing a study on Wideman's writing is in approaching the layers. As I suggest in the introduction, focusing on one or two of Wideman's works misses the breadth of his vision and the intricate workings of his layering—it would be akin to appreciating the bottom corner of a tapestry or a quilt or a mosaic. In the observation of Wideman's structures and themes, it is evident that pronouncing one work is only a family story or only a revision of history misses the larger picture it is portraying. His imbrications demand readers to look at more than one work as representative of his vision, and these layers illustrate that there are always stories hidden beneath our examination. Wideman alludes to this quality in his writing when he explains that "stories are onions": "peeling away layers turns them into something less, something other, always. Each skin, each layer a different story, connected to the particular, actual onion you once held in your hand."[133]

Analyzing one novel or one memoir can tend to diminish Wideman's artistic vision as a whole—at the very least the examination of layering discourses, texts, and stories is very difficult when only one or a few works are involved in the critique. Following Wideman's opus chronologically, when he deconstructs the acceptance of linear narratives in his own writing, also neglects some of the layers at play. Even proceeding thematically has its problems as many themes in Wideman's work reappear, are revised, even retracted, only to return again. Placing the works in categories of narrative types, as I have done in the chapters to come, also diminishes some thematic nuances and requires looseness and repetition in order to respect the layering and its place in Wideman's canon. Since I contend that Wideman bobs and weaves between multiple discourses, I illustrate where a work most clearly stresses particular narratives within its layers. In many cases, Wideman's texts, because they are interweaving so many different narrative types, focusing on and inverting multiple tropes, and repeating and revising several versions of Wideman's own stories, could fit in any category I could construct. Such boundaries are also necessarily fluid, allowing a text to appear in more than one category or chapter at once, occupying a simultaneous critical space in this study. But readers of Wideman's writing should not be surprised to discover such a possibility of being in two or more places at once.

Consider, for example, the short-story collection *Fever*. The collection includes stories that reflect every literary or cultural theoretical application I outlined above—there is even a story about theory and writing, "Surfiction." There are jazz stories, basketball stories, historical fictions, trauma narratives (linking specifically to Holocaust survivors and other victims of anti-Semitism), love stories, alienation narratives, and even a family story—if you accept the premise that the family dog, "Little Brother," needed a tale too. *Fever* is published roughly in the middle of Wideman's career, and its titular story, "Fever," sets the stage for the novel *The Cattle Killing*. "Fever" is repeated and revised within the novel. "Rock River" and "Doc's Story" are both re-envisioned in short stories and novels that Wideman will publish later. *Fever* is a collection of stories imbricated with other works, but this would be recognizable only if you know the Wideman canon. On its own, the collection is still a display of Wideman's virtuoso narrative styles, but without the context of Wideman's other work, it is more difficult to comprehend how it fits into Wideman's artistic vision.

The story "Surfiction" in *Fever* is not one of Wideman's more well-known works, yet this brief piece reflects the characteristic hybridity, layering, and multiple discourses within its own text. The work is composed of first-, second-, and third-person voices. It leaves visual margins and gaps (the image of Wideman reading notes on Charles Chesnutt) for the reader to engage the text and serves as a physical representation of Wideman's aesthetic desire for places to be cleared for new stories. "Surfiction" analyzes an African American writer, Chesnutt, and Wideman's own work in the light of men like "Barthes, Borges, and Beckett." The story tries to present a way of reading Chesnutt's "Deep Sleeper" (a work about which Wideman has written a critical study). It mixes passages from texts and theoretical work with journal entries. It includes a linguistic analysis of Chesnutt's orality. There are allusions to *Heart of Darkness*, the Bible (Pilate's *ecce homo* address), Godot, and Porky Pig—all within a single line. Woven within these literary moments are personal memories of teaching, of writing, of reading fiction and theory. There are footnotes and citations and conversations. The "plot breaks down" at the same time that the layers of snow obscure Laramie, Wyoming. Conventions of narrative are challenged by the "I" who tells us that he has "managed to embed several texts within other texts, already a rather unstable mix of genres and disciplines and literary allusions."[134] The "conventions by which we commonly detect reality" are replaced with "fictive reality." The "novelist/professor/reader" speaks from each position in the text: "hence the red-headed couple. Hence their diaries. Hence the infinite layering of the fiction he will never write (which is the subject of the fiction which he will never write)."[135]

The novelist/professor/reader informs us that at anytime we can "replay the tape at leisure. Can amplify or expand. There is plenty of blank space on the pages."[136] Though the story is only ten pages long, we hear a three-voiced structure. The discourses of history, literature, and theory are all phrased here (and challenged). The short story is also an illustration of Hutcheon's historiographic metafiction. There is a riff on the names of postmodern writers "Barth, Barthes, Barthelme." The title is an allusion to the work of Raymond Federman and the Fiction Collective, a group of postmodern writers and publishers that included Clarence Major. Most notable are those blank spaces on the page where the reader is invited to speak in the visibly present, cleared places of the text, where we are asked to "amplify or expand" the story. Wideman presents for us here a way of writing and a way of reading his work.

"Doc's Story" is in many ways a more traditional short story than "Surfiction"; nevertheless, it also exhibits many of the characteristics of Wideman's work outlined above. Not only does it take place on a court in Homewood, its title character has one of the nicknames that Wideman is known by—one of his other identities or doubles. Yet the narrator of the tale is not Doc. It appears to be a man more like Wideman himself—a storyteller. The story, like "Fever," is an incipient narrative. Later versions of this work will appear in *Two Cities* and *Hoop Roots*. Not only do both novels use basketball as a prominent metaphor and geographical literary space, they also have Doc characters, Robert Jones and Wideman himself, respectively. In *Hoop Roots*, the narrator and Doc of "Doc's Story" conflate into Wideman in his own memoir. Perhaps most notably, "Doc's Story" begins as a love story, a love story in trouble. The narrator goes to the court to hear stories to help him soothe the pain of the love leaving him: "He collects the stories they tell. He needs a story right now."[137]

The need to share and hear stories as a means to get over loss will be repeated throughout Wideman's career from Eddie and Bette Lawson in *A Glance Away* to works like *The Cattle Killing* and *Fanon*. While Doc's story is the one that disturbs the narrator the most because it is also about loss and failure—about the blues—it is also the one that ultimately fills him with the most hope. But even this is a cautionary hope:

> Would the idea of a blind man playing basketball get her attention or would she have listened the way she listened when he told her stories he'd read about slavery days when Africans could fly, change themselves to cats and hummingbirds, when black hoodoo priests and conjure queens were feared by powerful whites even though ordinary black lives weren't worth a penny. To her it was folklore, superstition. Interesting because

it revealed the psychology, the pathology of the oppressed. She listened intently, not because she thought she'd hear truth.[138]

The narrator listens to such stories and believes in them because he has faith in the power of stories to change the world. This is the storytelling magic he is wishing for when he muses: "*If Doc could do that, then anything's possible. We're possible.... If a blind man can play basketball surely we...*"[139] While this relationship is questionable, Wideman will return to revise these situations, characters, and themes in the other works emphasizing the connection between love and stories much more forcefully. In *Two Cities* and *Hoop Roots*, the narrator of "Doc's Story" gets a second chance at love.

Like "Doc's Story," other works in the collection reappear in Wideman's canon. This is the case with "Rock River." The story briefly describes the aftermath of a friend's suicide. The friend, Rick, and the speaker live out west, possibly in Wyoming. The speaker in the story arrives at Rick's home to help clean the truck that Rick shot himself in. The speaker tries to console Rick's wife, Sarah, during a conversation that reveals little about the types of relationships these characters had or the reasons behind Rick's suicide. This is a short glimpse into a life lost, one that no one seemed to notice—much like the "godawful racket" made by the bottles that Rick knocked over and broke at the last party they were at together. Yet even this short story implies the need to share stories. During the party, Rick tries to tell a story about a successful hunt: "No one was listening so Rick was telling it softly, slouched down in an armchair."[140] Soon after he knocks over the bottles. These attempts at being heard, of sharing his voice, are met with disregard by others. It is the one key to understanding Rick's choice. This is an incomplete sketch, a gap that remains to be filled. Wideman returns to this character and situation many years later in the short story "Sightings" in *God's Gym*, perhaps to address that silence.

"Little Brother" is not a story that Wideman returns to again, but it is populated by characters that we have seen before. The story is related primarily through conversation and talk. Its structure, language, and development are reminiscent of the Homewood works, of which it is a part. As a segment of the mythic cycle of Homewood stories, a tale about a dog may seem somewhat out of place, but Little Brother is seen as a member of the family. He also has had plenty of escapades that have risen to the level of family legend. But the story's significance lies in its reflection of how family stories are inevitably circular and how they reveal much more than could be anticipated when the story begins.

During the course of a tale about Little Brother, the story transgresses to stories of Uncle Otis, John French, other dogs, the streets of Homewood, marriages, and racism. The story is also interrupted by Geraldine and her audience, Penny, usually telling children upstairs to stop wasting water in the bathroom—which leads to other bathing stories, including the washing of the dog Pup-pup after he had been hit and killed by a car. The story is broken into several more times by more mundane details about saving a piece of pie for the writer's son, Dan, and then returns again to other serious matters, including the nature of love. Little Brother, as his name suggests, is just another character in the Wideman family history, but the work presents yet another narrative type in the collection that attempts to "gather up" all the voices in this family.

Even stories that do not have doubles elsewhere in Wideman or are not Homewood stories or historical fiction display many of Wideman's characteristic techniques. "The Statue of Liberty" balances multiple points of view and comments on race and sexuality in the American historical consciousness. The jogger, one of those points of view, admits he likes running by people's homes because it allows him to turn himself "into another person in another place."[141] "The Tambourine Lady" also employs multiple voices to tell its story. The story is set in Homewood but is not populated with Lawsons or Widemans, at least not directly. The story follows a young girl, and some of the narrative is layered with the language of children—how they hear parents and adults, game-playing, teasing, praying. Even in these child-like moments, the language of parental caution interrupts the narrative. The girl repeats several times the warning not to go play in Hamilton Avenue; she prays that she is able to hear the Tambourine Lady play again in church on Sunday. Is the child in danger? Is she another lost child in Wideman's opus? Or is it just a memory of a frighteningly close call? The work refuses to resolve any of these questions, but it develops through its structure the consciousness of the child as storyteller, a technique that Wideman will use again in "Newborn Thrown in Trash and Dies" and in segments of *Philadelphia Fire* and *The Cattle Killing*.

The emphasis on the power of music to make the child feel safe and connected in "The Tambourine Lady" echoes the significance of African American music in Wideman's writing. The other music stories in the collection, "Presents," "Concert," "When It's Time to Go," and "Valaida," also emphasize blues heroes and the tradition of the blues and jazz in African American writing. Each story follows a musician, a blues man who plays his music at the risk of his own happiness and peace. The blues hero is a consistent character, repeated and revised throughout Wideman's work. Even here we get variations on the theme. The first story, "When It's Time to Go," is a tale of a musician named Sambo, shared among men at a bar. The musician is a blind boy, born with a "caul over his head" that "turned him blue."[142]

The boy is able to see for a short time during his childhood but soon loses his sight even though he still has the memory of vision. People think his mother is a witch, and yet she trusts doctors with little care for medicine or children for an antidote for her son's blindness. The boy begins to dream, which he describes as "singing," and when the "light sings to" him, anything is possible. His singing allows him to be in "two places at once," a power that his mother fears. He eventually leaves home, still blind, to play piano in New Orleans. By the end of the story, the storyteller is revealed to be the boy himself, a man now, reflecting on his past. His life and his music have brought him suffering—the life his mother feared he would have when she understood that he had a gift of vision and "light" and singing that he would need to share with others. The sharing of his story and his identification with blindness and the blues illustrates his heroic status. He is a voice of the community, "thinking of that blood leaving you and running up in somebody else's arms, down into somebody's fingers black or brown or ivory just like yours. And listen to those hands playing music."[143] Whether he is playing or telling his story, it serves a ritual and communal function in the narrative.

Both "Concert" and "Presents" extend the image of the blues hero as a voice for the people. In "Concert" the musician is waiting for another set to begin when he receives a phone call about his mother, but rather than progressing from there in a linear manner, the story moves forward and backward in time. Other memories, other shows—the past interrupts the narrative. There is even a hint of a flash-forward that suggests what the phone call concerns ("I can't hang up because I haven't picked up yet").[144] This narrative appears recursive as well, going back and forward again to teach us something about music and the blues. While the power and magic of the sound transported the girl in "The Tambourine Lady" and the boy in "When It's Time to Go," the music here is not able to save anyone. It cannot stop time or transform reality. The musician seems to be playing this piece again and again in his memory as he recalls the night the phone call came about his mother's death: "If I hurry home, it won't have happened yet."[145] Most of the story replicates the sound and rhythm of jazz as well. Its pauses or breaks, repetitions, and circularity are all reminiscent of other Wideman works, but in "Concert," Wideman also tries to describe the hard life of the musician who is away from home, looking into the dark holes of his memory in order to tell his story.

The story "Presents" develops a similar type of character who from his birth is anointed as a future voice of the people. After he is born, his grandmother passes her "old hand once in the air over the crown of his skull" and her bed is a "throne."[146] The choice of words marks him as the blues hero, at least in his grandmother's eyes. He is a chosen one, who she "prophesizes" will "sing for kings and queens, but his gift for music will also drag him down to the depths of hell."[147] His talent will make "joyful noise" to the lord, but it will also cause him great suffering. His grandmother, Big Mama, teaches him to play, telling him that he should let the music take him to another place.

Again, the transformative power of music, like storytelling, is reinforced in this tale through the story of the blues hero who will follow in the steps of men like Robert Johnson and Buddy Bolden, but who will lead a lonely and isolated life. Later in his life, after Big Mama is gone and everything she has foretold has come true, the man "wishes someone would pat him on his head and say everything is gon be all right."[148] Without his family, his deeper connections to community are fragile and he feels alone. We are told that "the story has more skins than an onion and it can cause a grown man to cry when he starts to peeling it."[149] This line, later repeated in *Fatheralong*, further layers the alienation narratives common to the isolated artist figure who is bereft of connection.

Wideman transforms the image of the blues hero and alienated artist in "Valaida," a story that also more directly explores historiography beyond his family and Homewood. One of Wideman's most widely anthologized, this story falls more neatly into the realm of historical fiction. There is little of Wideman's autobiography here, yet he tells us that the story grew out of a biography on the musician Valaida Snow.[150] The story itself is dependent on the connections made between history, fictional characters, and the need to share stories. But it also juxtaposes the image of the isolated artist and the committed blues hero— "the articulate kinsman." The story is also another instance of a Wideman story that fills a gap. Little is known about Valaida Snow's whereabouts between 1940 and 1941. A jazz trumpeter and singer, Snow was an eccentric, colorful personality.

While on tour in Europe, she was apparently detained or possibly interned by the Nazis during World War II. Her biographer is even unsure about the history of these years, though there is some speculation that she suffered at the hands of the Nazis and was treated as poorly as European Jews in the concentration camps.[151] Snow returned to the states in 1943 and died in 1956, but apparently never revealed, on record, what happened to her during the war. Wideman fills this "blank space" in Snow's history; the "meaning" of Snow's life, Wideman suggests, is in the space that is silent.

In the story, Snow speaks from heaven, thirty years after her death, about a young boy she saved in a concentration camp. The story cuts to that boy, now a middle-aged man, Mr. Cohen. It is Christmas Eve and Mr. Cohen decides to share the story of his rescue with his African American maid, Clara Jackson. Cohen never knew Valaida's name, but he is touched by her courage and her sacrifice for a boy that she didn't even know. Her act and his sharing of this moment connect him to Clara: "When he looks at her, he imagines her family" and "the faces of her relatives become his."[152] Wideman uses a historical figure to examine a pivotal moment in the history of the twentieth century (another site of well-recorded cultural trauma) through a fictional character. This is certainly not a new technique, but Wideman is able to portray the heroism of an African American woman that most people don't even know. Whether or not Snow really saved a little Jewish boy ultimately is not a crucial fact. There are many unsung heroes in African American history. Wideman also connects other victims of trauma together whose stories may not be known.

"Valaida" also reiterates Wideman's belief that stories connect us in powerful and meaningful ways. It is not until Cohen shares his story with Clara that he feels a kinship with her (even though she is unsure of or uncomfortable with that connection). The story also is inhabited by many voices: Cohen, Valaida, Clara, and the numerous victims of both African American racism and the Holocaust whose stories and lives remain unknown. By weaving the voices of these victims together, Wideman illustrates the strands of racism throughout history, shown through two groups that are usually not seen occupying the same space, at the same time, in literature. The linking presents two crucial historical traumas that continue to haunt the world: the Holocaust and the African slave trade. While generally America has been more capable of speaking about the trauma of the Holocaust, it is still uneasy, and even unwilling, to see slavery as a comparable event. Wideman's story conflates these two historical moments and the post-traumatic influences they both continue to project onto the American consciousness.[153] While Cohen is the recorder of this silent space in Snow's life, their shared experience of trauma and her life-saving heroism invite him to speak on her behalf.

Wideman continues the associations between African American history and Jewish history in the story "Fever." Though I develop a more complete analysis of the work in chapter 4 as an antecedent text of *The Cattle Killing*, the story's position in the collection *Fever* is important to note here. In several ways, the story is a culmination of the ideas presented here in the first chapter of this study, but it is also the story that ties many of the earlier works in this collection together. As the centerpiece, appearing at the end, the collection moves backward to show us where the "fever" began—in the past. The fever is the disease of racism, spreading out from the "heart" of Philadelphia, as it is described in the epigraph. Everything that we have read in some way or another to this point has its roots here. The story layers several different discourses, which we will see repeated again in *The Cattle Killing*. The inclusion of scientific data to provide evidence of African immunity, the autopsy results, the letters from

Dr. Rush (one of the signers of the Declaration of Independence), and multiple narrative points of view provide a more complete picture of the yellow fever epidemic of 1793. The technique also calls into question the way that history is retold. The style of Wideman's writing here disallows a singular view of what happened. It constructs social and historical reality through several lenses rather than choosing the rational rhetoric or traditional historiography.

Like Wideman's archaeological project with his family history and the life of Valaida Snow, Wideman fills a gap in the story of Richard Allen. Though Richard Allen was not silent on the subject of the yellow fever and the treatment of African Americans in Philadelphia, Allen and Absalom Jones's pamphlet on the epidemic did not dislodge the stories promoted by Matthew Carey in his more popular pamphlet, which accused Africans of bringing the disease to the city and profiting from the death and destruction it wreaked on Philadelphia. In Wideman's story, Allen is an active and sacrificial blues hero, risking his life to combat not only the fever but the stories of African Americans that characterized them as animal, violent, diseased, without value. Allen and his followers help the city survive the epidemic, but he is unable to erase the racist perceptions of his neighbors, despite their residence in the "City of Brotherly Love."

One of the sick that Allen tends to is Abraham, a Jewish immigrant who admonishes Allen for not taking care of his own family and people. Abraham links the history of the yellow fever with the Palatine fever, equating the anti-Semitism that plagues European Jews with African Americans and their traumatic history. This shared "story" of victimization convinces Abraham that Allen is one of the Lamed-Vov (Vovnik)—one of God's chosen honorable and just men.[154] Like the blues heroes seen throughout the collection and Wideman's work, these characters bear the weight of suffering for their community. Abraham reminds Allen that God is a "bookseller" that only "publishes one book—the text of suffering,"[155] and the Lamed-Vovnik and the blues hero are forced to repeat the story.

The shared history of trauma and suffering between African Americans and victims of anti-Semitism is also reflected in "Hostages." The Lamed-Vovnik myth is retold here as well. The "Lamed-Vov are God's hostages. Without them humanity would suffocate in a single cry," and they are the "sponges drawing mankind's suffering into themselves."[156] Especially compelling is the description of men and women who have been kidnapped in the Middle East—other hostages or human commodities. Wideman draws connections between these hostages and others such as victims of the Holocaust and slaves. The narrator of "Hostages" makes these associations as he listens to an old friend talk about her history. A daughter of an Auschwitz survivor, she feels comfortable confessing her pain to the narrator: "She said she could tell me everything because I was black. Because I was black I would understand."[157] Both "Hostages" and "Fever" develop as shared narrative spaces between teller and audience, confessing their life histories and pain in order to connect to and instruct one another about surviving trauma. The necessity of telling stories as a means of addressing the "world's disorder and suffering" is a theme of the collection as a whole.[158] This sharing of traumatic histories as a step toward healing or surviving is found throughout many of the works in this collection and in Wideman's writing overall.

But Wideman does not suggest that storytelling is a cure-all for the suffering of the past. For those media pundits and call-in listeners who wish that we could just "forget the past and move on," who continue to misunderstand African Americans who "keep complaining about racism," who fervently believe we are living in a post-racial society, there is little understanding of the lasting effects of racism, of the post-traumatic impulse in America. The inability to "get over" the past is not a complaint lodged against Vietnam veterans or rape victims. But America's emphasis on progress and on popular culture's focus on the "healing process" neglects a close examination of the historical forces still at work, especially when it comes to the legacy of slavery and the effects of racism.[159]

In the postmodern trauma and apocalypse narratives prominent in the waning years of the twentieth century, artists and writers warned of the dangers of losing our memory and called for storytelling to protect the future, understanding that the "wounds of the past can never be healed, but can only be transcended."[160] The artists of the African American tradition understood this message that resounds in most of Wideman's work. They understood the need to tell their stories, to share them with others, to help soothe old wounds. Wideman's responsibility as a writer is the same as the blues artist who must "keep the painful details and episodes of a brutal experience alive in one's aching consciousness, to finger its jagged grain, and to transcend it."[161]

CHAPTER TWO

Deconstructing History

TRAUMA AND THE ALIENATION NARRATIVES

> Imagine how different we might be if we really listened to our father's stories. If we preserved them, learned to make them part of our lives. Wouldn't the stories, if known and performed over generations, be infused with the power of our music?
>
> —JOHN EDGAR WIDEMAN, *Fatheralong*

As we have already seen, much of the early criticism on Wideman operated on the premise that Wideman was alienated from the stories of his culture; his years as a Rhodes Scholar at Oxford University and his long periods of physical isolation from his family while living abroad and then in the Wyoming reinforce this notion. Critics and reviewers "read" Wideman, and thus his work, through the tropological lens of the "alienated African American intellectual." In Wideman's vision this is not the only "true" story for himself or others. He critically revoices this narrative and layers it among others, such as tales of lynchings, the experience of double-consciousness, the journeys North (and South), the Middle Passage, the flights from home, and the slave's escape, to name a few. He not only layers these narratives within his work, but also weaves in Western mythology, American romantic individualism, and the voices of European and American modernism. Any material is valuable in addressing the silences and the trauma of the past.[1]

We must consider whether or not Wideman accepts the Eurocentric influences on his work as uncritically as some have argued. Wideman's cross-cultural borrowing should not be viewed as "turning his back" on African American culture (a reading of Wideman that reiterates the alienated intellectual trope). Indeed, it is a characteristic of African American literature for writers to speak to and revise the white, mainstream tradition in their writing and for their works to be intertextual responses to both traditions.

Even in the early works, we see this characteristic in Wideman's writing, as well as the revision of images found in both modernist European literature and African American culture. Wideman's dialogic response to both traditions simultaneously in his work is an act of balance and equality, reinforcing the maxim "all stories are true." In this chapter, we will pay close attention to the revision of these "master tropes" in nearly all of his work, especially in the earliest novels. In works such as *A Glance Away*, *Hurry Home*, and *The Lynchers*, the trope of the alienated African American intellectual is particularly pervasive. However, the image continues to appear, even in his most recent novel, *Fanon*.

These master tropes of African American experience are produced by both the Western hegemonic tradition and the African American tradition. It is the dialectic between these discourses that imbues Wideman's work with its hybridity and its interplay of "all stories." Those images can be problematic, however, sometimes producing limiting metaphors and images of African American experience. These stories and tropes are reinscribed and revised throughout the scope of Wideman's work.

Wideman has stressed the need to understand what he calls "father stories." He reflects upon the description and the importance of these texts: "Father stories are about establishing origins and through them legitimizing claims of ownership, of occupancy, and identity. They connect what's momentary and passing to what surpasses, materiality to ideal."[2] "Father" and "son" are metaphors for the past and the present. Father stories are stories that connect all of us to the past—through literature or history. The past and the present share a dialogic relationship in Wideman's vision of storytelling. Time is once again seen not as a closed line of progression: "There is a circle and a flow. There's no difference between the stories of the fathers and the sons."[3]

One of the father stories that links history and literature and fathers and sons is the slave narrative. Many scholars argue that the slave narrative and its tropes created the foundation for the tradition of African American literature. Wideman has written critically on the slave narrative tradition,[4] and in his literature he addresses and revises the purpose of the slave narrative, the narrator's voice, and/or the images of the form. Henry Louis Gates Jr. calls this act "tropological revision." Tropes are repeated "with differences" between texts or between a text and the tradition. Gates goes further to suggest that "the revision of specific tropes recurs with surprising frequency in the African American literary tradition. The descent underground, the verbal 'ascent' from the South to the North, myriad figures of the double, and especially double-consciousness, all come readily to mind."[5]

When former slaves in eighteenth- and nineteenth-century America began inscribing their stories of bondage, escape, and freedom, they initiated a form that became a unique American literary genre. The slave narrative, subsequently, has influenced, directly and indirectly, generations of writers. James Olney's study of the slave narrative and subsequent African American literature leads him to conclude that the narrative, in such hands as Frederick Douglass's, "constitutes literary history and, specifically, the Afro-American literary tradition."[6] Hazel Carby reaches much the same conclusion: the conditions of slavery and its "cultural productions" are the basis of an "entire narrative tradition."[7]

Not only is the slave narrative an ancestor of the twentieth-century African American novel and autobiography, it has been revised as a new literary genre, the "narrativity of slavery," a term coined by scholar Ashraf Rushdy. These works include contemporary novels of slave's lives, such as Toni Morrison's *Beloved*, Ishmael Reed's *Flight to Canada*, and Ernest Gaines's *The Autobiography of Miss Jane Pittman*, and also novels that supplant the oppression of the slave plantation with that of the urban ghettos following the great waves of migration to the North. Reed refers to both types of writing as "neo-slave narratives."[8] Rushdy has gone so far as to categorize four types of "the narrativity of slavery" and to suggest that the growth and development of these works are rooted in the politics and cultural awareness of the 1960s.[9] The neo-slave narratives are perhaps the most figurative artifact of historical trauma in the contemporary period. Their appearance and popularity highlights the post-traumatic relationship between slavery and racism in American writing. Neo-slave narratives continue to be immensely popular with postmodern writers, like Wideman, who can critique and revise the historiography of slavery as well as creatively present "truthful" fiction and historical slave's lives.

Writers as early as W.E.B. DuBois discovered, in the words of Arnold Rampersad, that "only by grappling with the meaning and legacy of slavery can the imagination, recognizing finally the temporality of the institution, begin to transcend it."[10] The contemporary African American writer has transformed the nightmare of the past into a vision of imagining possibility. The neo-slave narrative offers a vision of history that can negotiate the traumatic past: "Most postmodern slave narratives reject the parodic aspects of the postmodern treatment of history (with the notable exceptions of Ishmael Reed and Charles

Johnson) and opt for a more serious approach even as they displace realism as the primary mode of history.... [W]hat results in these novels is a persistent faith in the power and ability of narrative (if used oppositionally) to achieve liberation for both the enslaved and the postmodern black subject."[11]

As the maxim "all stories are true" suggests, Wideman is deeply concerned with creating alternate possibilities to fight "the enemy's dream." The spectrum of his work encompasses the four categories of "narrativity of slavery" designated by Rushdy, a "form of writing which has emerged as the most amenable and most effective way of bringing to life the subject of hidden history of the black experience in contemporary African-American writing."[12] Since Wideman's literary project is the recovery of hidden stories and histories, his work exhibits many of the characteristics of Rushdy's four categories of "narrativity" and makes connections to the trauma of slavery explicitly through his fiction and nonfiction, even in those works of the Homewood trilogy.[13]

The Homewood books, especially *Damballah*, are examples of what Rushdy calls the "genealogical narrative," and *The Cattle Killing* fulfills the requirements of the fourth category.[14] Rushdy's second category is also significant in a consideration of Wideman's writings. This category is "comprised of narratives which set their action in contemporary, late 20th century America, which deal, implicitly or explicitly, with the lives and psychological make-up of modern men and women whose ancestors were enslaved. One could make the case that perhaps half the novels written in the African-American tradition deal with this scenario in some way or another."[15] Rushdy includes such representative works as Ralph Ellison's *Invisible Man* and Richard Wright's *Black Boy*; and, clearly, *A Glance Away*, *Hurry Home*, *The Lynchers*, *Brothers and Keepers*, and *Philadelphia Fire* reproduce these characteristics as well.

Another study that traces the connections between the slave narrative and African American fiction is Robert Stepto's, *From behind the Veil*, which illustrates the call-and-response relationship between the slave narratives and twentieth-century autobiography and fiction. His study is interested in how these "contrapuntal" texts speak to one another and how they "speak as one": "Afro-American culture, like all cultures, has its store of what Northrup Frye has called 'canonical stories' or what I call 'pregeneric myths'—shared stories or myths that not only exist prior to literary form, but eventually shape the forms that comprise a given culture's literary canon."[16]

Through the call-and-response mode that Stepto uses to frame the intertextual relationships within the tradition, there emerges a theory of African American literature that suggests that the characteristic of interrelatedness is endemic to African American culture. Henry Louis Gates's analysis of intertextuality in African American literature is based on such African American cultural practice as well. Gates's theory of signifying (or "Signifyin[g]") also traces the relationship between the slave narrative and twentieth-century texts (as well as between twentieth-century texts themselves).[17]

The similarity in content and theme between the narratives and African American literature and autobiography is illustrated by numerous other critics, including Houston Baker Jr., who describes the development of the African American tradition as a "journey back." Like their slave narrative forefathers and mothers, the writers of the twentieth century have still fixed their gaze "in the same direction—backward, to a time of chaos."[18] While this is by no means an exhaustive review of such criticism, one would have to conclude, as Deborah McDowell does, that the "assertions that the slave narrative begins the African-American literary tradition are repeated so often that they have acquired the force of self-evident truth."[19]

Despite such pronouncements that there are clear and significant relationships between the slave narrative and twentieth-century African American literature and that his work reflects such relationships, Wideman reminds us that the slave narrative is a problematic form, even if it is the progenitor of African American literature. Produced for a white, middle-class audience by abolitionists, the slave narrators, despite their considerable artistry, were often limited by the form and purpose of their work. The result, Wideman argues, is a repetitive pattern that reinforces Manichean construction and furthers hierarchal separation in America, forcing African Americans to choose between either one or the other:

> South to North, rural to urban, black environment (plantation) to white environment (everywhere, including the language in which the narrator converses with the reader), silence to literacy, are some of the classic crossovers accomplished by the protagonists of such fables. If you punch in modern variants of these dichotomies—ghetto to middle class, ignorance to education, unskilled to professional, despised gangster to enlightened spokesperson, you can see how persistent and malleable the formula is.[20]

Scholars have illustrated repetitions and conventions of the slave narrative at length, and many have concluded that the narratives possess a "sense not of uniqueness but of overwhelming sameness."[21] Most narratives do exhibit a set of conventions so standardized that they almost seem to have been published as a book of guidelines on "how to write a slave narrative."[22] Wideman's observation about the "persistence" of the formula reflects the overall nature of the narratives. The repetition of structures, content, and themes are another reflection of the shared traumatic legacy of slavery. Once the slave narrative appears as a genre, its conventions reify the experience of slavery in the consciousness of writers and readers alike.

However, one of the most pernicious aspects of the slave narrative and its descendants, Wideman suggests, is that "the fate of one black individual is foregrounded, removed from the network of systematic relationships connecting, defining, determining, undermining all American lives."[23] Because of the slave narrative's form and the circumstances of escape, the protagonist in most narratives is a singular, isolated character who escapes on his (or her) own. The slave journeys through the wilderness (physical and spiritual) and arrives in the North with a new identity and life. The "pervasive use of journey or quest motifs" in search of an identity is a practical and apparent result of the escaped slave's life. This will be a pattern repeated and revised in Wideman's *A Glance Away*, *Hurry Home*, *Brothers and Keepers*, *Philadelphia Fire*, *The Cattle Killing*, and *Fatheralong*.

This movement away from home and community into the wilderness to establish identity is a mythic feature of Western literature, heightened in the American imagination by the landscape and freedom of mobility found in the country. The birth of the American romantic hero of nineteenth- and even twentieth-century literature is the product of this mythic journey. In his study, *The American Adam*, R.W. B. Lewis describes this dominant figure as the hero of a new adventure: an individual "emancipated from history, happily bereft of ancestry, untouched and undefiled by the usual inheritances of family and race; an individual standing alone, self-reliant and self-propelling, ready to confront whatever awaited him with the aid of his own unique and inherent resources."[24] However, the slave narrators would not be "happily bereft" of their family, race, and their ancestry. These are the traumatic losses they suffered at the hands of slave traders and owners.

One of the dangers of adopting these tropes of American manhood is that the slave narrators "defined their humanity in the terms of prevailing conceptions of American identity."[25] The male is also cut off from community and family in the American literary model. This characteristic of the self-made man within the African American tradition has very different historical roots. It may be primarily the result of many men having already been removed from the community and displaced in the family structures. Few slave narratives illustrate a family on the run. When male narrators have families, they describe the "pain of leaving their families behind in order to escape as a pain they can bear only because the duty to escape bondage is even stronger."[26]

There is no argument that these models and motifs were forced upon the narrators and the narratives by the circumstances of slavery, flight, dislocation from the community, the need to establish a name and identity, and even the pattern of movement from the South to the North. The repetition of this movement in the slave narratives has a cumulative effect: it produces the repetition of tropes found in African American literature, and the narratives, in their form and content, support the "belief in efficacy and virtue of self-reliance," which has been a "crucial part of American popular thought. That belief is probably the common denominator in most variations of what we label the American dream."[27] The danger of such a belief, Wideman contends, is that it

> comforts and consoles those in power and offers a ray of hope to the powerless. Although the existing social arrangements may allow the horrors of plantations, ghettos, and prisons to exist, the narratives tell us these arrangements also allow room for some to escape. Thus the arrangements are not absolutely evil. No one is absolutely guilty, nor are the oppressed (slave, prisoner, ghetto inhabitant) absolutely guiltless. If some overcome why don't others?[28]

Several characters in Wideman's work have embraced this idea, and Wideman himself, in *Brothers and Keepers*, acknowledges that he had accepted this belief (though in a later interview he notes he "oversold" the idea of "running away" from home and his identity).[29]

The isolation felt by the slave narrators, as well as the form's reification of the ideas of American individualism and separation from community, is still a powerful strand in twentieth-century African American literature. In exchange for success in the white world, the American Dream, the African American protagonist (generally a male) in twentieth-century fiction and literature is cut off from his home, his community, and himself just as the slave narrator ancestors were. This dilemma is replayed again and again in the pages of many of the canonical works of the African American tradition. The characters in Jean Toomer's *Cane*, Richard Wright's *Black Boy*, and Ralph Ellison's *Invisible Man* narrate the flight away from the community in search of a new identity.[30] Thus flight from the community and the search for identity continued to be a predominant trope in the literature, reenacting the trauma of separation and disruption of family relationships.

The flight from community has been extended to another prevailing trope as well—expatriation or travel to Africa. W.E.B. DuBois, Langston Hughes, James Baldwin, and Richard Wright all narrate this experience. Baldwin expresses the motives and feelings of the alienated expatriate:

> When I followed the line of my past I did not find myself in Europe but in Africa. And this meant that in some subtle way, in a real profound way, I brought to Shakespeare, Bach, Rembrandt, to the stones of Paris, to the cathedral at Chartres, and to the Empire State Building, a special attitude. These were not really my creations, they did not contain my history; I might search in vain forever for any reflection of myself. I was an interloper; this was not my heritage. At the same time I had no heritage which I could possibly hope to lose—I had certainly become unfitted for the jungle or the tribe.[31]

Baldwin's description of a search for identity in historical places echoes the flight from home seen in Wideman's second novel, *Hurry Home*. The trauma and alienation of the African American intellectual/artist has also become a trope. Not only does the intellectual often physically leave home, he or she may also sever ties to the community.

It may be that the isolated artist, like the slave narrator, does not fully understand all that has been left behind until much later. Frederick Douglass tells us that he did not fully appreciate the value of the slave songs until after he had left the slave community. Looking back in the narrative, stepping outside "the circle," he tries to explain the beauty and the meaning of the songs. In his public, intellectual persona, he analyzes culture and society as reflected by these songs. But one senses his longing for the emotional sustenance that the songs and the community gave him. It is a moment akin to Wideman's realization that his time away from his family and community had caused him to lose "his Homewood ear."

Another trope that Wideman clearly responds to and revises is the division the alienated artist begins to feel between self and community. This division is classically expressed in DuBois's characterization of the "double consciousness" (and later Ellison's revised phrase "double vision") that afflicts the African American and, mostly keenly perhaps, the intellectual. After his first encounter with *The Souls of Black Folk*, Wideman saw an affirmative and recurring pattern of this characteristic in his own life and in others:

> When reading about two-ness, two souls, two thoughts, two unreconciled strivings; two warring ideals in one dark body, I felt a great sense of relief. My experience was being validated. What I felt as a black person in America counted, deserved to be on record. It wasn't simply my personality, my overwrought imagination that created the alienation and ambivalence dogging me.[32]

The first of his family to attend college, Wideman went on to become one of the first two African American Rhodes Scholars since Alain Locke. His achievements at Oxford prompted *Look* magazine to exclaim that he was the "amazing John Wideman."[33] "Amazing," it intimated, because he had excelled where few in America seemed to think African Americans could. He felt a similar "grim predicament" to what bell hooks and Cornel West described as facing all contemporary black intellectuals "caught between the American society and insouciant Black community; the Afro-American who takes seriously the life of the mind inhabits an isolated and insulated world."[34] This is not a phenomenon unique to the postmodern era, certainly.[35] Many of Wideman's works, particularly *Hurry Home*, *Brothers and Keepers*, *Reuben*, *Philadelphia Fire*, and *Fanon*, respond in some way to the conception of double-consciousness. Wideman's use of the double throughout his works is an echo and revision of this trope of African American literature.

Wideman's response to slave narratives, to the tropes and the archetypes of African American literature, to European and American literature, and to contemporary African American autobiography reflects his desire to recall little-known stories, revisit stories that people have forgotten, and revise stories that have limited and confined African American experience (no matter who has written them). In the individual lives that he portrays reverberate the lives that have gone before, linking past and present trauma, but also healing the community's wounds through the artistic weapons of the folk tradition—story and song.

The importance of story and song as theme appears in Wideman's first novel, *A Glance Away*. The work's jazz-like cadences and emphasis on the artist Eddie Lawson and his scat-speaking friend, Brother, illustrate these essential characteristics. The book begins with the birth of Eugene Lawson, the older brother of Eddie. Naturally, the events described happen before Eddie's birth, yet we see the forces of family and tradition that will shape him. His grandfather, "DaddyGene," his grandmother, Freeda, and his parents are all introduced, and most will never be seen again in the remainder of the novel. Many of the names will appear again in the Homewood trilogy and share similar or the same names as Wideman's own family. The relationships that Eddie has with the character Brother and his sister, Alice, echo Carl Lawson's relationship with Brother and his sister, Lucy, in *Sent for You Yesterday*. Martha Lawson is Wideman's real paternal grandmother ("Backseat"), but the character's isolation after the death of her husband and her son echoes the character Mother Bess in *Hiding Place*. Bette's and Eddie's caretaking of their mother also resembles Bette's and Carl's caretaking of their mother, Freeda, in "The Chinaman." These repeated stories illustrate once again the doubling and the layers of genre, story, and character in Wideman's work.

All that occurs here in the prologue—the novel's past—directly impacts the present time of the text. The past and the present act as dialogic voices. In the prologue, the despair and alienation felt in the rest of the novel is missing, and one senses that if DaddyGene was still living, the Lawson family would not be as fractured as it is. Equally, one perceives that if Eddie could remember this past, through the imagination, he could be saved. This is true of the character Carl in *Sent for You Yesterday* as well, who resembles Eddie in many ways.[36] In future works, we see that it is also clear that Eddie Lawson represents Wideman's father, Edgar, who Wideman repeatedly tells us was an isolated figure.

The first pages reenact the naming of Eugene, described in ritualistic language: "And he shall be called Eugene."[37] The prologue ends with the death of DaddyGene, which is also related through biblical language—"go tell it on the mountain" and "for thine is the kingdom"—that free-floats through the text. The importance of naming as a connection to the past (an act important in the African ritual tradition, but withheld from many slaves) is implicit when DaddyGene holds his namesake: "Off shuffling to tune of Gimme that wine spudie-udie he went, dedecorumed in glee of life renewed bearing his name, his flesh and blood redone forever in two bodies precious together under hospital blankets."[38] The prologue's illustration of the past is confirmed by the voices, languages, and discourses that have informed Eddie's life and that have shared equal importance. Interspersed throughout and in dialogue with each other are the biblical language and the voices of the family, free indirect discourse,[39] the authorial voice, nursery rhymes, allusions to T. S. Eliot's poetry, songs, and French words (and later in the novel there are sections of dialogue presented in dramatic form). All of these voices and texts are demonstrations of the novel's postmodern and dialogic form and its layering of discourses and texts. All of these texts reveal something about this family and the world that they inhabit.

Wideman has stated that one reason that he was attracted to Eliot's writing was because of Eliot's preoccupation with cultural collapse.[40] Of course, that doesn't mean that Wideman views that cultural collapse the same way or even that he is concerned with the same culture collapsing. Eliot's response to history was nostalgia for the past, a wish that the world would reconnect those fragments of the past.[41] If Wideman has any nostalgia for the past, it is the past of Homewood exemplified by John French's generation that sustained and celebrated the community. There is no indication that Wideman feels the loss of the European past that Eliot does. Wideman views the past as a postmodernist; it needs to be reevaluated, revised. There must be a "dialogue with the past in light of the present."[42]

Much has been made of Wideman's allusions to Eliot in *A Glance Away* and *Hurry Home*. Accused of relying too heavily on white modernism, Wideman's early novels have been dismissed as turning away from African American culture. However, Eliot borrowed heavily from African American language and music. Michael North goes so far as to suggest that Eliot and many other modernists saw African American culture as a paradigm for modernism; its subversive, alienated condition spoke to these artists' own feelings of isolation and loss of tradition and culture. Eliot re-imagined himself as a "racial" alien.[43] North points out the irony of African American critics and writers using Eliot as a model, when he, in fact, used them first.[44] That irony is extended even further when we consider Wideman is criticized for his allusions to Eliot.[45] Wideman has remarked on several occasions about the necessity of seeing the interrelatedness of both traditions and cultures in American history and art.

In essence, Wideman is revisiting his own language and revoicing it. Other contemporary writers are engaged in similar projects. Modernists other than Eliot, such as Ezra Pound, Eugene O'Neil, Gertrude Stein, and William Faulkner, were also influenced by African American models in terms of their style or in the examination of the theme of alienation.[46] Toni Morrison and, even earlier, Ralph Ellison return and revoice Faulkner's work.[47] And, of course, Ellison, like Wideman, also responds to Eliot. Many critics have also traced the influence of African American music, especially ragtime, on Eliot's poetry. James Weldon Johnson's "Under the Bamboo Tree" served as one of the important influences on Eliot's work, and Charles Saunders calls *The Waste Land* a minstrel show. The dialogic tendency between the traditions and their writers has led Gates to assert that African American literature has a "curious two-toned Harlequin mask of influence."[48] If this cross-cultural borrowing is a characteristic of writers like Eliot and Faulkner, then Wideman's style in this book could be called "jazz-like" as easily as it could be called modernist.

The jazz-like passages of *A Glance Away* occur most frequently in the prologue, and it is the language used to describe DaddyGene or other figures of the past not only to reveal the picture of the family and the community but also to approximate its music and its stories. It is also important that the only character who remembers family stories (and can retell them) and speaks in a manner similar to DaddyGene's is Brother, who is, at least by name, a double of Brother in *Sent for You Yesterday*, the scat-singing albino that is that novel's spiritual center. Wideman has suggested that the two characters are the same,[49] and he then later implied that they *could* be the same character, but more likely they were a "shifting spirit."[50] Wideman will return again to "shifting spirits," especially in the novel *The Cattle Killing*.

The main action in the novel begins with Eddie Lawson's trip home from a rehabilitation clinic. He has left his northern home to recover in a hospital in the South. Wideman inverts the trope of African American migration: Lawson is in the South but his home is the North. Why Lawson travels to the South is never clear—though Wideman infuses the South here as the site of both pain and healing. Lawson is anxious to return to his home, his family, and his former girlfriend, Alice: "I'm going home, again and again, repeated somewhere in his chest, from all of this I am going home."[51] However, the North, his home, has also been the site of his pain, despair, and drug problems and as such recalls the broken dreams of those who migrated to the "promised land." On the bus he notes the passengers and the "peculiar rootlessness visible in their eyes,"[52] and he calls the bus ride "the freedom train" going to the "promised land."[53]

Wideman's decision to send Lawson south to recuperate heightens our awareness of the pattern of North-South migration in African American culture. It is a conscious artistic rendering in the novel that reverberates with stories that have gone before. The South as a healing place also echoes a work like Jean Toomer's *Cane*. The southern journey acts as a post-traumatic repetition, returning to the site of original trauma. For the past to be successfully integrated into the narrative of African Americans, that journey, at least figuratively, must take place. Thus, the South is a text itself to be written on and by African American writers as a place of, paradoxically, trauma and healing. Wideman links Lawson's journey to the darker side of racial memory as well: "More than the hospital the thought of going to the South had frightened him. He had dreamt night after night of pursuit, torture, horrible death. Mutilated black bodies hanging from trees smoldering on charred crucifixes, debowelled, blinded, chopped by axes."[54]

The South occupies this dual yet paradoxical relationship in African American literature; it is "the land of cane and ancestral territory for most American blacks [and it is] both a hostile political field and an abundantly fertile cultural terrain. These tensions in nature and geography match the 'warring ideals' of being African and American."[55] Journeys to and from the South are equally symbolic, mythic, and ritualistic.

The ritualistic quality of Lawson's journey resonates in his description of himself on the bus considering the passengers around him: "He felt he had something to say, something they could understand. He wanted to roll up his wet sleeve, walk up and down the aisle like a preacher testifying."[56] Here Lawson sees himself as a possible voice in the community. He knows that he has been to the wilderness, has suffered for his knowledge, and can be a spiritual leader for his people. But he remains silent and sees only that the "negroes sat sullen and suspicious, and [he] shivered in the corner."[57] Lawson remains alienated from his fellow travelers.

But Lawson is seeking connection. He wants to come home. While at the clinic he has denied his past and his ancestry, however. We discover later in the novel that he told the hospital doctors that he had no family and no home. He admitted only that he lived in a city. He has separated himself from the ties of family and friends that could have sustained him. At several other places in the novel when he is facing despair, he removes himself from the company of others. Toward the end of the novel when Lawson is struggling against the need to get a "bag," he announces to Brother and Thurley that he has to leave the bar that they are in, that he has to "walk out of here by myself."[58]

Other characters are alienated in the novel as well. Thurley, the classics professor, is modeled on Eliot's Prufrock.[59] Lawson's girlfriend, Alice, is also an isolated figure in her neighborhood. As the recipient of a dance scholarship, she has been schooled in another neighborhood—a white, upper-class one. In a remembrance of the past, Alice explains to Eddie why she is attracted to him, that she senses that he, too, is different, apart from the rest of the community. She feels like "a fish out of water. But I know this is my water, my home, that I can't ever change."[60]

Alice's alienation is a characteristic of her role as artist, which is further exacerbated by her race. Eddie, too, is an artist (a painter) who quits his job at the post office and turns to drugs when he senses that there is more to the world, but the world will not let him have a part of it. Both are victims of the "crisis" facing African American intellectuals and artists; both suffer from "twoness." Again, Wideman layers within his novel the metaphors of the African American self. But unlike other African American intellectuals and artists in the tradition, such as Wright's *Black Boy* and Ellison's *Invisible Man*, Eddie returns home. He does not permanently leave his community. Even in this early work, Wideman illustrates the need to return home, even if, in the case of this novel, it does not seem to accomplish much.

Perhaps the most alienated figure in the novel is Lawson's mother, Martha. This was apparently not always the case. We see a very different portrait of her in the prologue. But after the death of her father, DaddyGene, her son Eugene (in the war), and husband, Clarence, Martha has lost her faith, her will to live. She becomes an embittered woman and is unable to leave the house or connect with Lawson or his sister, Bette.

Similar narratives and frames are present in *Sent for You Yesterday*, and Uncle Carl in that work is also a painter who returns home after World War II. As new waves of migration from the South arrived following the end of the war, men like Carl and Eddie Lawson found poorer living and working conditions as well as disruptions in the unity of the neighborhoods. Part of Lawson's despair (as well as his mother's) is his dislocation from home, community, and a past which had been kept alive before by men like DaddyGene, the storytellers. But Lawson, like his mother, prefers not to talk about the past. American history and culture tells him that he does not have a worthy one. Even the doctor at the clinic realizes the importance of the past in healing Lawson's psychic wounds. While playing chess with Lawson, the doctor states:

> This very set we're using has its personal history, a long line of ancestors from whom it has received the substance of these final rarefied and abstracted forms. What do you think about ancestors, Eddie? How far back can you trace your family, are there any traditions passed down through the male line which the men in your family relish as a sacred trust?[61]

This is a cruel conversation given the history of African Americans in this country. Much of Lawson's genealogical history has been obliterated by his status as a descendant of slaves. Doubly cruel is that the chess set has a more documented and well-known past than he does. Eddie does not remember the traditions "passed down through the male line." He cannot recall the "father stories" told by men like DaddyGene.

The most significant tradition that his family once possessed is storytelling. Both Lawson and Bette realize this to a certain degree, but neither is capable of sustaining the storytelling tradition. Bette states this need to hear voices and stories to fill the void of silence in the house she shares with her mother: "I would like to talk about Eugene. Brother can talk about anything. Stories about everybody—about DaddyGene who I barely remember, but when Brother talks sometimes so close, even closer than our real Daddy. Eddie too talked about Eugene and DaddyGene."[62]

Bette believes that the stories will erase the despair of her life. In her mind, she tells her mother about Eddie's return: "Mama we need his voice, we need to listen together, to stop the scream that holds us. Let him tell us about DaddyGene, about Tiny, about Eugene, and let Brother come too."[63] Bette never says this directly to her mother, however. Martha has cut herself off from stories; she would rather live in the past than remember it.[64]

Eddie remembers some stories of his grandfather, his brother, and Bette, especially when they were children, before DaddyGene died. Those were happy times, full of laughter, but their lives since then have been marked by despair and regret.[65] Martha has lost the past and her future; she is too old and sick now to tell stories and keep the family going. As Bette tells Eddie, "It must be the worst thing in the world to be old. Old so you can't remember stories like Brother tells, or so old that the people you know best all begin dying. Do you think that's why Mama's so lonely."[66] In this moment, Bette and Eddie share stories; they remember family members and friends. Eddie begins to tell the story of DaddyGene's friend, Tiny, to Bette:

Bette knew the story from beginning to end, she had heard it rehearsed a thousand times in this same livingroom. But it had become a private, almost mystical link between brother and sister. An experience shared so deeply that its content had become superfluous; they could both fasten on the narrative and wring far more from it than any meaning translatable to an outsider.[67]

But Eddie is unable to finish the story because "Tiny's gone." Lawson is trying to "erase his past" like his mother. He would rather forget the painful memories than relive them, and he is unable to refashion his painful past through the imagination. This is certainly what Wideman wants us to see; it is Eddie's failure to share his story and to tell his own that is the deepest source of his despair. The shared expression of grief and trauma, even in the brief moment that Eddie narrates the story of Tiny, mitigates the hold suffering has over this family. At this point, however, Lawson turns away from storytelling as a salve from his pain.

After failing to complete the story, Eddie asks Bette to run away with him, to leave the community and their mother behind. It is after this that Martha falls down the stairs and dies. There are indications that her fall was purposeful ("it seemed she smiled"), and Eddie feels responsible for her death because she most likely heard him say, "She'd be better dead, we'd be better dead."[68] In fact, Eddie does not know with certainty that his mother is dead; he runs out of the house the minute his mother falls. Brother asks him: "You killed nobody, you don't even know she's dead do you?" Eddie answers: "She's dead. I caused it. My words, my wish brought her down those stairs."[69] Death appears to be the only thing that Eddie can expect out of life. He suffers from a consciousness that many slaves possessed—a wish for this life to end.

Stories and words have an acknowledged power in the novel, despite the failure of Eddie's attempt to use them. The oral stories especially have the power to link brother and sister, to transcend misery. In a novel that has been so widely held by critics as privileging European narrative, it is noteworthy that it is the oral stories of the African American community that have the most power to save and heal in the text. Thurley's students have no interest in the stories that they discuss in class. He knows that they'll think *Oedipus* empty and dead.[70] And though he has surrounded his life with "beautiful" stories, they have not provided him with any meaning other than the academic. For Bette, stories can have the ability to save her life. This is true for Lawson as well.

Much of the criticism leveled at Wideman in the first novels surrounds the character of Robert Thurley. James Coleman calls him the "main character" of the work.[71] Yet the story of Eddie's family opens the book. We don't even see

Thurley until page 32. Eddie's character is developed in twice as many pages as Thurley. And significantly, much of Thurley's narrative before meeting Eddie is *about* meeting Eddie. Thurley's significance in the work is secondary and the world he represents is dead: "Everything dead, stinking to heaven, my task at best to loot the dead, finish the dying."[72] In his poetry journal, he notes that its pages look like "a mirror, a dark white mirror, refusing his image. Hopelessly confused but somehow ineluctably true the metaphors danced and persisted. Dark-white, transparency-opacity, returning-refusing his image."[73] If anything, these lines suggest that all that Thurley represents is meaningless to Lawson and the rest of the African American community. His culture, his traditions have lost their potency. The knowledge that Eddie is coming home—though he has never met him—is the only thing that seems to energize him. If Thurley is a Prufrock character, the voice of Eliot in the text, then it would be pertinent to remember Michael North's assessment of Eliot's use of African American language and music. Thurley's relationship to Eddie could be described as Eliot's relationship to African American culture.

It is Eddie's return home, the "glance" away of the title, that informs the themes of the book. Eddie must return home and create and share stories that will sustain his life and his family (even though it is possible that he will not accomplish this). Wideman does not view Thurley's world or his history as the vital one. Not only is he a Prufrock, he is obese, materialistic, epicurean, and a pedophile. His image is gluttonous, sterile, and diseased. Most of what he represents is portrayed as unattractive. The world he inhabits represents the history and the literature (he is a classics professor) that continue to control the culture that decides which stories get told and who writes them. He is the expression of what Eddie must confront and transcend in order to narrate his own vision.

Despite his insistence that he needs to be alone, Thurley and Brother accompany Eddie to a hobo camp at the novel's conclusion. They form a circle around a fire, and though they don't tell stories to each other, we experience their thoughts simultaneously, as their inner voices are interlaced on the page. Lawson is, in ways, for the first time in the novel, in a community, symbolized by their circle. He has needed this all along as he states in his letter to his mother and Bette: "I learned a man can only do so much alone, that he has to grab onto something outside himself, whether it be a good thing or a bad one."[74] At this point in the novel, he is dependent on the other two men, on a community, engaging in his own stories and surrounded by the stories of others. Throughout the book, Wideman has encircled Lawson with stories, those reminiscent of myth, literature, and history (in both the European and African American tradition) and those of his family, though these remain mainly forgotten or silenced. Significantly, those men surrounding Eddie represent the

European tradition (a classics professor) and the African American tradition (an oral storyteller who listens to the "rails singing"). Both speak and both sustain Eddie Lawson, and neither's voice has precedence over the other. They are, after all, in a circle.[75]

A Glance Away may not be as pessimistic as generally it is assumed either. Brother starts and maintains the fire that warms them and his storytelling voice may have the same positive force, for it is Brother's discourse that closes the novel, followed by an ellipsis that indicates the story (stories) will go on. It will not be until the works of *The Homewood Trilogy* that Wideman breaks the narrative frame and speaks more directly to the reader, as he does in the opening letter to Robby and in the short story "The Beginning of Homewood," showing the audience that stories can and must sustain the community. But the roots of this aesthetic (and the maxim "all stories are true") can be found even in *A Glance Away*.

The "spiritual communion of the hobo camp" in the novel reemphasizes another trope in African American literature.[76] The hobo is a liminal character who rides the trains in African American literature (and in the popular American consciousness), and the trains are a symbol of the crossroads.[77] We see the image of the crossroads elsewhere in Wideman's work (especially *Damballah*). The blues hero is associated with the hobo as both a wanderer and a liminal character. And the train is a trope of escape and promise for the African American, a revision of the chariot found in the spirituals.[78] The train and the hobo merge in the character of Brother and the circle at the end of the novel. Brother's voice, like a blues song, will fight the silence of Eddie Lawson's life. Wideman revises the traditional image of trains as a means of escape. This symbol, associated here with Brother, is firmly situated at home. Lawson has "glanced" away, but may now be glancing back to his home, his past. The novel's end does not clarify for us what will become of Eddie Lawson.

Wideman remembers, "One of the earliest lessons I learned as a child was that if looked away from something, it might not be there when you looked back."[79] This apprehension suggests a fear of leaving home and of looking away from your loved ones and the necessity to always have your gaze fixed on the past, or you might not remember it. Wideman describes the title, *A Glance Away*, as a way to think about time and history.[80] The consequence of "glancing away" is "hurrying home." Cecil Braithwaite, the protagonist of *Hurry Home*, is perhaps an even more alienated figure than Eddie Lawson. The novel opens with a quote, "the pain of being two." The quote sets up one of the major themes of the novel: the double-consciousness of its character. This double-consciousness is reflected in the journey that Braithwaite takes in the novel—to Europe and then to Africa. He is a child of both cultures. We have already seen that

Eddie Lawson suffers from a similar dilemma, though his double-consciousness is not punctuated by the same external events that Braithwaite's is.

Braithwaite studies the law and does so to escape his neighborhood and his past. One of Wideman's revisions of the trope of double-consciousness and flight in this novel is Braithwaite's ability to dream different lives for himself and his desire to return home after his journey to Africa (though this may be only an imaginative journey). The journeys in the novel operate not only as the flight away but also as a search for identity and history. The pattern in African American literature resonates in the novel:

> The individual, that archetypal figure of Western myth and fiction, journeys forth alone, usually bereft of family, as does the hero of *Invisible Man*. As he journeys ... imaginatively from a specific time and place into history and dreams, he seeks to know himself and to give form to his life.... [W]hereas Ellison's protagonist concludes his quest alone, the protagonists of his heirs' novels circle back to confirm their identity and dependence upon the black community and its traditions.[81]

Braithwaite's journeys are also akin to the image of the blues hero who leaves the community. Braithwaite does not yet have the capacity at the end of the novel to be a true blues hero—though he does return home (or he stops fantasizing about running away). Possibly Braithwaite will utilize his "two-ness" as a tool for discovery and art, something he has yet to do. He is still conducted by the "pain" of double-consciousness. Once he voices the suffering of two-ness he will achieve the "blues mind."[82]

Time in *Hurry Home* reflects the fractured quality of Braithwaite's life as well, and it questions the progression of the historical consciousness. Probably more than in any other novel of Wideman's, time is difficult to grasp. This is partially the result of Braithwaite feeling outside of time as a man with no past. It is also the reflection of Braithwaite's dreaming. Time has no structure in dreams. It is possible, even likely, that Braithwaite never actually travels to Europe or Africa. These journeys may be imaginary ones. The trauma that Braithwaite suffers propels him further and further away from home as an escape from the memory of pain.

Braithwaite's trauma is not alleviated by his escape; instead, his flight exacerbates his pain as he finds that no matter where he travels he does not belong. And as he meditates on the history of Europe and Africa, he is reminded of the historical trauma of his race. Wideman notes: "I hope that the reader sees that what was specifically Cecil's experience becomes conflated with the whole collective history of his race, that there is a thin line between individual and collective experience which permits one to flow into the other. It has to do with imagination. Cecil can suffer because somebody centuries ago suffered on a slave ship."[83] Wideman's description of Cecil's pain is indicative of the post-traumatic consciousness.

Wideman goes on to suggest that this is an imaginary voyage in the novel, but despite this believes that everyone has the capacity to travel between time and space. The difference between fantasy and reality is not important because art is a question of trying to "blur that line" between the two.[84] Braithwaite at one time contemplates Proust as a model for understanding himself and his relationship to Charles Webb, the white man with whom he travels in Europe: "I think of Proust in his corklined room, but a Proust who has lost the thread of his own experience and reads rather than remembers. Perhaps because I have so little past I know of, I am jealous, or at least hypersensitive to what Webb has accumulated."[85]

Braithwaite tries to explain to his wife, Esther, why he abandoned her for this journey. He writes that he feels directionless and that he "wanted to giggle at the moon. I wanted to run and watch it trying to catch me over the rooftops. I was afraid I was out too late, that I would be scolded, even beaten if I didn't hurry home."[86] Braithwaite leaves his home because he senses he belongs somewhere else. When he is abroad, however, he reiterates the need to go home and see his family, especially his Uncle Otis: "Go back. Return. Reprise. Repeat. About face. Again. Return."[87]

The return may also represent a post-traumatic cycle if Braithwaite does not face the loss and pain of his life more effectively. While on his journey, he remembers the spirituals that his wife is fond of, especially the song "Fartheralong" (which will appear in several more of Wideman's works). Though Braithwaite does not seem to value these songs at this point in the novel, he nevertheless remembers them, and for Wideman they signal what Braithwaite needs in his life to combat and survive his pain. The songs are also a signal that the voices from home will never leave him no matter how far he travels. In fact, he ruminates on his home the entire time he is away, especially on the multiple roles there that he is forced to lead:

> Herbert Philbrick, F.B.I. double agent, led three lives each week on TV in a perpetual turning of tables upon the communist conspiracy. Cecil had been bored by the show but identified with the numbers compartmentalizing the double agent's lives. Cecil defender of the faith: lover of Esther, diligent student of the law, advancer of banner proclaiming All Men Equal. Cecil conspirator: lover of love, student of their law, carrot wiggled

in front of the others, Equal Opportunity Lives. Cecil Cecil: neither of others, libra, seesaw, see soul, sees all.[88]

Braithwaite's identification with a double agent reinforces the two-ness that he sees as the tension in his life and marks him as a figure of the double. But it also suggests a doubleness that promises other possible lives—at least in the imagination.

Braithwaite is also connected to Webb by their dual desires to find a lost son. For Webb this is an actual investigation, for Braithwaite it is an imaginative recreation of what his son, Simon, might have been like if he had lived. A measure of the character that critics do not often discuss is Braithwaite's traumatic loss. The death of his son throws him into despair. His search for himself is an extended search for the history and the self that he can no longer pass on to another generation. Webb tells Braithwaite that Cecil reminds him of Hieronymus Bosch because "like him you've decided to wrap yourself in old sorrows. To be a kind of walking, talking *lest we forget.*"[89] The pain of losing his son connects him directly to the historical trauma he is reliving on his journey to Europe and later to Africa. If his son had lived, Braithwaite might have found a method to connect to his community and to his roots. In Wideman's canon, children are the source of connection between family and history; their loss is a destruction of that possibility.

While in Europe, Webb and Braithwaite visit art museums and libraries. Webb and Braithwaite both are searching for history, but Braithwaite cannot find his place in the stories or the art Webb shows him. He looks for black faces in the paintings, but the faces are usually shadowy or barely visible somewhere in the corner. His history will not be found by placing himself in the pictures that others have drawn of him. Wideman suggests elsewhere that individuals (such as Braithwaite) must see that "'black' history cannot be written by simply inserting the names and numbers of black folk into a conventional version of the American past."[90] Webb's need to find something in this historical search suggests the sort of nostalgic loss associated with Eliot, who has been alluded to throughout the novel. Braithwaite is looking for a past that was never available to him.

He discovers part of that past while in Madrid. Braithwaite hears the history of Tarik the Moor. Braithwaite feels a connection to the Moor, his blood, and his heritage: "*On that promontory My Friend is the seemingly impregnable citadel of the Black Kings. Defied all of Espana till on a white horse Iago Matamoros cleansed the dark plague from dis land.*"[91] Wideman recovers a moment of recorded history that heralds African heritage and tradition, yet it is a story that is not often taught, especially not in the systems that Braithwaite would have been a product of. After hearing Tarik's story, Braithwaite looks around to see the "brown life" of Madrid surrounding him, evidence of Tarik's place in the history of this European city: "I review the history of the Moors in Spain, in Reconquista, the pogroms."[92] Braithwaite realizes that he is on an important journey, one that will help him understand his own identity in the context of his history. Yet he can't quite grasp the meaning of his life because the history he is seeing is incomplete; it doesn't encompass everything that he is.

The story of Tarik and his victorious invasion of Spain offers Braithwaite a hero that resembles him. This story provides Braithwaite with a historical African man that evokes in him a sense of pride, a sense of heritage, but really reminds him most of home and Uncle Otis, who first told him about Tarik. The historical record and family stories are interdependent here. But, at this point in the novel, Braithwaite privileges the historical account over the family's oral tale. By the close of the novel, Braithwaite uses both to complete the vision of Tarik, illustrating that "all the stories are true."

Braithwaite also overturns the historical portrait of Tarik, who he claims as a proud ancestor. The Spaniards characterize Tarik as "dark" and as an animal. This image implies that, despite the Moorish influence on Spain, blackness is still associated with primitivism and bestiality. It also asserts that the European, on "the white horse," must conquer, subjugate, or destroy the "wild animal." His rendering of Tarik's and his uncle's stories acts as a counternarrative of the accepted European accounts of the Moor.

After the trip to Madrid and the remembrance of the story of Tarik the Moor, Braithwaite realizes that Webb cannot offer him what he is looking for, and Braithwaite leaves for Africa, searching for other "moorings." Their relationship has been a representation of white paternalism, as Webb has substituted Braithwaite for the black son that he has never known (Braithwaite's double), and Braithwaite has looked up to Webb as a father figure.[93] The relationship that Braithwaite has with Webb can also be read in terms of historical patrimony; Braithwaite cannot only look to the "white father" for his identity. He must also find his other history.

The traumatic forces of history are reflected in the numerous images of slavery found throughout the novel. Braithwaite says of his relationship with Esther: "I slaved as she slaved learning the law."[94] His own feelings of imprisonment and trauma breed his desire for escape through his education and his pursuit of the American Dream: "I could go no farther. Backward nor forward, nether side to side, just stand and dance in my chains.... I studied the law."[95] In the novel *The Lynchers*, Cecil Braithwaite is an attorney. Braithwaite's need drives him to Europe and eventually to Africa. He hopes to find a home in

Africa, and while on board ship, Braithwaite imagines the Middle Passage. He sees in his mind the slaves toiling. Anxious to reach Africa, he imagines himself as a "prodigal returning; he will be welcomed, understood, loved, be a man again."[96] However, when he arrives (either literally or in his mind), he realizes that "there is no Africa," at least not for him. He wishes that he could touch the "African soil. If it were allowed, he would plant himself in the sand. Stand like a flag that claims possession, satisfied to be forever possessed. I am part of it. It is part of me."[97] Wideman illustrates the need for Braithwaite to find history, to "possess" it somehow, to turn over the image of the Middle Passage.[98] Wideman rewrites the text of the Middle Passage by reversing its direction—Braithwaite is going to Africa (on a boat instead of an airplane, no less). But he controls the journey and the meaning of the voyage. This echoes Lawson's journey to the South in its inversion of the tropological journey of African American experience.

Robert Hayden's poem "Middle Passage" is imbricated in the novel in this section: "The narrow ship plies backward and forward relentlessly." Hayden, like Wideman, borrowed techniques from Eliot, and elsewhere in the novel Eliot is alluded to ("O O O you Shakespearean rag"). Wideman revises the line to "O O O you Shagspearean rug cuddled round my chin."[99] Eliot is reduced to bathtub shaving rituals and song. Wideman also includes an allusion to Prufrock: "I grow old, I grow old, should I eat my sausage rolled or pat it into patties."[100] Aldon Nielsen establishes the connection between Hayden and Wideman as authors both interested in revisiting and rewriting the modernists.[101] Clearly, there is little reverence in Wideman's treatment of Eliot here; he is riffing on Eliot and the tradition he represents. He does not accept the tradition uncritically; instead, he parodies Eliot to critique the Western tradition.[102] This is the same relationship that Wideman has with Eliot in the novel *A Glance Away*. In *Hurry Home*, however, the emphasis is on verbal word play as much as it is on the parody of historical consciousness.

Back home, his abandoned wife, Esther, has decided to educate herself to rise to the level of her husband. The dictionary becomes her university textbook. Wideman includes a page that she is reading: the words between "liberal" and "Libra." This is not a random inclusion. Esther memorizes the meanings of the words, and we see that the words "liberal," "liberal arts," and "liberty" all have common roots, but ironically seem at odds when we consider that Braithwaite's liberal education has been at odds with his "liberty," and he has lost his knowledge of Africa ("Liberia"). It has also forced Braithwaite into double-consciousness ("libra," representing duality and balance). Language is the weapon of oppression in the hands of those in power (and it has been used by Braithwaite to diminish his wife), but language and its multiple meanings reveal its possibility for change. Wideman puns throughout the novel, and one notable example is when poetry makes Braithwaite a "lyre." The image of the bard's instrument and Braithwaite's self-delusion about his identity conflate here. But the "lyre" also implies that Braithwaite is a possible bard who has not yet found his song.

After arriving in Africa, Braithwaite feels the need to return home to hear his Uncle Otis and his stories. It is his need to find something "familiar" in himself that encourages Braithwaite to "hurry home."[103] He has remembered the stories of Tarik the Moor that his Uncle Otis used to tell him as a child. When he hears about Tarik the Moor again in Spain, he recalls that he first heard the story from Otis. The conflation of the importance of storytelling, family stories, and the revision of the Middle Passage impress upon the reader Wideman's multiple responses to history and the characteristic way that he blurs the distinctions between genres and voices, implying the interconnectedness of all stories. This moment revises the tropes of the alienated artist and of the flight away.

Braithwaite's journey finally propels him home, where he goes first to Uncle Otis to hear a story, and he expresses the need to share with Otis the story of his voyage: "I need you to listen. Authenticate."[104] Otis's stories, whether fictions or nonfictions, are more important to Cecil than all the "real" history he experienced in Europe. Even the story of Tarik the Moor is more "real" for him now out of the mouth of his uncle. Wideman layers fiction, public history, and autobiography in this moment as Uncle Otis (a "historian") is also the name of Wideman's uncle, mentioned in *Brothers and Keepers*, who liked to tell stories. Otis is one of the many doubles in Wideman's work.

Braithwaite's desire to immediately see his uncle to share stories (suggesting that Braithwaite may be the poet that "lyre" implied) signifies the storytelling act, and it stands as a call-and-response moment. He replays, revises, and riffs on Otis's version of Tarik, creating his own version of the tale. Braithwaite's need to have other voices listen to his story, to give it meaning, connects him back to his community. He is also reconnected to his community through his job at the beauty parlor, where he "lays his hands" on people and listens to their stories.[105] He does not yet share stories with them; he is still in the process of imagining them, which is reflected in the novel's end, where we are told that "Cecil dreamed."[106] His dreaming is not action, so he does not fulfill the role of storyteller or blues hero, but he is less alienated by the end of the novel then he is at the beginning—and he has returned home. The "laying on of hands" image suggests that Braithwaite may yet become the blues hero. By the novel's end he changes from a seeker to a dreamer of possibilities.[107] Taking the job at the beauty parlor lacks the glamour he once sought for himself, and being in a place where he will be forced to interact with people everyday and listen to their talk and stories illustrates that Braithwaite is in a different place—his isolation from the community and from home is no longer as deep as it once was. He feels, for the first time "like a fish who has recovered his element."[108]

Wideman states that Braithwaite as a man "is not simply a product of a family; his family reaches out toward larger and larger circles ... [so] that individual memory becomes merged with someone else's from a past generation."[109] Wideman's intent is to revise the portrait of the typical alienated individual adrift from their community and their culture. He also says of Braithwaite that his search for an identity in Europe and a life that exemplifies that wandering in Europe was modeled on African American artists such as James Baldwin.[110] This suggests that Braithwaite possesses the vision of the artist—his dreaming and imagination indicate this—he need only find his blues voice. Braithwaite's fantasies echo in Wideman's claim: "What is history except people's imaginary recreation."[111] His novel *The Lynchers* attempts to dismantle and re-imagine the history of African Americans. It also has at its center a group of alienated intellectuals whose failure of communal vision condemns them and their mission.

Thomas Wilkerson is a history teacher, and his friend Littleman is a poet. Littleman conceives a plan to lynch a white police officer in a ritualistic attempt to change the forces of history that have limited, oppressed, and murdered African American men. This reversal of history will be a "lynching in black face."[112] As an artist, he understands the symbolism of the act, the need to dismantle master narratives, and the possible potential for mythmaking. He recruits Wilkerson and two other friends, Rice and Saunders, to help carry out the plan.

Littleman considers himself a student of history. As a failed writer, his artistic nature and his short, hunched-over body have isolated him from his people and from himself. His unsuccessful attempt at poetry foreshadows the failure of his vision of symbolic retribution for years of slavery and lynching. His desire to help his community is not real; he wants to show that he, a "little man," has power. He contends that his plot will help the community, but when he decides that the men must kill a young, black woman, Sissie, in order to place the blame on the white police officer, it is clear that Littleman's alienation from his community has traveled so far within himself that he suffers from a pathological self-hatred. Even her name, "Sissie," acknowledges that they are willing to kill one of their own "family" (and she is a sister-in-law of one of the men as well).

Littleman's anger, frustration, and self-hatred are so deep-seated that he even considers murdering an innocent boy that he thinks may be a spy. Littleman represents an ideology gone too far, one that destroys both the community it is trying to save and the individual man. Littleman is a noted orator; he could have been a Douglass or a King, but his personal traumas triumph over his talent.

Wilkerson shares some of Littleman's ideals. Also an intellectual, he connects through his community through positive work. But he decides to follow Littleman rather than believing in his own abilities and using his own talent and intelligence to influence those around him. As a middle school history teacher, he illustrates a position in the text that could affect positive communal change. And though Wilkerson has a strained relationship with his parents, he comes to his father's defense when the elder Wilkerson kills another man in a fight. Wilkerson's co-conspirators, however, see his father as a liability:

> A black man like Wilkerson trying his best to make good, to be somebody and he has to worry about his own kind pulling him down as much as he has to worry about the white man. Niggers are backbiters and spoilers. Ones at the bottom have no better sense than to try to keep everybody down.... You just have to cut them no count niggers loose and go about your business.[113]

Apply this sentiment to the community at large, and it is clear that these men are not interested in others so much as they are interested in their own rage. Wilkerson does not abandon his father, however; and after visiting him in jail, Wilkerson begins to see, finally, the futility of the lynching plan. It is a remembrance of his father's songs and stories that resolutely pushes Wilkerson to sabotage the plot. If Wideman illustrates the alienated intellectual as a failed leader of the community in Littleman, then Wilkerson represents the possibility of connection between the intellectual and the people through their shared historical traumas and their shared means of surviving those tragedies. It is through Wilkerson's family relationships—and through his "father stories"—that he is able to connect to the community at large. Scholars and reviewers have noted the emphasis on family primarily in the Homewood books; but, clearly, the importance of family as a means of managing grief and trauma has been a constant throughout Wideman's work, as we have already seen in *A Glance Away* and *Hurry Home*.

Littleman fails in his plot and as a visionary, because he cannot recall the songs and stories that Wilkerson remembers by the end of the novel. Ironically, Littleman has turned his back on African American history and culture. Littleman dreams that he will be present at the "birth of a new god," but in his dreams he can never see what form this god will take. He doesn't know what myth he is meant to produce; and because he cannot create a vision that is his own, he is forced to mimic the vision of the very forces of history that he is trying to overcome: "We are incorporating their understanding of history and power into our plan. We are saying crystally clear in the language they invented: we are your equals."[114] The "black face" image of the minstrel is repeated here, with its incumbent references and interrelated images of doubles, twins, and imitation. Littleman's desire to plan a "lynching in blackface" doesn't acknowledge that "blackface" was another way that white society portrayed the life of African Americans, stereotyping them as entertainers and buffoons. Littleman is unable to see that he is an imitator of the very stories he wants to condemn. Therefore, we understand, even when he cannot, that his attempt at changing history is doomed to failure.[115] The violence that Littleman and his co-conspirators wish to combat cannot be fought with the same violence that has been used against their race.

Wilkerson realizes that it is impossible to "form a plan in the world where all that mattered was accidental, a blind jumble of blind forces."[116] Both men understand the need for a symbolic act that will bring the community together, a new "passion play." As a history teacher, Wilkerson understands the traumatic past better than anyone else. He also must confront his own personal tragedies, but we see throughout the novel that he attempts to make more meaningful connections between the past and the present. In his planner, he notes books for his students to read and "presentations on current events he wishes to connect with their history lessons."[117] He entreats his students to "listen to the black voices from your past."[118] He instructs them about Olaudah Equiano and teaches them about African history, stories that they have never heard before. He tells them:

> We must learn not to shy away from the truth. Africa was dark only in the darkened minds of those who approached her with dark intent. When you come to steal, the past of your victim is of interest only in so far as that past may promote your plundering. But Africa lies swaddled in history and you are a part of its past, heirs of its legacy."[119]

Wilkerson initially tries to present a more positive approach to surviving the pain of the past. It is his intelligence, his connection to the community, and even his optimism that Littleman recognizes is the key to their plan. But he fails to see that African American history is populated with men and women like Wilkerson, who offered their best for the community. Littleman complains: "When have we ever risen up as a people, united, resolved, ready to die together. Never, never once in our pitiful history."[120]

Despite Littleman's claim to be a student of history, he is clearly ignorant of some significant moments of his African American past: Nat Turner, the

Amistad Rebellion, the peaceful demonstrations of the civil rights movement. Littleman neglects these stories because he has accepted the popular view of African American history that denies or hides such moments from sight. He calls his racial history "pitiful" and refuses to see the strength of the folk and their traditions. If these accounts were more popularized in the American historical record, they could be potentially liberating and empowering.[121] Littleman privileges the written historical records over the oral tradition of his people. He "scribbles away" at times, worried that no one will remember him because "my people have always written their history with their mouths."[122] Littleman does not seem to realize the power of this history; he devalues oral culture as European conquerors did in the past.

Littleman's paranoia, his problematic vision of history, and his later descent into madness foreshadow his failure as a leader and agent of creative change. Though "he sympathizes with Littleman's historical imperatives and existential choices, Wideman, as the tragic denouement illustrates, identifies more closely with his protagonist (Wilkerson's) internal changes, especially his moral and political decision to sabotage the plan."[123] Despite Littleman's inability to see the inherent dysfunctionality of his plan, he does see the need to question the systems that produce the stories that limit and enslave African Americans. He also realizes that the cumulative effect of these "stories" is that they begin to take on the appearance of truth. He tells Wilkerson, "We must say No, you cannot define us, you cannot set the limits.... [W]e will lynch one man but in fact we will be denying a total vision of reality."[124]

Wilkerson, Littleman, and the other conspirators, Saunders and Rice, are brought together not to work to save the community but to share their hatred and their frustration. They don't share sustaining stories; they plan a lynching. They complain about the older generation that just sits around and gets drunk, but those older men support each other, share stories, and play the dozens. The younger generation, the lynchers of the title, do not have this type of friendship. When Wilkerson tries to veer from conversations about "the plan," he attempts to joke around; he "wanted words to make them laugh, forget a moment the violence that drew them together."[125] Littleman accuses him of being silly, of trying to "play the dozens," reflecting the shame of his own culture.

Not only are the past and the present connected through shared pain, they are linked through a common ability to survive and transcend suffering through their artistic tradition—playing the dozens is one example of ways the folk tradition subverted authority and shared a common language and experience. The lynchers have not been able to reinvent themselves, and if African Americans continue to forget their stories, their shared historical traditions, as they do in *Hurry Home* and *A Glance Away* (and later in works like *The Cattle*

Killing in the Xhosa warning), they will be consumed by despair. Each of these novels can be understood as an effort to work through and beyond "racialized bodies,"[126] emphasizing the need to embrace the imagination as a powerful weapon against stereotyped and historical images of blackness. The lynchers desire to have society see them as more than their black bodies, but they use the physical body, rather than their own imaginations, to achieve this. Littleman, Eddie Lawson, and Cecil Braithwaite are all notably described as poets and artists who, in the course of each of the three novels, are unable to creatively re-imagine their experience of trauma and fail to realize their possible position as a blues hero.

The imperative of revisiting and re-imagining racial trauma opens the novel—the "Matter Prefatory." The record of slavery and lynchings projects an emotional repository of the unbearable weight and horror of the past. It effectively interrogates the connection between historical trauma and another generation's post-traumatic response. These conspirators, whether consciously or not, carry the fear, suffering, and anger buried within the "Matter Prefatory," within themselves—the preface acts as an objective correlative of their racial trauma. The past that the "Matter Prefatory" represents is dialogically related to present of the novel.[127] The public record of the "Matter Prefatory" continues to haunt African Americans, not just the men in the book. Wideman examines the history of lynching to understand the attitudes that still have the power to control the lives of the African American community, particularly males. Like other contemporary historical novels, this work is characterized by a "sense of urgency—sometimes even a sense of desperation," as it probes the past to explain its "chaotic" present.[128] Trudier Harris's study of *The Lynchers*, one of the first critical examinations of Wideman's work, contends that

> for Wideman, lynching is a metaphor for the psychologically and physically destructive ways in which blacks and whites have interacted with each other; the long term effects of those interactions can either stifle the growth of his characters or allow them the means of self expression—if they have the ability to control the extent to which the past influences them. In their desire to find a symbol for their own liberation by reaching back into the past for one which usually meant degradation and death for them, they play simultaneously with the possibility of freedom as well as for further enslavement.[129]

This is evidenced by Littleman's continuous remarks that they need a plan, that there is some logic or order to his thinking: "If there is orderliness, precision, cleanliness, rhythm in the world, they are most visible in action, a plan such as I have conceived. Formulating a rite totally consistent with the logic of history, yet harnessing the blind rush of events, opening a momentary wedge so a new myth can shoulder its way into the process . . . to tear such a hole in history."[130]

Littleman goes even further, indicating that his plan has a "mathematical precision" and that he has "circled" and "numbered incidents" that could be "strung together by the immutable logic of history."[131] As we have already witnessed, Wideman views historiography as a postmodernist: it is not "immutable" or rational or "logical." It is random, fluid, even chaotic; it does not follow a "plan" of development. Littleman's view of history is "objective" and scientific, and this is the type of privileging of genre that Wideman is refuting in his work. Littleman does observe that the "holes" of history can be places where new stories and myths can emerge. Yet he fails to see, because his imagination is unable to do so, that he can use his art to address these gaps; he doesn't have to use violence to create them. He refuses to acknowledge the unknown yet significant stories and lives around him (for example, his dismissal of the young orderly, Anthony, and Wilkerson's father). He suffers from the "racial melancholia" described by Anne Cheng—he is a man whose subjectivity has been formed by rejection, loss, grief, and racial injury.[132] He wants bloodshed and destruction to ease his own personal pain. However, his downfall represents Wideman's unwillingness "to give up black humanity for racial revenge. . . . [M]ost importantly of all, he is not willing to create a new mythology in the black community which would be based on violence."[133]

Littleman first meets Anthony after he is beaten during a rally. Anthony works as a hospital orderly where Littleman is recovering. Littleman decides to use Anthony in the plan somehow, but he first must convince the boy that he is ripe for revolution. He insists on calling the boy Anthony, even though the boy is more comfortable with Tony. The only other person that calls him Anthony is his teacher, Miss Collins. Littleman is suspicious of what Anthony is learning in her classroom:

> A white teacher of social studies. She . . . displays posters of black heroes on her classroom wall. The class listens to recordings of Paul Robeson, Malcolm X speaking; they read Richard Wright and Eldridge Cleaver. She has drawn him in. . . . What grasp does she have of history? Of the larger context that destroyed the black men whose words and music are now being exploited by their destroyers?[134]

Despite what he thinks of Miss Collins and her motives, Littleman clearly identifies with her as an intellectual and authority as evidenced by his insistence on referring to the boy as Anthony. The name is more formal, more suited to Littleman's style and tastes.

Littleman really doesn't care about Anthony; he appears most concerned in his own cause and turning the boy to it. As well, he belittles what Anthony is learning about his past, when he should be encouraging the boy's education. He fails to tell stories to Anthony that would teach him about his ancestry or give him the weapons against the negative portraits drawn of young black males in the society. A few days later, Littleman is convinced that Anthony is a spy and considers killing him. All of the conspirators seem to be moving to the edge of insanity. Wilkerson is certain that someone will discover their plan; Rice locks himself in a room with guns and becomes so paranoid that he shoots (and probably kills) Wilkerson when he knocks on the door; and Saunders is also becoming increasingly violent. When Wilkerson is late meeting him, Saunders imagines choking him when he comes in the door. Their behavior demonstrates "how thoroughly antithetical such actions would be to black human nature; Wideman allows the mere contemplation of them to drive almost all of his characters mad."[135] Even though Wilkerson's father kills a man, his best friend, it happens during a drunken fight. The other conspirators are ashamed of the type of man Wilkerson's father is, but Orin Wilkerson is distraught by his actions and is willing to suffer for them. He is not a murderer in any sense that the younger men intend to be.

Saunders is willing to sacrifice his sister-in-law, Sissie, for the plan and exhibits no guilt about such a cold-blooded choice. Sissie is a prostitute, and the fact that Littleman was earlier humiliated by another prostitute implies that his reasons for killing Sissie have less to do with reversing the forces of history and more to do with personal vengeance. When Saunders goes to Sissie's home to observe how difficult it would be to kidnap her, he finds his niece, Lisa. He contemplates the possibility that he may have to kill her as well, so that there will be no witnesses. The destructive and futile nature of the plan is ensured when Littleman considers killing Anthony and Saunders thinks of killing Lisa. Children are the connection to the future, as Wideman suggests elsewhere. To use them, or to lose them, cancels out the race and concedes to the social forces that have tried to destroy it. In embracing the violent revolution, these conspirators unravel the future. Wideman does not share this thinking. He clearly suggests that "this dynamic of intraracial violence is just what is most dangerous and ever-present in nationalist thinking."[136]

By the end of the novel, Wilkerson has found the possible means of connection, revision, and salvation that the others could not. When Wilkerson goes to see Sissie, he hears Lisa singing a song he remembers from his childhood. The child, the song, and the memory persuade the already irresolute Wilkerson that the plan cannot proceed. He remembers that his father had sung the same song to him. He concludes from his memory that Lisa's singing illustrated that "someone had loved this child,"[137] recognizing that he had been loved himself. He realizes that he has never sung a song with a child, and he resolves that he is unwilling to sacrifice this child, or any, for the revolution.[138] Wilkerson's dedication to children has been illustrated all along. He shares history with them, like his father shared stories with him. On some mornings, he can only get out of bed "for the children." After he hears Lisa singing, he realizes how his father had given him something as a child with that song: love and a key to survival. Wilkerson fully comprehends, finally, the sustaining power of stories, the rituals that families and individuals have created to overcome the apparition of the "Matter Prefatory." He recognizes that the power of those survival stories, the "father stories," "couldn't all be lost. Shouldn't be lost. He would sing to the children. They would sing together."[139]

Wilkerson has chosen dignity and responsibility over violence. But he has probably done so too late. His likely death is not a failure of his vision, but of his seduction by a false prophet, someone who is "dreaming the enemies' dream." This image is repeated again by Wideman in *The Cattle Killing*, where the Xhosa girl warns against following the false prophecies and living the enemies' dream. Wilkerson has not heeded such a warning and that is his tragedy. His death will probably ensure that his students will be lost as well. The loss of these men is a necessary step in realizing what will aid the African American community in the future: Wilkerson's final epiphany prevails as the philosophy of the work. His embrace of the power of stories and of the imagination over history and over bloodshed and cultural immolation implies Wideman's belief in the veracity and strength of all stories and their ability to address collective and personal trauma.

Looking back at *The Lynchers* after more than thirty-five years of a publishing history that includes numerous novels, short stories, and nonfiction, it is remarkable how often this early work reappears in some form or another in Wideman's oeuvre. Consider the portrait of the character Reuben (in the novel of the same name published in 1987). Reuben is a double for Littleman. Both men have a small, hunched-over physical shape; they are intellectuals; and they have suffered scorn and abuse. They both have had troubled and painful relationships with women. In the novel, Reuben reveals he has a twin. Unlike Littleman, however, Reuben is able to overcome his anger and hatred in ways that Littleman cannot envision. Wideman creates this double to revisit the traumatic history symbolized by Littleman and the lynchers as well as the trope of the alienated African American intellectual. This use of *doppelganger* or the "double," as suggested by scholar James Berger, is a "symptomatic return of trauma."¹⁴⁰ The conditions that created a Littleman have not been erased; the historical and cultural suffering embodied in the desire to enact the symbolic lynching will continue to return and repeat in the post-traumatic impulse.

The double, found throughout all of Wideman's work, is also an emblem of the "all stories are true" axiom. Reuben is an example of the possible life that Littleman could have had if he had not succumbed to his traumatic past. The work and its characters are doubled in other ways as well: Cecil Braithwaite is the group's lawyer; Orin Wilkerson, or Sweetman, is a friend of Wideman's father in *Fatheralong*, and Littleman is his father's cousin; Saunders is the name of Eddie Lawson's roommate in *A Glance Away*; Darnell, a basketball player in *The Lynchers*, used to play against Cudjoe in *Philadelphia Fire*; and there's an entire scene in *The Lynchers* repeated in *The Cattle Killing*.¹⁴¹ Why so much seemingly insignificant doubling? In this work, perhaps the darkest and most oppressive of all of the novels, readers of Wideman's canon will recognize the desperate need to see that there are other possibilities, ones that can be transformed and created out of shared trauma through the power of storytelling.¹⁴² Wideman's literary doubles across the scope of his work reaffirm this need. The revision of the trope of the alienated individual often occurs within the relationship between Wideman's doubles. Wideman inscribes and revises the trope of the alienated intellectual and his or her flight from the community as an imaginative means of surviving the trauma of the past and confronting the continuing legacy of racism and cultural annihilation in the present.

Notably, the image of the alienated intellectual and his flight away or isolation from community can be found everywhere in Wideman's writing even after the first three novels, including those works in the Homewood trilogy that are published after *The Lynchers*. These tropes still linger in Wideman's novels and nonfiction, despite the critical readings that argue that Wideman has put such stories behind him and that the issues raised by the earlier works have been resolved.¹⁴³ In the mythic tales of the Homewood trilogy, the alienated intellectual does return to the community, but his isolation does not completely disappear. For example, Doot Lawson, in *Sent for You Yesterday*, transforms from alienated intellectual to blues hero—reconnecting to the voices of the past and the community, but his newly acquired status as the blues hero necessarily requires a removal from the community as well.

In *Damballah*, the story "The Beginning of Homewood," which appears at the end of the collection, is an origin tale that links the family's traumatic past with its painful present. A story that begins as a letter to Tommy becomes an account of Sybela Owens's escape from slavery. The linking of the two characters' flight and imprisonment is a post-traumatic narrative: Tommy's story is also somehow Sybela's: "One was the root and the other the branch but I was too close to you and she was too far away."[144] The root and the branch images address the continuing history of racism in this country. Tropes of enslavement in the stories of Sybela and Tommy reflect the relationship between common metaphors found between slave narratives and African American autobiography (both forms are revoiced and conflated in this piece).

Lawson remembers seeing Tommy in "old-time leg irons" and remarks that "if they captured Great-great-great grandmother Sybela Owens, they would have made a spectacle of her return to the plantation, just as they paraded you, costumed, fettered through the halls."[145] Little has changed in the hundred years between their lives, "so the struggle doesn't ever end. Her story, your story, the connections."[146] The repeated images of slavery, alienation, escape, and imprisonment continue in Wideman's work, even after the publication of the first three works, because Wideman's works collectively speak to the post-traumatic narratives in African American literature. Even if the alienated individual returns home, the history of racism and its traumatic effects are still felt within the community and in the life of the protagonist.

Tommy is also an important character in the second of the Homewood books, *Hiding Place*. On the run from the law, Tommy hides out at Mother Bess's home. Mother Bess has retreated from the community following the untimely deaths of her son and husband. She has gone into hiding. She is bitter and angry at the world. As a character, she is very reminiscent of Martha in *A Glance Away* and Martha in the story "Backseat." But as the epigraph to the novel suggests: "Went to the Rock to hide my face / Rock cried out. No hiding place"; neither Mother Bess nor Tommy can remain isolated or escape for very long. Tommy and Bess aren't the novel's only alienated figures. Tommy's brother, Doot Lawson, who has moved out West, away from Homewood, is also an isolated figure and a writer. The recurrent patterns of flight and alienation found in this novel reveal how running away from your home, your family, and, ultimately, yourself is unnatural and unhealthy to the spirit. It is Tommy and Bess's interaction that saves them, their sharing of stories and selves. It also rewrites the image of flight and escape found in the narratives and in subsequent works in the tradition.

The images of flight and return are recursive throughout the trilogy—there is also no clear beginning or conclusion to the trilogy. Characters are leaving and returning and leaving again throughout the course of the works as a whole. This circular pattern can be found throughout the work as a metaphor of history, of memory, and of the post-traumatic experience.[147]

The last book of the trilogy, *Sent for You Yesterday*, opens with Brother Tate's dreams of trains. Trains remain a predominant image as the work unfolds. Carl and Brother chase them as children, and Brother ends his life wishing to teach the train songs to his dead child, Junebug: "He wanted to teach it to Junebug. The scare game on the tracks."[148] Trains signal the promise of freedom exemplified by the train's association with the chariot of the spirituals and the migration to the Promised Land, the North. Yet neither Carl nor Brother feels free in the novel. Instead, they are trapped by the racism of their society and the trauma and loss that permeate their lives. Brother (another double, seen previously in *A Glance Away*), because he is unable to pass on his stories and his train songs to his dead son and because of the tragic betrayal of Albert Wilkes, fails to emerge as the blues hero of the work and help Homewood survive its shared traumas.

Albert Wilkes's extended departure from the community years ago damages the identity of Homewood. When he returns and is killed, his death further unravels the community's ties to one another. With Wilkes and Brother dead, Doot (the writer, Lawson) must become the blues hero, but he is the alienated intellectual, living out in Wyoming. His listening to and telling of stories will eventually reconnect this community to their traumatic pasts as well as to their cultural traditions. He accomplishes what Lawson in *A Glance Away* (a "different" character and yet another double) is unable to.[149]

The works of the Homewood trilogy are the literary double of *Brothers and Keepers*. In trying to answer the question how his brother ended up in prison, Wideman uncovers his own questions of identity that have plagued him and other African Americans, especially artists and intellectuals, throughout history and literature. The question "Who am I?" has been one of the central concerns in the canon of African American literature. The search for identity in the wake of double-consciousness is particularly salient in the tradition, as we saw in *Hurry Home* and here again in *Brothers and Keepers*.

In seeing the patterns of flight and alienation in the life that Robby led, John discovers his own flight, to college, to Wyoming: "Nothing new in my tactics. I'd adopted the strategy of slaves, the oppressed, the powerless. I thought I was running but I was fashioning a cage. Working hand and hand with my own enemies."[150] Reviewing the work, Ishmael Reed reiterates that Robby's run from the law and John's flight to Wyoming are as "old as the oldest slave narrative," though John's "flight is of a different nature. Like Toni Morrison's memorable New Woman, Jadine, he is in flight from his background and from his community."[151]

Wideman sees his writing as an escape from his background as well and acknowledges his own complicity in the either/or propositions that determined his life and Robby's: "Just two choices as far as I could tell: either/or. Rich or poor. White or black. Win or lose. I figured which side I wanted to be on when the Saints came marching in."[152] Robby is on the other side of this construction, the "dark" brother, a mask—another possible self, or double for Wideman. Wideman comes to realize that "the problem was in order to be the person I thought I wanted to be, I believed I had to seal myself off from you, construct a wall between us."[153] These are the same choices that many of Wideman's characters face: Cudjoe in *Philadelphia Fire*, Cecil Braithwaite, Littleman, and Eddie Lawson all struggle with this hierarchy, out in the world and within themselves, and all are in some way destroyed by it.

Wideman acknowledges that this entire family history may be founded on "running away":

Did our grandfathers run away from the South? Black Harry from Greenwood, South Carolina, mulatto white John from Culpepper, Virginia. How would they answer that question? Were they running from something or running to something? What did you figure you were doing when you started running? When did your flight begin? Was escape the reason or was there a destination, a promised land exerting its pull?[154]

Brothers and Keepers, more than many of Wideman's other works, shares the most common patterns and influences of the slave narrative and African American autobiography. Besides the motifs of running away and search for identity, *Brothers and Keepers* reenacts metaphors of enslavement, tropes that tie slave and prison narratives together.[155] Drugs, pain, hopelessness, despair, alienation—all of these enslaved Robby before he was ever behind bars, like they enslaved the characters Uncle Carl and Eddie Lawson. Wideman realizes that Robby's prison sits on the Ohio River. He asks, "Is this somebody's cruel joke?" Viewed "from barred windows, from tiered cages, the river must call to the prisoners' hearts, a natural symbol of flight and freedom."[156] Wideman reveals to us within the layers of these images from racial memory that such freedom still does not exist. Until the forces of racism are vanquished in America, the patterns that tie Robby and John and all African Americans to the slave narrative will persist, and even then, in the post-traumatic consciousness the connections will continue.

Even following the publication of *Brothers and Keepers*, Wideman revisits these images and themes. His next novel, *Reuben*, also presents other alienated and isolated figures. Wally is a college sports recruiter whose biography somewhat resembles Wideman's. Consumed with overwhelming hate and murderous rage, Wally describes to the lawyer, Reuben, either a real or imagined violent killing of a white stranger in a bathroom. Wally also feels guilty about his success and acknowledges that it has come at a high price. Despite his fortunes, however, his status as an African American has not changed in his eyes. Wally states: "You ain't part of where you land, you ain't really no part of what you left behind. You float. You're a floater. People begin to see you that way. Which amounts to not seeing you at all. Invisible."[157] This is a description of the "pain of two-ness" that plagued Cecil Braithwaite in *Hurry Home*. On the road for his job, Wally constantly feels that he is being watched, that "they" are making sure to "keep this nigger running."

Reuben, the other intellectual in the novel, does remain intimately connected to the community, despite the traumatic experiences of his life. He recognizes the folly of leaving the community in a passage that alludes to Wideman's biography and moments in other novels: "Home, home on the range. Blue Wyoming sky, gray waves of sage. Stars and stripes crackle like tinsel in a fabulous sky. Everybody's happy, wherever they are, whatever they are doing, daydreaming, climbing of stars and bars to heaven and back."[158] We can see here that no such place exists. The West is no more the Promised Land than the North was.

The guarded optimism of the Homewood books and *Reuben* begins to evaporate by the time Wideman publishes the collection *All Stories Are True*.[159] Wideman returns to stories and situations where characters suffer from the pain of double-consciousness, disconnection, and traumatic loss as the focus of his writing. Family is present in these stories as well—as it was even in *A Glance Away*. But these stories present situations where characters re-experience traumatic events or face new suffering, and family and community stories offer much less solace and connection. In *All Stories Are True*, Wideman continues to develop the narratives of alienation and in some cases even returns to Homewood stories previously written to reintroduce and reemphasize some of these tropes and themes. Usually, the Homewood stories are read in terms of restoring balance to the creative imagination. Wideman's return to these stories—as well as a renewed focus on the alienated African American individual/intellectual—reminds readers of his overall work of the precarious nature of African American life in American society. Bette Lawson tells her son, the writer, that a neighbor has had a very difficult past year, comparing him to Job; the same comparison could be made with any character in the book.

While in some cases it is difficult to discuss a collection of short stories as having a common thread or theme, *All Stories Are True* can certainly be said to have a predominant tone. Few of these stories are hopeful and nearly all of them consider a world haunted by lost children and lost family. Take, for example, the title story, "All Stories Are True." Considering the prevalence of the saying in Wideman's work, we should expect the story to resonate with many of Wideman's themes and layered narrative style. Yet, those familiar with the Homewood books may see a different direction in this new Homewood story.

The story is still a family story—one of those works associated most directly with Wideman's family and the Homewood community. Unlike the Homewood books, however, the alienated intellectual has already returned home and discovered his place within the community. This narrative progression is discussed more fully in the following chapter, but what we have here is not a story that illustrates an artist and family healed by shared stories and able to move on past their shared trauma. Instead, we are presented with a story that will suggest within the context of Wideman's works as a whole a repeating and cyclical message—one that reflects the post-traumatic nature of Wideman's canon. In "All Stories Are True" Tommy is still in prison for life—and we are told that his appeals for parole have been repeatedly turned down. Any hope we may have had for a happy ending when we read about Tommy's situation in *Damballah* has been dashed. Homewood itself is still suffering from economic woes and hard times. But the times seem to be getting even harder when Tommy and John's mother, Bette, complains about someone stealing her beloved flowers right out of her garden to sell and the troubles besetting her neighbor, Wade. And Bette has become ill, now often too ill to face "the evil prison" where Tommy is kept. John sees her as "frail" and "vulnerable."

Despite these changes and losses, John consoles himself by thinking about the Homewood street names: "The song of the street names a medium in which we all float, suspended, as if each of us is someone's precious, precious child, who must never be allowed to slip from the arms cradling, rocking."[160] The one constant is the strength of the home. John describes the tree growing near the house, whose "roots must run under her cellar. The sound of it drinking, lapping nourishment deep underground is part of the quiet when her house is empty."[161] But the flowers that "grew feet" one night and left the yard counter this image of rootedness. The tree is grounded in the past, in the home, but the loss of the flowers represents a disintegration of the neighborhood as a whole.

This image is further developed when John visits his brother in jail, which also acts as a clear representation of the post-traumatic in the work. The story illustrates that traumatic wounds can never be completely healed, and the pain associated with the original suffering always returns. This is symbolized most poignantly in the account of a leaf that "escapes" the prison yard and flies beyond the walls. The prisoners and their families who have come for a visit cheer on the leaf and its escape, seeing in the moment a symbol of their own hopes. But Tommy reveals to John the true story:

> The leaf. I told you how it finally blowed free over top the wall. Couldn't see it no more. Denise grabbed my hand. She was crying and was bouncing up and down. People shouting. Some even clapped. But you know

something. I'm gonna tell you something I don't tell nobody when I tell about the leaf. The dumb thing blew back in here again."[162]

The leaf's return, Tommy's failure at parole, Bette's illness and her resignation toward the loss of her son to prison, the allusion to Job, all suggest the inevitability of suffering.

We see this same attitude in one of the other Homewood stories in the collection, "Welcome." Seemingly another story about the Lawsons, this one focuses on a young mother whose daughter, Njeri, died when she was still a young child. The child's loss frames the story as Njeri's mother and grandmother discuss the impending arrival of Njeri's uncle (who appears to be another alter ego of Wideman). The uncle, named Tom, is visiting for the holidays—an event less frequent since he moved away and since the loss of his own son to jail. Names and situations from other stories are doubled in this work—in yet another variation or possibility of these characters and their narratives.

But Tom's noted absence implies that he has not stayed in touch with his family, despite his troubles. His loss of his son and his sister's loss of her daughter do not seem to bring them closer together to share their grief or to help one another cope. It is the mother who is the vessel for such communication, the one who carries the "weight" of the family's suffering—a characteristic of Bette Lawson that will be expressed in the short story "Weight," included in *God's Gym*, published a decade later.

The matriarch seems incapable of holding the family together here. The two women tell stories about Tom; and he has, in turn, talked about how pleasant it is when the family is all together at home, but Tom is clearly a phantom now, someone they recall through past stories. When Tom and his sister try to talk about their shared trauma, she reaches out to him, but "he wasn't asking for that. Eyes in another country that quick."[163] She calls him "Tom, Tom the piper's son / Stole a pig and away he run."[164] Thinking about her brother's problems reminds her of the father that deserted them and the grandfather who held the family together, but in the end there is not a moment of expression between brother and sister that actually occurs, that connects them and soothes their pain. Instead, she muses on the "silence" between them, broken only by "the old toothless man" shaking his bell under his blankets on the corner of the street.[165]

The next scene offers a moment of understanding between Tom and his sister when he at last reveals his feelings:

I'm home again and it's the opposite of a new shiny world because I feel everything closing down. Blam. I know nothing has changed and never will these streets swallow me alive and hate everybody and that's how its going to be.... You'all remind me of what's good here. Why I need to come back.[166]

The lines are expressing contradictory emotions. Being home sustains Tom but it also exacerbates his loss. Tom finally is able to slightly share his grief and admits how much he misses his own son when he sees a man and his son on the corner and imagines them freezing to death, the "whole dreary storyline."[167] He comes to realize that the girl singing while she is waiting on him at a restaurant and the man on the corner who is lucky to be alive and is hugging his son are the ones that have the answers. Even though Tom is able to understand these key moments, he remains isolated and alone at the end. His loss separates him, perhaps irrevocably, from others around him. Every encounter emphasizes his loneliness and emptiness.

The mask that Tom wears to hide his pain is a tool employed by many characters throughout Wideman's fiction and nonfiction. Wideman describes it as a method for dealing with feelings of alienation in *Brothers and Keepers*. It is also a skill nurtured by the father and grandmother in the story "Backseat." The story is another Homewood work; however, this one centers primarily on the writer's paternal grandmother, Martha. Martha lost a husband and a son as well. The son, Eugene, died in World War II. The names and events can be found in various forms in *A Glance Away* and *Hiding Place*, serving as yet another literary double. There are several stories within stories here as the writer reflects on his youth and on his grandmother's life and recent illness.

He confesses he knows little about her life; her stories have been hidden from him by her. When he tries to encourage her to explain her origins, her unwillingness or inability to share her stories with him leave the writer with the need to "devise a history I don't know."[168] Her losses and her pain are an emotional mystery to him, and yet he feels he must know her past in order to understand his destiny: "I'm left to construct what I need from her thoughtful silence."[169]

"Backseat" bobs and weaves between the writer trying to grasp his distant grandmother and recollections of his own teenage years, especially the moment when he had his first sexual experience. The story moves backwards and forwards much like memory, but ultimately the pieces of the story do not coalesce into a coherent picture of his grandmother. The stories that he has written about her, the gaps he has filled in about her life, become what he knows best about her.

He realizes he also has the "power to separate" himself from others. This trait is characteristic of his grandmother and his father, and his description sounds very much like the double-consciousness that we have seen in Wideman's other trauma narratives:

> My father's definitely her son. Aloof, detached, self-sufficient. A habit of masking emotion that's so thorough-going, so convincing, you wonder sometimes if emotions really are percolating behind the mask or if the elegant, stylized mask itself has become an emotion, the ultimate, unchanging protective shield of cool indifference.[170]

In this story, as in most of the works of the collection, Wideman is unable (or unwilling) to revise many of the tropes of African American literature as he has done in other works. Still, "Backseat" does offer us a multilayered identity of the writer—a sign of narrative possibilities. His grandmother "anointed" him with many nicknames, including "*Doot, Spanky, John-Edgar, John, Doodlebug, Mr. Wideman.*"[171] Even though he states that there were many times when he did not know his grandmother's last name (due to her remarriages), many of his family members have multiple names or identities. The lack of cohesion in his grandmother's identity appears to bother Wideman, but the numerous titles counter the typical image of a fixed, stereotypical African American identity. This is one "true" story that Wideman succeeds in revising in the work.

But multiple names and identities can suggest a very different meaning in other works in *All Stories Are True*. In "Everyone Knew Bubba Riff," Bubba Riff is known by many names in the community and within his family. He also inhabits many roles, several of which paint very different portraits of the character. The reflection on Bubba Riff and his place in the neighborhood and on the "riffing" of his names takes place at his death. Looking back over the course of Bubba Riff's life, it is clear that everyone in Homewood had their own perception of the man. Here, as in "Backseat," no cohesive history of the character appears. Again the reader is presented with a complicated image, one that allows all possible readings to be true. Bubba Riff becomes a text to interpret. One reading implies that Bubba's ability to occupy different spaces in his family and his community is transformative, countering the image of a singular African American identity. Bubba then would be a trickster figure of his own tale.

The other reading suggests a different slant on Bubba's character. This reading sees Bubba as a mysterious figure—a paradox, given the title. His identity is unknown, and ultimately his death is tragic, because his true self is too remote from the people around him to acknowledge. He has not developed close, meaningful relationships because he has masked his real face from others. In fact, *nobody* knew Bubba Riff. Wideman transforms him into the "Richard

Cory" of Homewood. There is evidence in the story to argue for either reading of Bubba Riff, but given the overall tenor of the stories in the rest of the collection, "Everybody Knew Bubba Riff" illustrates the loss of another Homewood son, fractured by the forces of history still operating in the community and within the consciousness of Bubba Riff.

Other mysterious and unknown figures can also be found in the short story "Loon Man." The Loon Man of the title may be a character out of local folk/ghost stories. Or he may be the new handyman that Foster believes is one and the same. Or Foster may be the Loon Man (or at least as crazy as the moniker implies). The Loon Man may be responsible for the disappearance of several children—either to save them or to kill them, depending on which version of the narrative you agree to believe at any one point. Again, we are presented with wildly disparate versions of the same character or multiple versions of a Loon Man. Is he a ghost, a pied piper, a monster? Is he even real? He appears to be a character out of myth or the unconscious. The only thing that can possibly be agreed upon is that either the character or the narrator, or both, have suffered psychological damage of some sort. Has Foster created another identity for himself, a manifestation of his double-consciousness, or is he so traumatized that he cannot present a coherent narrative, like Clement in *Hiding Place*?

Whichever version of the story is true, neither provides its reader with a healing story, a cohesive identity, or characters integrated into their community. The Loon Man is one of the "three bears" or from a family of ghosts. He is a marginal figure; and, unlike some of the other isolated characters in Wideman's work, he lacks the necessary empathy and imagination to be a possible blues hero—unless Foster and the Loon Man are one in the same. In which case, Foster's psychological trauma has so unraveled his mind that he cannot offer the community an effective artistic vision.[172]

The image of lost children found in many of the other stories in the collection becomes the focus of "Newborn Thrown in Trash and Dies." Told from the point of view of the newborn on her way to her death, the work offers a double of the story "Daddy Garbage," from *Damballah*. In "Daddy Garbage" two older men (one of whom is John French) from Homewood find a newborn that has been thrown in the trash. Distraught by their discovery, the men—strangers to the baby—lovingly bury the child as they mourn the death of family and communal bonds in Homewood. Given the tone of the stories in *All Stories Are True*, it is not surprising that no such redemptive act occurs in this narrative. In fact, the newborn asks where are the people, even strangers or the media, to care about her or even watch her.

The child, falling down the garbage chute, imagines the lives on the floors she passes, and the life that she will not get a chance to live. Even her imagined future in the "Floor of Love" sequence is grim, another violation of family and love. In this vision, the home is not a sanctuary; it is a violation. A stepbrother, not yet born, she sees shot and dying in a schoolyard when he is just a boy. Unlike the baby in "Daddy Garbage," this is a child that no one loves, not even in her own imagination. There is no anger expressed in her own death, only resignation and certainty that this is what life has to offer. The newborn expresses the only hope in the story when she confesses: "One thing bothers me a lot. I regret not knowing what is on the floors above the one where I began my fall. I hope it's better up there. Real gardens perhaps or even a kind of heaven for the occupants lucky enough to live above the floors I have seen."[173] The hierarchy of value implied here reminds us of other Wideman stories at moments where he argues about America's calculation of the worth of African American children against all the rest.[174] Even the baby comprehends that her life has little importance, but there might be some children, some who are entitled to a beautiful life, whereas others seem to deserve the pain and suffering that she has seen and experienced in her flight downward.

Nevertheless, she thinks her story needs to be told—and her mother's—whose motives she tries to understand. She does not want to be another statistic, another unknown child: "The newspaper account is not enough, why I want my voice to be a part of the record. The awful silence is not truly broken until we speak."[175] Wideman's fiction allows for this story to be heard, and it provides another medium for an examination of alienation and trauma. What has happened to this mother that she feels too alone to ask for help? Where are well-meaning strangers? Why was there no one to rescue this child, to tell her story? These apartments and floors are separated from one another so deeply that his child's birth and death have gone unnoticed.

An alienation narrative of a different character is the work "Signs."[176] Kendra, the protagonist, is a young African American graduate student at a small, nearly all-white liberal arts college. An orphan, she has been raised by her two aunts, who are supportive of her goals and have nurtured her as she was growing up. She is the center of their warmth, generosity, and love. In their presence, she feels at home, but when she is at school she is out of place. Only one of a few African American students, she connects to no one—especially not the students she teaches. She even expresses alienation from the material she is teaching—John Milton in a Western literature course. Trying to explain Milton's significance to a blond, blue-eyed male who could care less about Milton or any other literature, she muses about her own disorientation when reading the works on the syllabus (from Oedipus to Eliot). She has never been able to find herself there and has little sympathy for the student in her office:

> I know it's not easy, Bobby Baby. See these wounds in my palms. If I unbuttoned this desk from my waist and let it float down around my slim ankles and lifted my naked foot for you to inspect you'd find a ten-penny hole bored through my instep. Of all people I know how easy it's not.[177]

Her entire career has been "marked" by professors who felt that she did not belong. One critiques her essay with a red "X." She writes a letter to her dead mother about the traumatic experience that she connects to the past suffering of African Americans:

> Those marks he put on my paper, Mama, it was as if he tattooed my body. Scarlet slashes on my chest. Rusty iron hook in my back. Felt like I was walking around naked and everybody could see. This nigger gal don't belong here. She ain't worth the time of day. Doesn't write or speak our language. We gotta use signs to communicate with her. An X like her daddy signed on the dotted line when he sold her. I can't come home, Mama. I can't stay here."[178]

The reader also sees that Kendra has a poor self-image; she fantasizes about having a lover with the "power to change the way she looked at herself."[179] Shortly after arriving at school, she begins to receive threatening and anonymous signs designed to scare her into leaving and prey on her own feelings of low self-worth. The language of the signs is the language of historical trauma—words and images meant to wound her further. One merely reads, "K K K"; another says, "Whites only." Each sign steals her confidence and reminds her that America has always promoted these "signs" in order to diminish African American life. The signs tell "her story as if she'd never had another."[180]

After receiving several signs, she has a dream of her dead mother. The image of love and comfort degenerates when roses in the vision turn into "big behinds, a big bouquet of jiggling backsides that spill from the cradle of her mother's arms and split and bleed sticky red juice and black roachy seeds."[181] The iconic image of the watermelon, seen as a sign of everything black and "down home" in *Damballah*, is repeated here by Wideman to illustrate Kendra's alienation from her past and her identity—connecting to the discomfort with these "letters from home" that plague John Lawson in the Homewood books. Kendra also suffers from double-consciousness. She wonders herself if she is "fatally divided" and later describes her realization as an "uncontrollable rage exploding when you discover the enemy outside is also inside."[182] As the signs continue to appear, and as she feels more and more disconnected from her past, she struggles to maintain her identity.

Being at school, apart from her family and cultural experiences, Kendra's feelings of isolation intensify. Looking back at life with her aunts, she remembers the comfort of going to church with them, their unquestioning love of her, "squeezed between them, their soprano voices a starry roof over my head."[183] They protected her as an orphan, but she is orphaned once again at school. The final "sign. The one [she] heeded," is the death of both of her aunts in a car crash.[184] Three times an orphan, this final event leads to her confession. The "truth" of the story is revealed at the end, as it is in "All Stories Are True" in the brother's story of the leaf. Her entry in the diary (a text we had not seen previously in the story) represents the discourse of autobiography and confessional. This is where we expect true stories to be told—but, of course, we should know better. Kendra admits to being the one who wrote and left the signs. She hasn't shared her feelings in the diary with us before. Why now? She also acknowledges that she had all the necessary writing materials to make the signs. Her inclusion of the "yellow writing tablet" is a sign for the readers to decipher themselves. Has the whole story been an imaginative creation in the mind of the character? She tells us she knows all the "ugly words used" against her and that she knows how to read texts and look for patterns. She "could have been the one." The events are all "unverifiable as a dream."[185]

Kendra's story appears to be an alienation narrative—a story where a character's own mind has been struggling against itself as it struggles with the tragic loss of family and double-consciousness. Her own voice possesses her and "rapes" her. Like other characters such as Littleman and Cecil Braithwaite, Kendra has been living the "enemy's dream." But like her alter ego, Wideman, she has written a fiction, a story that helps her survive her experiences, her trauma. She is the writer of the "signs," the story that helps her survive her experiences, her trauma. In the end, she reveals that the writing has been therapeutic and has helped silence those voices of self-doubt and those stories that exclude her identity: "If not healed, I'm cured."[186]

Kendra is yet another of the lost children in the collection whose tragedies in their childhood follow them as they grow. She serves as a reminder of the necessity of teaching children stories of survival. The son in "Casa Grande" is the most poignant and painful example of this need. The writer discovers a story that his now twenty-one-year-old son wrote when he was ten. The tale is a science-fiction fantasy that is typical for young adolescents. The story within the story "A Trip to Jupiter," expresses the son's need for acceptance and the wish for special powers—usually a common sign that the child feels like he cannot control the universe. "A Trip to Jupiter" illustrates a boy who feels alone in the world. The writer finds his son's long-lost story in a folder eleven years later but immediately connects the isolation the boy felt years ago with his current situation as a prisoner. He is cut off from his family as if he is on a "planet ten million light years away."[187]

The writer makes further connections between his son's story and the Pima Indians of Arizona, where his son's prison is located. He muses on the Pima Indians' stories of the Hohokam who occupied the land a thousand years ago. *Hohokam* means "used up, gone." These unknown people are "named *hohokam* by archaeologists because the ones who dwelt here are gone, gone, gone and cannot speak their own names, sing their songs."[188] Throughout the remainder of this very short story, the writer/father thinks of his son only in terms that reflect how isolated the son is and how far they are from one another. His son is one of "the lost ones, the outcasts, the *hohokam*."[189] The writer also feels lost as if he is missing something, like the cacti sitting along the Arizona road that look as if they are missing limbs or heads: "Clearly each cactus is incomplete."[190] "Casa Grande"'s brevity offers little solace or resolution; it is a snapshot, an expression of longing and loss.

The loss of a son and its traumatic response also structures the novel *Philadelphia Fire*. Continuing in a tone even more deeply distraught than *All Stories Are True*, *Philadelphia Fire* follows Cudjoe, another alienated figure who seems to lack the skills to survive his personal traumas and whose tendency is toward flight when suffering erupts. He is an expatriate writer, a "son" of such literary fathers as Baldwin, DuBois, and Wright. He is one of the types of men that the character J. B. complains about toward the end of the novel, one that "exited for goddamn parts unknown. Kathmandu. Wyoming."[191] As such, Cudjoe is another double for Wideman. When we meet Cudjoe, he is living on a Greek island, isolated from friends and family and community. He returns home to Philadelphia after he has heard about the MOVE bombing. Seeking to understand what happened in the MOVE house and what has become of the boy seen running from the flames of the MOVE house, Cudjoe goes to interview witnesses of the MOVE bombing and is confronted with his feelings of alienation from the African American community: "How, after the briefest of conversations, did they know his history, that he'd married a white woman and fathered half-white kids? How did they know he'd failed his wife and failed those kids, that his betrayal was double, about blackness and about being a man?"[192]

It is noteworthy that two of the European texts layered into this novel, *The Tempest* and *Oedipus at Colonus*, are also about exiled men. They are also the "father texts" of Western, humanist civilization and the texts that an African American writer must continually confront. Cudjoe is connected in the text to both Caliban and Prospero from *The Tempest*. All three characters are dispossessed and exiled, which links them to the other literary figure in the text,

Oedipus. Cudjoe does come home from his island escape, but so much has already been lost. In searching for the lost boy, Simba, he reflects on his own relationship with his sons and other lost children in his past. We are presented throughout the text with multiple fractured conversations, especially between the "writer" and his son who is in prison. This moment conflates a metafictional voice with Cudjoe's to suggest what can be lost if fathers and sons cannot communicate. And yet Cudjoe still proceeds in a symbolic and fruitless quest for a forgotten "son" when he could be caring for his real ones. The history and patterns of alienation and isolation of African American men in narratives is repeated here between fathers and sons and seems to be threatening to continue into the future.

More than any other novel, *Philadelphia Fire* illustrates, through its narrative disintegration, what happens when the artist remains isolated. He is unable to communicate the pain and suffering of his own experience in any meaningful way for the community. Wideman does invert the trope of flight by bringing Cudjoe home, and by the novel's end he appears to be recommitted to family and community (*"Never again. Never again"*),[193] but it is unclear if Cudjoe will be able to conquer the familiar trauma and alienation "rumbling" toward him in the concluding lines. The novel is, nevertheless, an accurate depiction of the failure of storytelling during the most traumatic of situations. Cudjoe, despite his closing words, is trapped in a post-traumatic narrative.[194]

The alienation between fathers and sons and their lack of shared storytelling are the impetus for Wideman's travels with his own father in *Fatheralong*. The two journey to Promised Land, South Carolina, close to the seat of the Wideman clan. The journey is an immersion ritual, an inverted historical image that is necessary for communal and personal recovery. Wideman hopes to better his relationship with his father as well as learn about his past and himself.

As a boy, Wideman hadn't wanted to visit his grandfather's family, to go to "a place where they lynched black boys like Emmett Till."[195] Now, however, Wideman sees an opportunity to learn more about his past and the history of his people. Driving through South Carolina, looking out the rental car window, Wideman realizes: "I've been here before. I'm not simply summoning up some reactionary, ole-time, morbid stereotype of slavery days to mock the New South. I've been here before. My skin recalls sensations I can't name yet."[196] This is a scene from Wideman's racial memory, a story as essential as any that he has experienced firsthand.

His father has been for the most part an isolated member of the family. The family stories at the center of most of Wideman's work are matrilineal. His father's world, he writes, represents the governing principle of his life: "You stand alone. Alone, alone, alone."[197] We see this in "Backseat," from *All Stories Are True*, and in many of the portraits of Wideman's fictional characters. Wideman also writes that his father was physically separated in Wideman's imagination when he was growing up. The father lived somewhere else, apart from the women and alone. Wideman became a different person when he traveled to the "other side" to visit his father.[198] In the present, Wideman describes where his father lives now—alone and growing old. The father's high-rise building makes Wideman wonder: "Did somebody consciously seek to erect an image of isolation."[199] Wideman hopes to close the gap between his father and himself by traveling with him to recover their history, but he learns little about his father's past despite the fact that they are sitting right next to each other on their long road trip. Closing the gap on their physical space does not close the other gaps between them.

Wideman further examines his father's life and his own in his discussion of literary fathers. He observes the predominance of fatherless boys in the African American literary tradition (Richard Wright, Ralph Ellison, and Frederick Douglass, for example) and that the writers of the past, particularly Wright, cut themselves off from their real and literary fathers. The danger in this is losing yourself, your past. Wideman argues that Wright in "repudiating his father ... comes perilously close to repudiating all people of color" and that "another form of running away is substituting the white father for the unreachable or unknowable or unacceptable black one."[200] Wideman has been writing about his father since the beginning of his career—Eddie Lawson, for example, serves as a double for his father. His characterizations of his father through fiction—through his imagined father stories—represent Wideman's search for his father's identity. In his attempt to gather his father's history, to "gather him up as family" as the god Damballah would have, Wideman hopes to recover some portion of his own history.

Wideman reiterates, in the course of his journey down South, the importance of "father stories," those stories that establish manhood, stories that strengthen ties to the past, stories that have been denied through history to the African American father and son. These stories must be passed on to the next generations, an act that we have been told is important as early as *A Glance Away* and is reflected in the Homewood books; but *Fatheralong* signals a return to the power of storytelling as a means of survival following *Philadelphia Fire* and *All Stories Are True*.

Fatheralong presents a realization that the feelings of isolation and alienation are not imposed only from the racism outside of the community. The necessity to share "father stories" isn't an easy task in a society where African American fathers and sons are separated by a history of racism, alienation, and despair that can sometimes perpetuate self-loathing and diminishes the value and worth of the African American individual and community in American culture and history.[201] Nevertheless, Wideman and his father have taken this journey together; it has not been a solitary flight into the wilderness, revising the trope of the solitary fugitive slave and their narrative.

In *Fatheralong*, Wideman has a vision of his place between the past and the present, between all stories and voices, when he sees before him a path that leads to the land owned by his ancestors in South Carolina as the same path that leads to the Arizona prison where his youngest son will spend his life. It is a visual crossroads of myth and time, a vital intersection between two worlds presided over by the god Damballah, which links the past with the present and the future. That same crossroads appears in *The Cattle Killing*. The past, present, and future intersect in the story of an itinerant preacher, a former slave in late eighteenth-century Philadelphia at the time of the yellow fever epidemic. Wideman retells this historical event through the eyes of the fictional, unnamed protagonist (reminiscent of other unnamed protagonists in African American literature). He wanders the countryside looking to testify and learn the will of God. The novel revises the form and character of the typical slave narratives of the eighteenth century, especially those modeled on the popular picaresques of the time.[202] The "black picaroon" is a character who suffers because he must learn to repress his traumatic past. The price that is paid is "alienation, lack of identity, and the incapacity of love."[203] Wideman revises most of these elements of the black picaroon in the novel. In *The Cattle Killing*, the unnamed narrator decides to preach "the word" to his fellow brethren. He is not the typical isolated figure, even though he is wandering throughout the countryside of Philadelphia. His character, despite his nomadic nature, connects to his community and his race—living with them and serving them through acts of charity and the sharing of stories. Unlike most picaroons, he is not in search of an identity or freedom or to return home: "I took to the road to spread the Lord's good news."[204] In the end, he chooses love and connection—and storytelling, his anathema to the fever and violence spreading across Philadelphia.[205]

With the publication of *The Cattle Killing*, alienation narratives become less prominent in Wideman's work. Like the preacher in that novel, Robert and Kassima in *Two Cities* ultimately choose love as a healing weapon against trauma. Robert, Kassima, and Mr. Mallory all begin the novel in a post-traumatic space, but Robert and Kassima are able to move forward and survive their past while Mallory ultimately succumbs to it. As the artist of the work, Mallory represents a slight shift in Wideman's work. Robert appears to be the alter ego here, not Mallory, who is not even the novel's protagonist. Mallory has chosen art and isolation over love, and it condemns him because he is never able to truly confront the horrors of his past.

To preserve the true identity of the African American community, Mr. Mallory in *Two Cities* has turned to photography. Like other Wideman characters, Mallory has suffered several personal traumas, one during World War II. His desertion of his wife after the war because of the pain he experienced there is a classic post-traumatic narrative. His further isolation from the world signifies his inability to reintegrate into society following his experience. When we meet him in *Two Cities*, he is a senior citizen, living in the house of Kassima, who has suffered numerous personal tragedies as well. The two soothe each other's pain by talking. In Kassima, Mallory sees his young wife he could no longer live with. He says to Kassima: "Believed I had to leave if I wanted a life. Stole myself. Like a runaway slave. Stole myself and the price was leaving my family behind, my people behind."[206] Mallory's relationship with Kassima expresses a desire to reconnect and to heal the wounds of the past—perhaps to help her in her time of suffering. Until he lives in Kassima's house, Mallory has hidden behind a camera, distancing himself from others. But his art reflects his need to record the past as he snaps photos and layers images to capture the lives of the people in his community.

The characters in Wideman's later works realize late in life the necessity to reconnect to their family and their community. In his latest novel, *Fanon*, Thomas, one of Wideman's alter egos, receives his head in a box—a sign that everything the head represents, the imagination, intellect, and memory, has been severed. Now, perhaps, the "other" Thomas can move forward. These later characters or revisions of characters find ways—usually through love—to reconcile the pain of their history. The past they are trying to move beyond is not only one filled with personal suffering. It also stems from the slave past and the continued racism plaguing the African American community. Knowing the father stories is not enough; you must also be able to pass them along. The storytellers must also be aware that father stories are not without their problems. They often have embedded within them images of trauma, alienation, the pain of double-consciousness, and the impulse to "fly away from home." Revisiting and rewriting the painful narratives and images of history ultimately allow Wideman to clear a space for characters that seem more aware of healthy ways to survive. These later characters finally achieve the status as blues hero that seems just beyond the reach of many of the younger characters in Wideman's novels. Those characters never quite achieve the status of the DaddyGenes or John Frenches whose storytelling, whose connection to community and the past, whose experience, and whose love of others help the family and the individual survive and even thrive.

CHAPTER THREE

The Return Home

MYTHIC NARRATIVES AND FAMILY HISTORY

> Sometimes the god wears a woman's face, sometimes a man's. Both suffer the same fate. Betrayal, dismemberment, the body pieces scattered, interred in a thousand, thousand, unknown places. Then she comes, always she, inconsolable, her tears a frozen rain drenching the land that has not cycled past winter since the lost one disappeared. She will scour the whole wide world until she finds every fragment of her beloved. And when she has gathered them and united them and breathed life again into the body, the earth too, as if it has been kissed, will begin softly to stir again, bud, bloom, warm as she does, her outstretched arms and smile open wide as a horizon in welcome.
>
> —JOHN EDGAR WIDEMAN, "Malcolm X: The Art of Autobiography"

More has been written about Wideman's "family stories" and genealogical history than on any other characteristic of his work. The novels of the Homewood trilogy (*Damballah*, *Hiding Place*, and *Sent for You Yesterday*), *Reuben*, *Brothers and Keepers*, and *Hoop Roots* all center on Homewood. Other works depict the lives of Wideman's family, including *Fatheralong*, and there are family stories in the short-story collections and in *Philadelphia Fire* as well. Family names are used in *Hurry Home* and *A Glance Away*; and even in the novel *Fanon*, Wideman interweaves portraits of his mother with the fictional Thomas and the story of Frantz Fanon's life. It is clear that Wideman believes that the family—literally and figuratively—is the source of the story, and he has confessed: "All of my books are about my family, family relationships, and reordering and transformation of family."[1]

Several of these "Homewood" works are classified as autobiography or memoir, including *Brothers and Keepers*, *Fatheralong*, and *Hoop Roots*, yet even they admit to some fictionalizing. The novels of the trilogy and *Reuben* are also examples of autobiographical fiction. Seen as a whole, these works reveal some of the postmodern philosophy in Wideman's writing—there is a meaningful blurring of the boundaries between fiction, autobiography, and history.

Wideman's emphasis on family history in these works serves multiple purposes. These stories operate as a lens by which Wideman views the history of his race and the historical consciousness of America, and Wideman uses these family narratives—these stories of home –to directly refute the stories written by outsiders to describe what it means to be an African American in this country. This has been his "calling":

> I have had to read experts on African Americans my whole life. Although it may not have been about John Wideman, per se, it's about my family, about my neighborhood, about what made homeboy tick. About the athletes that I admired. I've had to deal with that bullshit from day one. The few little stories that I've been able to get into the web don't even begin to equal—they're a drop in the bucket compared to what's out there, and some of the things I am trying to reverse, or change.[2]

Wideman works both within and outside the family circle to tell their stories, to refute what others have written, to install new "true" stories into the historical mainstream. In this sense he is a liminal figure using both autobiography and ethnography to recall and remember family history. His descriptions of the lives of the individuals in the community and in his "fictional" family testify to the trauma that they have suffered historically. These works, acting as examples of autoethnography, bear witness to the legacy of slavery and racism in America. Their illustration serves to offer solace to the family and community, and it speaks to the audience beyond Homewood who fail to see the human suffering outside the realm of the history books and the nightly news.

The autoethnographic quality of many of these "Homewood stories" reflects Wideman's desire to produce counternarratives to dominant or institutional texts. Such a violation calls into question the authority of the "scientific" ethnography over autobiography and fiction. In his vision, ethnography is just a "story" that may also happen to be as true as an autobiography or a novel.

These "objective" accounts reify the trauma of slave history as they cage and control the portraits of black life.

Clearly, the way we apply the term "autobiographical" to a work must be carefully considered, especially with a writer such as Wideman. Therefore, we should be cautious whenever we discuss Wideman's fiction within the context of the family. Trying to decide what is fiction and what is nonfiction in his work is like wading through quicksand and, ultimately, misses the goal of Wideman's aesthetic.[3]

Most critics have focused on the novels of the Homewood trilogy as the sites for Wideman's recovery of family history.[4] But Wideman does not ignore family history or Homewood itself as a topic in earlier novels. Even the first novel, *A Glance Away*, set in an anonymous neighborhood in an unknown city, uses Homewood street names. Those works set outside of Homewood, including *Hurry Home*, *The Cattle Killing*, *The Lynchers*, and *Philadelphia Fire*, have references to the family that appears in the Homewood books. Also, all four of these books are set in Philadelphia, where Wideman went to college and where he later taught after returning from Oxford. Wideman's "homes" are both represented in the novel *Two Cities*: Philadelphia and Homewood (Pittsburgh) are the "cities" of the title. Even in *Fanon* the action is centered in Homewood and Wideman's new home, New York City.

Wideman is interested in all of the works, to different degrees, in preserving family and communal history, whether this takes place in Homewood, Philadelphia, Martinque, or Africa. The community of Homewood and the African diaspora are as much a part of the family as are its actual members: "Think rather of circles within circles within circles, a stone dropped into a still pool, ripples and wave motion."[5] Every descendant of slaves and of the black diaspora is bound by common traumatic experiences. These family stories return to a mythic space and time.

We are told in "The Beginning of Homewood" that the community was started by Wideman's ancestors, the runaway slave Sybela and the slave master's son. Stories in *Damballah* center, primarily, on the members of the family shown in the begat chart in the prefatory material. Between and within the stories of *Damballah* are the tales of neighbors, friends, enemies—the inhabitants of Homewood. *Reuben*, also a Homewood book, published after the trilogy, centers on individuals in Homewood outside of the Lawson or French families (though Mrs. Lawson speaks briefly to one of the main characters, Kwansa).[6] Family history is not limited to Wideman's own immediate kin; by celebrating the lives of those closest to him, he reconnects to a larger family—one composed of the neighborhood, the community, and the race.

Wideman's concentration on Homewood over several generations has led to inevitable comparisons to William Faulkner's Yoknapatawpha County.[7] Both Wideman and Faulkner are interested in analyzing the ways in which the communities have changed over time, and each author expresses a profound sense that something essential to the vitality of the community has been lost. Wideman's work takes a different turn beyond these parallels, however. While one could suggest that Faulkner mourns the loss of tradition and cultural collapse, records the end of an ancestral line, or is haunted by the past, Wideman reminds us that the dominant culture has suggested that African Americans have no history, no significant traditions, or culture.[8] Recovering lost or silenced stories of his family's past and of the beginning of Homewood enables Wideman to address those gaps in the narrative of American history and consciousness. Revoicing his family's and community's ancestral history into the written record helps ease the burden of their traumatic past and refutes the claims about African American life from outside of the community. It is by remembering these stories of the past that Wideman discovers he has one: "If I don't speak, I have no past."[9]

Before history there is myth. In the battle for Irish independence, William Butler Yeats and other Irish writers embraced the Irish mythic past as a significant step in the creation of new, self-determined cultural identity. Early American writers such as Henry Wadsworth Longfellow and Washington Irving promoted a similar artistic and cultural project. Wideman understands that artists must first either recover or create a pre-historical mythology before they can record or rewrite new histories and cultural narratives. Homewood itself is a text, a "mythopoetic space" that must be remembered and revoiced in order to ensure the survival of its people and their traditions.[10] The writing of Homewood, the mythic text, must serve as communal memory that has combated the world of racism through its oral storytelling and music.

Most of the scholarship on Wideman's work has focused on the books of the Homewood trilogy. And in most cases, as I noted in the introduction to this study, critics have focused on Wideman's return to Homewood and his regaining his "Homewood ear." This is certainly the case with Wideman's earliest readers. The story of the loss and recovery of the Homewood ear and Wideman's "running away" from his community have been read more biographically than as tropes of African American experience and mythmaking. James Coleman argues that "the most important thing Wideman does in *Damballah* is to describe the black intellectual writer's arduous movement back toward the black community and black culture."[11] Numerous other readers have seen the Homewood trilogy as Wideman's return to his family, his roots, and his identity. His emphasis, it is suggested, is on the black folk culture that he has forgotten.[12]

As scholars have repeated and retold the story of Wideman's return home, it has taken on the appearance of truth. But it is possible that fact and truth have been used interchangeably here. The return home is an essential episode in mythic narratives. Wideman, the blues hero/ artist, must return home in order to accomplish the task of this role in the community (and, conversely, he must also *leave* the community). This is certainly true of the alter egos in the fiction, such as Lawson in the Homewood stories. He must leave and learn and return again—as we will see in chapters 4 and 5 of this study—and share stories with the community of Homewood and the community beyond. The story of the Homewood ear is an apotheosis; it is the event within the mythic narrative that transforms the young protagonist into the mythic hero. Wideman/ Lawson could not become the blues hero if he had not taken this journey. And Wideman the writer is conscious of this rhetorical step in the development of his metafictional character and alter egos. While all of these aforementioned scholars have called Wideman a blues artist, I think they may have overlooked the possibility that Wideman's "biographical" confession might be a fiction meant to invoke a mythic genesis of a heroic storytelling voice. He is now the tradition bearer in the Wideman clan in the Homewood books, and, as Keith Byerman proposes, he "claims for himself in this sense the role of Damballah."[13] But the African American cultural influences and stories were always there in the vessel that is Wideman the writer.

A student once told me that he never understood what W. E. B. DuBois was describing in his picture of double-consciousness until he left home and went to college. Leaving home made this student feel the isolation, the pain of double-consciousness. This student's story reminds me of Wideman's account of his time at the University of Pennsylvania in *Brothers and Keepers* and how the blues meant even more to him in this world where he was only one of two African American students.[14] Wideman and the other African American student, Daryl, would leave campus and look for neighborhoods that reminded them of home. It is no accident that the titles of Wideman's first two novels, *A Glance Away* and *Hurry Home*, signal that loneliness. The pain of being away from home even after college, the death of his grandmother, Robby's imprisonment, all of these traumatic experiences called out for the language of grief and longing for family. Clearly, his personal life may have had a part in looking for comfort in the voices of home, but it was also an artist's creative engagement with the common experiences of others in his community. His story of surviving the pain of double-consciousness may speak to them as well. His stories fulfill the need for heroic myth in all cultures: How do we grow up? Who will we become? What are our responsibilities? How will we survive the traumas ahead of us?

Wideman's Homewood is also a symbol of a Golden Age, one that likely has been romanticized in the process of mythmaking. In discussing the litany of street names in the Homewood stories, Wideman makes the connection to epic catalogues out of Greek mythology.[15] The use of the name Orion in the story "Damballah" (and later the multiple appearances of Oedipus in Wideman's work) also draws from the Western tradition—in order to balance classical Greek mythology with that of African cosmology. Damballah is a god, and the reference to an ur-history might imply a similar Golden Age that has been lost. But the course of the stories in the collection does not reveal any such particular moment. There were times when things were *better*, but they do not ever seem to have been idyllic. Wideman warns that it is not the place itself that is important in the Homewood stories, it is how the "people created it through their sense of values and the way they treated one another, and the way they treated the place."[16] This is what Homewood has lost—people no longer remember or seem to care about *place*. Wideman recalls the names of the Homewood streets to invoke memory of place and community.

In the foreword to *Damballah*, Wideman quotes from Maya Deren's work on Haitian culture and voodoo, *Divine Horsemen: The Living Gods of Haiti*. Deren's description of the god Damballah is a reflection of Wideman's project not only in this work, but in all of his writing, even those stories that on the surface seem to go beyond the reaches of his immediate family. Damballah, Deren states, is the father, the god of the sky. His presence (along with the other sky gods) reminds one of "historical extension, of the ancient origin of the race." Deren implies that to remember Damballah is "to stretch one's hand back to that time and to gather up all history into a solid, contemporary ground beneath one's feet." She tells us in a footnote following this statement that one of the songs to Damballah requests that he "gather up the family."[17] Wideman juxtaposes these quotes in the foreword, clearly linking them and, by extension, family and racial history with a mythic creature and cosmology.

Wideman must share the means of survival over painful experience with the community—to "gather them up." His position as artist requires him to be the recorder of the horrible tragedies of the past, as well as find stories that have given the community and the family solace. This has historically and even universally been the role of the artist. The family stories also record what has happened to address the post-traumatic present. Like narratives of the survivors of the Holocaust, Wideman's work testifies to the suffering of silenced victims and reaches back into past cultural practices that sustained the community in other dark times.

Wideman continues the legacy of the blues artist who recounts tales of suffering and survival. Several portraits in the stories of the Homewood trilogy fit the description of the blues artist: Albert Wilkes, Brother Tate, Reba Love Jackson, and Doot Lawson, one of Wideman's alter egos. Each character uses art to embrace all of the stories of the community, past and present. It is not the individual voice that takes precedence; the solo animates the chorus. In the Homewood trilogy novels, it is only when the blues hero leaves the community for good or the community forgets his music or the artist forfeits his role that despair and destruction prevail.

Wideman uses the blues idiom, the blues stanza, and the blues hero to refute the hegemonic portrait of African American families. Wideman, in the preface to *The Homewood Trilogy*, tells us that music is a "dominant, organizing metaphor" for the trilogy and that all the works act as a "continuous investigation ... of a culture; a way of seeing and being seen."[18] The writer in this regard is seen again as the "tradition bearer" or the individual given the responsibility to ensure that the stories of the community are heard.

Wideman, as an example of Robert Stepto's "articulate survivor" or a "blues hero" or a *griot*, addresses the suffering of the community and the self by recounting family stories of survival.[19] The conjuring of Damballah as a story and a character calls forth such power to address current trauma. The return home for Wideman is not just about an alienated intellectual going back to Homewood after he has run away, it is about finding a way back to the beginning of African American history, before the European story displaced the African imagination.

Wideman's position as storyteller exists within his texts as metafictional moments, and they are clearly structurally significant in his autobiographical work, *Brothers and Keepers*. Its designation as a nonfiction text is called into question in its own preface. Wideman tells us that the work is a "mix of memory, imagination, feeling, and fact."[20] It is also a collaborative autobiography, one whose purpose is to salvage something from the "grief and waste" that has left Wideman's brother, Robby, in prison. While on the surface the work appears to be engaged in depicting the life of Robby, it really reveals as much or more about Wideman and the Homewood community. The work's imbrication of genres—autobiography, history, ethnography, and fiction—attempts to capture a continuous, coherent (if not unified) picture of its subject, to present all stories. However, Wideman is uncertain where to begin the story or how to tell it. He digresses on to other topics, topics that, to a reader of traditional autobiography, would seem unrelated. Ultimately, the work is more an artifact of the attempt to tell the truth then the truth itself. Nonetheless, it is still a more accurate reflection of Robby's life than the prison statistic he has become.

Wideman proceeds further in his attempt to capture the "true" portrait of his family and of Robby with the publication of the Homewood books. These works add another version of the story. The interplay of discourses, genre conventions, and categorizations within Wideman's canon, evidenced most strongly in the relationship between *Brothers and Keepers* and the Homewood trilogy, is the probable cause of the overwhelming amount of biographical criticism on the works as a whole.

With the rise of the postmodern autobiography, we have seen the concurrent rise of the "indigenous ethnographer."[21] The writing of the indigenous ethnographer examines the culture from within the circle in an effort to preserve traditions and to address ethnographies written by the outsiders or the "experts." In this context, Wideman's work can be seen to reflect such a project. Even when he suggests that the books of the Homewood trilogy are a "continuous investigation of a culture," we are reminded of the discourse of an ethnographer. We are also reminded of another hybrid work, Zora Neale Hurston's *Mules and Men*. In this work, Hurston is the ethnographer, stringing together folktales that represent the community and its art, but she's also an autobiographer and fiction writer. The subjective "I" in the text disrupts the rules of ethnography, as do the descriptive passages of characters and events that seem more at home in a work of fiction. Hurston is narrator, listener, and collector. She occupies in *Mules and Men* much the same space that Doot does in the Homewood trilogy. The position of an indigenous ethnographer raises numerous questions about the relationship of the writer to the material. Such a writer would necessarily be liminal, speaking in two languages simultaneously. A form that voices both the position and discourse of the autobiographer and the ethnographer would be an autoethnography. The term "autoethnography" was first coined and defined by Mary Louise Pratt, who describes it as a text in which people undertake to describe themselves in ways that engage with representations others have made of them. Thus, if ethnographic texts are those in which European subjects represent the lives of Others (usually their conquered Others), autoethnographic texts are representations that the so-defined Others construct *in response* to or in dialogue with those texts.[22]

The genres of autobiography and ethnography (an "I" and an "eye," the same positions that Wideman takes as the writer in the beginning of *The Cattle Killing*), blur, blend, and speak to one another; Pratt asserts that one of the best examples of an autoethnographic text is the slave narrative.[23] In essence, the genre allows the writer to form a gap or clear a space within the narratives of the dominant culture to tell an alternate history. The audience of the autoethnographic text is not just the mainstream; the autoethnographic text also reminds the community from which it originates that their culture exists concurrently with the dominant one. Thus, the discourses of the autobiography and the ethnography, both stories, occur simultaneously. The effect is balance and equality—all stories are true.

Though Wideman has yet to use the word "autoethnographic" to describe his work, there is evidence that he is aware of the term and its reverberation in his writing. Wideman's essay "Malcolm X: The Art of Autobiography" opens with the quote from Francois Lionnet's work, "Autoethnography: The An-Archic Style of *Dust Tracks on a Road*." Wideman frames his discussion by echoing Lionnet's words: "We urgently need to retrieve those past traditions that can become the source of reconciliation and wholeness, for it is more important to learn from those traditions than to dwell on pain and injustice."[24]

Lionnet extends Pratt's definition of autoethnography to include that the form "establishes connections among the children of the diaspora, and remembers the scattered body of folk material so that siblings can again touch each other."[25] The project of the autoethnographer can be likened to the invocation of Damballah that "gathers up the family." Lionnet also argues that the form allows an unusual dialogue between the self, culture, and history. In fact, the ethnic self cannot be realized without an understanding of itself in relation to the culture and history. This is an idea echoed by other critics of ethnic autobiographies, such as Arnold Krupat, whose notion of the "synecdochic self," constructed by ethnic autobiographers and their narratives, directly undermines the authority of anthropologists, sociologists, and historians.[26] Wideman approaches the project of making the Homewood myth to develop and recover sustaining stories for his community, *and* he also creates the Homewood mythology as a counternarrative to the master narratives written about himself and his African brethren.

The portrait of the African descendant has long been drawn by European and American culture as a singular or essentialist image. As Frantz Fanon posits, the "European has a fixed concept of the Negro." The "black body" and its "Manichean darkness" is an "artifact" of the "white man's imagination." The black man has been "woven" out of a "thousand details, anecdotes, and stories."[27] The African's characteristics have included either some or all of the following: primitive, savage, ignorant, natural, and bestial, to name a few. This image comes to us as early as Montaigne's essay "Of Cannibals" and Shakespeare's *The Tempest*.[28] These pictures were revisited in early America in eighteenth-century pamphlets and treatises that condemned African and African American intelligence, morality, and character. Such examples of characterization continued well into the later years of the twentieth century, as is evidenced by the publication of works like *The Bell Curve*[29] and practices such as racial profiling.[30] And in 2005, former secretary of education William Bennett's remarks about abortions and African American children ignited a firestorm of virulent discussions about race and family values.[31]

Particularly damaging have been the studies done on the African American family. Even those sociologists who have had the best intentions are guilty of portraying African American life as fragmented, despairing, and devoid of culture. The motives for such renderings have sometimes been to bring attention to the problems of the African American race or the conditions of their neighborhoods. E. Franklin Frazier, the noted African American sociologist, even argued that "because of the absence of stability in family life, there is a lack of traditions and hence life among a large portion of the urban Negro population is casual, precarious, and fragmentary. It lacks continuity and its roots do not go deeper than the contingencies of daily living."[32] Much of the writing done about the African American family and its traditions implied this same conception—that there was not a great deal to praise in most of these communities.

Other important examinations sprang up in the late 1950s and 1960s that further characterized African American life in stereotypical and damaging ways, including Stanley Elkins's *Slavery: A Problem in American Institutional and Intellectual Life*, Nathan Glazer and Daniel Moynihan's *Beyond the Melting Pot*, and Kenneth Clarke's *The Dark Ghetto*. These works portrayed African American life as "substandard" or "impoverished" and "diseased."[33] *Beyond the Melting Pot* speculated that "the Negro is only an American and nothing else. He has no values and culture to guard and protect."[34]

No sociological study provoked more controversy, however, than Daniel Moynihan's other work, *The Negro Family: The Case for National Action*, which quickly became known as the "Moynihan report." The study argued that the problems of the African American family lie within its structure, essentially blaming African Americans rather than the system for the community's material impoverishment.[35] Moynihan made sweeping generalizations about the reasons behind his statistics, and the report is still referred to today, either implicitly or explicitly, whenever we talk about "the African-American family."[36] The report was roundly criticized by African American leaders upon its publication in 1965. Moynihan argued that he had based his work on the foundations of E. Franklin Frazier and that of another African American, Kenneth Clark.[37] Writer Albert Murray asserts that such studies base their interpretations wholly on statistics and "add up to what functions as a folklore of white supremacy and a fakelore of black pathology."[38]

Even in his early novels, Wideman indicates that the imagination is essential in dismantling these types of assumptions about African American life. He states in an interview from 1973 that the imagination plays such a powerful role in the relationship between blacks and whites in America, which is also a predominant theme in my work. It's not what we are, it's what we think we are. From the very beginning Western civilization has had an idea of what black men are, and that idea has come down to us generation after generation, has distorted and made impossible some kinds of very human and basic interaction.[39]

The Homewood trilogy addresses some of these issues directly. It presents an honest portrait of the suffering and despair that often accompanies the harsh lives of the family and the community, but it also chronicles the means by which the inhabitants of Homewood refute those images offered by such studies as the Moynihan report through the blues, through humor, through family history—by re-imagining themselves in story. Wideman calls attention to the goal of the Homewood trilogy in his preface: "In these three books bound as one, I have set myself the task of making concrete those invisible planes of existence which bear witness that Black life for all its material impoverishment continues to produce the full range of human personalities, emotions, aspirations."[40]

Wideman makes a direct connection between the trilogy and the Moynihan report in another interview while discussing the goals of the Homewood books:

> Another way of looking at it is connected to statistics about broken homes, a definition of family codified in the Moynihan report. If you look at black culture, the black culture is deviant and delinquent because it does not have a family structure which reproduces the Moynihan model. But of course that is just a stipulative, narrow, and arbitrary definition of what a family might be.[41]

His short story "Daddy Garbage" (in *Damballah*) draws this argument further, illustrating the refutation of negative portrayals of African American life and impoverishment. Finding a dead and discarded baby, the two characters, strangers to the child, anguish over its loss as if they were its own fathers and commit to giving the child a burial.

Nor is the Homewood trilogy Wideman's final word on the subject of the Moynihan report. Following the MOVE bombing, Wideman revisits the persistence of the report in the American consciousness. Wideman blames the report for confusing race relations in this country:

> It took the view that the American Dream was not failing, it was failing only for blacks. A false description leading to false remedies: Let's

determine what's wrong with blacks so that we can cure them, bring them or some of them aboard our Good Ship Lollipop. Hadn't Mr. Moynihan heard James Baldwin's eloquent refusal to be integrated into a burning house? The plethora of Great Society social programs that perpetuated a doctor-patient, patron-client, master-slave relationship between whites and blacks remains a withering testament to a failure of vision.[42]

Wideman's revision of Ellison's "invisible man" into a "divisible man" (the title of the essay from which these lines come) argues that African American life is no longer "invisible" in this country; it is all too visible, but only as a subject of sociological study, debate, dissection, sound bytes, and fear. Not only is "divisible man" an allusion to double-consciousness, it is Wideman's argument that African American life is used as a "body double" for white, mainstream America—the same image that he suggests that Europeans represented Africans as when they came into contact with the Other.[43]

It is an image that places African American life as a standard that the "rest of American society" measures itself against in terms of education, family relationships, and economic status. Instead of the status that white middle-class America wants to attain, it is the status that the "mainstream" wants to avoid—at all costs. Wideman implies further that words like "urban" and "ghetto" "have become code words for terrible places where only blacks reside."[44] He also adds that "prison" has become "re-lexified" to indicate that same status. These words are paraded by the media, social scientists, and historians whenever anyone wants to talk about the decline of American life and its values. The implicit reference, if we accept Wideman's argument, is that danger and depravity in this country is "black." It resides in its families, in its neighborhoods, in its traditions.[45]

Clearly, Wideman's work strives to disprove such portraits of African American life, and we need to consider Wideman's characterizations of the Moynihan report and other descriptions like it as essential in realizing the axiom "all stories are true" in the chronicles of his family and Homewood. African American autobiography continually refutes "the white ideas of America, of both the white concepts of white character and the white concept of black."[46] If American society creates and reifies such negative stories of African American life, calling them sociology or history and, by extension, therefore true, then Wideman as an indigenous ethnographer must present the other true stories of the African American family and its culture, expressed in its music, its folklore, and its intrahistory. As Amiri Baraka has suggested, if you want something "more precise and specific than the Moynihan report," go the stories and the music of the blues.[47]

Wideman tells us that even his first novel, *A Glance Away*, is about his family and his past.[48] It includes descriptions of streets that we recognize as the streets of Homewood, though we are never told in the text that this is where the novel is set. The novel opens with a description of Eugene Lawson's birth (though it sounds a great deal like the description of Lawson's or Wideman's in *Damballah*). The baby is welcomed into the world by his grandfather, Eugene. The prologue establishes the ties of family here. DaddyGene, the grandfather, is clearly a mythic figure for this family. He is the fountainhead of their strength and their love. The prologue ends with his death. The figure of DaddyGene is also reminiscent of John French in the Homewood trilogy.[49]

Whether it is the same character or not, DaddyGene's death, foregrounded as it is against the rest of the novel, indicates that the loss of this man disrupts the flow of family history. The loss of the ancestor destroys the characters of *A Glance Away*. We see a similar sentiment echoed by Lucy Tate in *Sent for You Yesterday* regarding the death of John French.[50] What the family loses when DaddyGene dies is its sense of itself. DaddyGene was the family storyteller, and his loss represents the family's loss of its history, of the story of itself. *A Glance Away* does not retell family stories in the same manner that the Homewood trilogy does; its intent is to illustrate the results of loss and trauma.[51] The works of the Homewood trilogy present an alternate version of the story of loss that opens *A Glance Away*. It is not that Wideman did not write about family before the Homewood stories; he just had not yet begun to construct Homewood as mythic text.

Even after the Homewood books, Wideman remains concerned with the importance of family stories. *The Cattle Killing* includes an introduction with a writer delivering a story to his father and sharing the same story with his son. The generations represented here could very well stand for Wideman's own family and situation. More importantly, the idea that the sharing of stories is essential to the family's survival is expressed in this book as well. Even in *The Lynchers*, a work from the pre-Homewood trilogy era, this theme is represented. Saunders, one of the lynchers, is cut off from his family and community. The reason lies in his past and his connection to the storytelling practices of his mother:

> He alone had spent time listening to his mother's stories. Perhaps, he later conjectured, her stories had amused him, perhaps, since he realized they were the Saunders' sole legacy he had been hoarding them, seeking an advantage over his brother and sister, perhaps he had experienced a momentary victory watching the hard circumstances of his past shredded, destroyed, refashioned according to the whim of a frail, babbling

woman old before her time. Any of these motives could not explain their long sessions together, his fascination as she unraveled version after version of the family history.[52]

Saunders never shares these stories with anyone else. That act condemns him to the self-destructive behavior that leads to his involvement with the lynching plan. Wilkerson, on the other hand, by the end of the novel, remembers his father's songs and stories and vows that he will share them with the children he teaches.[53] It is by the *sharing* of family history that all of Wideman's characters, in some way, survive. The family's need to share stories and the role of storytellers in the community are also both defined by Wideman explicitly:

> The novelist or the writer is a storyteller, and the process for me that is going to knit up the culture, knit up the fabric of the family—all of us—one crucial part of the process is that we tell our own stories. That we learn to tell them and we tell them in our own words and that they embrace our values and that we keep on saying them, in spite of the madness, the chaos around us, and in spite of the pressure not to tell it. And so that storytelling activity is crucial to survival, individual survival, community survival. So the storyteller, the artist, is a crucial member of the community. He is also someone who perhaps by definition is outside the community—and should be and will always be—and so that yearning to be part of it may be one of the natural conditions of being a storyteller. Storytellers are always inside and outside the story by definition.[54]

Here Wideman sees himself as both storyteller and autoethnographer.

The first book of the Homewood trilogy, *Damballah*, establishes the framework for the rest of the books of the series.[55] Its prefatory material—the letter to Robby, the begat chart, the family tree, and the description and invocation of the god Damballah—establishes the family as the center of the work. It also initiates the work as one that is meant to "gather up the family" and to remember history (making it a logical opening chapter to the trilogy).

The material in the preface also echoes the "authenticating documents" of the slave narratives. These documents included marriage certificates, manumission papers, letters from abolitionists verifying the life of the slave, slave auction announcements—all of the legal documents were historical artifacts that supported the slaves' claims and represented the voice of objective truth in the tale. The documents' appearance asserts its authority over the experience of the "I" or the community of slaves that had produced volumes of narratives. It was the voice of the white American legal discourse that finally had the power to prove or disprove in a page or two the validity of this life and the lives of all slaves. This layering of prefatory material alludes to the intersection of literary history, institutional history, and family history as early as the opening pages of *Damballah*. Here the material provides another equally valid recording of the family history that is as true as the stories about to commence (even if they are fictional).

The begat chart and the family tree provide dates for marriages, births, and deaths, which stand as parallels to the certificates in the narratives that documented the same events, but provide a clear, historical lineage from the time of slavery—something that was difficult for many families to achieve. The prefatory material also includes a letter, but it is not from an outside authority; it is from within the circle. The letter is from the writer to a member of the family. The letter authenticates the stories as gifts to Robby. The writer's authority as its creator verifies its contents. The material in the preface as a whole concludes that the family is the authority of its history. Readers outside of the family and the community depend on the prefatory material for historical knowledge about the family; the outside readers do not depend on the material for the authentication of the text. The definitive historian of the family is not a voice from the hegemony; it is a voice from within the circle of the community. Wideman parodies an already autoethnographic form, the slave narrative, and reinscribes it in a way that removes the power of the outside audience entirely.

The letter to Robby also sets the stage for a further reading of the importance of family and its history. Wideman asks Robby to recall shared family memories:

> I think it was Geral I first heard call a watermelon a letter from home. After all these years I understand a little better what she meant. She was saying the melon is a letter addressed to us. A story for us from down home. Down home being everywhere we've never been, the rural South, the old days, slavery, Africa . . . a history we could taste and chew.[56]

There are several essential points that this letter addresses. The first is the iconographic image of the watermelon. Wideman states later that he never liked watermelon because of the image it produced, "of becoming instant nigger, of sitting barefoot and goggle-eyed and Day-Glo black and drippy-lipped on massa's fence."[57] He now realizes its significance—as a letter from home. Wideman recovers the image of the watermelon by retrieving it from those negative portrayals that had turned it into a racist stereotype of African American life, and he revises it into an image of family and racial continuity and history: a symbol of the past that he and his family can own and "enjoy." The moment is akin to the yam cart that the "invisible man" visits in Ellison's novel. The smell of the yams makes him remember home. When he bites into one, he's homesick. But the act also reminds him that the yam and the South connect him to his past and are his "birthmark" ("I yam what I yam").[58]

The letter also unites Robby and Wideman with their racial past through their shared family history—down home in the South, in Africa, where they never lived. The watermelon reminds them where they have come from, where they have been, and the sites of shared traumatic history as well as shared traditions of survival. A writer's voicing of places historically essential to African American history, even to places they have never been, has a specific purpose: by "calling themselves to remember" the South, Africa, and /or the racial past, "black Americans are actually re-membering."[59]

This image is reflected in Wideman's description of the "beloved" in the quote that opens this chapter. The beloved travels the world "remembering" and "re-membering" her children. The image is also reminiscent of the god Damballah. Damballah (the god), Orion, Sybela Owens, and Aunt May are mythic ancestors and storytellers, and they serve for the rest of the family, neighborhood, and, by extension, the culture as models. They are the gatherers of family history. Wideman and his fictional counterpart, Lawson, assume the position of gatherer as well. They collect and recall stories to bring the family together and, by doing so, refute the notion that these families have nothing of value—no tradition, no history.

The preface also includes the description and the invocation of Damballah. Wideman quotes from Deren's *Divine Horsemen: The Living Gods of Haiti* and includes two references to that work that illustrate his theme in the Homewood trilogy, observing Damballah's dual ability to gather up history and the family.[60] Wideman does not include the iconography of Damballah in this description; however, it is important to note that Damballah is represented as a snake arched across the sky and that sometimes the arch of the snake is created by his female counterpart, Ayida, the representation of the rainbow. In most drawings of Damballah, the serpent is drawn with both the male and female aspects and is "sometimes represented as a pair of twins." As well, the reptile in Haitian mythology is an animal that can commune with both the living and the dead.[61] The book *Damballah* is composed of many repeated stories and twin figures, especially in the context of the other books in the trilogy.

The doubling here evokes the possibility of lives other than what someone else has written for you; it connects two brothers; it expresses the voice of the individuals and the community; it represents the voices of the dead and the living in the family and in the community; it links the past to the present (and to the future); and it reflects the two positions of voice in the book—the first and third person (the *auto* and the *ethno* discourses). All of these voices address each other throughout the book, reinforcing its dialogic quality. The representation of many voices in the community also affirms the work's polyphonic quality, and its unwillingness to "compromise the chorus of voices into a performance of one" reflects its deconstruction of master narratives about African American history.[62] The oral voice, the free indirect discourse, is balanced with the standard literary voice throughout the work.[63] All of the voices and discourses that inform the text and offer multiple versions and points of view echo the maxim that "all stories are true."[64] And by imbricating oral forms and speakerly text within the literary framework, Wideman hearkens back to Zora Neale Hurston, Jean Toomer, and Charles Chesnutt's conjure tales.[65]

These multiple discourses have made it difficult to categorize the work (and Wideman as a writer). Is it a novel? A short-story collection? I would argue that the stories are more intimately connected than a collection implies. I prefer the term "short-story cycle" or "composite novel" to describe the work. It has more in common with Toomer's *Cane*, Sherwood Anderson's *Winesburg, Ohio*, or James Joyce's *Dubliners* than it does an arbitrary collection of stories. The stories in *Damballah* are interwoven to the extent that they support one another, like members of a family or community, thus the themes of the work constitute its form. Most of the stories in *Damballah* are on equal footing; no one voice is more prominent than the other. The stories, with the exception of the first and last, do not progress throughout the collection in a linear fashion. The work as a whole is a mosaic of these stories and the voices that they represent. The Vintage paperback edition of the book (the 1988 printing) literally illustrates this as well. The cover is Romare Beardon's *The Street*, a collage of photos and paintings representing the people that reside in a community. The artwork itself is a composite of various artistic mediums, and Bearden is one of the artistic models for Mr. Mallory in *Two Cities*.

The first story in *Damballah* is the titular narrative. Orion, a slave, has recently been captured and brought to America. Naturally, he still embraces the culture and traditions of Africa. This makes him dangerous in the eyes of his slave masters. Throughout the tale, a young boy who is a slave on the plantation follows Orion. The boy is curious about who Orion is and what he is doing, about the unknown African past that he does not remember and that Orion represents. Orion senses that this boy "could be the one. This boy born so far from home. This boy who knew nothing but what the whites told him. This boy could learn the story and tell it again."[66]

Orion draws a "cross in the dust."[67] The drawing is the symbol of the crossroads—where time is multidirectional and where past and future meet. Several essential descriptions of the crossroads will illustrate its importance in this story. We have already seen in previous chapters that the crossroads is an African symbol as well as an image of the blues. The symbol also reflects the god Damballah: "The crossroads can be understood to include the entire cosmos, below and above the earth; the sky, or life-principle, represented by the serpent rainbow reflected in—hence encompassing—the waters, thus comprehends the abyss as well as the sky; the abyss or underworld, is the actual domicile of the ancestors."[68] The crossroads is the intersection of two worlds, the living and the dead. It is the soul of life, and the daily life of man and the community depends on the constant communication with the world that the crossroads represents. It is the individual's and the community's source of "memory, intelligence, imagination, and invention."[69] It is the source of story and history in a culture where the distinction between the two does not exist.

The word "Damballah" recalls something deep in the boy. It is "a place the boy could enter, a familiar sound he began to anticipate, a sound outside of him which slowly forced its way inside, a sound measuring his heartbeat then one with the pumping surge of his blood."[70] The word, its representation of story and possibility, stirs in the boy a racial memory that connects him to a world that he has never seen. Though Orion and the child have lived different lives, they are connected by the traumatic story of slavery that binds them. They both long for the language of home. Orion decides to teach the boy the power of stories. Orion is later killed by his master for refusing to give up his African ways. The boy carries Orion's decapitated head to the river: "He knew they had been waiting. He knew the ripples would touch him when he entered."[71] The boy returns Orion back to the land. Orion's death and the boy's "burial" are reminiscent of ritualistic sacrifice for the community. Orion's duty has been to teach the boy about Damballah and about the necessity to pass the stories on to the community. The story's appearance at the beginning of "Damballah" opens the past to the present time of Homewood.

The next story in the cycle is "Daddy Garbage." John (Doot) asks a family friend, Strayhorn, about the dog he used to have named Daddy Garbage. Doot wonders how the dog got its name; he asks for its history. Strayhorn tells him that the name comes from the fact that the dog was always in the garbage. He remembers a particular time when Daddy Garbage found a dead baby that had been thrown in the trash. What begins as a simplistic, even comic tale, takes a drastic turn that Wideman uses as another meditation on lost children.

Strayhorn tracks down his friend John French (Doot's grandfather) to help him bury the child. French cannot believe that the baby has been thrown away. Times were bad in the past, back in the South, he says, but something new is happening. There's a difference growing in the community that worries French. He is established in this story and will remain throughout the Homewood trilogy and *Brothers and Keepers* as an ancestral voice (a family elder) whose wisdom the following generations are forgetting. It is a storytelling voice that ultimately holds family above all else. The death of the unknown baby and its subsequent burial in subfreezing temperatures by two old, slightly drunk men is a striking image of the possible loss of the future if the community doesn't remember their stories and traditions. The men treat the child as one of their own, and the story is passed down to their children and grandchildren, thus all the children of the family and the African American community are linked in some way in this piece through storytelling. The discarded baby becomes, through the storytelling act, a member of their family. This story appears in an alternate version in the short story "Newborn Thrown in Trash and Dies" (in *All Stories are True*). Here the newborn baby is the narrator of its tale. These two versions told from different points of view allow for a broader understanding of such an act.

"Lizabeth: The Caterpillar Story" also appears more than once in Wideman's canon. It is repeated in *Sent for You Yesterday* and is briefly referred to in the novel *Two Cities*. This story begins with Lizabeth (Doot's mother) sharing stories of her deceased father (John French) with her mother, Freeda. Point of view shifts several times in the story. We have the sense that Wideman is presenting the tale in the voice of both the autobiographer and the ethnographer. We are told that as a child Lizabeth needed "her mother's voice to make things real (years later when she will have grandchildren of her own and her mother and father both long dead Lizabeth will still be trying to understand why sometimes it takes someone's voice to make things real)."[72] The storytelling that takes place here is presented in fluid time. The tale moves across the generations and across history. The story is also imbricated with several other stories that we will see in more detail in other works, including Albert Wilkes's return; the man chasing her father with a gun; and her mother's subsequent smashing of a window with her hand to warn John French, Lizabeth's father. Each story is interconnected as a way to understand the primary story—the love of John French for his daughter.

Another repeated story is the anecdote about Freeda's scar, which she got by smashing the window. This story is woven into *Sent for You Yesterday* (and briefly in *Two Cities* and in *Hoop Roots*). We also see the image of a soap bubble that will be repeated in the same novels. Sometimes the image of the bubble is described through different points of view. The rainbow and the circle that are associated with the soap bubble connect back to Damballah (the god of the rainbow) and the circles of time that connect all these stories to Lizabeth and to her parents, her children, and her grandchildren. The image is conflated even further in its echo of Damballah the god's role (to "gather up the family"). By presenting this story through so many different points of view, this story gathers up this family.

Many selections in *Damballah* concern distant family relations or community members. Wideman, nevertheless, indicates that these people and their portraits are equally important as the Lawsons. The story "Hazel" is such an account: Hazel and her brothers are cousins of the Lawsons. In this story we are offered a picture of a young Bess, the main character in *Hiding Place*, before she goes up to live on Bruston Hill. "Hazel" is a story of extreme suffering, of a family that let tragedy divide them and ultimately leave them all to die alone. Their tale is an example of a family that has given up on itself; it is an example of how a family should not react to their shared trauma.

Other Homewood stories include "The Watermelon Story" and "The Songs of Reba Love Jackson." "The Watermelon Story" echoes the image of the watermelon in the letter to Robby. Its appearance among the sketches repeats the image and gives us another story about watermelons (actually, several stories about watermelons). Doot Lawson's Aunt May tells him this tale. May is the supreme storyteller of the family. She narrates the anecdote of a man whose arm was severed when the "throne" of watermelons he was sitting on tumbled, and he was thrown through the plate glass window of the A & P. This story triggers another in May's mind, an old folktale from "slavery days." The slave story bears a resemblance to the conjure stories of Chesnutt (and with the association of the watermelon, particularly "The Conjurer's Revenge"). Unlike most of Chesnutt's stories, this conjure tale produces happy results. In the story, a childless couple finds a baby in a watermelon. Truth and fiction are contested by May when she tells her incredulous listeners: "You all don't believe in nothing. Old man brings home a baby first thing you do is call the police or start wagging your tongues and looking for some young girl under the bed."[73] May implies in her tale that her listeners don't have faith, and by association they do not, therefore, have the power of conjure, the power to transform words into deeds, the power to re-imagine their lives. It is a mythic talent. But they have lost the faith in the power of story and in the past. Such transformation tales also belong to the realm of mythology, and May uses the tale to instruct her listeners about the need to share stories.

"The Songs of Reba Love Jackson" briefly traces the life of a woman who grew up in Homewood and is now a popular gospel singer. In a story that also resonates with the importance of faith in daily lives, we hear Reba's biography interspersed among the songs that she sings. The connection is fairly explicit; her suffering has made her a singer and has made the songs she sings more meaningful for others. She is a blues hero. She has transformed her pain, and the pain of others, into a survival story. As she explains to an interviewer about her fans, "They hear their stories in my songs, that's all."[74] Her relationship with the community, with Homewood, is a reflection of the spiritual itself. The last section of her story is titled "This Last Song's for Homewood," which further illustrates the spiritual singer's relationship to the community, and its title also reflects the purpose and structure of *Damballah* as a whole. The speakers in each of these stories, as well as Lawson and Wideman, all share a relationship to the audience similar to Reba's. All of these stories, these songs, are for Homewood.

"The Chinaman" opens with Freeda remembering Lizabeth's birth. Freeda is "telling stories. Telling herself."[75] We find out a little later that she is very ill. The stories combat her illness and let her reflect on both the sorrow and the joy of her past. The story of Lizabeth's birth is also repeated in *Brothers and Keepers*. Like the version in that book, this story is well-known family history that is an event that others mark their lives by. A third-person voice opens this piece, but then we soon switch to first person as John Lawson's voice interrupts the narrative to include his commentary on why the story of Lizabeth's birth is important: "The first born, Lizabeth, our mother, saved by May in the snow. May's told the story a hundred times but each time it's new and necessary. If she didn't tell the story right, there would be no baby shuddering to life in her arms when she runs through the crashing door."[76] Lawson's retelling of the oft-told tale further confirms that family stories help heal and even help give birth to the promise of the future. The story itself appears to bring forth Lizabeth and, therefore, the next generation's storyteller, her son, John.

Narratives and voices glide through time here as well. Freeda is alive at the beginning of this story, then we hear about her funeral, then we return to a time before she died. The experience of his grandmother's funeral forces John to think about his family connections and the need to hear them: "I wished for May's voice and the voices of my people in a circle amening and laughing and filling in what I didn't know or couldn't remember, but it was just me whispering in the dark motel room."[77] The circle image is repeated here, and the structure and purpose of the ring shout is reflected in John's desire to hear his people speak within the circle. Before he finishes the tale of Freeda's death and the Chinaman, John realizes that he doesn't have all the facts, all the necessary points of view to complete the account. His wife falls asleep after he stops narrating, but he hears "paddle-wheeled steamers packed with cotton and slaves" on the river all night.[78] The traumatic past of slavery associates emotionally with the personal loss he suffers when his grandmother dies. Telling her story keeps her alive and keeps the connection to the past that she represents alive as well.

Just as John wishes for other voices to help him finish the tale, the narrative breaks to let other voices "fill in" the spaces that John cannot. Both Lizabeth and her brother, Carl (of *Sent for You Yesterday*), contribute to the story. The voice shift takes us back before the funeral when Freeda is in the hospital and is visited by another patient, a "Chinaman." She has foreseen this as an omen of her impending death. John's voice concludes the tale, admitting that the story has different meanings for each speaker who tells it. In the hotel room, after his wife has fallen asleep, John hears silence: "The silence is an amen." The silence is also a voice in the story; it is the space where "the past and lives other than mine" may fill in the story as well.[79] Many voices, heard and unheard, construct this tale; the only true portrait that Lawson will ever have of his grandmother is one that draws her from multiple perspectives.

The story "Across the Wide Missouri" is repeated in the work *Fatheralong*. It is the only story in *Damballah* that is about Lawson's father at all. Most of the stories in the Homewood texts are about his mother's side of the family, as Wideman points out in *Hoop Roots*. Nevertheless, this story also gives us a portrait of Homewood and offers us a voice of authorial intrusion, a second-person narration, a metafictional account. Wideman tells us that when he wrote the story before there was more crowd noise. And he tells us how we should see his father in the piece. This story is a precursor to *Fatheralong* in other ways as well. Wideman finishes the story by relating a time to us when he missed an important event in his son's life. The connections that we see between fathers and sons over generations in *Fatheralong* appear more than ten years earlier in this short story. Wideman "plays" this story again emphasizing different notes and chords—it is another example of his jazz-style.

The story "Rashad" is told through Lizabeth's voice. It centers on the young man who is the father of her daughter's children. Rashad shares many of Tommy's character traits. Rashad returned from Vietnam a junkie. The story connects to the larger view of family, however. It goes beyond the streets of Homewood to illustrate that there are certain constants in human relationships throughout the world. Rashad, when he was in Vietnam, asked an old man to draw a picture of his daughter, Keesha, from a photo that he had of her.[80] Lizabeth notices the child's sad eyes in the painting and wonders about all the possible stories that could be behind that sadness. She imagines that her granddaughter reminded the old man who did the painting of one of his own children, one that he had lost. She connects the loss of her own children and grandchildren with this man's. She even imagines him in her house: "She saw him clearly at that turning of the stairs and understood the sadness in the eyes. The lost child she would pray for too."[81] Like the dead newborn in "Daddy Garbage," a lost child outside of the family circle is brought into their stories, almost as one of their own.

The story "Tommy" reappears in *Hiding Place* almost verbatim. In *Hiding Place*, it acts as a chapter, a flashback of the crime that Tommy has committed—the one that has led him up Bruston Hill to hide from the police. This story is followed by "Solitary," which is the story of Lizabeth visiting Tommy in prison after he's been captured by the police. "Solitary" is told from Lizabeth's position (though it is a third-person voice). In the first few pages, she chronicles the journey she must take to visit Tommy. It is an agonizing one. The portrait gives a name and a voice to the men inside prisons and to the consequences of that imprisonment to their families. Both "Tommy" and "Solitary" echo *Brothers and Keepers* and refute the sociological and media reports of the lives of men like Tommy. The stories show us the very human side behind the statistics. Following her visit, Lizabeth wanders through the streets of Homewood, thinking about her family, the past. She tracks down her brother Carl and the two of them share stories that help Lizabeth cope with Tommy's situation, that help her begin to regain her faith in family and in God.

The final story of the collection, "The Beginning of Homewood," is a mirror of the first story, "Damballah." Both have slave stories at the center, but Wideman moves from "Damballah," which could be the story of all slaves and all families, to the story of Sybela Owens, which is the cornerstone of the Lawsons and of Homewood. Why is a story about the beginning of Homewood at the end of the collection? It is another reflection of Wideman's notion of circular time. The beginning is inexorably connected with the present and the future: the past is the "root" and the present and the future are the "branch."[82] Sybela's escape as a slave makes her, according to the laws of the land, a fugitive, and Tommy's crime and flight make him a fugitive as well—what Lawson calls the "root" and the "branch." Wideman (and Lawson) connects the two lives throughout the story, further echoing the metaphor of the "root and the branch" in early African American literature—the connection between slavery and the racism that persists despite the abolishment of the institution.[83]

Like Orion, Lawson passes on stories in this piece. He shares with Tommy the story of the beginning of Homewood, of the escape of Sybela Owens, of her position as the family's matriarch. Each story is meant to give Tommy sustenance, like a blues song. The sharing of painful memories allows Tommy (and John Lawson) to transcend his own. Lawson tells Tommy that he first heard Aunt May narrate Sybela's story:

I heard her laughter, her amens, and *can I get a witness*, her digressions within digressions, the webs she spins and brushes away with her hands. Her stories exist because of their parts and each part is a story worth telling, worth examining to find the stories it contains. What seems to ramble begins to cohere when the listener understands the process, understands that the voice seeks to recover everything, that the voice proclaims *nothing is lost*, that the listener is not passive but lives like everything else within the story. Somebody shouts *Tell the truth*. You shout too. May is preaching and dances out between the shiny, butt-rubbed, wooden pews doing what she's been doing since the morning somebody said *Freedom*.[84]

May's stories are "webs" or circles that connect the family through the generations, through time. Lawson's description of storytelling and the power it possesses to transform experience, to keep alive the traditions and the family itself, reverberates though all of Wideman's work. It is the truth; it is freedom. This is the reason why Aunt May keeps telling the story and why Lawson must continue the tradition that Orion started and she has continued. The associations here with the church and the spiritual reassert that storytelling is an act of faith and that it has the same ability as religion to sustain individuals. Lawson addresses Tommy here, but the audience is also being solicited to think about the power of story and the African American family and culture. There *is* something valuable within this family, something worth preserving. It continues in spite of adversity, in spite of the other stories that have been told about it. *Damballah* has a double purpose: to preserve family history and deny the history and story that others have written about the family, the race as a whole.

The repetition of "bearing witness" and "tell the truth" reinforces the autoethnographic project of the work. Aunt May tells the family that when she met Sybela Owens that she "told me to live free all this time and be a witness all this time. And told me come a day her generations fill this city and need to know the truth."[85] Truth resides in the family, in the members' remembrance of their own past. Sybela is another image of the beloved and of Damballah, a mythic figure that connects the family and the past: "The old woman watches her children fall like stars from the night sky, each one perfect, each one a billion years in the making, each one dug from her womb so the black heavens are crisscrossed infinitely by the filaments of her bright pain which no matter how thinly stretched are unbreakable and connect her with her progeny and each point of light to every other."[86] By remembering Sybela and remembering Homewood, the family "re-members" its roots and its past. By building Homewood, both as a physical site and as a mythic text, the family builds a meaningful historical past. They, too, have constructed a city on the hill, both literally and figuratively.

Two figures estranged from the family's past are the focus of the second work in the trilogy, *Hiding Place*. This brief rendering of Tommy and Mother

Bess on one evening further crystallizes the themes of *Damballah*. Tommy hides out with Mother Bess in her house on Bruston Hill following the robbery and murder in which he has been involved. The novel is so compressed that it could be considered a novella. The story follows three characters in a short time period. The third character, Clement, does little to further the action of the plot, but his voice operates as a distant narrative reflective of the community at large. Clement is an adolescent boy who delivers groceries to Mother Bess on the hill.[87]

Most of the action takes place on Bruston Hill, the site of the beginning of Homewood, where Sybela and Charley Owens moved when prejudice forced them to isolate themselves from other members of their community. We briefly see the hill in *Damballah*. But here the hill takes on even greater significance; not only is it the historical site of the neighborhood, but it is, simultaneously, a place of refuge, self-imprisonment, and spirituality. The "mountaintop" in African American literature has served varied purposes. It is the height of consciousness as well as the inversion of the underground. It is the place where African Americans are not forced to hide.[88] If this is the case, Wideman, in part, is parodying this image. Sybela and Charley essentially went there to hide, though they transformed the hill into their home and a place where future generations could be free. Both Bess and Tommy have gone to the mountaintop to hide, to flee society and their problems, ironically becoming prisoners. By the end of the novel, the usual trope of the mountaintop is reinstated. Both characters are enlightened about their condition and return to society. But even this is a revision of the usual journey. The quest to the mountaintop, including the knowledge and spiritual guidance that is gained there, is generally thought of as a solitary experience. In *Hiding Place*, this journey, this enlightenment, not only comes from the experience of going to the mountaintop, but also is achieved by sharing stories and creating community. Neither Tommy nor Mother Bess could have reached an understanding of themselves without the other's voice.

The novel opens with Clement listening to stories at the barbershop where he sweeps floors. The barbershop is the site of communal voices. Clement understands the power of the stories around him even if he doesn't understand the stories themselves. In his own mind, he constructs a story of a mother he has never known. Even a boy like Clement uses story to create a world that he can control. His imagination helps him survive.

Survival is also the key to understanding Tommy. He has come to Bruston Hill to escape the police. He expects that Mother Bess will help him, but she is reluctant to let him break her self-willed silence. She has come to Bruston Hill to escape as well. The deaths of her only son, Eugene (a story already seen in *A Glance Away* and repeated later in "Backseat"), and of her husband have made her lose faith in God and in the world. The only way she can survive, in her mind, is to hide. But her flight has also made her lose her faith in the power of storytelling. In one of her sections, she remembers a time when she was at church, listening to the "Fatheralong" song. The song and her memory remind her in the present what she has lost: "The singing is part of the story she is watching and hearing as somebody tells it, somebody not her because she doesn't believe anything anymore. Not even enough to make stories."[89]

The only stories that Bess is interested in are the old ones. The problem is, however, she doesn't just want to remember the old stories; she wants to imagine herself in the past. Her imaginative life is reminiscent of Cecil Braithwaite in *Hurry Home*. The image of the wise, old woman on the hill is inverted here because she is not on the hill to dispense knowledge and wisdom. She is there to deny that life is still going on down the hill. Tommy's appearance brings her back to this realization. He is the son of Lizabeth, whom she remembers as a child. In her mind, she repeats the story of Lizabeth's birth, which we have seen already in *Damballah*. These repeated stories, layered in the texts, connect the works as well and reflect one of Wideman's theme of the necessity to remember and pass on family stories. Remembering Lizabeth reminds her of other family stories, ones that she has purposefully forgotten. Lizabeth, she recalls, is Freeda's daughter, and Freeda was raised by Bill and Aida Campbell. Thinking about these family connections brings her to memories of Bill Campbell's music, the blues. He could play "that guitar named Corrine he brought from down home, said it was full of letters from home and he would read them when he played and you'd listen and know just what he was talking about even though you'd never been South yourself."[90] The image of "letters from home" from *Damballah* is imbricated in the text of *Hiding Place*. In *Damballah*, the letters allude to the stories of the collection. Here, the blues is also an illustration of letters and their connection to the past. Remembering Bill Campbell also makes her think of her dead husband, and Tommy's arrival signals to her that time has gone on without her. She "couldn't stop making the connections she knew she'd have to make."[91]

While hiding in Bess's shed, Tommy flashes back to the events that led him up the hill. The recollection here is also nearly identical to the short story "Tommy" in *Damballah*. That story is layered within this one. Wideman's decision to repeat the story here is important for several reasons. First, it links to works in the trilogy. And by placing the story in *Hiding Place*, it gives the piece a different direction and perspective from *Damballah*. It offers us another possible story of Tommy's life. We see the story from a new angle, another possible truth of this character and, by extension, Robby.

The possible versions of Tommy's life may have led some critics to believe he dies at the end of the novel.[92] Though the text does not indicate this (Mother

Bess hears sirens and gunshots, but beyond this she does not hear or see anything to suggest that he is dead; she's not even sure if he is still in the area), the repetition of the stories between *Damballah* and *Hiding Place* could suggest that Tommy survives. In "The Beginning of Homewood," the story that closes *Damballah*, John writes to Tommy in prison to tell him that "Mother Bess is down off Bruston Hill now. She talks about you and asks about you and says God give her strength she's crossing that river and coming over to see you."[93] And Lawson visits Tommy in prison in "All Stories Are True," so it is true that in some versions of the tale Tommy is still alive. However, given the elasticity of many of Wideman's versions of story—all resolutions of Tommy's narrative are feasible.

Wideman uses *Hiding Place* to depict the inner workings of two very different people who must find some common ground if they are going to survive. The text reflects the polyphonic quality associated with the different voices reverberating within it, and it reveals that sharing of traumatic experience alleviates if not erases the pain of the past

In the course of the novel, we discover that Tommy is a storyteller; he needs to hear Mother Bess and he needs to talk to her.[94] He tries, unsuccessfully at first, to get Bess to talk to him, but she is annoyed by his presence. When he fails to get her to talk to him, he retreats to his own mind and the memories that reside there. Every time he does this, he remembers the pain that the stories indicate in his life. This thrusts him out of his isolated meditation, returning him to the desire to speak with Mother Bess: "Stories are lies and Mother Bess pigging down her soup brings him back."[95] He is also reminded of the stories he would tell his little boy, Clyde. It was a way for them to share father-son stories. He realizes that "telling a story makes Clyde happy. No fairy tale or nonsense like that. Telling him about life. Real life. When life was good. When life full of good things and safe. And the story ain't just words. More like it is in them old songs. What made the story so good was that other me listening too." Tommy describes his "other me" as a "god" floating over everything in his life, controlling it, making sure that everyone in his life was safe. The "other me" is the other story that Tommy has imagined for himself, one that isn't the story that the "trigger-happy cops" are certain they know.[96]

The cops' story is exactly what Tommy's Uncle Carl fears. Carl and Tommy's brother, John, are talking to each other about Tommy in the next section of the book, entitled "Clement." In Clement's sections other communal voices speak in the novel. Carl expresses to John his concern about Tommy: "Whose going to believe Tommy's story? Chester's story? You got the cops' story and that's the way it will go down."[97] Wideman establishes here that authority in storytelling is given to those in power, but authority is not equal to veracity. *Hiding*

Place and its nonfiction relation, *Brothers and Keepers*, are a direct refutation of the story that the cops tell about Tommy (and Robby). Tommy's point of view, like the "other me," is more in control of this narrative; it draws its own picture of his identity.

As Tommy and Bess spend more time together, the walls between them begin to come down. Bess finally reveals to Tommy what finally drove her up to Bruston Hill. It was the death of his niece: "What kind of world give that baby beautiful eyes and then put in a drop of poison so they roll round like crazy marbles and she can't see nothing and can't hear and can't swallow her food? What kind of world is that? Ima tell you what kind. It's the very kind run me up on this hill."[98] Bess removes herself from her family because she's lost faith and because she's lost the power to transform suffering into survival.

Tommy helps Mother Bess plant seeds outside in her garden. The act is a symbolic rendering of the bond they have made. It is a ritualistic event that connects them to each other, their family, their community, and their world. The seeds represent the future that can be secured if the family renews its storytelling practices. It is right after the planting that Tommy announces that he has to leave. Mother Bess informs him, without her past annoyance, that he has "disturbed" her out of "her usual ways."[99] Both have been hiding from themselves, from their family, and from their past. Tommy tries to convince Bess that she has to come down off of the hill; she shouldn't continue to live in "some damn slave cabin."[100] This is a literal description of Bess's house on one level; Sybela, a former slave once lived there. But the image also addresses Bess's own complicity in her oppressive existence. She is somewhat responsible for the sorrow that she continues to experience. In the community, around the sustaining stories of her family, some of her wounds may have healed; she could have been, as Aunt May would say in "The Beginning of Homewood," "free."

Tommy implies that he understands why Bess has chosen to hide; he too has lost faith in himself and in storytelling: "I was scared a long time. Ever since my granddaddy, John French, died and his house fell to pieces and everybody scattered I been scared. Scared of people, scared of myself. Of how I look and how I talk, of the nigger in me."[101] Like in *Damballah* (and even in *A Glance Away*), John French's death has initiated the death of the family. They have stopped telling their own stories and have started to listen to others' stories of their lives and of their identities. This is evoked by Tommy's confession that he's "scared" of himself and the way he looks. The stories constructed about African American men and African American families have nurtured Tommy's self-hatred. Tommy leaves, and Mother Bess makes the decision to put the pain of her past behind her by burning down the house on Bruston Hill. The act will ensure that no one will ever be able to come up there again, to hide out, to remove themselves from the sustaining circle of the family. She's also going to come down off the hill to bear witness to Tommy's story, to tell them that he didn't kill anyone and that "he ain't scared no more and they better listen and they better make sure it don't happen so easy ever again."[102] Her destruction of Sybela's slave house symbolizes her transformation into the mythic figure and storyteller that the family matriarch historically represented.

The final work of the trilogy, *Sent for You Yesterday*, also repeats several stories that we have already seen in *Damballah* and *Hiding Place* (and, to an extent, also in *A Glance Away*). The effect of the repetition among each of the books of the trilogy is at least twofold. As in *Hiding Place*, repeated stories deny singular, essentialist notions and constructions of African American life. That the stories repeat themselves through each text magnifies that refutation. Also the three works act not as a single story from a single point of view but as a chorus of voices, texts, and experiences that, as a whole, challenge the assumptions of the mainstream.

Several different voices construct the text as well, including characters who are no longer alive during the present time of the novel. Doot (John), the narrator, accumulates these voices and time periods to represent the life of the family and the community, but he does not control the narrative in any sense—he is one of the voices in the conversation. Sometimes he does comment on the action, giving background information, filling in spaces that other voices have neglected. In the text, his voice is the response to the call of the other storytellers, especially Carl and Lucy. Doot's circular, rhythmic memory gives shape to the book, with its spiritual interlinking of characters, metaphorical descriptions of places and events, and convoluted sense of time.[103] The novel, like the trilogy, is a call to remember the past and the family; here, however, more than in any other work of the trilogy, Wideman replicates the act of multiple remembrances in the narrative.

The novel opens with a memory of Brother Tate's train dream. We have seen in the discussion of *A Glance Away* that Brother is linked to trains because of his position as a blues voice or hero in the texts. The trope of the train in African American literature is evoked here, especially in its revoicing of the image of the chariot from African American spirituals.[104] The train in Brother's dream is carrying "lost souls" to an unspecified destination. The dream frightens Brother, and he doesn't understand its meaning. Later in the novel, when he is waking from the train dream, he "counts the parts of his body. He is remembering." He is meant to call forth to the lost souls, the children of the diaspora, and "re-member" them.[105] The dream signals to us Brother's role in the novel—he is its spiritual voice. It is a role that frightens Brother and one that ultimately leads to his betrayal of Albert Wilkes and his own death. It also connects him to the suffering of other lost souls. It is his human suffering that makes him a candidate for a blues hero, a voice that represents the stories of trauma in the community.

Whether Brother in *Sent for You Yesterday* is the same character as Brother in *A Glance Away* is never clarified.[106] He is associated in both works with trains, and he's called a ghost in the two novels because of his albino features. His designation as "a ghost" evokes the mythic position that Brother has in the text; he is the embodiment of an ancestral spirit. But as a "ghost" he embodies a figurative image of the traumatic past, linking him with everyone in the novel, past, present, and future. His name, Brother, connotes this universal quality as well. Carl envies this quality because Brother has "no color. No name. No job. No father you got to find."[107] Freeda, Carl's mother, states that "she had been born and raised in Homewood and if there was a time in her life when Brother hadn't been around, she couldn't remember it." Yet Brother is "just a boy but sometimes he seemed older than she was. Sometimes he was older than old Mr. and Mrs. Tate who they say had found him and raised him in that big old house of theirs."[108] Brother's timelessness, his unknown lineage and age, and his ubiquitous appearance in the neighborhood all suggest that he is a mythic character in the text. He is also a liminal character who can speak from multiple positions in the work, except, of course, Brother doesn't really speak. He scats, which further emphasizes his blues hero image.

This image is also inherent in Brother's relationship to John Lawson. It is Brother who nicknames Lawson Doot as a child.[109] The musical sound reflects Brother's position in the novel, but it also implies that Doot has also been christened a blues hero-to-be, the "articulate kinsmen." Brother's renaming of Lawson expresses a passing of the torch. Lawson senses this himself, at least to a degree: "I'm linked to Brother Tate by stories, by his memories of a dead son, by my own memories of a silent, scat-singing albino man who was my uncle's best friend."[110] Lawson, too, will accept a liminal position then in the text.

Lawson's voice enters the narrative early, in the middle of a description of the day Albert Wilkes came back, when Carl Lawson was still a child. His voice interrupts to announce: "I am not born yet."[111] Then the narrative continues describing a morning in Carl's and Brother's life. Lawson's break serves here in much the same capacity that a break in a jazz composition does. It is a bridge, a bridge between the generations and between the characters that will construct this novel. It is also a way for Lawson to enter the "weave of voices." A few pages later Lawson's voice appears again following three paragraphs voiced by three different characters: Freeda, Brother, and Carl. This time, however, Lawson comments on the action, explains who the characters are and what the setting looks like. His voice is trying to "remember" what

Homewood in the 1930s and 1920s looked like, even though he is not yet born. The lives and homes of the community seem to him to be "islands, arks, life teeming but enclosed or surrounded or exiled to arbitrary boundaries."[112] The description is not a personal one; it is culled from the stories he's heard as the autoethnographer. The image reflects two different versions of Homewood. One is fairly positive—the homes are arks. They keep the community afloat. The other suggestion is more ambivalent or even negative: "enclosed or surrounded or exiled." The community saves and sustains itself, but the implication is that it must to protect itself from dangerous external forces. The reference to arks also implies a time of mythic significance and the beginning of a new history.

The caterpillar story from *Damballah* reverberates within the novel. The story this time is told by a different voice than it was in *Damballah*. Wideman's position as autobiographer, novelist, historian, and ethnographer is highlighted here as well. He appears to be collecting versions of this story and then presenting the "family folklore" through an objective, third-person voice. The story is about the day that Albert Wilkes comes home. The point of view shifts to Carl Lawson (though it is still presented in first- and third-person point of view). Carl tells himself that he has to wake up, because "if I don't wake up, Homewood will be gone."[113] Carl constructs Homewood as a text, the way a storyteller would. It is its own story; the people of its neighborhood make it what they will through their own imagination and perseverance.

The image of the soap bubble trapped between Freeda's fingers, which we see in *Damballah*, is repeated here as well. She holds the bubble from the dishwater between her thumb and forefinger. She's enchanted by its shape—a circle. And she knows that with one "puff she could set the room and the rainbow free." But the soap bubble breaks before she can do anything: "She couldn't remember what had pulled her away, but it continued pulling, drawing her past the edges of herself. Since that day, whenever she looked away from something, she was never sure it would be there when she looked back."[114] The last line echoes the title *A Glance Away*.[115] The bubble is an image that evokes both the circular version of history that Wideman represents elsewhere and the rainbow image of the god Damballah.[116] The bubble also symbolizes Homewood itself: a beautiful, perfectly-shaped "bubble" protecting the neighborhood, like the arks described before, but the bubble is about to burst.[117] The image of *Damballah*, also implied in the rainbow colors of the bubble, evokes Wideman's previous characterization of history, family, and community. Wideman speculates that the community will not continue if we glance away from it, from its history, from its reservoir of family stories. If we don't imagine it, or dream it everyday as Carl must, it will disappear.

Albert Wilkes's story is developed in the next pages. The narrator comments on the silence between the notes.[118] This version of call-and-response allows a place for the stories of the community to be played. Characters constantly comment on how they could hear themselves and their stories in Wilkes's music; when he played, "it was like a mirror anyway."[119] As one of the works' blues heroes, Wilkes is a liminal, even mysterious figure. He is necessarily isolated from the community in his role as artist, as Wideman has said even about himself as a writer, but Wilkes's alienation is not pathological. The community depends on his voice, and his absence has nearly destroyed Homewood's imaginative response to trauma.

Lucy Tate needs Wilkes's music. His song is so familiar because "everything she's ever heard is in it, all the songs and voices she's ever heard, but everything is new and fresh because his music joined things, blended them so you follow one note and then it splits and shimmers and spills the thousand things it took to make the note whole, the silences within the note, the voices and the songs."[120] Lucy's description of Wilkes's music explains why Wilkes focuses on those "silences within the note." It is the break, the bridge that "joined things."

This could describe Lawson's storytelling technique in the work as well. Whenever his voice breaks in, it is at a stopping point or a silence in the story that is being told to him. His voice comes in and tries to fill in the gaps. Brother is described early in the text in a third-person voice. The text tries to chronicle when Brother became silent. The third-person voice does not have this answer, so Lawson breaks in.[121] He tries to imagine Brother and then what Brother and Carl were like as boys; he creates a story for them in an attempt to understand Brother, a man he really knows primarily through stories about him rather than his own experiences of the man.

Wilkes's music shapes the community, just as Lawson tries to "shape" the figure of Brother. Wilkes tries to capture all the fragments: "the phrases, chords, runs, teasing little bits and pieces." The music even shapes the external world of Homewood. John French intimates that there is a "moody correspondence between what [Albert's] fingers shape and what happens to the sky, the stars, the moon."[122] The music also informs the text and the trilogy according to Wideman.[123] Wilkes's music has mythic power. The portrait of him and his effect on the community suggest that he is a mythic figure as well. When he arrives, everyone has a story about who first spotted him, about what he said and what he did. The community searches for him; and through him, they reconnect to their faith, to the story of Homewood. People will later argue that they saw him that day he came back, and they weren't even alive yet. His death has mythic significance as well. If he is a blues hero, and we accept Albert Murray's argument that the blues hero is reminiscent of the

Fisher King story, then Wilkes's death should signal chaos and destruction in the community. And it does.[124] The death of Wilkes and the death of this generation disrupt and nearly destroy the next generation. This next generation (Brother, Carl, and Lucy) are lost. They have no surviving children, and they either die young or live an empty existence compared to their fathers and mothers, who survived equally tragic times yet still connected to each other and to their past.

This novel is also part detective story. Who betrayed Albert Wilkes? Lawson can find no definitive answers. If you "gather all the stories, listen to every tale and all of Homewood guilty."[125] Later in the novel Lawson will imagine a narrative (spoken by Brother) that implicates Brother in the betrayal. This might be the result of Lawson's need to fill that space and of the stories that he's heard about Brother's almost supernatural ability on the piano. Carl and Lucy tell him that Brother just started playing one night. They never knew he could play. He played for about five years, and then he stopped just as abruptly as he began. Lawson breaks into the narrative again at this point:

> I was born about six months before that evening in 1941. So already I was inside the weave of voices, a thought, an idea, a way things might be seen and said.... If I missed Brother playing between '41 and '46 then I missed him forever, because after Junebug died Brother stopped playing the piano just a suddenly as he stopped talking.[126]

Lawson connects his life to Brother's here, though the linear progression of the story did not require it. And he offers a reason for Brother's silence (Junebug's death, even though he doesn't have confirmation of this). Lawson imagines a story that will complete family and communal history. This story asserts that all stories have no conclusion, no closure, and offers many possible reasons for any event. Lawson is also consciously illustrating the mythmaking process.

When Lucy and Carl are young adults, Lucy shows Carl something that she has kept hidden, a piece of Wilkes's skull (he was shot to death in her home). She has held onto the skull fragment like a totem. It represents the myth and the sacrifice of Wilkes. And as a "fragment" it should remind us of the fragments of story we see in the text and the fragments that Wilkes hears in his music. To collect these fragments is to reconstitute a life of the community, a myth, and to remember the stories and songs that Wilkes brought to Homewood. Like Damballah, remembering Wilkes brings the family and the community together. But Homewood's despair over his death and what they lose when he dies silences them. That is until Doot wants to hear their stories, record them, understand them, and share them with others.

Lucy's and Carl's voices inhabit most of the middle section of this book. They argue with one another about how the stories should be told and what the other is leaving out. Lucy isn't even sure why they are dredging up the past and why Carl says that something happened just like it was yesterday when it clearly was not. Carl's answer to her (and to readers following the narrative style of the book) is this:

> Cause that's the way the world turns. Circles and circles and circles inside circles. Don't you understand nothing, woman? Doot don't make me feel old. Don't make me feel young neither, sitting there with children when I remember him in diapers. Point is I can see him back then just as plain as I see him now and it don't make no difference. Just a circle going round and round and round.[127]

Lucy tells her own story of Brother as well. Layered within her version of Brother's story is Samantha's story. Samantha is the mother of Brother's dead son, Junebug. Lucy understands that in order to tell Brother's story, you have to know Samantha's; and in order to tell her own story, she has to tell Brother's. Lucy's voice, in fact, structures most of the middle section and a large portion of the third.[128]

Lucy's "side of the story" is her own version of what happened between Samantha and Brother. Brother is dead and Samantha is in the insane asylum. Neither can offer "true" accounts of the events of their life together or Junebug's death. Lucy has to re-imagine the story, fill in the numerous gaps with her own voice. Considering this is a text of many voices, Lucy's emerges as one of the strongest and most memorable. She is also often the character that makes connections for us between Brother and Albert and Doot. She is a blues hero herself. Her story is intimately connected to the "men in her life."

We are presented with several possible versions of the events that led to Junebug's death, including one from the dead child himself. Junebug is another lost child in Wideman's canon. Hated by his mother's other children because of his albino appearance, he may have been a victim of fratricide. There will never be a true story of his death, only imagined ones. Yet Wideman (and Lawson) collects all of these versions to argue once again that all stories are true. Even those we must imagine ourselves.

Carl describes his years back following the war and his decision not to pursue his interest in art because a teacher told him that an African American artist could never make it. Carl believed the lies that others constructed of his life. Carl gave up. Lucy and Brother gave up. This is expressed in the image of the three of them when they were younger, getting high and breaking John French's records. They destroyed the entire collection: "Shame about those records. Got destroyed just like a lot of innocent bystanders got destroyed by junk. Shame about Daddy's records and shame on us all."[129] The importance allotted to music in the trilogy alerts us to the waste and destruction that this act foretells. These characters destroyed the very stories that could have given them comfort and guidance and that could have connected them to a larger community.

That loss is further illustrated by Brother's death and the loss of his blues voice. Brother's voice animates the beginning of the final section. It is a riffing, steam-of-consciousness style at times. After Junebug dies he tells us that he "*sang to him to save his life.*"[130] He speaks mainly to Junebug in this section. He tells his dead son that suffering is human; it is what connects father and son, individual to community, the past to the present:

> *I had been through it before. That nothing stopped. That I had crossed the ocean in a minute. That I had drowned in rivers and dangled like rotten fruit from trees. That my unmourned bones were ground to dust and the dust salted and plowed. That I had watched my children's brains dashed out against a rock. That I had seen my mother whipped and my woman raped and my daddy stretched on a cross. That I had even lost my color and lost my tongue but all of that too was only a minute. I sang to him. I let him know I didn't understand any more than he did. Except I had been a witness. I had been there so I could tell about it. . . . Listen, son. Listen, Junebug. It all starts up again in you. It's all there again. You are in me and I am in you so it never stops.*[131]

Brother speaks here as a man who has moved through time and space, a mythic character, a Damballah figure. Historical and personal histories conflate here. Brother's life has been tied to the history of his people. He knows that his son is listening; he's "breathing so there's little spaces for the words to fit and Brother whispering in the spaces."[132] Brother, like Lawson, must fill in the spaces of Junebug's life that he cannot know. He imagines his son listening to his train songs. Brother tries to teach his dead son the "scare game" with trains. It is here, we find out later, that Brother dies. His sorrow overcomes him. He cannot connect to those very stories that he should have been sharing with the rest of the community.

As the middle generation, Lucy, Carl, and Brother have listened to stories other than their own. Elsewhere, Wideman calls them "stillborn." This generation barely survived, Wideman suggests; they tried to leave behind the generation before them (John French's), but "society said no, there's no place for you to go, we don't want you here, you are no good, you are wasted. So that generation became sacrificial."¹³³ This trio, this generation, is based on the same family members and friends that Alice, Eddie, and Brother represent in *A Glance Away*. While Wideman states that he made no conscious attempt to rewrite that novel, the characters in *Sent for You Yesterday* are a "prolonged meditation" on the actual people that they are based on. The members of each trio cannot rewrite their own story; they cannot imagine a better self, and that is their tragedy. While many critics have concluded that the Homewood trilogy is an illustration that shows Wideman has found the site of sustaining stories, these characters do not seem to fully realize where those stories are and what their power is. If they do come to this realization, it happens too late.

Doot, however, through his position in the text, can see what the others have missed. His gathering of stories is an indication that he values them and sees that they are essential. This is the message that he wants to impart to his community and that Wideman wants to describe to the dominant mainstream as well. Doot is connected, in the final pages of the novel, with the stories and traditions that have sustained African Americans throughout slavery and in the wake of prevailing racist attitudes regarding their character and their life. Doot is also an alienated figure who has come back to claim his position as the family storyteller.¹³⁴ The novel reflects the voices of the entire community presented through the voice of the blues hero. This goes directly to the autoethnographic project. Wideman uses the forms and voices of the community that he is writing about to preserve its traditions, but also to directly illustrate that this community has a unique language, a culture, and a tradition. Wideman names and renames Homewood, not as a ghetto, but as a site of heritage and history that is intimately connected with his own family.¹³⁵

Homewood is also the site for much of Wideman's nonfictional work; *Brothers and Keepers* retells many of the stories of the Homewood trilogy.¹³⁶ In the foreword to *Brothers and Keepers*, Wideman suggests that he has written this work in an effort to "salvage" something from "the grief and waste" that surround the events that led to the incarceration of his brother, Robby, for murder. Throughout the book, Wideman seeks reasons for his need to understand the forces that led him to college and a successful career as a teacher and novelist and led Robby to prison. Foremost to Wideman is the need to "break out, to knock down the walls" that stand between him and his brother. This is a highly personal and emotional work that in the end reveals as much about Wideman as it does Robby.

Personal and historical traumas are inexorable in Wideman's confessional reflection on his brother's crime, imprisonment, and the silences that separated them throughout their lives. Woven into the narrative of his brother's story is Wideman's own and his need to escape the traumatic past of his "blackness":

"Just two stories as far as I could tell: either/or. Rich or poor. White or black. Win or lose. I figured which side I wanted to be on when the saints came marching in.... [M]y mind was split by oppositions, by mutually exclusive categories. Manichean as Franz Fanon would say."[137] Wideman's description of his own double-consciousness engages the ontological wound that W.E.B. DuBois suggests African Americans all suffer from. Wideman states that his move to Laramie, Wyoming, was "running away from Pittsburgh, from poverty, from blackness," and, ultimately, from his family and his own suffering.

Repressing the trauma has not soothed the post-traumatic pain; only now, writing about Robby—which reminds him of his grandfather's past, his mother's growing bitterness, his daughter's difficult birth, and his own isolation from his community—can Wideman rediscover the power of the blues, his Homewood ear. This can never change what has happened to Robby or to Wideman; the original wound will never really heal: "I realized no apotheosis of Robby's character could occur in the final section.... [M]y brother was in prison. A thousand books would not reduce his sentence one day."[138] Writing the book will, however, reconnect Wideman to his brother. Even though these are only stories, and they often stand in for real communication between the men, they do remind them of their shared suffering: "Silence does not stretch between us separating us. It joins us, a common ground."[139] Readers can see Robby's own feelings of alienation, whose sources are somewhat different than Wideman's, but they are nevertheless as responsible for his despair.[140] In the end, the sharing of their common experiences is the only way to weather the pain of the post-traumatic burden.

The work violates boundaries of the traditional autobiographical modes through its confessionals, dialogues, alternating narrative voices, histories of families and communities, social commentary, and even, possibly, fictional constructs and use of African American literary tropes. It presents a family and culture that directly oppose the limited and racist portrait often painted in the dominant culture's history and sociology of the African American. Wideman succeeds for his brother where society failed: he creates a space for Robby's voice to be heard. In *Brothers and Keepers*, Robby Wideman rises above a statistic, beyond a category, and is permitted, at last, to be a flesh-and-blood man.

The style and form of *Brothers and Keepers* reflect the polyphonic chorus of voices that have shaped Wideman, Robby, their family, community, and race. In the beginning it seems that Wideman wanted to approach this project in terms of traditional autobiography. He talks about rooting out his "fiction-writing self." But as he began, Wideman foresaw that traditional biographical/autobiographical methods would not work if he wanted to capture the complexity of Robby's life and the historical and social forces that contributed to his trouble. The text ultimately "rejects the conventions of autobiography in its rejection of the assertion of the individual" as a cohesive, singular entity at odds with the community."[141]

The form of the work, its hybridity and its polyphonic narratives and discourses, reflects its desire to abstain from the traditional autobiography that is controlled by a single narrator who argues that the life being presented is a complete and finished product. Several times in the text Wideman tries to begin the story of Robby's life, trying to determine where and when things went wrong. His point of origin is different than his brother's idea and also different than his mother's opinion. Of course, Wideman's vision of Robby's life contrasts most sharply with that of "the keepers," but he includes even this perspective in his narrative. Wideman allows these various origins to play in his text, never giving any precedence. Each is a possibility. The work itself is an illustration of "all stories are true."

In fact, the story of Robby and Homewood, Wideman's old neighborhood, as we have already seen, will be told in *Sent for You Yesterday*, *Hiding Place*, and *Damballah*. These various versions of Wideman's and Robby's lives further reveal Wideman's questions about "truth" and "history" as a writer. *Brothers and Keepers*' form not only resembles a jazz composition, but also embodies postmodern refutations of the master narratives of verifiable truth. The form that emerges is a multivoiced text that embraces the values and culture of the family and the community over the privileged notions of the "individual" extolled in traditional autobiography. Wideman argues in the work that it has been the idealization of the individual that has led to his estrangement from his family and his race. He explains to Robby: "The problem was in order to be the person I thought I wanted to be, I believed that I had to seal myself off from you, construct a wall between us."[142] Success in mainstream America, as Wideman sees it, demands that African Americans sacrifice identity, family, and race. Their achievement is measured by their ability to overcome their past and their environment, to "become like the man."[143] Wideman feels that it is formulas such as these that have isolated him.[144] He uses the fluid text of *Brothers and Keepers* to reconnect to his past, to his community, and to his brother. He "takes notes like an ethnographer" as he writes the work.[145] He also finds himself struggling against his "fiction writing self," questioning as to whether this too will exploit Robby and other members of his family. And the reader can never be certain where that fictional voice is entering if Wideman is unable to control it. Did Wideman run away from Homewood or is he echoing the trope of the alienated intellectual or the solitary mythic hero?

As the work progresses, its clear that Wideman adopts and retains these and other writing voices and styles and incorporates these into the text. Again, this addresses his reluctance to write in the traditional modes that have too often silenced marginal voices like Robby's. Wideman moves between "I" and "eye," a play on words that he uses throughout his fiction. Wideman accepts a liminal position in the text, and he emerges as an autoethnographer once more. For Wideman's purposes, the autoethnographic form moves beyond the boundaries imposed by traditional narratives and allows Wideman to speak to his brother through the text, which addresses the still-problematized silences between the two of them. By sharing the page, the "narrative space" is transformed from silence to empathy.[146]

Many of the aims of *Brothers and Keepers* do intersect, however, with the goals of a traditional ethnographic project. Wideman, at times, even seems to want to adopt the role of the ethnographer. Initially, looking at observation and detachment as the style that might best be used in the making of this work, Wideman states several times that he wishes that he could rid himself of his fiction voice. Even more importantly, Wideman is concerned with presenting the history of a community, the history of a place, the history of family, kinship ties, religion, institutional practices, mythology, folklore, and music. We also hear the voices of the elders in this work (grandfathers Harry Wideman and John French) and the description of day-to-day living in the community of Homewood, past and present.

While Wideman's ultimate goal is different than a traditional ethnographer, in the course of his journey to reconnect with his brother, the audience is educated about the world of Homewood. In a sense, Wideman is reeducating himself as well. For in answering the questions: "Who is Robby? Who am I? Am I my brother's keeper" (the biblical allusion that resonates in the text's title), Wideman rediscovers his and Robby's place in the web of relationships of his family, neighborhood, and race, past and present. He senses that each of us is responsible for our brothers, both literally and figuratively.

Stories from home characterize much of *Brothers and Keepers* as well. Here, however, Robby is also a storyteller, contributing to the history of the family and of self. Robby's voice, Wideman's voice, and their mother's voice construct the first-person narratives of this work. Other stories are told through Wideman's fiction and nonfiction third-person voice. All of these voices are engaged in the project of describing family and history in a way that a traditional autobiography or ethnography could not accomplish. Hence, the control of the narrative is not singular but communal.

Brothers and Keepers begins with Wideman hearing the news about his brother's trouble. He sits down to write a letter to Robby, knowing that he has no idea if Robby will ever be able to see it. The letter talks about old times and new news and emphasizes the "deep roots of shared time and place and blood" between the brothers.[147] Wideman begins to see that Robby's "flight" from Homewood and the authorities in some way mirrors his own "flight." Both brothers wanted to escape the harshness of their world; they merely chose different routes. Wideman asks if their grandfathers had also run away from their worlds.[148] Wideman links the present with the past in a way that reverberates not only for his own family but for the many African American families past and present that have had to run away from something or to something in the search for freedom. Wideman also thinks about the connections to his family's past when he describes the birth of his daughter, Jamila, and envisions in her ties to his brother and ties to his mother. He understands through his daughter's birth the frailty of human lives and what he has already lost with his brother. Her birth, like Lizabeth's, also creates another mythic tale in the history of the family.

A family photograph also encourages Wideman to link the past and the present. In his family's faces he sees not only the generation before and the promise of generations to come, but also the history of black and white relations in American in the fair skin and light eyes of some of his family members, "the underground history of interracial love, sex, and hate."[149] This prompts him to remember his mother's family's arrival in Homewood: how Charley Owens, the son of a slave owner, escaped with one of his father's slaves, Sybela, and they began their life and their family in the community that would later become Homewood.

His family history is inexorably linked with the history of the city and with the history of other African Americans. This knowledge connects him to the past and the present communities. It also connects him to a racial past and, in doing so, questions the very essence of differentiation in this country based on race, a problem that he blames for many of the reasons for Robby's incarceration and his own alienation from his community. Here Wideman uses personal and family history not only to connect to Robby, but to question the history produced and maintained by the dominant culture.

Wideman speaks and writes and allows others (especially Robby) in the text to tell their stories as well. These stories and traditions are at the core of the family and its stability in the face of a racist America:

> No matter how grown up you thought you were or how far you believed you'd strayed, you knew you could cry *Mama* in the depths of the night and somebody would tend to you. Arms would wrap round you, a soft soothing voice lend its support. If not a flesh-and-blood mother then a mother in the form of a song or story or a surrogate, Aunt Geral, Aunt Martha, drawn from the network of family members.[150]

As he has elsewhere, Wideman suggests that it is the family and community that have been the means of survival for African Americans in this country and that these traditions reach back to the African past:

> None of us knew how traditional West African families were organized or what values the circular shape of their villages embodied, but the living arrangements we had worked out among ourselves resembled the ancient African patterns.... [T]he high wall of the family, the collective, communal reality of other souls, other huts like yours eliminated some of the dread, the isolation experienced when you turned inside and tried to make sense out of the chaos of your individual feelings.[151]

Arguing against the claims of unstable families, the lack of tradition and history, and incipient racial inferiority, Wideman presents Homewood and his family as a more accurate (or at least as accurate) representation of African American life. He also reclaims "blackness" as an image of "celebration" and "endurance" as opposed to a sign of urban decay, violence, and depravation.[152]

Much of *Brothers and Keepers* is devoted specifically to revising the portrait of the African American prisoner and to indicting the prison and legal system at large. Several times Wideman draws connections between slave narratives, the autobiographies of African American political prisoners of the 1960s, and his brother. Robby's incarceration reminds Wideman that he could have easily been the imprisoned brother. The brothers are doubles; and Robby, especially, is a mask, another possible self for Wideman. Even Robby's crime condemns Wideman when detectives pick him up for questioning following Robby's arrest, believing that he may be an accomplice to a crime that they are trying to link to Robby: "No matter that I lived four hundred miles from the scene of the crime. No matter that I wrote books and taught literature and creative writing at the university. I was black. Robby was my brother. Those unalterable facts would always incriminate me."[153]

Wideman discovers that his "charmed" life in Laramie, Wyoming, cannot protect him from the racist assumptions that still exist in this society. For Wideman, the very act of writing the book flies in the face of the stereotypes that have been constructed by the dominant culture. The forces that led Robby to prison are largely also a product of such racism, Wideman believes. Welfare, poverty, ghetto life, and the feelings of despair and resignation that accompany them have all contributed to Robby's troubles. Again and again, Robby is told he is not a "man" by society. And he is not alone. Even Wideman, who has gained the measure of success usually celebrated by society, has not been protected from voices that question his humanity. The police interrogation is just one example from the text. He also feels the forces of such assumptions when he visits the prison with his children, wife, and mother: "I'm one hundred percent behind them, prepared to make anyone who threatens them answer to me. And that posture, that prerogative remains rare for a black man in American society."[154]

Wideman's other nonfiction work, *Fatheralong*, reiterates many of the same ideas that *Brothers and Keepers* voices. The two are linked by their paternal roots (a brother and a father are echoed in the book titles), and both consider the ties between fathers and sons. His father is a lesser-known figure in Wideman's autobiographical pieces and even his fictional accounts. His mother's world "was ruled by love, by encircling arms, by overlapping circles of generations." It is an image that he connects to Damballah: "unbroken circles expanding, contracting, rainbow circles you can visualize an instant if you don the mask of Damballah, hold all time, Great Time in your unflinching gaze."[155] It is his mother's stories that connect him to the past and to the future. His father's stories are still unknown.[156] As such, the father stories occupy a different position within Wideman's canon; nonetheless, they must also be transformed into mythic narratives—but these stories emphasize isolation, solitary quests, and exile.[157]

In *Fatheralong*, Wideman briefly discusses again that Africans and African Americans are body doubles for Europeans and white Americans.[158] He uses this image in an interview with Ishmael Reed as well to suggest another version of the image of double-consciousness.[159] Wideman's varied and multiple use of doubles throughout his canon operate most explicitly in *Reuben*.

The title character of the novel is a lawyer who operates out of a trailer in Homewood. While this story does not include family stories, it does present the stories of the Homewood community. Reuben tries to help those people in his community most in need. Though he is a respected person by many, we don't observe him in any situation that really illustrates the position that Kwansa and Wally place him in. He is only visited by these two, and he does not appear to be treated well by anyone else he comes into contact with. He's actually an isolated figure, another of Wideman's alienated intellectuals. In this case, however, Reuben is able to transcend the tensions confronting the African American intellectual primarily because he has assumed a mythic role in the community and in the novel itself. But as it is with all mythic heroes, Reuben necessarily remains isolated as he works to help Homewood. He is physically similar to Littleman in *The Lynchers*; both men share an emotionally painful experience with a prostitute. Reuben's history is far more traumatic than Littleman's; he has much more reason to hate, yet he turns those destructive feelings into ones that can change the lives of those in his community.

Early in the work, Reuben examines the photographs of Eadweard Muybridge, especially his photos of Egypt. Reuben has always been interested in Egypt and for a moment contemplates its ancient religion and culture. He is reminded of the Osiris and Thoth myth.[160] The figure that Reuben wears around his neck is probably Egyptian in origin. He notes the connection between Osiris and Thoth especially in relationship to his own twin brother (who may or may not exist). Though Reuben only mentions explicitly that Thoth protected Osiris, the two also signal to us other stories and images found in Wideman's work. Osiris is the Egyptian god that was dismembered and scattered throughout the world. Thoth helps "re-member" Osiris. Thoth is also the god of writing and hieroglyphics. If we extend the image, the god Osiris can only be remembered through the deciphering of codes and through writing.[161] The symbolic implications of the Egyptian brothers illuminate Wideman's own work and the god Damballah: the remembering of story, family, and history through the act of mythmaking or storytelling.

Reuben's interest in Muybridge is also a reflection of Wideman's project. Muybridge's photographic studies try to capture motion in still photography. Reuben realizes that the photos examine the "illusion of motion."[162] The linear chain of events or the "illusion of motion" could explain, could give order and meaning to the chaos of the streets of Homewood; to "arrive at this bad dream of Homewood and lost children and mothers grieving you needed a chain of events, one after another didn't you?"[163] But Reuben knows that this is the illusion, that nothing follows a logical pattern.

Later Reuben imagines a conversation between himself and Muybridge, who is always in a rush to chase the "god of motion." Muybridge tells Reuben that nothing changes in history except our perspective: "One age, one set of assumptions, wears itself out, but there is simultaneously a concentration of vital force, incandescence, a final focused energy ... exhaustion, depletion ... but also a final, life-sustaining flash of spirit." In this context, history is an illusion, a new story for each age. What lasts is not history, but the "flash of the spirit." That spirit is the need to tell stories; once the old assumptions or stories are dispensed of, "one vision of the world reaches its limits, blows itself to smithereens. The air is clear, rushes away, free to be shaped again according to a new dispensation." New stories must constantly be told, rewritten.[164]

It is the flash of spirit that is timeless and transcends history. Muybridge admits that his pictures could never capture the true essence of time. The photos isolate time and history into "cubicles," marooning us from the "twin living next door."[165] Muybridge argues here that the minute we try to capture a moment in time, we limit its possibilities and our own. The twin "next door" is the other possible version of our story, of our lives. This conversation is revelatory for

Reuben. Earlier he viewed "possibility [as] just a name for another chain" meant to fool you into believing in freedom. But after this conversation he embraces the other version of himself, a possible twin.[166] Another possible story of himself denies the motion of history; it argues against a singular defined truth, of a way of seeing. As Muybridge has suggested to him, the only way to escape the burden of history and the past that limits the way we see ourselves and the way others see us is to "let go of our stony notions of starts, stops, beginnings, middles, ends."[167]

In order to connect to our other selves, our other stories, we have to look at time not as discrete units but as

> a bottomless bowl of cherries. Or a snake with its tail in its mouth. Or a turtle shell. Or a sacred hoop. Or the round face of a clock, the circle of numbers from one to twelve to one, spinning invisibly over and over again. Still, yet always moving. Perfect representations of time. Everywhere and nowhere at once. Eternally moving, eternally still. The same numbers on the clock face can tell today's time, tomorrow's, yesterday's. A clock's face registers every moment, past, future, present. It expresses our true relation to time. How time mothers us and orphans us. Our immersion in a great sea, drowning, spewed forth endlessly. Each sounding we take connects us to all the soundings. Each time different, each time the same. Many in one; one in the many.[168]

Muybridge's notion of time echoes other images of time we have seen in Wideman's work, but it also describes the many voices, the many stories that exist in each of us and connect us to one another. It is this image of the circle as both a reflection of history and an icon of community that is voiced simultaneously in Wideman's writing. The image of the circle and of time here also brings us back to an evocation of the phrase "all stories are true" ("each time different, each time the same"), no matter when they are told or where they appear on the circle of time.

Wally tells Reuben about the man he murdered in the washroom. Reuben asks him "is this story true?"[169] Wally isn't really sure, but the feelings that drove him to commit the act or imagine he committed it are the same. Truth lies in the story not as a factual account of the event but as the emotion that it tries to explain. The "other" Wally who may be a murderer is a possible story of his life. The image of the double throughout this work is voiced in this way. The doubles represent other possible stories that are as true as the ones that are verifiable, accepted as truth by the outside world. The double, and his or her story, acts as a way to combat the limited stories that are often portrayed of

African American life and to open up history to prevent it from being conclusive, fixed, and stable. We have seen Wideman use the double this way in other texts. The double also reflects Wideman's position in the text as a voice *speaking to* Homewood and *speaking for* Homewood.

Reuben's position in the community is akin to the African American artist who must re-imagine stories and who is "expected by his ethnic community to create a counterversion of the reality as propagated by the dominant white society."[170] Reuben does this throughout the novel. Kwansa believes that she has "no story," and Reuben sees his task as not just aiding her in keeping her son, but helping her "change her story."[171]

The need to change "the story" even influences the form and structure of the novel. The work is voiced by several discourses: philosophy, the novelistic tradition, poetry, and drama. There are times in the text where the story switches from one discourse to another. Prose is interrupted by dramatic dialogue.[172] The genre of the story has to be changed to accommodate something in the story. At other times the novel includes stage directions and notes on how to read a passage.[173] The hybrid quality of the text illustrates the multivocal and communal nature of Wideman's work. *Reuben*, like other works that we have seen, is a text that "resembles a choir of seemingly converging but often parallel or diverging voices reminiscent of Mikhail Bakhtin's theory of the polyphonic novel."[174]

The double-voiced discourse of such novels resonates in the multiple images of doubles in *Reuben*. These possible other selves represent other voices layered within the novel, both heard and unheard. This begins early in the novel where Kwansa repeats the nursery rhyme "Reuben, Reuben." She is not certain what to call him when she first meets him. Is Reuben a first or last name? Should he be addressed as a doctor? She isn't sure who he is because she's heard so many contradictory stories about the man. Which one is true? Reuben himself offers few answers.

It is uncertain, even to Reuben, if his twin is real or exists only in his imagination. There was a time when he wasn't aware of the twin's existence; he had "heard only one heart, strong, firm, its beat a fire within him, warming, pumping light. Then the sound was halved. Two hearts beating, the slightest syncopation, his brother or himself by a quarter beat as he discovered he was two, not one."[175] We are reminded of *Brothers and Keepers* when Reuben remembers that in a "dream or a vision or during one of the extra lives he grew more certain he had lived, Reuben had learned his brother was in prison. In a vast, gray prison in a cell too small for a dog, from which he'd never be released." *Brothers and Keepers* is layered further in this novel by Reuben's continued analysis of his relationship to his brother: "Had he somehow helped cause his brother's plight? Did years of neglect, careless stowage on the bottom layer of a bottom box, burial under sheaves of yellowing pads, did all that equal turning a lock, throwing away a key?"[176] These lines echo Wideman's sentiments in *Brothers and Keepers*. Robby's and Reuben's brothers are buried under yellowing pads (writing paper?) and are, consequently, lost. The language appears to be an intentional reverberation of the nonfictional piece. At the least, it reminds us again how often Wideman repeats and imbricates stories within stories among his own work.

The work also reinforces Wideman's autoethnographic project. He suggests that one way to critique American culture and to "have choices" is to illuminate past traditions and racial memory in the African American community:

> The books have to reflect the deeper spiritual values that animate, for me, what's good and what should be preserved about Afro-American life. The rituals are a manifestation of some spirit force, which runs much deeper. That's why the outward shape or description of the culture can change. But it can maintain its integrity because of the forces that run underground. Those forces have always been there. And those are the ones I'm trying to touch upon. I might do something like try to show how Kongo cosmology might be relevant to what Reuben's doing—how it's tied up—the notion of doubles, the notion of two worlds.[177]

Wideman suggests here the Yoruba belief that gods exist in all of us, a manifestation of the *ashe*, "the power-to-make-things-happen, a key to futurity and self-realization."[178] *Ashe* is also the ability to multiply, to embody different realities. The deity that first exhibited this ability was Esu-Elegbra, who shares a relationship with Damballah as the guardian of the crossroads and is represented by a "double face," a Janus figure who can occupy two roles at the same time.[179]

The ability to live in two worlds, the one constructed for you and the one that you imagine, is at the center of this novel and at the purpose of autoethnography. Wally sees his friend Bimbo as two people, the one stuck in the wheelchair and the "one free." The hardest thing for Kwansa to believe is "the dream she carried of a better Kwansa, the Kwansa she'd find one day and throw her arms around and they'd cry and laugh like long-lost sisters."[180] Everyone here needs to re-imagine a life that challenges the one that's oppressing them, killing them. The autoethnographic writer tries to bring to the attention of the mainstream those other lives that exist in the margins of society. The autoethnographic writer presents another story to counterbalance the hegemonic story. It has been a necessity of African American writers to do this since the beginning of the tradition, as Reuben affirms: "If your life's not a memory or a tale you concoct at will, playing it fast-forward or reverse, stopping and starting in the middle or end, if your life's more than this mix of yes no and maybe and skipping and losing and somebody else working the dials then who are you?"[181]

The only way that one can refute these stories where "somebody else [is] working the dials," Wideman argues again and again, is to let the community be heard, let all of its stories be told. Toward the end of the novel, a metafictional second-person voice interrupts the narrative to tell us: "From a great distance, longer than the time it's taken all the voices that have ever told stories to tell their stories, in the welcome silence, after so much lying, after so much wasted breath, the women's voices reach us. Where we sit. Imagining ourselves imagining them."[182]

Reuben transcends his past and acknowledges the power and necessity of storytelling to become a mythic figure of his community. He follows in the tradition of other Wideman characters like Orion, Sybela, Albert Wilkes, Brother, and even Doot Lawson. While other works written by Wideman after the Homewood books concern family or illustrate family stories, including *Hoop Roots*, many of the characters in these later works fail to realize their blues potential. Cudjoe is such a character in *Philadelphia Fire*, and even Wideman in *Fatheralong* cannot successfully share stories with his father (at least not in the way he seems to desire). Interestingly, *The Cattle Killing*, which follows *Fatheralong* in publication, allows fathers and sons to share written stories—manuscripts—in a fictional recreation of the figures in Wideman's memoir. These protagonists have more difficulty in finding home or seeing it as a site of healing. Even the notion of what and where home really is becomes a complicated question. In fact, *Philadelphia Fire*, *Fatheralong*, and *The Cattle Killing*, unlike the Homewood books, all follow the pattern of a quest story (with Wideman's typical inversions and revisions). The plot follows them on their journey to the past, to the site of trauma, and sometimes to greater awareness of the power of story.

CHAPTER FOUR

The Journey Back (Again)

THE POST-TRAUMATIC NARRATIVES

> Past lives live in us, through us. Each of us harbors the spirits of people who walked the earth before we did, and those spirits depend on us for continuing existence, just as we depend on their presence to live our lives to the fullest.
>
> —JOHN EDGAR WIDEMAN, *Sent for You Yesterday*

Perhaps no area illustrates Wideman's aesthetic more effectively than his dialogue with recorded or popular history. Through the imagination, he can fill the gaps and silences of African American life in the historical consciousness—celebrating the unknown men and women who survived and kept a tradition alive in the wake of slavery, racism, and oppression. Reaching back into the past allows Wideman to confront the site of trauma and the "original sin" of America—slavery. Wideman seeks to question, deconstruct, and displace those histories of the hegemonic culture by revising them or imbricating them within his own fictions, autobiographies, and re-imaginings of the past.[1] He buries the recorded history in his writing as historians have often buried the stories of African Americans in the official chronicles.

In these moments or in these works, the lines demarcating discourses become even more blurred and indistinct, as is the case of *Philadelphia Fire* and *The Cattle Killing*, especially. The layers of story (and the respective genres they traditionally represent), are indistinguishable and embody within the texts a dialogic and contrapuntal relationship. Wideman has pointed out that the slave narratives collected by the Works Project Administration in the 1930s also have this characteristic. They are an example of personal testimony and a history of slavery, yet the narratives exhibit techniques and structure that are novelistic in design. Wideman also argues that the fiction of Charles Chesnutt embodies the desire to balance the discourses of Western tradition, the language of the folk, and the history of slavery, ultimately to argue that black speech and culture (and, by extension, black life) is as valuable and authoritative as the Western tradition.[2]

The historiographers of slavery, lynching, and racism in America were sometimes the very men who had perpetuated the system that created and reinforced these conditions. Or the histories were written by men who had little firsthand knowledge of slavery or the terror of the post-Reconstructionist South. In *Fatheralong*, Wideman expresses unease as he is being helped by a historian in South Carolina: "Hadn't the historian's career been one more mode of appropriation and exploitation of my father's bones, the pearls that were his eyes. Didn't the mastery of Abbeville's history, the power and privilege to tell my father's story, follow from the original sin of slavery that stole, then silenced, my father's voice?"[3]

The work of official historians is a site of contradiction and revision, according to Brian McHale in his study of postmodern fiction. McHale argues that historical fiction in the postmodern era is characterized by the violation of the "seam" between fiction and history and that postmodern historical fiction visibly contradicts the documented accounts by "redress[ing] the balance of the historical record of writing histories of the excluded, those regulated permanently to history's dark areas."[4] By exploding history's linear structure, its realistic conventions, and its claims of accuracy, postmodern fiction, especially what Linda Hutcheon calls "historiographic metafiction," questions the nature of history and historiography itself.[5]

Clearly, Wideman's purpose for the inclusion of history in this work is to "redress the balance," to ensure that all stories are told. Through the imbrication and interplay of autobiography, autoethnography, fiction, and history, he removes the hierarchical structure of genre that privileges historiography as authoritative, accurate, and scientific, and, therefore, more valid. This, too, is one of the purposes of postmodern historical fiction, according to McHale: "One of the thrusts of postmodernist revisionist history is to call into question the reliability of official history. The postmodernists fictionalize history, but by doing so they imply that history itself may be a form of fiction."[6]

Wideman's open-ended structure and hybridity emphasize that history is not linear or discrete. This is not, however, a style exclusive to postmodernists.

Indeed, Wideman suggests that it is a characteristic of African thought and culture: "My notion of history is not linear, but more like traditional, indigenous versions of history—African, American Indian, Asian—that see time as a great sea. Everything that has ever happened, all the people who have ever existed, simultaneously occupy this great sea. It fluctuates, and there are waves, and ripples."[7]

Balancing versions of reality is most important for a writer such as Wideman, who is interested in combating the stories told about his family and his race, stories that are accepted as history, yet provide very little accuracy or truth about African American life. As other postmodernists have done, Wideman sees the Enlightenment philosophy as a source for the privileging of the "master narratives" over oral culture, personal testimony, and fiction. One of those master narratives popularized in the eighteenth century is the scientific pamphlet. Numerous eighteenth-century treatises, such as Samuel Stanhop Smith's "Essay on the Causes of the Variety of Complexion and Figure in the Human Species," Richard Colfax's "Evidence against the Views of the Abolitionists, Consisting of Physical and Moral Proofs of the Natural Inferiority of the Negroes," and David Hume's "Of National Characters," to name just a few, were accepted as scientific observations of the African American character. Even Thomas Jefferson, who saw himself as a natural scientist, practiced this type of observation of African American biology and anthropology in his *Notes on the State of Virginia*.

The authority of such "qualified" scientists and their writing foregrounds the narrative and life of the unnamed protagonist in *The Cattle Killing*, who as an eighteenth-century former slave is victimized by these widely held "scientific" assumptions about the African mind and character. Wideman notes that Martin Bernal in *Black Athena*

> has traced the link between European theories of race and language. How nineteenth-century theories of language development parallel, buttress, and reinforce hierarchical concepts of race and culture. How social "sciences," the soft core posing as the hard core of academic humanities curricula, were tainted at their inception by racist assumptions and agendas.... How uncritical absorption of certain hallowed tenets of Western thought is like participating in your own lynching.

Wideman proposes that we have the power within us to make and live by our own stories and warns that the only way to survive is through the imagination, through story, by "carrying an alternative version of reality in our heads."[8]

According to Wideman, the view of African American life and culture found in the history books written in the past affects the present portrait. Wideman has indicated throughout his work that he does not observe time in a linear fashion. It is circular—where past, present, and future converge and exist simultaneously—so each time is interdependent on the other. *The Cattle Killing, Philadelphia Fire, Fatheralong,* and even *The Lynchers* especially reflect the "post-traumatic loop," a story repeated upon itself, returning always to the site or sites of trauma. In Wideman's aesthetic those sites reach further back than his immediate history, or even his mother's and father's history. They reach back to slavery, to the "birth of the nation's blues." Wideman has noted connections between his family and the slave past before—Tommy's incarceration, for example. Wideman also includes the story of Sybela Owens in "The Beginning of Homewood" and Orion in "Damballah." And the characters of *The Lynchers* directly discuss these links. These works in Wideman's canon, however, leave behind the mythic sustenance of Homewood to journey back to where it all began. Notably, all of the works mentioned above involve the character (and the writer) taking a journey—often leaving one home and traveling to another ancestral home or searching for a new one.

Wideman, in order to understand the present, must understand the past. He has said: "I think certain public events occur and they have lots of significance, and they are very important, they define powerful currents, they are events we shouldn't ignore, that we shouldn't forget, that we should try to make sense of."[9] Most of Wideman's work contains some moment out of the official record of history. In some cases these moments are brief: a name, a date, a place, within a passage about his mother, his brother, himself. Other instances develop a connection between a past event and a present, personal moment at length. One could argue that this dialogic relationship is the foundation of the novel *Philadelphia Fire*. Wideman's use of the MOVE bombing in 1985 becomes the lens by which he examines his own life, the forces that have imprisoned his son, and the relationship between son and father. Often, Wideman will juxtapose recorded events and the private lives of his characters, most notably, the yellow fever epidemic and the travels of the unnamed former slave/preacher/narrator in *The Cattle Killing*. Fiction, autobiography, and recorded history all intersect in this novel.

It is important to consider how Wideman has addressed recorded history before in his work as we consider *The Cattle Killing, Philadelphia Fire,* and *Fatheralong*. His analysis of historiography is evident when he is writing about Robby in *Brothers and Keepers*. *Brothers and Keepers* is characterized most strongly by its use of family history, but it also illuminates how Robby's and Wideman's private lives are governed by the forces of the past. While Wideman searches for the reasons from Robby's past that have led to his imprisonment, he discovers the limitations of traditional history and discards the linear, progressive model:

> You never know exactly when something begins. The more you delve, backtrack, and think, the clearer it becomes that nothing has a discrete, independent history; people and events take shape not in orderly, chronological sequence but in relation to other forces and events, tangled skeins of necessity and interdependence and chance that after all could have produced only one result: what is.[10]

In some cases Wideman considers how history has helped his brother and himself. He describes the structure of West African villages and their emphasis on community. Even in highlighting the connection between the lives of slaves and his own life, Wideman suggests that if he had known and understood his past, he could have overcome its hold over him:

> Knowledge of my racial past, of the worldwide struggle of people of color against the domination of Europeans, would have been invaluable. History could have been a tool, a support in the day-to-day confrontations I have experienced in the alien university environment. History could have taught me I was not alone, my situation was not unique.[11]

Wideman also acknowledges the darker side of history and its control over his and Robby's lives. He talks about the history of Pittsburgh, especially at the time when his grandfather, Harry Wideman, first arrived in 1910. Wideman describes the life of the African American community at the time, the Pittsburgh Steelers, and the effects of the steel industry on the growth and deterioration of lives in the city. He draws a portrait of Homewood between 1910 and 1930: its streets, music halls, boarding houses, and people. If you were too drunk to go home, there was always a place to stay.[12] If you were a lost child, the community took you in, looked after your welfare.[13]

Wideman's picture of the community is not only as an ethnographer here; he also practices historical cartography, drawing the history of the growth of streets and avenues—where they used to stop, where the railroad crosses, where the pavement now ends.[14] He chronicles his family's name and their neighbors', along with the names of streets and Pittsburgh history; but that's how it is done: "You heard things like that in Homewood names. Rules of etiquette, thumbnail character sketches, a history of the community."[15] Wideman represents the history of a community to provide a place that has always served as sacred ground to its inhabitants, despite its recent trials and deterioration. He also collects the lives and stories missed by the traditional historian.

However, Wideman's knowledge of history and his racial past—which he suggests would have helped him survive the pain of the present—is already there. That history has come to him through songs and family stories. Wideman is referring to the silence about African American and African life in the recorded history of America and Europe—what Wideman was reading and studying at the university. Wideman's remarks are about historiography and its privileged place within the culture as a monolithic and stable document. These written academic histories, the mainstream history, as well as his "father stories" are the silent spaces he is seeking to address.

When Wideman visits his brother, he remarks at the jail's place along the Ohio River, a place historically connected to freedom, not imprisonment. Wideman recounts the history of the jail and its ancestors: "Western is a direct descendant of the world's first penitentiary, Philadelphia's Quaker-inspired Walnut Street Jail, chartered in 1773."[16] He develops the history of the prison at length, equating historiography with imprisonment. The way historians have catalogued African American life becomes a metaphor for slavery and the prison.[17]

Despite the "good intentions" of rehabilitating rather than torturing prisoners, Walnut Street Jail was not exempt "from the ills that beset all societies of caged men. Walnut Street Jail became a cesspool, overcrowded, impossible to maintain, wracked by violence, disease, and corruption."[18] Wideman equates the problems of this jail with the present one that has been accused of similar trespasses. Nothing has changed. He also includes numerous statistics on prisons in America, Supreme Court cases regarding prisoner's rights, and the media coverage and attitude toward jails; all of this is layered with the family stories and with Robby's story in an attempt to rescue Wideman's family and brother from being just another statistic, another limited portrait of African American life.

Wideman visits the problems of the Walnut Street Jail again in the short story "Ascent by Balloon from the Walnut Street Jail." An African American who accompanied Jean Pierre Blanchard on the first hydrogen balloon flight in 1793 narrates the tale. This event also appears within a letter in *The Cattle Killing*. "Ascent by Balloon from the Walnut Street Jail" opens with a newspaper announcement of the flight. The newspaper mentions the duration of the flight, where it began, where it landed, and the fact that George Washington was in attendance, but nowhere is Blanchard's companion mentioned. He is a forgotten pioneer. We discover that he was also a prisoner at the Walnut Street Jail, where the balloon took off. He is also anonymous in the historical records of this jail and of the Cherry Hill Jail, where he was later transferred. He was little more than a number:

> I'd been transferred from Walnut Street Jail to the new prison at Cherry Hill. There, too, I would have the distinction of being the first of my race,

> Prisoner Number One. Charles Williams: *farmer, light black; black eyes; curly black hair; 5′ 7 1/2″; foot, 11″; flat nose, scar on bridge of nose; broad mouth; scar from dirk on thigh; can read.*[19]

Williams is characterized in terms that echo descriptions of slaves on the auction block, yet he is a "free" man (his freedom is further emphasized by the fact that he has flown above the ground). But he is still a prisoner, literally, and figuratively, because he cannot escape his blackness. Other people, journalists, wardens, and social scientists (DeBeauchamp and DeTocqueville visit him at Walnut Street to see if the "experiment" is working), tell his story. Williams's need in this piece of fiction is to tell his own tale about the balloon, about the torture at Walnut Street Jail, but he keeps getting events and time confused. His story and history are not linear, and he apologizes for "muddling time": "No. Beg pardon. I am confusing one time with another. Events lose their shape, slide into one another when the time one is supposed to own becomes another man's property."[20] His traumatic experiences have resulted in a post-traumatic shaping of time and events.

Williams is treated as property, whether he's a prisoner or the participant in the launch. He is a "guinea pig" in both instances, expendable. He remarks on the decision to have him on board the balloon with irony:

> Dr. Benjamin Rush, a man of science as well as a philanthropic soul, well known for his championing the cause of a separate Negro church, had requested that a pulse glass be carried on the balloon, and thus again, became a benefactor of the race, since who better than one of us, with excitable blood and tropically lush hearts, to serve as a guinea pig.[21]

Despite his position in the experiment, Williams finds his own victory in the moment: "Born of a despised race, wallowing in sin as a youth, then a prisoner in a cage, yet I rose, I rose."[22] Williams "muddles" the balloon ride with a day at the prison, creating a slippage that allows these two disparate moments in his life to connect and converse. This dialogic passage invites the reader to see that, despite Williams's ascension into the sky, time and history conspire to keep him imprisoned; he cannot escape the prejudice that exists below. The traumas he has experienced as a black man in eighteenth-century America and his time as a prisoner cage him in a post-traumatic experience to the extent that he confuses the present with the period of the original moments of his past pain.

As this passage begins, Williams is above in the balloon looking down at the Walnut Street prison yard when, simultaneously, he emerges from his cell:

> My eyes adjusted to the glare and there it was, finally the balloon hovering motionless, waiting for someone it seemed, a giant, untethered fist thrust triumphantly at the sky. From the moment it appears, I am sure no mere coincidence has caused the balloon to rise during the minute and half outdoors I am allotted daily to cross the prison yard, grab tools, supplies and return to my cell. If Citizen Blanchard's historic flight had commenced a few seconds sooner or later that morning, I would have missed it. Imagine. I could have lived a different life. Instead of being outdoors glancing up at the heavens, I could have been in my cell pounding on the intractable leather they apportion me for cobbling my ten pairs of shoes a week. In that solitary darkness tap-tap tapping, I wouldn't have seen the striped, floating sphere come to fetch me and carry me home.[23]

The passage is reminiscent of stories from African American folklore where slaves are taught the secret of flight so that they can fly back home to Africa. In the story, recorded history does not take precedence. Factual reality and imagined reality both exist. His imagination sustains him through these experiences. The story itself and this passage in particular show the burden of historical events and the power of the imagination to re-envision them. Is this story true? We may never know for certain. But by allowing for the possibility of truth, Wideman has filled a gap in history that speaks for all the unknown true stories that will never be heard.

The balloon launch appears in this short story and in *The Cattle Killing*, while the yellow fever epidemic that is the center of "Fever" and *The Cattle Killing* is alluded to in "Ascent by Balloon from the Walnut Street Jail" as well. This repetition and revision is yet another example of Wideman's layering of doubled or multiple versions of a story within his larger narrative. Whether or not these stories are true is not an issue finally. Their repetition creates a collective force of history. The stories feel true because we have heard them before; they confirm one another—which one could argue gives history its feeling of veracity. If you repeat a story enough, there will be some who will accept it as authoritative.[24]

Wideman first examined the yellow fever epidemic in his short story "Fever." When asked why he returned to it again in *The Cattle Killing*, Wideman answered that he hadn't "figured out all the things that the plague might mean."[25] Wideman says that both of these works "attempt to bridge, to synthesize past, present, and future sources of this fever, which to me clearly is the unresolved question of slavery, the unresolved question of racism, the unresolved question of majority rule that leads to majority domination and oppression."[26] In both works, Wideman layers the past, present, and future in order to see the necessary connections between them: "It struck me that, boy, we need to understand what happened then if we're going to begin to try to understand what's happening now." Wideman sees *The Cattle Killing* as a historical novel despite its lapses into the present, and he understands that the fictitious moments create a problem with the work being accepted as history: "The historical incidents that take place in *The Cattle Killing* and the impressionistic cuts into contemporary culture, as far as I am concerned, are absolutely documented, on record, and are powerful elements in history and present life. I am a reporter in that sense."[27] Wideman journeys back to the site of the epidemic and to slavery to understand the problems of today.

The novel's hybrid nature makes it difficult to categorize and, perhaps, to navigate as a reader. One critic queried: "Is this a story of a heroic quest? Is it a detective story with multiple solutions? You're better off recognizing that you inhabit a dreamscape where belief itself—in God, in science, even in imagination—is constantly challenged."[28] The work does not fit neatly into any prose genre and, in fact, questions such distinctions. The story of this preacher and his experience should be as valid as any history of this period. Very few firsthand accounts of African American life in the eighteenth century exist; Wideman is trying to fill one of these silent spaces.

Wideman populates the terrain of the novel with verifiable, historical figures such as George Whitefield, George Washington, and Phyllis Wheatley. These figures provide the atmosphere of the novel, validating the world that the unnamed slave/narrator/preacher inhabits. Other historical figures are active participants in the work: Richard Allen, Benjamin Rush (the doctor who treated many of the victims of the epidemic, though he is called Dr. Thrush here), and the artist George Stubbs. These historical figures and characters serve a more important purpose in the terms of the novel's content and structure. They test our notion of what we accept as history and truth. If finally we acknowledge that the stories that have been written about these historical figures are accurate, aren't we also obligated to accept the veracity of the stories of the unnamed preacher, Kate, Liam, and his wife?

The novel begins not in the past, but in the present, where a writer is on his way to give the manuscript of his new book to his father. Even here at the beginning of the work, Wideman's concern with the need to share stories is emphasized. The writer tells us that he is also reading at a literary conference. This act of sharing will be repeated at the end of the novel when the same writer's son writes a letter to his father about the new novel that his father has just sent him to read. The son is a historian; his father, a fiction writer; and the story of the unnamed preacher is framed by their voices. The bookends of the novel reflect the balancing act that Wideman embraces in his aesthetic: the end does not clarify whether the work is fiction or history, and through the genealogical relationship of the historian and the novelist, we can infer that both discourses are related. The historian son tells the father that he has found documents that suggest that the unnamed preacher's lost brother wound up back in Africa. But if the brother is supposedly a fictional character, how can a historian find letters that verify his existence? There is no resolution offered; fiction and history are equally valid, and each authorizes the other. The structure of the frame reflects Wideman's content and his themes. As well, Wideman suggested in an interview before the publication of the novel that the Cudjoe of *Philadelphia Fire* (a writer) and the Cudjoe of *Reuben* (a small boy in the context of that work) would meet in his next novel, *The Cattle Killing*.[29] Are the father and son here their doubles? Are they the doubles of Wideman and one of his sons?

It is noteworthy that the era in which this novel is set is also the period in which many of our ideas about historical and scientific writing were formed. It is also the time that saw the development of the novel as a genre. The split between the discourses has its roots here. *The Cattle Killing* returns to the same questions about art and the imagination that were explored by such eighteenth-century English novelists as Henry Fielding, Samuel Richardson, and Laurence Sterne. Mrs. Thrush writes in her journal that she is reading *Pamela* and that the digressions of the unnamed preacher when he tells his story are worthy of *Tristram Shandy*.[30] The unnamed preacher is also reminiscent of the picaresque characters popular in eighteenth-century fiction. Eighteenth-century slave narratives, such as those written by Olaudah Equiano and, to an extent, Briton Hammon, were influenced by the picaresque.

The unnamed preacher is unlike the typical *picaro* character, however. The picaro within the tradition is an isolated figure. The preacher's identity is defined by his relationships with others, especially the African spirit that inhabits many lives in the novel. The emphasis on the community and the race is evident here, even in a book that does not center on Homewood or the Lawson family. His adventures as a picaro include his residence with an interracial couple, the Stubbses (living under assumed names) and his encounters with parish churches. His most remarkable adventure is his meeting with a mysterious African who drowns herself in front of his eyes. She represents all of the African women in the novel and the African girl whose vision caused her people, the Xhosa, to kill their cattle (the "cattle killing" of the title) and, in doing so, destroy their way of life and themselves.

It is not a coincidence that *The Cattle Killing* has at its center a picaro character,[31] that sections are epistolary in nature, and that, as a whole, it is a mix of journal entries, the picaresque, medical discourse, and conversion narrative—all genres and/or characteristics of eighteenth-century writing. The novel also layers within the literary documents and reportage the historical documents of the era and of the actual cattle killing in South Africa. Wideman studied the eighteenth-century novel at Oxford, and he is alluding to these works of this era for specific reasons; these early novels tackle some of the same concerns that their twentieth-century counterparts do. Specifically, Wideman's work questions scientific knowledge (especially as it is applied to the writing of history) and challenges the linear and fixed quality of history. *Tristam Shandy* also examines historical knowledge, and its structure represents its examination of such processes through self-reference and fluid timelines.

Wideman enters into the British eighteenth-century tradition, uses its language and techniques, and signifies on it by disrupting its linear progression and by weaving together its seemingly disparate genres. As one critic has pointed out, postmodernist novels owe a great deal to eighteenth-century works and their characteristic mixing of fact and fiction.[32] The eighteenth century is the date of the "birth of a nation," the moment of the original trauma of institutionalized slavery, condoned by the same people crying for freedom and human rights while denying those rights and humanity to African Americans.[33] The post-traumatic narrative is born out of the "disparity between the Enlightenment ideal and social practices" in our "democratic ideal that still haunts us today."[34]

Wideman has called *The Cattle Killing* a

> parable about texts. It's a parable about actual life, the fictional life, invented lives—about fathers and sons who invent lives for one another, generations who invent lives for their ancestors. All that comes into play. It's also a kind of carnival of texts—of letters, novels, reminiscences, research, historical documents—and how those interact and click together at certain times for readers, writers.[35]

The fiction writer (Wideman? Wideman as character? Another writer?) in the introduction suggests himself that this is what characterizes the work (the work that we know as *The Cattle Killing*). He cautions us that this new novel is composed of stories that are "not quite stories. True and not true (check out the facts, dates, murders). Not exactly a novel. Hybrid like this new ground under your feet as you pound up Wylie."[36] The writer offers us a legend to follow the work he is about to present. We are even told, if we are interested, to "check the facts." The metafictional voice challenges us to find out for ourselves, to learn a little history in the process, and informs us that the point is not to deliver the same story, but to recover little-known moments from history and revise our perceptions of African American life in the past. Wideman is showing us in

The Cattle Killing, and elsewhere, the possibilities beyond the stories we already know or think we know.

The writer in the introduction also intimates at the connections between the past and the present (and their meaning for their future). A news story in the morning paper has made him think about the story he has written:

> *The boy shot dead on the hill last night. His ancient African lad meeting his brethren as he thinks the meeting, as he unleashes himself from his time, this moment beginning the climb to his father. What is the name of the space they now. All of them. The black boy always fifteen, the two boys freshly dying, the long-gone African, his father.*[37]

Wideman connects and layers different times and histories in this single passage. This temporal density will occur in other passages of the novel when a preacher talks about the fever, his life, the imprisonment of Mandela, and the memorial for the victims of the MOVE bombing. Wideman will later trace these different moments in time to the Xhosa's killing of their cattle, filtered through the African spirit whose description opens the story of the preacher and the yellow fever. The novel also moves back and forth between and within its own time, which the narrator himself realizes when he explains to the woman listening to his stories that his tales sometimes get ahead of themselves and that sometimes his stories "jump around." The listener tells him, "I thought all stories go backward." And the narrator replies:, "Backward to go forward. Forward to go back."[38] This discussion in the novel describes Wideman's own discursive style.

Wideman "goes backward" into history to explain the problems of his present, a characteristic of the post-traumatic narrative as well as much historical fiction. Throughout the novel, he connects the fever of 1793 with his own time, comparing it to the violence and racism of today. In an interview, he links the yellow fever, which during the epidemic was believed to have been brought to this country by escaped Haitian slaves, with other plagues of our time:

> Now the plague that is besieging the city is AIDS. If you think about it, in the popular imagination, who's blamed for AIDS? Where did AIDS come from? It came from Africa. It came from black people, people of African descent.... [I]n terms of science the way that it was perceived in the public imagination was not as a microbe, but as one more menace that the black body contained.[39]

The yellow fever epidemic is a historical fact; numbers and dates can be verified. The fever hit Philadelphia in July 1793. Within a month it had reached epidemic proportions. Thousands of prominent citizens fled the city and took refuge in the countryside, leaving the fever to devour the less fortunate. The epidemic began to subside at the end of October with the arrival of cooler temperatures. But by then nearly twenty thousand whites, along with representatives of the national and state governments, had left Philadelphia. The fever had claimed more than one-third of the city's population, and it is still considered the worst epidemic in United States history.[40]

Buried within the official record are the lesser known histories of Richard Allen and Absalom Jones, the founders of the Free Africa Society and the A.M.E. Zion Church, who at the behest of Dr. Benjamin Rush helped wage a war against the fever. They became, along with their followers, the "most heroic figures of the plague year."[41] Though there are very few histories about their actions during the plague, Allen and Jones volunteered the services of themselves and their followers to nurse the sick and bury the dead. They were assured by Rush that descendants of African blood were immune from the disease (presumably because there had not been any African Americans afflicted in the early weeks).[42] They bled patients by day and drove carts to the cemetery by night.

Allen and Jones, both preachers, had founded the Free Africa Society in 1787 when they were forced out of St. George's (even though Jones had preached there). Rush had supported them in their decision to establish their own church. Despite the prejudice they had faced in the community, they saw their help during the epidemic as a

> God-sent opportunity to prove their courage and worth and to show that they could drive anger and bitterness from their hearts. Perhaps they could dissolve white racism by demonstrating that in their capabilities, civic virtue, and Christian humanitarianism they were not inferior, but in fact superior to those who regarded former slaves as degraded, hopelessly backward people.[43]

Allen and Jones also had prisoners released from Walnut Street Jail to serve as nurses, though we are told by Williams in "Ascent by Balloon from Walnut Street Jail" that he was not one of those released. Unfortunately, Rush was not correct in his assessment of the African's immunity to the fever, and soon the nurses and grave diggers were dying more quickly than their charges. Allen became sick himself.

When the epidemic subsided, however, Allen and his followers were not viewed as heroes. Matthew Carey's pamphlet "A Short Account of the Malignant Fever" accused African Americans, such as Allen and Jones, as profiting from the disease. Many did profit: "Rates offered for nurses and attendants, black or white, were exorbitant, and the Negroes were blamed for it.... Many blamed them for carrying contagion, or preying upon the diseased."[44] Stories began to circulate that Haitian slaves from a French ship brought the fever with them. There was no scientific evidence, but the stories inflamed the tensions between the white and black population, and Carey's pamphlet only fueled the fire. Yet few questioned the fact that Carey had himself fled the city during the epidemic and that his pamphlet went through four editions in a month, providing "a lesson in deriving profit from mass misery."[45] Allen and Jones refuted this public account with their own pamphlet, where they described the acts of heroism performed by African Americans.[46] Like Wideman, they wrote to produce a counternarrative to the one being accepted by the young American nation.

Despite numerous stories of African American sacrifice and heroism, their pamphlet sold poorly and tensions between whites (mostly immigrants) and African Americans in the city still rose, leading to several altercations. In *The Cattle Killing*, angry whites burned down the African American orphanage, where children of the fever victims were living. While this does not seem to be a "historical" account, it does reflect the tenor of hostilities at the time. As Wideman suggests in *The Cattle Killing*, that tension, "the fever," continues to reverberate. These children, like the young men at the beginning of the novel, are the casualties of this traumatic racial past.

Wideman uses the fever to examine the racial tensions of the past that continue to haunt us today. He outlines this relationship before the publication of *The Cattle Killing*:

> Like Antonin Artaud, I think that societies, in some metaphysical sense, create the diseases that they need and that those diseases are metaphors for the basic problems of those societies. It is no coincidence that the yellow fever epidemic, described by many at the time as the end of the world, was allegedly brought to the Americas by slaves from the West Indies. We need to stop the wheel and look at things again, try to understand what they mean.[47]

The "fever" is the same despair, violence, and self-loathing that accompany the long history of racism in this country; it is a manifestation of the cultural post-traumatic illness.[48]

Wideman's preacher sees manifestations of the fever wherever he travels in the novel. Once a slave, the preacher is freed, but soon his mother dies and his brother disappears. He has no home, no place to return to. Following these events, he experiences a religious conversion. Conversion narratives, popular in eighteenth-century America, are another discourse that Wideman layers in this novel. Conversion was important to the slave narrator as well, as we can see, for example, in Olaudah Equiano's narrative.[49] The preacher decides at this time to travel the country and spread the word; he is not the typical picaro or quest hero.

He spends a significant amount of time at the farm of Liam and his "wife." The couple masquerade as Mrs. Stubbs and her slave to keep their true (and illegal) relationship a secret. Liam has been an isolated figure because of the nature of his existence, saying that they have been "forced to quarantine" themselves. Liam is further isolated by his position as an artist who is not allowed to pursue his art. Liam's word choice reflects the metaphor of fever as racism. Racism and the fear of miscegenation keep Liam and Mrs. Stubbs separate from the rest of the community. They cannot have children or their secret will be revealed. If they don't remain separate, they could lose their lives (as they do later in the novel).

Liam connects to the preacher by sharing his history, and the preacher gains a deeper understanding of his own past through Liam's stories. Liam sees that he needed the preacher to talk to, someone who could share similar experiences and feelings, another like himself: "I didn't know how deeply I missed another like myself beside me until you arrived. So many stories to tell. Too much bitter silence for too many years. Too much lost. I couldn't begin to talk, son, till I learned you were willing to listen."[50] Liam tells the preacher about his time as a slave and as a servant of Mr. Stubbs (the name Liam's wife has taken to hide their identity), who owned and supervised a slaughterhouse.

Stubbs orders Liam to attend to his son, George, an artist (a historical figure) interested in anatomical drawing. George Stubbs learns about anatomy by observing births, deaths, and dissections. His fascination sometimes leads him to criminal activities as he is forced to use whatever means necessary to find proper specimens for his study. Liam is often dragged along with him to these haunts. On one such occasion Stubbs and Liam are brought to the body of a young African woman who had been pregnant. As Stubbs and the other white men in the room (mostly doctors) view the body, Liam realizes that Stubbs and his father actually share a similar occupation—both trade in flesh. Stubbs, the father, slaughters cattle, and his son sees people, particularly African Americans, as no more than animals. George Stubbs joins the group of eighteenth-century scientists, mentioned earlier, in reinforcing racist assumptions through their ideology. The dead African girl is sold, even in death, to the highest bidder. And the doctors debate, in front of Liam, if such "creatures" feel pain. The question of the "feelings" and "human" qualities of people of African descent was a popular pamphlet topic, as evidenced above, and it continued well into the twentieth-century, as evidenced by the numerous accounts of African Americans used in medical experimentation.

This scene brings into question not only the science of the times, but also its art and imagination. George Stubbs is an artist, as is Liam, we are told, but it is Stubbs's art that is valued by society; his position as artist is solidified in the tradition of Western culture. And his contributions are historically recorded. But at what price does this art come? Wideman intimates that it is at the same price of most Western art and culture, as it placed itself above all others, through blood, violence, and death. The imagination of the culture, as Wideman points out in his earlier reference to the *Black Athena*, reified racist ideology more often than it questioned it or sought to change it.

It is when he is staying with Liam that the preacher joins the congregation of Radnor, the small village near Liam's farm. On one occasion, the preacher has one of his visions. The vision reinforces the temporal density of the novel and is expressed in different narrative voices: a third person and a first person. During the vision, he loses a sense of himself; he joins in the "Great Sea of Time":

> This world and a multitude of others whose existence had been hidden until the walls of the church fell away and he found himself seated at the center of a disc upon which the universe was shrunken and arrayed. Nay, not shrunken. There was no diminishment of scale or distance. Better its immensity rendered available. The miracle was that near and far had become interchangeable. Things close at hand, things separated from him by a continent, were blended. One. He roamed everywhere at once.[51]

The preacher's vision could describe the structure of *The Cattle Killing* itself. The preacher enters into the fabric of time, where past, present, and future intersect, revealing their interdependence in a way that is not progressive but interrelational: "In the clearing I witnessed two worlds crossing. One for people like us, who worshiped at St. Matthews. The other a thoroughfare frequented by ancestors, our generations yet to be born."[52]

The vision of the crossroads connects the unnamed preacher to the past and future, and it draws him closer to his present community, particularly, a young woman who is the next embodiment of the African spirit haunting him and who may also be Dr. Thrush's servant, Kate. The preacher sees his life echoed in other lives: "He was all the others. They were thinking with his thoughts. Their thoughts were his. He lived uncountable lives. Breathed for all of them, dying, and being born so quickly life never started or ended. It flowed. One continuous sweet breath."[53] Not only does this moment unite the unnamed preacher to his community, it places him in the "Great Sea of Time" and reminds us that all the possible lives he's living and not living, those known and unknown, are true. His wish to share his vision and the voices he hears link him to the African American artist and their necessity to connect to the past.[54]

We have seen the image of the crossroads before in Wideman's work and its relationship to African cosmology and to the Haitian god Damballah (the title of the first installment of the Homewood trilogy).[55] The image of the crossroads also appears in *Fatheralong*. Its frequency in Wideman's work not only reflects multidirectionality, but also indicates the collapse of linear time and, subsequently, history. In these places of the novel, the style not only suggests a post-traumatic loop or cycle, but reflects the possible stories of African American life conversing. It provides a separate, mythic space for the African American storyteller to re-imagine the world.[56]

The preacher believes it is during his vision that he first meets the mysterious African girl who is the embodiment of all the African women in the text, including Kate. As the quote at the beginning of the section indicates, "certain African spirits" inhabit many different bodies, and the preacher is certain that the women he encounters in the novel are all one woman. The spirit has many doubles in the novel, many possible lives, including the African girl who called for "the cattle killing," the woman who drowns herself in front of him, the woman at the church, and also Kate. A young, African woman helped him the day of his vision (Kate? Or just another version of the spirit?), tending to his fevered state. The preacher believes that she was from the other side of the crossroads and that by stopping to help him she got caught in his time. He reminds Kate of this meeting when he tells her stories: "Let me relate to you our first meeting, itself also, strangely a return. To memory, possibility, life. As all stories are."[57] All possible versions of this woman are true.

The first encounter with the African spirit (called an *ogbanji*) links the protagonist to his traumatic past. Before the woman drowns herself, she walks in the forest with the narrator and the dead child she is carrying. As they journey through the woods

> he recalls the sound of heavy footfalls, panting, piles of leaves exploding, crackling branches. They were escaping together, a family on the run. Men on horseback with baying hounds pursuing them. They must plunge deeper into the forest, slip into the briars and tangled undergrowth where horses can't follow, splash through marsh and swamp so the slobber-jowled dogs will lose their scent.[58]

However, they are not being chased. The preacher's imagination fixes on the moment as an echo of past slaves' escapes through the wilderness, a post-traumatic repetition of racial trauma. This was not his own individual experience. His meeting with the woman, and hence his relationship with the spirit she represents, connects him to this vision of racial memory.

He tells Kate (when she is ill) of this encounter with one of her "selves," the young woman who drowned herself. When he hears stories of a young African girl who sounds like the one he met along the road, he believes each of them, no matter how differently they describe the circumstances of the girl's existence, because it is his "way of reckoning learned from old African people, who said all stories are true."[59] The unnamed preacher spends much of his time in the novel in search of this woman, trying to find her, looking for clues of her existence, much like a detective might. This woman's appearance in different places, in different times, and in different bodies connects the events in the novel across time and space, revealing that not only are all these stories possible, but they are all part of a larger narrative.

One manifestation of the girl might actually go back further in time and farther away in space. In the novel, all the spirit's selves exist simultaneously despite any physical distances. This same spirit could be the girl who prophesies the cattle killing. The preacher hears the girl, Nonggawuse, speak to him in a vision. She tells him the story of the cattle killing and her part in the false prophecy that destroyed her people. She warns him to be alert to lies: "Beware. Beware. Do not kill your cattle. Do not speak with your enemy's tongue. Do not fall asleep in your enemy's dream."[60] Prophecy weaves its way throughout the tapestry of the novel. The writer tells us in the introduction that he is called "eye" or Isaiah. A quote from Ezekiel opens part 2, and the preacher is plagued with visions. Even Mrs. Thrush's blindness alludes to those prophets in history and literature who possessed second sight yet could not see.

It is the prophecy of the cattle killing that is one of the defining moments of the novel. The writer alludes to this prophecy in the beginning of the work when he warns that people are listening to new prophesies, believing in new lies. The prophecy of the cattle killing is a metaphor, not only in this novel, but for all of Wideman's work. It is those stories which perpetuate a vision of African American lives that is "false" that must be revised, dismantled, balanced by new stories and by new visions, otherwise the fate of the Xhosa, the destruction of their lives and their culture, will be the fate of all children of Africa. Wideman layers every event in the novel with the cattle killing and with the present self-destructive attitudes and actions embodied in the shooting death of the fifteen-year-old at the beginning of the novel: "Shoot. Chute. Black boys shoot each other. Murder themselves. Shoot. Chute. Panicked cattle funneled down the killing chute."[61]

The past and the present are threatening the future of children, of the race. The novel opens with the image of more lost children. Wideman makes this connection explicitly: "If you believe the lies of your enemies, this is a sure path of self-destruction. If you internalize those lies, you're on the way out. It's analogous to the 'cattle killing' that's going on now."[62] We see this "cattle killing" in other works of Wideman as well; characters in such works as *A Glance Away*, *The Lynchers*, *Sent for You Yesterday*, and *Brothers and Keepers* have believed "the lies of their enemies."

The Xhosa's self-destructive act has been described as "probably the greatest self-inflicted immolation of a people in all history."[63] And yet this tragic story is not a well-known tale. Its choice as the controlling metaphor in the novel indicates that it is not just the uplifting, sustaining, and heroic stories of African American life that must be recovered. Wideman suggests that the traumatic past must be revisited in order for any healing to begin; by

> recalling the horrors of African American history, accepting the challenges our history presently places on us, [it is] like acknowledging a difficult, unpleasant duty or debt that's been hanging over our heads a very long time, an obligation that we know in our hearts we must deal with but that we keep putting off and evading, as if one day procrastination will make the burden, the obligation we must undertake, disappear.[64]

The story of the cattle killing is certainly one of the most difficult to recall and accept.[65] The Xhosa had weathered the incursion of white settlers, the loss of grazing land, and the introduction of Christianity. They had managed to survive all of these events where others had failed. But in April or May 1856, Nonggawuse, the niece of a Xhosa holy man, saw two ancestral spirits that instructed her to tell the people to kill their cattle, promising a new world free of white invaders and disease. This event happens chronologically more than sixty years after the yellow fever epidemic, yet it seems to predate the fever in the novel. Wideman is transgressing linear time to emphasize the crossroad-like connections that exist outside of time and space. This violation of linear time also illustrates the persistence, throughout history, of what destruction follows when you believe false prophecies and the false stories others tell about you. The relationship between historical events and the fluid time remind us once again of Wideman's use of circles; all events exist at the same time and place on a circle—there is no chronological connection, no "point" in time.

This is made clearer when the preacher connects through time to the Xhosa and Nonggawuse while he is drifting asleep in an open field:

Beneath that African sky I tried to will my body to rise, rise closer to the energy uncoiling from the stars, the circles within circles within circles nearly reaching me, almost audible. If my body would take me just a lit bit higher, I'd hear the song, become a part of it, the stars that blackness over my head.[66]

Wideman has also used the image of the circle to show connection, to question the linear progression of time and history. There are other instances in the novel where time moves in a circular motion. The present often flows into this story of the past. As we have already seen in the Homewood books, the names of Mandela and Mumia Abu-Jamal are intoned alongside the Xhosa of Africa and the victims of violence and racism in 1793. This temporal density illustrates the past and present continually merging. The racial violence found throughout the years of the epidemic and in the preacher's account is connected to the young men dying in the present time of the novel, seen in the prologue.

The preacher sees his own time and the treatment of African Americans as a cyclical event—linked through time and space to the Xhosa, to the *ogbanji*, and to Nonggawuse. Nonggawuse's uncle, Mahlakaza, had taken Anglican Communion and was known to have revered much of the Bible. He accepted what his niece had seen, despite the fact that the Xhosa did not believe in "secret communication." The consequence of accepting his niece's prophecy was civil dissension. The Xhosa divided themselves into believers and non-believers. Violence erupted between the two groups; Xhosa began destroying their own land and each other. The controversy tore at the fabric of Xhosa society. That "life itself was inextricably bound up with their cattle was expressed by a Xhosa saying, *Inkomo luhlanga zifile luyakufa uhlannga*, cattle are the race, they being dead the race dies."[67]

As the cattle herds began to diminish, Xhosa social structure began to deteriorate. Men no longer had enough cattle to exchange for wives; marriage and polygamy were threatened. This in turn affected kinship rites and the fealty to the chiefs. Planting and harvesting dropped off. Xhosa began to leave their homeland and were forced to work as cheap labor in the colonies. Most of the English colonists refused to help; either they believed that the prophecy was a Russian plot (the cattle killing took place during the Crimean War), or they were forced by laws forbidding private charity to turn away starving and sick Xhosa. Starving Xhosa, depleted in numbers by famine, disease, and the exodus, were finally moved off their homeland by the British and indentured to colonial farmers. Mahlakaza died of starvation, and by the end of 1858, the entire Xhosa nation was either dispersed, displaced, or dead.[68]

The apocalyptic tone of both the Xhosa story and the accounts of the yellow fever epidemic reverberates out from the novel's opening pages. We begin in the present during a time when the young people are killing themselves, killing each other, listening to "false prophecies." Wideman's bleak outlook throughout most of this novel (as well as in *Philadelphia Fire*) signals the post-traumatic culture of America toward the end of the century. Even before the events of September 11, 2001, Americans were absorbed in end-of-the-world rhetoric, as most Western cultures have been in the past two thousand years whenever a century is about to change—what Wideman refers to earlier in the novel as the "prophets of Kool-Aid." Reflecting on the Xhosa prophecy and apocalypse and looking out onto a present landscape of violence, death, and despair, Wideman's work illustrates that the world is out of joint, the future is in question, a day of judgment is approaching. The tone of *The Cattle Killing*, *Philadelphia Fire* and, to some extent, even *Fatheralong* is apocalyptic; and the narratives in each focus on the ends of history. Bombings, fevers, fires, murders, plagues, the loss of sons—all signal an imminent, even biblical Armageddon. These works together not only suggest a fear that the world is getting worse, but negotiate the "desire for the world to end and the desire for the world to be as it should be." Writing about these types of narratives, scholar James Berger reveals:

> The wish to end the world, or to represent the end of the world, arises in each case from more particular social and political discomforts and aspirations. In the wake of some catastrophe, the apocalyptic writer creates a greater and conclusive catastrophe. Surely, he thinks, the world cannot—and should not have survived such destabilization and horror. And it has. The world, intolerably, continues. But it should, it must end.[69]

Berger states as well that even at the end of the world, stories continue. Wideman's characters continue to share stories throughout the epidemic, after the bombing, after traumatic loss; and even when they are not capable of doing so, the attempt is still made to understand, to narrate, to speak. The Xhosa girl, even after the end of her world, has come across time and space to tell her story.

The writer at the beginning of the novel believes that the story of the Xhosa can save the world, if people listen to their tale:

> Love song once. Then a dirge. The image haunts him. Xhosa killing their cattle, killing themselves, a world coming apart. A brave elegant people who had resisted European invaders until an evil prophecy convinced

them to kill their cattle, butcher the animals that fleshed the Xhosa's intricate *dreaming of themselves.*[70]

Because the Xhosa believed false prophecies, they tried to "become something else, something they could never be."[71] Wideman also connects the cattle of the Xhosa to the slaughterhouse that Liam once worked in. Mr. Stubbs and his son both are peddlers of flesh (whether they are buying and selling cattle or dead women); the allusion to slavery is clear. They, and their society, have also benefited from the bodies, lives, and deaths of Africans, just as British colonists benefited from the new land that was available for consumption after the Xhosa died or were moved off. Those Xhosa who lived and remained provided cheap labor on the land that once belonged to them. The cattle were an integral part of Xhosa life, and, as such, the animals were well-respected. The linkage between the Xhosa herds, the slaughterhouse, and the dissection of the African woman shows the disintegration of the Africans' image in the European consciousness from men and women who owned cattle to those who became treated as if they were cattle.

This is illustrated further when an African American male is selected to be an experimental animal (the "guinea pig") in the first hydrogen balloon launching. The launch is shown here in *The Cattle Killing* as well as in "Ascent by Balloon from the Walnut Street Jail." Dr. Thrush's (Rush) letter notes the African American's presence on the balloon, but he does not name him. Thrush (Rush) also confirms that the man is there only because of the experiment. He does not see the irony of his own following statement: "I believe this balloon and other ingenious inventions open boundless prospects for our new nation in the coming century."[72] The nation will indeed prosper, built on the lives of men like the unnamed African American on board the balloon. Countless, nameless African Americans will serve as the raw material in the construction of the new republic. As well, the coming century will only bring more of the racial tension that spurred Carey's pamphlet. The City of Brotherly Love has proven to be anything but that. Throughout the city's history, racial tension and violence will continue to trouble its legacy. Liam and his wife, along with the African American community of Radnor (outside of Philadelphia), are destroyed by a fire set by white neighbors. While this is a "fictional" event, the essence of it rings throughout the record of racial violence in America. It is the trauma of that violence that Wideman writes into the historical record by revisiting and re-imagining these events.

Even in the years directly following the epidemic, racial violence was a common occurrence in Philadelphia. In 1825, two white men started a fire in Allen's church that killed two people. In 1834, the Flying Horse Riot marked a two-day assault on African Americans. The houses in a neighborhood of middle-class blacks were burned down in 1835. Another church was burned because white Philadelphians were disturbed by the "noise of emotional religious services."[73] In May 1838, the newly opened Pennsylvania Hall was assaulted during an Abolitionist Rally by over a thousand rioters who burned the building down. Rioters also stormed an orphanage for African American children. In 1850, African Americans were mobbed during a Fourth of July celebration, an event that will appear in the final pages of Wideman's *Philadelphia Fire*.[74]

In recent years, Philadelphia has had to weather the civil rights violations of Mayor Frank Rizzo's administration and the MOVE bombing in 1985 (which is the focus of *Philadelphia Fire*). The MOVE bombing is hinted at in *The Cattle Killing* as well, along with the imprisonment of Mumia Abu-Jamal (another violation of the linear historical record). The preacher looks forward through time to these events that show him that the fever will continue to infect the future. It is revealed to him in the course of the novel that the epidemic is only one of the many plagues that have scoured (and will scour) the city in the past, present, and future:

> I found in that city of brotherly love the country of sickness and dying the African woman's dream foretold. And Philadelphia was a prophecy of other cities to come, as my stay in the village of Radnor had been prophecy and fulfillment of the city. Circles within circles . . . a circle without and within, the monstrous python swallowing itself, birthing its tail.[75]

This image of eternity presented here is not the vital and sustaining one that we see elsewhere in Wideman's work. It is the cycle of trauma, the reenactment of the post-traumatic narrative forever looping upon itself in the vision of the *ouroboros* and the birth of the "fever" in America. It is a symbol of the history that African Americans cannot seem to escape, that seems to be their burden to bear.

Because the past cannot be reconciled, the future is in peril. The boy shot at the beginning of the novel is a double for the orphans tended to by Mrs. Thrush and Kate. While these children have survived the fever, they are left without parents, without a home. The voice of one of these children in the book is full of violent hatred. His other double lays outside the text—the lost boy, Simba, in *Philadelphia Fire*. This unnamed boy in *The Cattle Killing* is also a child lost through fire to the flames of history: the children of the orphanage are killed when their shelter is set on fire. The hatred set aflame by Carey's pamphlet destroys the reminders of the past and the possibilities of the future. The fire in Philadelphia at the time of the fever still burns by the time of the MOVE bombing in 1985. Layered within the images of fire here are also implicit allusions to James Baldwin's *The Fire Next Time* and, by extension, the Bible and the destruction of human history.

The historian/son at the end of the novel writes to his father, the novelist who has "created" *The Cattle Killing*, that he has discovered letters from a man who may be the preacher's brother; these "historical" letters once more violate the boundaries separating genres. The letters also speak about the cattle killing in South Africa that the brother is witnessing firsthand (which we know is a breach of the historical timeline). He writes in the letter, quoted at the end of the novel, about the "children that are dying" because of the cattle killing. In each time, in each space, the children are being lost and with them the future. The relationship between these events, the fiction and the history, causes the historian/son to remark, "The circle's too neat."[76] Indeed, the hierarchical boundaries between the genres have been removed, and Wideman's "fictional" creation speaks for all those unknown African American men and women who were real, who did walk the streets of the diseased city in 1793, but whose stories have been forgotten or have never been recorded until now.

The preacher's view of the future (our present) is an alarming one, but within the novel, Wideman offers us the hope to change the present course:

> There are prophecies in the air, prophecies deadlier than machines. If you deny yourselves, transform yourselves, destroy yourselves, the prophets say, a better world will be born. Your enemies will be dismayed, disarmed by your sacrifice, and be your enemies no more. From the ashes of your sacrifice a new world of peace and plenty will arise, they say. The prophets of ghost dance, prophets of the cattle killing, prophets of Kool-Aid, prophets of bend over and take it in your ear, your behind, prophets of off with your head, prophets of chains and prisons and love thy neighbor if and only if he's you; prophets of one skin more equal than others and if the skin fits, wear it and if it doesn't strip it layer by layer down to the bone and then the prophet sayeth a new and better day will dawn.[77]

The preacher finds that the only way to combat this disease and his anger is through sharing stories with Kate. The stories soothe both her literal fever and his figurative one, stories that sustain and embrace us.[78] Part of the urgency of the novel lies in the feeling that these sustaining stories are being lost in America and that the loss is possibly a fatal one. This idea resonates in the tale of the Xhosa. The act of cattle killing destroys their past traditions and their future—the history that Wideman sees repeating on the streets of present-day Philadelphia.

The preacher shares his stories to combat his feelings of frustration and loss as well. Kate teases him, saying that all his stories sound as if they are about a lost love:

> Come, you owe me, sir, a trip to Philadelphia. Love's another story.
> Philadelphia. Love is buried in the name you know.
> Love. Love, sir. Surely not during the season of plague. A most unlovely time, by your word.
> Very little love. Yes. Yes. But love was there. The city would not have survived without it.[79]

In an interview following the publication of the short story "Fever," Wideman proposed that the fever represented a "misunderstanding not only on the individual level, but on a cultural level. These stories [of the collection titled *Fever*] are also about the ways of combating that malaise through love, through talk, through rituals that families create."[80] One of those rituals, as we have seen previous chapters, is the act of sharing stories. Any good storyteller, especially an oral storyteller, embellishes the tale that has gone before. Even a story of their own making develops, changes, improvises—the work of the jazz musician, of signifying. This is the case with "Fever" and *The Cattle Killing*; they are each other's story doubles, sharing a relationship similar to the Homewood books and *Brothers and Keepers*.

We have seen throughout Wideman's work the repetition of names, characters, and stories that emphasize the loose boundaries between genres, the slippage of time and space, and the inescapable connections in our lives. The earlier work "Fever" lays much of the groundwork for the novel *The Cattle Killing*. The short story opens with Allen's refutation to Matthew Carey, "who fled Philadelphia in its hour of need and upon his return published a libelous account of the behavior of black nurses and undertakers, thereby injuring all people of my race."[81] The opening of Allen's church is interposed with the growing epidemic. Dr. Benjamin Rush is a character in this story, and many of his letters are imbricated into the text. Here Rush's name has not been altered. There are some important differences between "Fever" and *The Cattle Killing*, however. Allen, in this version, is much more involved in the action of the plot. His voice is present throughout, unlike in *The Cattle Killing*. And one of the main voices in the piece is an ailing Jewish man who, like the figure of Cohen in the short story "Valaida" (in the short-story collection *All Stories Are True*), draws implicit connections between the racism suffered by both African Americans and Hebrews throughout history.

Throughout the short story, the etymology of the disease is traced. The fever exists everywhere in the world, not just on American soil. It is also known

THE JOURNEY BACK (AGAIN): THE POST-TRAUMATIC NARRATIVES   169

as the Palatine fever; the description of its effects in Europe sound like the yellow fever epidemic in America:

> They lay blame on others for the killing fever, pointed their fingers at foreigners and called it Palatine fever, a pestilence imported from those low countries in Europe where, I have been told, war for control of the sealanes, the human cargoes transported thereupon has raged for a thousand years.[82]

The speaker informs us that he has seen this fever before in many places, at many different times. The speaker appears to be Abraham, a ailing Jewish man being tended by Allen during the yellow fever plague. As a victim of prejudice himself, he sees the power the fever has to control and determine our destinies:

> I hear the drum, the forest's heartbeat, pulse of the sea that chains the moon's wandering, the spirit's journey. Its throb is source and promise of all things being connected, a mirror storing everything, forgetting nothing. To explain the fever we need no boatloads of refugees, ragged and wracked with killing fevers, bringing death to our shores. We have bred the affliction within our breasts. Each solitary heart contains all the world's tribes, and its precarious dance echoes the drum's thunder. We are our ancestors and our children, neighbors and strangers to ourselves.[83]

Abraham goes on to trace the sources of the fever and its history: "It grows in the secret places of our hearts, planted there when one of us decided to sell one of us to another. The drum must pound ten thousand years to drive that evil away."[84] The speaker repeats names that the fever has been known by (its "twins"); it has had different names throughout countries and history—too numerous to count. The fever is a historical constant of the human condition, a sign that history has always been about trauma.[85] Allen, at the end of the story, describes the end of the epidemic and Philadelphia's road to recovery, but in the middle of the passage a moment of temporal density occurs. Allen informs us that the mayor has made a statement regarding the events of the plague, but the event he narrates is the 1985 MOVE bombing and the leader is Mayor Goode:

> Philadelphia must be rejuvenated, refueled, rebuilt, reconnected to the countryside, to markets foreign and domestic, to products and pleasures and appetites denied during the quarantine months of the fever. A new century would be dawning. We must forget the horrors. The Mayor

proclaims a new day. Says lets put the past behind us. Of the eleven who died in the fire he said extreme measures were necessary as we cleansed ourselves of disruptive influences. The cost could have been greater, he said I regret the loss of life, especially the half dozen kids, but I commend all city officials, all volunteers who helped return the city to the arc of glory that is its proper destiny.[86]

The MOVE bombing is just another manifestation of the fever and of the cycle of trauma reappearing. The idea expressed in *The Cattle Killing* of lost children and the threat to the future is echoed here as well (as it will be in *Philadelphia Fire*). Abraham admonishes Allen for tending to him when he should be home with his own family, protecting them from the fever: "Fly, fly, fly away home. Your house is on fire, your children are burning."[87]

This warning is repeated in *Philadelphia Fire* when Cudjoe, the story's central character and its writer, remembers the children's rhyme as he returns home, himself in search of a child, one of the survivors of the MOVE bombing.[88] Cudjoe revises the line a few pages later: "Runagate, runagate, fly away home."[89] The change indicts Cudjoe for choosing self-imposed exile over staying in his community and remaining close to his own sons. The fire described at the end of "Fever" is the center of this novel. The repetition of dying children and fire is so pervasive in these three works that, taken together, it carries the force of an extended metaphor and myth. This is noteworthy given that also embedded in this novel are the stories of Oedipus, Caliban, and Prospero—all figures from Western mythic narratives. Wideman needs to revisit and rewrite these mythic figures and stories as sources and sites of trauma. These are "textualized pasts" (a term coined by Linda Hutcheon). History and literature are seen here as intertexts, as they are in *The Cattle Killing*; and the incorporation of *The Tempest* and *Oedipus at Colonnus* is a method of reinvestigating representations of the past in an attempt to understand their hold over the American consciousness.

Wideman plays all these stories at once, exploring, revising, and layering all simultaneously. The overall effect can be breathtaking and somewhat discordant. Some critics argued that the "novel is grounded too deeply in the chaos it means to re-create to leave its readers at ease."[90] Ishmael Reed commented that the book was "reader unfriendly."[91] Wideman breaks the rules of narrative and historical accuracy in the novel, but in a manner that embraces possibility.

The work has also been compared to *Invisible Man*.[92] This analogy is useful in understanding the possibilities of language, identity, and story that the novel hints at. John Africa is known by many different names in the text: James Brown, Mr. Brown, Reverend King, and it is likely that he is J. B. at the end of the novel. His character, though we see little of him, flits in and out of the text and is marked by the shifting possibilities of name and personality, much like Rinehart in *Invisible Man*. Wideman, the writer, assumes a position as a character in the novel as well as one of its narrators. He is a "metafictional Rinehart"[93]—shifting identities, stories, and subject positions in the text (as he does in many of his works). The narrative's movement and Wideman's place in it violate reality and the tenets of the realistic novel but also, in doing so, question our assumptions of art, truth, and personality. Since all of these stories can be true, Wideman can assert multiple authorities. This is reflected even in his language play: "He would cast about. Cast himself as a caste. A cast in his net. Catch of the day. Fresh. Castanet."[94] The possibilities of words and language here indicate that there exist many different possibilities for structure, narrative, and ways of seeing.

What critics respond to in *Philadelphia Fire*, its chaos and its unfriendliness, is the condition that allows all the possible stories, discourses, and meanings of words to play at once, without authorial guidance. We are forced as readers to make meaning in a world and in a text where the writer (writers) are having difficulty doing so themselves. Critics' misapprehension about the novel's nature and its discordance sounds a great deal like early criticisms of the "new jazz," bebop. Rudi Blesch vilified the form: "The irrelevant parts of bebop are exactly what they seem; they add up to no . . . unity."[95]

Cornel West compares African American postmodernism and its writers, including Ishmael Reed, to bebop and its revolt against the "museum of modernism."[96] Wideman echoes these descriptions of bebop in a discussion about his own writing and its relationship to the conventions of literature: "I think it's only natural that when you internalize these rules some of them become part of your conscious repertoire, so you're learning to manipulate and play with them and be silly about them—in the same way that the jazz musician interrogates traditional, conventional music."[97] The discordant narrative is most evident in the voices that structure the novel. Each of the voices establishes some narrative authority. As illustrated earlier, those voices belong to Wideman the character, Wideman the author or narrator, and Cudjoe. Mae Gwendolyn Henderson calls such literary voicing "speaking in tongues."[98] In the postmodern era, especially, African American writers have embodied in their texts double or triple consciousness, expressing their narratives in multiple voices. Particularly, the three voices operating as one within *Philadelphia Fire* represent the three tenses of narration in a work. A structure of this kind "undercuts the traditional, verifying third-person, past tense voice of history."[99] The polyphonic nature of this novel makes it difficult to embrace the narrator as the most accurate and reminds us once again that all the stories must in some way be valid.[100]

The three-voiced structure of *Philadelphia Fire* might also reflect the three genres that we have seen operating within other Wideman texts: autobiography, fiction, and history. In this view the voices of the texts are not distinct hierarchical discourses; they are imbricated simultaneously throughout the text. The public record of the MOVE bombing (literally "recorded" here on the news; eyewitness accounts are "recorded" by Cudjoe); the literary texts, *The Tempest* and *Oedipus at Colonnus*; the fictional narrative of Cudjoe; and Wideman's autobiographical voice all speak to one another. The voice of the text "Fever" is echoed here as well, as it was in *The Cattle Killing* (though this book was published later). These three works are, in essence, different phrasings of the same song and are another example of a three-voiced structure; in this case not within a work but between works. It is, in fact, the interplay of all of these voices that allows Wideman to question the validity of privileging one text over others. In the book, the text that Wideman believes has the most prominent place within the culture is *The Tempest*; but placed alongside these other stories, it loses much of its power and its position. The play is shown to be as much a fiction as any other of the other stories in the novel.

Many critics see *Philadelphia Fire* as "significantly different from the early [works] both thematically and structurally."[101] We have seen in previous chapters, however, that many of Wideman's other works reflect a polyphonic structure, though certainly not to the degree that *Philadelphia Fire* does. Sometimes three voices (and discourses) are layered in a single paragraph or on a single page, as it is in *A Glance Away*. But even as early as *Brothers and Keepers* and *The Homewood Trilogy*, Wideman clearly raises questions in the text about the interplay of voices within his work. Thematically, *Philadelphia Fire* deals with many of the same issues presented in Wideman's earliest works: the alienated individual in the African American community, the need to reconnect to that community through story, the loss of children, and the need to redress historical and cultural assumptions. This novel, however, through its structure allows each of these concerns to be voiced simultaneously.

Both Wideman, as the writer's voice, and Cudjoe are suffering from traumatic losses and are drawn to the story of the MOVE bombing and the loss of the child, Simba. Wideman (the character? the writer?) asks in the text: "Will I ever try to write my son's story? Not dealing with it may be causing the forgetfulness I'm experiencing."[102] And later, he asks another metafictional question: "Why this Cudjoe, then? This airy other floating into the shape of my story. Why am I him when I tell certain parts? Why am I hiding from myself? Is he mirror or black hole?"[103] In the novel, in what appears to be an autobiographical moment, Wideman describes his son's illness, adult schizophrenia. In responding to the illness that has destroyed his son's life and the madness of history and society that is exemplified by the fire, Wideman creates "a schizophrenic text" that cannot mask its inability or unwillingness to place order on such a feverish and diseased world.[104] The text reflects both the son's illness—the source of another trauma—and the father's post-traumatic response. All roads will lead back to this pain—as it almost literally does in *Fatheralong* when Wideman imagines a road in South Carolina leading up to the prison in Arizona where his son is incarcerated.

It is important to see that Wideman is not only the writer of this text, but also a character. Autobiography is, after all, a fiction we create of ourselves as well as a reportage of the facts of our lives that could be considered historically accurate. Cudjoe is an alter ego for Wideman, as Thomas is in *Fanon* and Lawson is in *Sent for You Yesterday*. But the lines between autobiography and fiction are too fuzzy here to assume that we can accept the truths reported on in the text. Wideman directly cautions against confusing his life and work in an interview:

> When I write, I don't open up my life for people to see; I open up what I want people to see. Writing is both revealing and an act of concealment. It is deciding to construct a public persona. It is often a preemptive strike. One might write because one doesn't want people to know one's life. So that should be clear first.[105]

Cudjoe states in *Philadelphia Fire* that "maybe this is a detective story" when he considers the type of story that he is writing about the MOVE bombing. That classification is applicable not only to the story he is writing but to Wideman's entire literary project. Both *Philadelphia Fire* and *The Cattle Killing* are detective stories, and their protagonists are solitary, heroic figures on a quest.[106] *Fatheralong* follows this pattern as well. Here Wideman "searches" for his father, for his father's stories, even though the man is sitting right next to him in the car. Each one of these works imbricates the historical discourse with classic Western fiction and mythology—the search for one's self, for identity. Cudjoe has no idea who he really is because he is so used to seeing himself through the eyes of others—like Ellison's invisible man. Madelyn Jablon points out that Easy Rawlins, the detective of the Walter Mosley novels, describes his work as a detective as being a discoverer of "little pieces of history" that have "previously been 'unrecorded.'"[107] The postmodern detective story is a reworking of the traditional genre. Its clues lead to more clues, but rarely closure. These novels do not accept that clues lead to truth; they question whether truth can ever be known.

Albert Murray argues that the detective story hero is a "species of blues idiom hero." The hero "plays hunches" and is "a researcher whose open-mindedness is closely geared to precisely the sort of riff-style improvisation that typifies the blues idiom sensibility."[108] Houston Baker also suggests that the "blues detective" is a trope of African American literature. These characters reveal a "critical orientation that looks, not to real history, but to the limitless freedom of myth and fictive discourse."[109]

If we see the genre in this light, Wideman's project as writer could be seen as similar to that of the blues detective—even Cecil Braithwaite in *Hurry Home* imagines himself as a detective. What Wideman is searching for here is not just the truth; he is questioning the very narratives by which we discover truth and the narratives that argue that it can be readily resolved and put on a shelf by the close of a novel. This investigation, then, is not only the search for the boy and what happened the day Philadelphia dropped the bomb, but also Wideman's hunt for those fragments, those clues that are left behind because they seem to have no meaning to the one ordered, monolithic vision of reality. The detective story, in this text, inhabits the fictional realm, along with the genres of scientific and historical writing and personal meditations—all of which seek an answer, a resolution (or possible answers). For Cudjoe and for Wideman the search for truth is a search for "where the trouble began," the site of historical trauma.

Cudjoe records his conversations with Margaret Jones as a reporter would. He wants to get the facts straight, to see if she can give him clues to the whereabouts of the boy who escaped the fire. But while listening to the tape he "fast forwards her story. Would she tell more about the boy this time? Or would the tape keep saying what it had said last time he listened?"[110] Cudjoe is ultimately more at ease with imagining what happened than he is with discovering the facts. We get very little factual information about the MOVE bombing or the boy that Cudjoe is looking for. And the facts do not allow a space for him to connect to this public event, whereas his imagination does. The dream he relates to Timbo about a lynched boy hanging from a basketball rim indicates this:

> "Who killed him?"
> "It was a dream."
> "Well, make up something then. Wake up and make up. You got my attention. Don't leave me hanging."
> "Damn you, Timbo."
> "I ain't trying to be funny. But it ain't fair to start telling me a story then just stop in the middle."
> "The dream stops there. Everything surrounding it's gone. I want to know the rest too. Thought telling you might help. But it doesn't. I

feel myself beginning to invent. Filling in the blanks are real. Part of a dream."[111]

Timbo asks detective questions (whodunit?) and is more interested in the solution and in the narrative than he is in the dream as a dream. He wants an ordered reality, but for Cudjoe the dream offers him blanks to fill, the spaces to fill the gaps of his own life. All along, Cudjoe's interest in the bombing and in the boy has been to "do something about the silence."[112] The structure of the novel reinforces these silences or blanks that occupy Cudjoe (and Wideman). Created by the fractures in the narrative, these intentional gaps are call-and-response moments. They ask us to fill these spaces with our own stories, stories that will be valid and true because they will exist beside the historical or literary ones of the text. More than any other of Wideman's novels, this work demands communal involvement. It is only though the actions of the community, both within the text and outside of it, that meaning and wholeness can be achieved.

The silence is created when the unknown stories remain unheard. But this is not just a literary or historical dilemma. It is also a personal one for Wideman (or at least his character in the novel). The novel is obviously more than an attempt to understand the MOVE bombing. It is interested in recognizing the connections between the bombing and racism and lost children:

> [*Philadelphia Fire*] wasn't a piece of investigative journalism about MOVE. There are lots of books that attempt to look at that organization—the history of that organization—and what happened to the people and the biographies of the members. That isn't what I was after. The book is not even a fictionalized biography or history of the MOVE cult. It's a book about many things.[113]

The novel is ultimately more concerned with the silences—not only the silence of history about the bombing, but also the silence that rushes to fill the void that words couldn't when he speaks to his son over the phone: "I breathe into the space separating me from my son. I hope the silence will be filled for him as it is filled for me by hearing the nothing there is to say at this moment."[114] The meaning, for Wideman's aesthetic, lies in the gaps of the novel where possibility lies. But while Wideman "praises" silence elsewhere,[115] these spaces in *Philadelphia Fire* reflect the failure of language when it attempts to address the unspeakable and unutterable in post-traumatic narratives. Even family stories cannot fill these silent moments. These spaces do not appear to be the cleared areas where discourse can take place.

Wideman links this section of the novel with the MOVE bombing and with a riot against blacks in 1850 described in *The Annals of Philadelphia* (a historical record that is mentioned several times in the text). These events are imbricated in the novel through the imagination, an imagination that has the power to reenvision the painful stories remembered here: "Pretend we can imagine events into existence. Pretend we have the power to live our lives as we choose. Imagine our fictions imagining us."[116]

One of the historical moments that the novel tries to re-imagine is European colonization through the work *The Tempest*. As an artifact of colonization and as a literary work, this text is a powerful vision that has, in the eyes of Wideman and Cudjoe, silenced the stories of others. The play is the text, the ur-story, of Europe's relationship to the New World and the aftermath of its first contact. Cudjoe sees *The Tempest* as the "birth of the nation's blues" just as the "fever" was present in the nation's infancy.[117] Cudjoe appears to argue here that this play is more than a literary work; it has informed the historical consciousness of Europe and the Americas. It is the one of the sources of "postcolonial melancholia."[118] Its story portrays a limited vision of African American experience. Caliban, "your great, great, great grandfather," is presented as a weak, vulgar, lazy, sexually driven, ignorant, violent, and illiterate creature. Caliban "is anything but a Noble Savage" in *The Tempest*.[119] Cudjoe tells the children he is preparing to perform the play because it influences the world they live in now. Shakespeare

> scoped the whole ugly mess about to happen at that day and time which brings us to here, to today. To this very moment in our contemporary world. To the inadequacy of your background, your culture. Its inability like the inability of a dead sea, to cast up on the beach appropriate role models, creatures whose lives you might imitate. So let's pretend.[120]

Cudjoe and his students attempt to rewrite the text. Doing so "would change an important root source of much western discourse and change the oppressive circumstances of black Americans, particularly those of black males."[121] Caliban is also the forefather of Bigger Thomas and of the image and stereotype of the African American male that is seen as an inarticulate rapist and brute animal. The name "Caliban," as an anagram for cannibal, portrayed an image of Africans and those of African descent that has lingered even into the twentieth century. Wideman tries to dismantle this story, one that the novel implies is the phylogenetic narrative of the African in the Western consciousness, to allow other stories of African Americans to be told. In Cudjoe's version of the play, Caliban speaks to the audience about the themes of the work and his role in it.

The character reclaims his voice and its power to transform his story, because "everybody knows can't nobody free Caliban but his own damn self."[122] If Caliban can tell his own story, then his version offers another possible truth.

The play is meant to empower the children as well: "The play was the thing. To catch a conscience. To prick pride and dignity and say, Hey, we're alive over here."[123] The metafictional voice implies further that *The Tempest* is an important key to understanding the writing about the bombing:

> This is the central event. I assure you. I repeat. Whatever my assurance is worth. Being the fabulator. This is the central event, this production of *The Tempest* staged by Cudjoe in the late, late 1960's, outdoors in a park in West Philly. Though it comes here, wandering like a Flying Dutchman in and out of the narrative, many places at once, *The Tempest* sits dead center, the storm in the eye of the storm, figure within a figure, play within a play, it is the bounty and the hub of all else written about the fire though it comes here, where it is, nearer the end than the beginning.[124]

The Tempest is a central text within the text; it is a "master narrative," the master plan for the European treatment of indigenous peoples; it is the "central event" of the fire; and its portrait of Caliban is one of the most persistent images of the African American man in the historical consciousness.

Caliban loses his island, his heritage, and his freedom. His world is forever altered by the presence of Prospero. Prospero alters Caliban's very perception of himself when he teaches him to speak in Prospero's tongue. We are told in *The Cattle Killing* of the danger of learning the "master's" language, and it bears repeating here. The prophet of the cattle killing warns the preacher in a vision: "Do not speak with your enemy's tongue. Do not fall asleep in your enemy's dream."[125] Caliban's story of himself is replaced with Prospero's story of Caliban. Wideman implies that seeing yourself through another's eyes, having their story replace your own in your consciousness, is a deadly historical event, as evidenced by such stories as the cattle killing, the MOVE bombing, and even his brother's life in prison.

Language itself is equally responsible for the historical and traumatic oppression of African Americans. The master's tongue represents the cultural assimilation that can produce self-doubt and self-loathing in African Americans. We have already seen this in several of Wideman's characters—Cecil Braithwaite, Littleman, Wally, and even Wideman's self-portrait in *Brothers and Keepers*. As Wideman intonates in essays as early as "Charles Chesnutt and the WPA Narratives" and in "The Black Writer and the Magic of the Word," African Americans must keep the oral roots "alive and kicking" in fiction. Throughout

Philadelphia Fire, Wideman uses contested linguistic spaces to illustrate his version of "all stories are true." Rap lyrics, black vernacular, and verbal puns keep the oral alive in this written space. As well, they provide another story through different discourses and language styles—the "high culture" of *The Tempest* and *Oedipus at Colonus* exists alongside the "low culture" of the Kiddie Korps, rap music, and Caliban's voice. These moments are more evidence of Wideman's polyphonic style.[126] The multiple discourses existing together also critique the popularly accepted notion that American history and culture owes everything to the European tradition. Wideman reminds readers of the prominence of the African and African American traditions within the American story—"the submerged history."[127]

In the section of the novel voiced by the character Wideman—the metafictional chapters—Wideman relates going to a production of *Oedipus at Colonus.* Breaking into the narrative is a quote from *The Tempest*: "This thing of darkness / I acknowledge mine."[128] The lines are spoken by Prospero in the play to Caliban, but the meaning of the lines is revised here. Cudjoe calls himself the "fabulator,"[129] and for all the possible associations between Cudjoe and Wideman and Caliban that are possible, we cannot forget that Cudjoe and Wideman are also linked to Prospero. All three characters are fabulators. As fabulators, they are imagining their worlds and creating their stories, the same position Prospero holds in the play. This, in itself, is a revisionary act of historical assumptions. If Prospero can make a myth from the life of Caliban, then Cudjoe and Wideman can also make a new myth of Caliban. The perception of Caliban as an animal that leads to the cultural image of African American males is clearly what Wideman wants to deconstruct.[130] Its image controls the ways that Robby is treated in prison; the ways slave traders viewed the Africans; the way the police and the media see urban, male, African American youth. This is the image that the city government had of the MOVE members before they bombed their house—it is the fever and it is the fire that continues to spread.

The image of Caliban has been revised elsewhere as well, in the work of Clarence Major, Aime Cesaire's *A Tempest,* and in African American playwright George Wolfe's production of *The Tempest* in 1995, to name a few. In Wolfe's production, which emphasized Afro-Caribbean art and music in its sets and costumes, Caliban is fiercely articulate—the opposite of how he is portrayed in Shakespeare's version—but trusts in Trinculo and Stephano's ability to lead the revolution rather than in his own abilities and voice. Even Prospero's lines, "This thing of darkness / I acknowledge mine," are revised, at least in their performance under Wolfe's direction. Prospero does not see Caliban as property—which is the traditional way to view these words. Here, Prospero speaks the lines as someone who takes responsibility for Caliban's condition. He indicates that the violence that Caliban attempts in the course of the play is his fault: the result of Caliban's enslavement and disenfranchisement by Prospero.[131] This feeling of responsibility is also echoed by Cudjoe: "Oh. He was precious. Oh. How did the shit get piled so high? And here he was responsible for it."[132] While it is not clear exactly what he feels responsible for (His isolation from his community? The loss of his son?), Wideman suggests, as he has before in *Brother and Keepers*, that he has "fashioned the cage" that is imprisoning or enslaving his characters.

Missing and lost children are also one of the primary thematic elements of this novel. Throughout his work, we have seen that Wideman examines this situation from different places and different times, yet the answer is always the same. If the children are lost, the future is lost: "A child lost cancels the natural order."[133] The fever, the bombing, and its ensuing fire are responsible for most of the lost children in *Philadelphia Fire*. Hearing about the survivor, the boy Simba, is what brings Cudjoe home ("Your house is on fire, your children are burning").

Almost all of the mainstream newspaper reports mentioned the boy, Birdie Africa, who did, in fact, survive the bombing. The mainstream press was also quick to blame Mayor Goode and to paint MOVE as a threatening, militant group that posed a viable threat to the community. They presented stereotyped images of the "notorious" MOVE members. But there were conflicting reports about what actually started the explosion and the fire, and investigations into the disaster, at the time, never produced a clear picture of what transpired. All that was "known" at the time was that the Cobb's Creek section of Philadelphia was destroyed by the very officials sent to protect it. It was the worst fire in the city's history, leaving 240 people homeless and 11 dead, including 4 children. This act of destruction echoes later in Wideman's description of the Xhosa cattle killing. Read together, we see how Wideman retells and replies to the same story in a new chord, showing us the inescapable connections between the traumatic past and the post-traumatic present.

The dramatic image of Birdie Africa running through the flames was a popular one in the press following the days of the bombing, but what happened to the child afterwards received little or no attention by the major newspapers or magazines. He, like the other children of the novel, was used and tossed aside. Nobody in the society at large seemed to really care about what happened to this child or to the other children who died in the fire. Only *Jet* magazine issued a follow-up, and it amounted to little more than a few lines of copy about the boy's reunion with his father.[134] Before *Philadelphia Fire* was published, Wideman spoke about the MOVE bombing: "I think that's a very crucial event in our history and we can't afford to forget it. And so I am doing what I think is my bit in trying to keep it alive."[135] Wideman's novel is an attempt to tell those silent stories of Simba, but also to reveal the connections between this child and the stories of other children.

Cudjoe is unable to find Simba in the novel; he disappears after the fire. He hears stories about a boy called Lion (the meaning of Simba) traveling with a gang that has published a pamphlet outlining their grievances against society. This is clearly a gang that has revolution on its mind. Cudjoe sees their "sign" KK (Kids' Krusade), or sometimes KKK (Kaliban's Kiddie Korps), painted throughout the city. The latter sign signifies both on *The Tempest* presented here in the novel and on the Ku Klux Klan, suggesting perhaps that both references are equally destructive toward the African American community. Timbo summarizes the pamphlet for Cudjoe:

> The fire's in it. In a list of atrocities that prove adults don't give a fuck about kids. The lousy school system, abortion, lack of legal rights, child abuse, kiddie porn, kid's bodies used to sell shit on TV, kids on death row, high infant mortality. In that list as one of the latest signs. Cause the fire burned up mostly kids. And also because a kid managed to survive. Survived the bullets and flames and flood and bombs. Superkid, dig. City used everything in its arsenal but the little mothafucker got away. Simba right? He's a symbol of kid power. He's a hero, magic, they say. Went through hell to show others they can do it. Do anything.[136]

These dispossessed, abused, and neglected children join the list of other lost children in the novel: Wideman's son, Sam's daughter, Cudjoe's sons. The children are also reminiscent of the boy shot in the beginning of *The Cattle Killing* and the orphans burned to death in the same novel (and countless other lost children in Wideman's work). The grievances outlined above speak to a system that promotes "family values" in political rhetoric and on the airwaves, but clearly fails to value the children living at the margins of society. The overall message, even when it comes to children, is that an African American life is not as significant as a white life, even today.

When Cudjoe goes to meet Timbo to ask for help in finding the boy, he looks at his watch, wondering if he will be late for the meeting; he sees that there's "time, but none to spare."[137] *Tempestas*, means "time," Wideman later tells us.[138] The various signified meanings conflate here: the play, a storm, time. The time to stop the fever from spreading is running out; it is "conspiring, expiring." "Time, but none to spare" also echoes the final line of Charles Chesnutt's *The Marrow of Tradition*: "There's time enough, but none to spare."[139] *The Marrow of Tradition* is a work also concerned with lost children and the continuing trauma of racial history. Wideman sees Chesnutt's novel as one that emphasizes that "history is not simply progressive but cyclical, and that personal, family, communal, national and finally global history are part of the same process."[140] Wideman's post-traumatic narratives reflect the same characteristics and concerns that he notes in Chesnutt's work.

The connections between the past, present, and the future are dramatized in the closing section of the novel. Cudjoe waits at Independence Square for the memorial service for the bombing victims to begin. Few are in attendance; Cudjoe notes the silence and the absence of any city officials making a statement. Looking around, he is reminded of an incident that took place in the square in 1805 on July 4, where African Americans were chased and beaten during the holiday celebration. He feels the ghosts from that incident brush by him. The square is populated by them. The past and the present meet when Cudjoe

> hears footsteps behind him. A mob howling his name. Screaming his blood. Words come to him, cool him, stop him in his tracks. He'd known them all his life. *Never again. Never again.* He turns to face whatever it is rumbling over the stones of Independence Square.[141]

Cudjoe is there in 1805. Even though this event occurred historically in 1831, the dates are not significant. The fever that caused that incident and the racism and hatred that spurred it on have followed Cudjoe all his life. The burden of that history has always been "the footsteps behind him." But now Cudjoe is finally ready to confront that history no matter how painful. He is no longer the "runagate." If the future is to be saved, the past must be remembered and understood—new stories must be told; new myths must be made. "Never again" can there be silence about incidents such as the riot of 1831, the MOVE bombing, the loss of boys like Simba. Ultimately, Cudjoe does not find the boy, nor does he write his book: because of "the influence of Calibanism," Cudjoe's story and Caliban's story cannot replace the Western myths.[142] But in the novel, Wideman manages to deconstruct and dismantle these narratives, if not completely replace them with his own myths, as he did in the Homewood trilogy. Things must first be torn down, or burned down, in order to be rebuilt—before new myths and narratives can be installed. The narrative structure itself suggests the necessity of the revision of language and the Western modes of discourse and methods of storytelling.

What happens to those who don't confront their history in positive and potentially liberating ways we have already seen in Wideman's earlier work,

The Lynchers. The characters of this novel fail to see that they must create a new story, a new myth, one that enables them to rewrite history rather than continue to be its victims. They are the descendants of Caliban, forced to speak their master's language; they don't understand that they need to rewrite such texts, not imitate them. While the call to rewrite history is a postmodern act, the actors in this piece are in search of truth and order, which makes them sound more modernist: they wanted to "cage time in the red lines that marched across the page."[143] Most of the characters essentially view history as stable, yet their world is in chaos, Wideman argues here, because they cannot see history for what it is; they cannot reenvision it. They cannot connect to their past; they cannot connect to their future, to each other, or to anyone else in their families or in their communities. Wideman, however, illustrates that this is a failure of their vision; they are too grounded in the very language and ideology that they wish to rebel against.

The "Matter Prefatory" that opens *The Lynchers* includes twenty pages of quotations from actual documents recording the treatment of slaves, lynchings, or commentary about the response to post-reconstructionist terror. This record of initial trauma initiates the post-traumatic narrative of the men who plan a "lynching in black face." Included in the "Matter Prefatory" are passages from slave narratives and other writings by former slaves that discuss racism, torture, and the rape of female slaves; a petition from an African American community in Kentucky applying to Congress for protection against lynchers; and accounts from newspapers covering lynchings, as if they were sporting events. The extensive sources and quotations offer an encapsulated view of the treatment of African Americans in this country. The history of the "Matter Prefatory" is, in fact, the basis for the whole novel; it is the world that the lynchers of the novel inhabit, from which they can't seem to escape.

The architect of the lynching plan, Littleman, desires to seek revenge for centuries of white supremacy, but his description of history lies at the heart of what Wideman tries to deconstruct in his novels. Littleman's need for "order" is that evidence of his inability to see that the systems that he is trying to dismantle inform his view of the world. He comments about a new building's colonial architecture: "They want the Enlightenment, the Age of Reason, as if they don't know what those delusions cost, who paid for their leisure and elegance. How many black bodies were cast into the sea to finance what those damn merchants call culture."[144]

Wideman's assessment of the historical consequences of the Enlightenment appears implicitly in *The Cattle Killing*, while in *The Lynchers* Littleman explicitly characterizes and condemns the philosophy of the Enlightenment as demanding "sublime order. Everything, everybody in its place."[145] However, this description of the same system that he has just been condemning sounds analogous to the words that he uses earlier to describe his own plan, his own view of history:

> If there is orderliness, precision, cleanliness, rhythm in the world, they are most visible in action, a plan such as I have conceived. Formulating a rite totally consistent with the logic of history, yet harnessing the blind rush of events, opening a momentary wedge so a new myth can shoulder its way into the process ... to tear such a hole in history."[146]

It is Littleman, not Wideman, who sees history as a modernist would. His apprehension of history (shared by most of the conspirators) is a monolithic and relentless document (embedded as the lynching stories that open the novel), and that is precisely why he feels burdened by it and why he cannot imagine another story.

Littleman's failure of vision arises from his inability to escape the "language of Caliban," as we have seen in the previous chapter. He can only imagine the world within the parameters of Western discourse. Cudjoe reaches levels of understanding that Littleman can never achieve, though clearly he still has far to go. History in each of these works represents the "masterplots Americans have found acceptable for black lives."[147] And in *Philadelphia Fire* and *The Cattle Killing*, as well as *The Lynchers*, Wideman acknowledges his responsibility as a writer is to deconstruct history.

Of course, Wideman is not only engaged in this act of historiographic demolition, but also, as we have seen previously, devoted to "cultural preservation." Clearly, Wideman desires to retrieve and celebrate family and Homewood history in the trilogy, but one of the blank spaces in his own history that he needs to fill are his own personal "father stories." The search for those father stories inspires *Fatheralong*.

Once Wideman decides he needs to learn these stories, he encourages his father to travel with him to the Wideman ancestral home in South Carolina (both grandfathers, John French and Harry Wideman, were from the South). It takes three years for the excursion to finally take place, and even then the two experience some early bumps on their road trip—the quintessential father-son story—to his father's birthplace.

The first bump is the theft of Edgar Wideman's car. Wideman describes his father's broken-down old car (stolen only for its parts) and its loss and then follows it with an illustration of his father's own fragile state: "growing old, alone, and poor."[148] Wideman's tone suggests a shift in his perception of his father from the "deity" the young Wideman imagined growing up to the realization that his father is vulnerable, is falling into disrepair, and, like the car, is seen as worthless by the world around them. Even though Edgar Wideman's car was not the vehicle they were going to drive down South, the loss of a car at the beginning of a road trip foreshadows the failure of Wideman's plans to reconnect to his father during their time together. The image also suggests the impotency of African American male relationships to move forward in a society formulated by the "paradigm of race" that Wideman discusses at the beginning of the work.

Wideman also remarks on the disintegration of the city in this section and the ways that urban renewal has failed African Americans and their families. His father is "excited" and "anxious" to get on the road, but Wideman assumes the reason is because he wants to get out of his small and miserable apartment. A road trip, even to the South, symbolizes freedom that Edgar Wideman feels is no longer available to him. For Wideman, the journey to the South for his father and him will be a journey to healing. Readers of *A Glance Away* might wonder if Wideman had this trip with his father planned in his imagination for sometime. The novel's main character, Eddie Lawson (Lawson is Edgar Wideman's mother's maiden name), travels from the North to the South as part of his drug rehabilitation—to heal the wounds of the past. Since Wideman has not known much of his father's stories growing up, did he fill in some of those blank spaces with his early fiction, creating an identity for his silent father?

It is significant that we actually learn very few of his father's stories here; the early images in the work projecting the journey's failure prove to be accurate symbols. The two men have a difficult time connecting, a difficult time sharing. His father is able to talk very freely with strangers but does not say much to Wideman. Much of the book, consequently, meditates on other events and related subjects, but it does not present us with many family stories. We do hear repeated the "Across the Wide Missouri" short story from *Damballah*. Its appearance here in *Fatheralong* reflects that Wideman and his father spent very little time together when he was a child, nor has much been added over the years to their shared stories (at least as it is represented here).

Wideman tries to preserve what stories he does hear along the way, preserving what he can to combat the "conspiracy to prevent the stories of black men from being transmitted from generation to generation."[149] Wideman's own experience with his father (and later with one of his sons, as it appears in *Fatheralong*) argues that there is some pathology, some inability for these men to break down the walls that separate them. Conversation of any kind can barely get into those silent spaces (which we also see in the phone conversation between father and son in *Philadelphia Fire*); they cannot manage to share stories.

When Wideman's father speaks to strangers, however, he seems to have no problems communicating his past all. Wideman is a little miffed, especially since his father has added one of Wideman's stories to the history/story he is creating for the stranger:

> He was making up the story as he went along, embellishing fragments I'd learned and shared with him, drawing from his own reading, from TV and movies, and barbershops, and hanging on the corner, communal lore and anecdote, a metahistory of the South, slavery, the Wideman clan's heroic resistance to oppression, a tradition of family solidarity my father claimed as his inheritance and vowed to pass on.[150]

There is some irony here when Wideman admits to being "annoyed" by his father making up stories about real people and events. The scene reveals that Edgar Wideman could weave a fine tale, layered with multiple narratives, mixing fact and fiction. His storytelling abilities may not have been apparent to his son over the years for a variety of reasons.

Some of those reasons will always be hidden to us—as they may be to Wideman. But one reason may be embodied in Edgar Wideman's cousin, Littleman. Wideman does not recall ever having met Littleman when they are first introduced. Slowly, he realizes he has heard a story about the cousin and then remembers that Littleman accompanied him and his mother on a trip once. This meeting, significant enough to have an entire section named "Littleman," is noteworthy for a number of reasons.

First, Littleman quickly establishes himself as a storyteller, indicating that there is a talent for the art throughout the Wideman family—something Wideman did not seem to know before. It also is significant that the man's name is the same as the character from *The Lynchers*. Though Wideman tells the reader that he did not remember the man, he appears to have remembered the name. Not only does this provide us with another double of Littleman from *The Lynchers*, it also reconstructs that character's lack of vision and imagination. This Littleman does not want to burn down the world; he seems content to re-imagine it through stories.

Also Wideman recalls that Littleman left the South to move to the North, only to eventually return. As Jackie Berben-Masi points out, the journey from the South to the North to the South was once seen as a failure but now in this work "provides the key that unlocks the mystery John and Edgar need to unravel together."[151] Littleman represents an inverse historical journey that counters the image of the South in Wideman's family and in his own imagination. If Wideman and his father can piece together the history of the South and of the African American and re-imagine it, they can reconnect with one another. Wideman understands: "The South is a parent, an engenderer, part of the mind I think with, the mind thinking me. My history begins here, at least my history in this hemisphere."[152] In order for the process of deconstructing history to happen, Wideman must journey back to this time and to his father's beginnings—if not literally then metaphorically—to the clan and the community of Promised Land.

He has tried to recover the history of Abbeville and Promised Land, South Carolina, before. But the work suggests that he has invited his father on this journey so that by rescuing the historical record, Wideman can save his father and their relationship. If he can find his father's history, he can finally find his father. This is further emphasized in the photography exhibit that Wideman attends in the work. The photos are of long-dead residents—many unknown—of Abbeville. The patrons who visit the exhibit are searching for an ancestor, for their likeness with a ghost from the past, for a recognition of their own past and their own identity in the face of a historical stranger. Wideman is hoping to find out something about who he is by discovering his father's identity on this journey back.

Wideman has not always wanted to make this trip. His grandfather Harry Wideman invited him many times to go back home with him to visit the South and learn about family history when Wideman was a boy. He recalls his reaction: "Going to South Carolina was about as appealing as going to Africa and living in the jungle."[153] He also expressed a cultural anxiety about the South, embodied in the story of Emmett Till. For Wideman, as for many young African American men, the South was where they lynched black boys. As a youth, he did not want to "travel back to slavery days."[154] Denial of his grandfather's wish haunts Wideman in this text, and part of this present journey is to heal his personal feelings of guilt, as well as seeing the South through his grandfather's eyes as home. He admits now, "The shape of South Carolina reminds me of Africa."[155] The shape of Wideman's memory and the shape of African American history conflate in the knowledge that this journey is giving him.

Such a search for the father, for knowledge, and for identity is common in literature, a staple of the quest journey. But Wideman knows who his father is—he's brought him along for the ride. Unable to find the family history that he is looking for in his father's conversations and his minimal recollections of the past, Wideman leaves his father behind within the structure of the narrative in search of the known and unknown history of the Promised Land. While most of the works discussed in this chapter have a solitary quest character on a search for understanding, *Fatheralong* begins with a revision of that trope as both father and son travel together. As the work shifts from a typical quest story to a meditation on the nature of history, race, and his own position as father, Wideman realizes that his hopes for the trip and a new closeness with and awareness of his father are not going to happen. Once again the dreams of the Promised Land remain unfulfilled even within the margins of the text.

The past that Wideman uncovers while in Abbeville is not unusual. He finds that few records exist of the slaves who lived on the Marshall Plantation that later became Promised Land. They were either never kept or destroyed by a fire. What he is unable to find prompts Wideman to turn Promised Land into his own story—a tale of loss and deceit, of "false promise": "You won't find Promised Land on most maps, just as you won't discover any mention of Africans or slaves or slavery in the closely printed eight-page outline of the 'Chronological History of South Carolina' (1662–1825)."[156] The former plantation, rewritten as the "Promised Land" for former slaves as reparations, as "forty acres and a mule," transforms into yet another broken promise that stretches from the false prophecies of the Xhosa cattle killing and the promise that it would send the colonial Europeans packing to the Declaration of Independence and the Constitution, to post-Reconstruction, and to the civil rights era. Even his father's apartment—a promise of the Great Society and urban renewal—has turned into the despair and the blight of the cities. Wideman notes that these images are reminiscent of Ellison's character in *Invisible Man* who sells "discarded blueprints"—another sign that such broken promises perpetuate the traumatic history of slavery.[157]

Wideman transforms this vision of absence and loss into guarded hope just a few lines after telling us that Promised Land is not on any map: "Maybe Promised Land lies where it does to teach us the inadequacy of maps we don't make ourselves, teach the necessity of new maps, teach us how to create them, reimagine connections others have forgotten or hidden. Maybe we need Promised Land to be born again."[158] His deconstruction of the Promised Land trope in literature and history allows him the "blank space" to write his own history.[159] Once again, Wideman locates and clears a space in the historical narrative to allow other voices to speak.

Wideman's meditation on historiography and African American history allows him into another space—the sea of Great Time, the crossroad of Damballah. Here Wideman witnesses the road under his feet in South Carolina leading to the road to his son's prison in Arizona. He connects to other moments in history as well—the dust under his feet is the dust of bones of African Americans in Natchez, Mississippi, who died in settlement camps following the Civil War. This camp reminds him of other similar places, including concentration camps. He immediately comments on the connections between the trauma of slavery and the Holocaust: "The South was a winnowing of people," the Middle

Passage, African wars, the "forced march to the coasts," and then "the South as a test just as brutal for the mind."[160] This scene in Wideman's historical imagination dissolves into the "archetypal scene of German officers" and Jews being forced on trains, forced into lines in the concentration camps—one direction hard labor and starvation, the other death. If we understand the history of trauma and survival across national boundaries, something can be salvaged: "The underground history of the camps must be remembered, written, and celebrated. The story of how strength of mind, individual and collective, altered the genocidal master plan, how the horror that destroyed so many could be transformed into a rite of passage for some, then for a people, a nation."[161]

Later in *Fatheralong*, another camp is recalled. This one had been the site of love, family, peace, and nature—an Edenic spot like Promised Land was supposed to be. This space has also been transformed into a site of trauma through personal history. Wideman's father-in-law's camp in Maine—a retreat from the violence and craziness of the world—is a further symbol of lost innocence in the work. Perhaps even a recollection of how others have survived grief and suffering in the past can recover this space, perhaps not. It exists in *Fatheralong* as traumatic memory and the loss of something both "golden" and "green." This moment in the text also brings together the two fathers—Wideman's and his wife's. One never had this space of freedom and ease; the other one's space has been "tainted" by trauma.

In *Fatheralong*, Wideman attempts to write a story of his time with his father in the South, but it is as incomplete as the historical record of African Americans: "I am setting down a part of a story, a small piece of what needs to be remembered so when we make up the next part, imagine our lives, our history, this piece will be there, among the fragments lost, found and remembered."[162] Wideman's description of the story/history that he is working on describes the text as a whole; it feels unresolved, much like the trauma of slavery and racism in the United States. There are gaps in the text, multiple blank spaces, but it is not always certain what Wideman wants us to do with them. The work reflects the failure of communication between black fathers and sons, exacerbated by the traumatic past and the "paradigm of race." But these silent or blank spaces do not always represent a wholly negative experience. The tension between deconstructing and preserving history clears a space for new histories to be written on again and again. Even Wideman's own stories can be rewritten, as he sees firsthand when his father writes over them with his own tales. This palimpsestic quality of the book and of the nature of storytelling and historiography is a reflection of all of Wideman's work, especially in the ways that he has attempted to respond to the past through his writing: "Learn facts, the official documentary evidence, witness, proof. Simultaneously, I must not neglect the many other ways the past speaks. Through my father's voice."[163] By balancing and imbricating historical accounts with his own fiction and his own autobiographical voice, by listening to all stories, and by disrupting linear time, Wideman tries to dismantle the "masterplots" of history to open spaces for new stories to emerge and to address the wounds of the past.

CHAPTER FIVE

Truth and Reconciliation

THE BLUES AND THE HEROIC ROMANCE

> Tell me, finally, what is a man. What is a woman. Aren't we lovers first, spirits sharing an uncharted space, a space our stories tell, a space chanted written upon again and again, yet one story never quite erased by the next, each story saving the space, saving us.
>
> —JOHN EDGAR WIDEMAN, *The Cattle Killing*

The circular narratives in Wideman's canon have been ever-widening. In the last few years his novels have steadily encompassed worlds beyond his immediate family and their history, moving to his old neighborhood basketball court, to American history, to Africa, to Martinique. The cultural collapse and traumatic events that beleaguer the characters of the early novels spread further to considerations of global chaos, genocide, and terror. One could argue that Wideman's later novels merely reflect the times, but the relationship between the world outside the doorstep and the world inside your own home has always been a factor in Wideman's novels and nonfiction. The most marked change in his work in the last ten years is not in its illustration of our post-traumatized culture or in the local/global apocalypse that waits at the margins of his narratives. It is not in the darker times that haunt his pages. Nor is it in the survival and healing power of shared stories or the necessity of remembering the past. These have all appeared before—perhaps in different versions, but they have been consistent characteristics of Wideman's epic vision. Since the publication of *The Cattle Killing*, Wideman's writing not only has emphasized the importance of sharing stories in addressing the wounds of the past, but has also introduced love, intimacy, and trust as fundamental to soothing the chronic, feverish plagues ready to engulf the planet.

Those "fevers" we have seen elsewhere emblemize grief, racism, greed, hatred, and not giving people the benefit of the doubt, as his mother and grandfather, John French, would do. The lack of humanity exemplified in the kidnapping, slavery, and torture at the birth of the nation; the victimization of the poor; the systematic destruction of cultures and people; and the irrecoverable loss of children are the traumas that play and repeat in the post-traumatic narratives that we have seen thus far. Wideman's strategy of recovering the past in order to understand and survive the past proves to be insufficient to heal the pain or remove the burden of history. It does, however, begin the process of truth and reconciliation. While uncovering hidden histories may not change the world overnight, the need for storytelling—of bearing witness—is still urgently expressed, but there has been a notable change in our storytelling characters. In these later works, Wideman and his fictional doubles are less isolated and less alienated.

The need to share stories to alleviate suffering and stave off death and the end of the world resonates in *The Cattle Killing*. The preacher tells stories to a woman, Kate, a victim of the yellow fever epidemic, who may also be an African spirit seen throughout the novel and throughout history. Kate's imminent death—signaling the end of the African spirit and people as well—cannot be stopped by conventional means. The preacher shares his stories to soothe her fever and his own rage at the racism and hate that he has encountered in Philadelphia. These stories will save her and thus keep alive the African spirit and, by extension, the African culture and its people. Wideman revises the notion that the "Black picaroon" (that the preacher represents) loses his ability to adequately love. He finds love, and that power transforms his storytelling into the vehicle of the blues hero. Wideman argues that storytelling helps to heal the trauma of the past—in Africa, in the South, in Philadelphia, in our personal lives.

Indeed, from *The Cattle Killing* onward, the protagonists are involved in mature, fulfilling, and emotionally intimate love relationships. Wideman discusses this element of *The Cattle Killing*:

> Love of others is connected to the love of self. Until you have that transcendent—how can I say it—the transcendent experience of feeling internality and eternalness of another person, you can't respect those qualities, and you won't find those qualities in yourself. I think when we get paired up with someone else, paired up with a certain kind of spirit,

that's when our spirit begins to flourish, begins to take on solidarity and determination.[1]

As the preacher and Kate talk and share stories to combat the traumas they have suffered and her illness, he reminds her that in the end "love was there. The city would not have survived without it."[2] This also illustrates how finding Kate has saved him as well from his own despair, from his own feelings that maybe the world deserves to end. Kate may be a manifestation of the *ogbanji* spirit, the spirit that takes on many lives and stories, or she may just be a human woman; in either case, their love, expressed through their storytelling, saves our protagonist and will possibly save Kate as well.

In the interview above, Wideman equates love and intimacy with personal enlightenment, but he goes onto to say in that same interview that this type of "transcendent love" can create families, communities, and nations. It can connect people who might not otherwise be connected. At the surface, this philosophy is not unlike the ideals of the Enlightenment and its emphasis on brotherhood and human rights. It also echoes Platonic ideals, but the philosophy of love expressed by Wideman above, and that is found within the later novels, especially, also embodies the elements of the blues romance and the hero's journey. In the course of the narrative, the blues hero will transform his own suffering into an artistic representation of the community's voice.

In the Western version of the epic and later the romance, the hero undertakes a journey that will forever alter his comprehension of the world. In such cases, the hero is on a singular quest, removed from family, community, and love. By the end of such journeys, the hero returns to these "human" connections a changed man and, in some cases, a better man. He is often a better leader, father, and husband. We see such patterns repeated again and again in literature, and even in Wideman's works. Characters like Cudjoe in *Philadelphia Fire* and Doot in *Sent for You Yesterday* follow such a pattern, though not always successfully. But the hero from the blues romance embodies a link between the past and the present that is far more significant than in its Western analogues. Wideman further practices his palimpsestic style by balancing the blues with the literary styles of the Western epic and romance. This also points out the links already addressed between Wideman's work and the theories of Mikhail Bakhtin. Wideman's layering of the blues and the romance highlight the dialogic relationship in his writing between the discourses of "low" and "high" culture, what he has called the "street" and the "academy."

It is important here to reiterate and develop Robert Stepto's definitions of "articulate survivor" and "articulate kinsman." The articulate survivor is a questing hero who must isolate himself or herself from the community. These heroes are found in the slave narratives and other early autobiographies. Their isolation is ultimately a positive act for the community as a whole. Douglass's flight, while it separated him from his community, produced a narrative that spoke for the lives of those left behind on the plantations. The work could not have been produced if Douglass had remained in the South, in his community. The articulate kinsman takes a symbolic journey South and "seeks those aspects of tribal literacy that ameliorate, if not obliterate, the conditions imposed by solitude."[3] The articulate kinsman eventually must forsake his or her individuality for group identity. Stepto categorizes these two types as conditional of the type of narrative they inhabit. The ascension narratives (the slave narratives, the progenitors of the tradition) establish the pattern of movement in these characters in literature (away from the community).

The immersion narratives are the descendants of the ascension narratives (the response to the call). Most of these works are produced in the twentieth century (for example, *Invisible Man*). The characters in these works give up their identity for the community. I would suggest here that in the spectrum of Wideman's work, his characters have moved increasingly from articulate survivors to articulate kinsmen. Not only do characters try to merge back into communities and families from their space of isolation and alienation, but they are now better suited to "speak" for these groups as an artist figure. The articulate kinsman is a wiser character, a tribal elder.

In *A Glance Away*, Eddie Lawson takes the symbolic journey South, but he is unable to achieve an adequate position even as an articulate survivor, let alone as an articulate kinsmen or blues hero. This is also true of Cecil Braithwaite and Thomas Wilkerson in their respective novels—even though they possess the desire to become these characters. Cudjoe in *Philadelphia Fire* is even more motivated to achieve this status, but the novel ends with only a small glimmer of hope that he can reach his potential. Before *The Cattle Killing* and *Fatheralong*, only Doot and Reuben seem to succeed in becoming this figure, and even they remain essentially alone at the end of their novels. A certain amount of isolation is necessary for the heroic figure, but without continued and deep connection to the community they cannot be effective voices.

Brother Tate nicknamed John Lawson "Doot" when he was a little boy. The naming links him to the role of blues hero by the association with Brother, and hence with Albert Wilkes, and the name is itself a musical sound. Doot is also a character who has left his community but may be back to stay. He sees himself inside a "weave of voices."[4] Through collecting the stories of his family and their neighborhood, he connects to the community on a level that many blues heroes do not. He is composed of other voices; he must inhabit the community. Doot is Ashraf Rushdy's exemplar of the blues mind.[5] Rushdy describes the blues mind as one that exhibits the themes of the blues, transcending sadness, for example, but does so not in the individualistic mode that is usually associated with the blues. This blues mind model is "premised on an engagement with a collective (historical) and communal past that helps explain a personal present."[6] The blues mind is also influenced by the communal chorus of the gospel.[7]

Elsewhere we have seen the blues hero described as an isolated individual, necessarily removed from the society because of his status as artist and, possibly, sacrificial victim.[8] Albert Wilkes and Brother both fit this description of the blues hero in the novel. Doot—and Wideman's work, as we have seen in chapter 3 of this study—returns to the mythic home for stories that help revise damaging traumatic histories. However, in this novel, Doot is not the wise hero or tribal elder yet, he is still the apprentice, learning the songs, the stories that he must pass on.

In *Philadelphia Fire*, Cudjoe returns home from a period of exile, attempting to tell the story of the MOVE bombing and the lost boy, Simba. He is estranged from his family members in this work for various reasons; he is also isolated from much of the African American community. Cudjoe is making the attempt to reintegrate into his community, to take responsibility for what he has done. He feels especially guilty for his absence from his sons' lives and for never staging the performance of the revised version of *The Tempest* with his students. The imbrication of the text of *Oedipus at Colonus* within *Philadelphia Fire* works here as a revoiced historical artifact, but also signals that Cudjoe's story is one of redemption. Wideman, as a character, sees the play and notices at the end that Oedipus is "one quarter in from extinction, there's time for forgiveness, peace and understanding."[9] Cudjoe feels it might be his fate to find the child Simba to atone for his trespasses against other children. His redemption lies in his search for the child and his telling of his story: "He must find the child to be whole again."[10] Though he clearly regrets his past choices that have led to this alienated existence and clearly wants to recommit himself to family and community, the reader is left uncertain of what Cudjoe will achieve as a blues hero. Like Cecil Braithwaite in *Hurry Home* (a text that reverberates throughout *Philadelphia Fire*), Cudjoe does not quite reach the potential of the blues voice.

Significantly, the possible failure of Cudjoe's ultimate quest is replayed and inverted in the work published immediately following, *Fatheralong*. The loss of sons and the damaged relationship between fathers and sons are not only the thematic focus of the work, but also the structure of the quest toward reconciliation between Wideman as the father and Wideman as the son. It appears that until the relationship to his father can be addressed and resolved (or forgiven), the relationships with the sons cannot be fully realized—at least metaphorically, in the text. The journey to reconciliation takes place as an actual journey South, to the past, to reimmersion, to understanding, and even to healing.

Though Wideman hopes to reconnect with his father, most of the trip is a silent one. This quiet has affected the relationships of the fathers and sons of the Wideman family. When Wideman's father lived apart from the family when Wideman was just a boy, Wideman would try to sneak over to see him. He wonders, "[Did] the prospect of finding my father over there beyond Hamilton put my flight in a different light? Not so much deserting or shaming the women as it was seeking him."[11] In Wideman's imagination, the world of his father, of men, began to inhabit a different space than the world of his mother, of women. He develops this further in *Hoop Roots*, when he goes to the basketball court to "find fathers."

Wideman clearly seeks to find more than his father in *Fatheralong*. The work, subtitled "A Meditation on Fathers and Sons," considers the relationship between history and race as well. Hoping to reconcile himself to his father, Wideman searches for reconciliation with the racial past, a hope symbolized by the journey itself, so that he can move on. At one point in the work, Wideman compares African American slavery with the Holocaust. He has made such associations in the past, especially in the short stories "Hostages," "Valaida," and "Fever." By layering these images and stories within a search for his "father stories," Wideman "posits that the ancestral story he seeks to recover is one about genocide and survival."[12] The connection between the "ur-trauma" of the twentieth century and Wideman's collective and personal past reframes this memoir as a search for philosophical meaning and hope in a world scarred by unbelievable trauma.[13] This is a characteristic of several other contemporary African American novelists as well. When Toni Morrison opens *Beloved* with the dedication "Sixty Million and More," she "clearly signifies on the 'six million' victims of the European Holocaust . . . and just as the narratives of the Holocaust are gestures at speaking the unspeakable, of bearing witness to an evil beyond imagination, so too this figuration of black history recasts that experience as one beyond the rationalist discourses of historiography and social sciences."[14] Wideman's work has consistently attempted to forge images of African Americans beyond the mainstream, but that urgent need grows at a more rapid pace in the later works of his canon. This need also becomes less localized within his family's and the nation's past, as we infer from the closing scenes of his son's marriage to a young woman from Sierra Leone, whose own past represents traumas that continue to plague the world.

Ultimately, Wideman is unable to recover a meaningful relationship with his father, at least in the confines of the text. However, the resolution of

Fatheralong offers a struggle that balances the hopeful union of one son in marriage, surrounded by Jewish, African, and African American voices and cultures and ancestral spirits, with the irrevocable loss of another son imprisoned in Arizona. Danny's wedding, portrayed with effusive love—matrimonial, parental, familial—and global and cultural harmony, contrasts with the letter to Jake that closes the novel. Love is as deeply expressed in these pages, but it is expressed by pain through Wideman's ex-wife Judy's loss, by Wideman's loss. While the personal trauma cannot be healed, it is navigated within the daily act of surviving by recalling stories of Jake's childhood: "a love story finally, love of you, your brother and sister, since no word except love makes sense of the ever-present narrative our days unfold."[15] *Fatheralong* ultimately reconciles love and pain to manage trauma in ways that the fictional characters of *Philadelphia Fire* cannot achieve.

If *Fatheralong* acts as a complementary piece to *Philadelphia Fire*, *The Cattle Killing* may be thought of as the coda to these stories and a bridge to Wideman's last four works. The writer's relationship between his father and his son frames the novel. It opens with the writer, another fictional self of Wideman, walking up the hill to his father's house to deliver a manuscript that is *The Cattle Killing*. The novel ends with the same writer's son writing a letter to the writer after having read the same manuscript—it is important to note here that this structure echoes the relationships in the previous two books. The writer/character/autobiographer who has been isolated in the last works from fathers and sons reverses the patterns in his past by, first, attending to those relationships in the book, and then concluding with a scene that illustrates these connections and shows that the sharing of "father stories" continues. Here the fictional counterparts achieve what is only hinted at by the end of *Philadelphia Fire* and not fully realized in *Fatheralong*: the fulfilled quest of the blues hero. Interestingly, Wideman has had to go further back in history to reach this moment. He meditates on history in the previous works, layering its presence within his texts to show the relationship between the post-traumatic present and the traumatic past. *The Tempest* and the antebellum South are haunting figures in those works, but in *The Cattle Killing*, the historical stage, the "birth of the nation's blues," takes front and center.

The other blues hero in *The Cattle Killing* is its narrator, who also takes a journey, this time into the heart of racism and the yellow fever epidemic. Having no real home, part of his mythic quest is to find his own identity and place in the world. He finds not only himself on this journey, but also despair, death, and apocalypse. But he also discovers love. This loves grows through its intimate recollections of self and of the past. It is a microcosmic relationship of the power of storytelling that Wideman has voiced elsewhere. In the midst of enormous global and historical traumas expressed in the novel, it is remarkable that Wideman focuses on the most private, most human moments between two people in love. It is not unusual to see such patterns in literature when the historical moments are so fraught with danger, fear, and emptiness. Love poetry often flourishes in the worst moments in human history.

For the past several decades, American culture has also supported the notion that words and stories have therapeutic power, especially in the case of victims of abuse, trauma, and genocide. And the Truth and Reconciliation Commissions of countries like South Africa encourage victims of torture to recount their experiences to bear witness, to help with the prosecution of crimes, to make certain that this history never repeats itself, and to encourage the "process of healing a traumatized and wounded people" so that they can move forward.[16] These characteristics of healing stories, of redemption and revelation, all merge in *The Cattle Killing*, and in later works as well, to save characters from destruction and despair over their losses.

The novel *Two Cities* also uses conversation and storytelling to forge love relationships and to begin a process of healing or reconciliation. As in other works that we have looked at, the novel resonates with the loss of children. The book opens with a dedication to Omar Wideman (1971-1992), the son of Robby. The central character, Kassima, has lost a husband and both of her sons. Disease and violence have infected her life. She meets Robert Jones in a bar, beginning a relationship that we know will at some time have to address the painful losses that she has barely survived.

The other main character in the novel is Mr. Mallory, a boarder in Kassima's house in Homewood. His personal history is also traumatic. As a photographer, he has tried to capture the images of African America life in both Homewood and the other city of the title, Philadelphia. The two cities have always been implicitly linked in Wideman's fiction. Novels are either set in Homewood (Pittsburgh) or in Philadelphia. Homewood is usually the site of the stories of family history, and Philadelphia is for the stories of official history. Here Wideman brings the two cities together to embrace the community at large and to illustrate the connection between family and official history in his vision.

Another character that appears periodically in the novel, through flashbacks and memories, is John Africa—who also appeared in *Philadelphia Fire*. He is a friend of Mr. Mallory's in the novel, and it is John Africa's death that makes Mallory desert Philadelphia. He moves to Pittsburgh, living quietly and silently in Kassima's house. He remains isolated, using only his photographs to express himself.

The novel opens with Mallory imagining a conversation with his dead friend, John Africa. His reminiscences of John Africa prompt him to think about other young men who were killed by a city inflamed by hate. John Africa especially reminds him of Emmett Till.[17] At times in the first few pages, it is hard to distinguish if John Africa is alive or dead. Mallory also moves fluidly between times and places: "two cities, two places at once."[18] The fluidity of time is compared to a circle: "Would the mirror shatter, would ripples skim across the surface of the water, ending one scene, forming another, one circle climbing out from another, chasing the other, chasing itself."[19] Time is conflated and circular throughout this novel as it is in others that we have examined, illustrating the repeated circles of history, the continuing recursive relationship between past and present.

There are several doubles in the novel, including repeated stories. In the early pages we hear a replay of "The Chinaman's Story" from *Damballah*. Mallory's photography is characterized by its "double exposure." Robert Jones is clearly a double or alter ego of Wideman. Jones talks about his grandmother breaking a window with her hand to warn her husband that he is in danger,[20] which is a scene in several works of the Homewood trilogy and appears again in *Hoop Roots*. Jones talks about growing up in a house full of women's stories on Cassina Way. He is the first male child, spoiled by their attention. And he is a basketball player. All of these instances are indications that Jones shares many autobiographical connections with Wideman (this is illustrated even more clearly in *Hoop Roots*, which seems to be the memoir version of these moments in *Two Cities*).

Jones expresses what it was like growing up with a household of women:

> He's reminded of his mother's hand, the hand of his grandmother and aunts in the details, the little extras that change nothing, add more clutter to the clutter, but also add space, space blessed because its touched by something of them, from them. Space the women open. Space beckoning him, saved for him, space for his daydreams to fill.[21]

It is their storytelling voices and unconditional love that open a place for him to dream and speak, but it is also a place to re-imagine possibility and share intimacy—between family and especially between Jones and Kassima.

Jones and Kassima begin their relationship with sharing stories of family. Their relationship is clearly reminiscent of the preacher and Kate in *The Cattle Killing* (which immediately preceded *Two Cities*). Part of this sharing act helps Kassima deal with the pain of her loss. The other voices she hears in Jones's stories remind her of the other lives that do survive in the face of adversity. She also reads stories from the Bible to console her. The end of this section disrupts time, as Jones interrupts the narrative to tell us about how he met and lost Kassima. He tries to explain the breakup to an audience (us?) through the metaphor of the big-fish-that-got-away story:

> Something I never understood before I met her and lost her. The guy's not lying. He feels the empty between his hands growing each time he tells the story, each time the damn fish gets away again. You see, the funny thing is the sorry motherfucker's right. No matter how wide apart he spreads his lying hands, he's right. The story's true.[22]

Kassima's voice begins the next section, "Lamentations." She narrates her discovery of the stories of the Bible. At first she is surprised to see stories of suffering similar to hers in the book.[23] As she reads the stories of loss and "lamentation," she contemplates the importance of storytelling: "Never thought about something like being a writer. Hell. Just halfway learning to read but I wondered if I wrote down my story would a woman lost a son in Detroit or Cleveland or Philadelphia or Los Angeles, California know just what I was talking about."[24] Kassima, unknowingly, defines one of the tenets of writing for Wideman—the need to share stories of suffering because of their ability to connect to others. It also marks Kassima as a blues hero, whose voice may someday be able to soothe others and help them through their grief and loss. Kassima's narrative moves from first person to a second-person voice when she addresses us directly: "Ask me why I lost three men in my life in the space of ten months and wound up alone with Mr. Mallory in this haunted house and I have no answer for you."[25] Kassima is also a woman who has borne the burden of loss; her discovery of the Bible and its stories may indicate her transformation into an articulate survivor who may in turn become an articulate elder, like Wideman's own mother, whose suffering has been an equally difficult burden to bear (her "weight," as he describes it in a short story in *God's Gym*).[26] The voice here asks us to engage with Kassima, to share her story and perhaps our own as a way of healing and answering unanswerable questions.

Kassima later describes the events that ended her relationship with Robert Jones. Robert invites Kassima to watch him play a game, a place where he can display his manhood. The basketball court in *Two Cities* is both a site of love and urban violence, as it is in *Hoop Roots*. More than an arena for mere showmanship, it is a space where Robert feels in control in a world where he clearly has no real power. On the court he can confront the failures he sees in himself as a man and the limited identity he has been handed by society. He sacrifices his sore, aging body to prove to himself and to Kassima that he's more than the chances he has been given. Kassima acknowledges:

> Nothing he could do would make me love him more. Loved him enough. More than enough. More than enough to last us both forever and ever and he should have understood but they never do. I don't need him to be any better than he already is, but men don't understand love is love and if it's love it's enough. Men always got to prove something. Or have you prove something to them. So I walked up to the basketball court that day against my better judgment just to be with him because he asked me to. Why do men have to pretend they are better than they are.[27]

Jones is playing on the court when two much younger men start a fight. One has brought a gun. Kassima is certain that they are in a gang, perhaps the ones that killed her son. Shot, but only wounded by the boy, Robert realizes that even on the court the violence and despair of the urban world can intrude. And even here someone else can try to define who you are: Robert is called "old nigger" by the youth who shoots him. Some of the tension shown here between generations appears in the short story "Doc's Story." Though in that story Wideman's alter ego seemed to be the younger narrator (as well as "Doc"). In *Two Cities*, Wideman's double is clearly Jones, the older man. In "Doc's Story," the conflict does not erupt in violence; in fact, the younger men respect Doc. The basketball court and the world have grown steadily unstable and even more violent.

The incident reminds Kassima of the frailty of life, and she discovers that she can't let herself be hurt again. She's tired of "sad stories." The narrative flows instantly into Robert's retelling of their breakup with his friends, almost at the same place that Kassima's story ends. Both voices and stories occupy the same space almost simultaneously. Kassima's desire to remove herself from her relationship with Robert because of a fear of losing someone again echoes other characters we have seen in Wideman's work, including Martha and Mother Bess. We know what will lay ahead for Kassima if she does not find a way to reconcile herself to the outside world.

The next section of the book is heard through the voice of Mallory. Mallory's death compels Kassima to call Robert for advice. She's not certain that she can keep her promise to Mallory to burn his photos. She explains to Robert why Mallory and she had become so close in the last days of his life. He needed to talk: "Talk, talk, talk about everything. . . . He talked and I liked to listen. Enjoyed listening. And he'd listen to me."[28] The two have kept each other going by sharing stories of their lives. Mallory dies when Kassima is out of the house. He has wandered around looking for her, wanting to tell her one more story before he goes.

Linear time is interrupted again in the text when Kassima's description of Mallory's death is followed by another letter from Mallory to Giacometti. In this letter, Mallory asks "Mr. G" if he knows Romare Bearden. Mallory describes Bearden's work as

> many paintings in one, overlapping, hiding, and revealing each other. Many scenes occur at once, a crowd hides in a single body. Time and space are thicker. I'm seeking the truth of his painting when I stack slices of light onto each square of film. Different views, each stamped with its own pattern of light and dark but also transparent, letting through some of the light and dark layers beneath and above. Like a choir singing. Each voice distinct, but also changing the sound of the whole, changing itself as it joins other voices.[29]

The link to Bearden is a salient one for many reasons. Bearden's work is layered, a collage of people and pictures, mixing mediums to create a textured and "multivoiced" portrait. The description fits Wideman's work as well. Bearden's work graces the cover of *Two Cities*, as it did on the Vintage paperback versions of the books of the Homewood trilogy. The comparison of Bearden's work also highlights the relationship between the layering in Wideman's writing and the dialogic hybridity that Bakhtin asserts is the nature of the novel. It is also the description of Mallory's photographs: "So I snap, snap, snap. Pile layer after. A hundred doses of light without moving the film. No single, special, secret view sought or revealed. One in many. Many in one layer."[30]

Mallory also makes a comparison between Bearden's work and Thelonious Monk: "Though I lack words to say how, our homegrown African music, like your sculpture and Mr. B's paintings, helps me with my picture-taking. In the piano solos of Mr. Thelonious Monk I hear familiar tunes drifting in and out, hiding and uncovering each other, old songs, playing something new, music's no one's ever heard before."[31] The comparison illuminates that the layering of Bearden and the silence of Monk have allowed for spaces that Mallory feels his own art can address: "snapshots one inside the other, notes played so they can dance away, make room for others."[32] This is a space where sharing stories can occur, and there are places where new stories can be heard. Robert's response and help during Mallory's death show Kassima that he does love her and that maybe that love could survive the streets of Homewood. Realizing this, she is reminded of a story Robert told her about the love his grandmother had for his grandfather. She loved him so much she put her hand through a window to warn him that his life was in danger. Kassima knows that the grandmother's scar will "become a story grandmother will tell grandson and then one day long afterwards the grandson will tell it to her."[33] The story, of course, we have seen before, and here and in *Hoop Roots* it represents shared intimacy and storytelling as a sign of love and connection. The story illustrates to Kassima the power of love and the inherent pain and sacrifice that accompany it. The story reminds her that her own experience of loss and love is not new, and others have survived it. The sharing of the story brings her back to the community and to life.

Later in the novel, we see one of several letters that Mallory has written to Giacometti. In it, Mallory explains the purpose and character of his art. Mallory suggests that he converses in two languages.[34] The implication is that those languages are oral and written, African American and European American (what he calls a "minstrel tongue"). But it also, in Mallory's aesthetic, recalls voices of history buried within him. His duty as an artist is to recover what "the old voices taught me. I keep working to keep myself alive, the voices alive inside my work."[35] He also calls himself the "best blues singer in the universe."[36] All of these descriptions could easily depict Wideman's own writing project. This idea is further extended in various passages in the text when Mallory contemplates the MOVE bombing and pictures of Emmett Till. Mallory even revoices the "ladybug" song that is alluded to in the short story "Fever" and *Philadelphia Fire*. Mallory's time confusion, reminiscent of the structure of *Philadelphia Fire*, is likely evidence of his traumatic past or a sign of "a psychic wound from which [he] is unable to heal."[37]

As a blues artist, he has chosen to isolate himself to escape his pain, but also, in his mind, to perfect his art. However, he confesses in a letter to Giacometti: "I decided to live alone. Suffered the loneliness and pain of cutting myself off from other people only to discover when I started taking pictures, others still lived inside me."[38] Like other typical blues heroes, Mallory has chosen to separate himself from the community in order to better tell their story. He even leaves behind his family: "believed I had to leave if I wanted a life. Stole myself. Like a runaway slave. Stole myself and the price was leaving my family behind, my people behind."[39] The trope of the alienated artist replays here and is eventually inverted when Mallory begins to see a connection between Kassima and the wife he left behind. His alienation is further relinquished as he seeks out Kassima to "talk" to her and share stories. In a significant shift from many of the other alienated figures in Wideman's work, Mallory realizes too late that he could have been more effective if he had stayed connected to the world. In his absence, Kassima will develop her blues voice, and in her relationship with Jones, she will embrace love and intimacy as methods of survival and transcendence in the face of trauma.

Mallory connects moments like the MOVE bombing (and the photographs he carries of them in his mind) with his personal history, especially that moment in World War II that forever changed his life—when white men in his own company purposefully shot him and killed another officer, physically and mentally wounding Mallory permanently.[40] The intersection of personal history with recorded history is reminiscent of many of Wideman's works, but Mallory is a walking embodiment of Wideman's artistic project as well as its greatest sufferer of post-trauma. His portrait as a traumatized World War II veteran and artist recalls Carl in the Homewood books as well. Carl never realizes his potential as an artist, but Mallory's work is a testament to his position as a "blues singer," even if he is one that remains isolated from most of the community. His work, at least, has captured the community's stories and voices.

There are other moments in *Two Cities* that revise earlier Wideman novels, even the first novel, *A Glance Away*. At one point, Mallory considers how snapshots are like memory, how they order and shape our lives:

> We believe in them. Depend on them. See a world out there, separate from us. Force of habit turns to certainty. We forget how spirit and mind piece the world together glimpse by glimpse. We forget our power. Forget that one naked, sideways stare, one glance away changes everything."[41]

And then later in the novel, Mallory states:

> Was he learning to look at life the way Giacometti looked at his models. A head stranger, more mysterious each time the sculptor's eyes returned from a glance away . Starting over with each look, each time, each day. Failing always. Always a clean, scrubbed slate, a yawning emptiness, a chance. Clarity returned. Goodness of all things merging, blending into one. The one always many.[42]

Why the references to a work that so many critics think that Wideman has moved beyond? Wideman's work is still questioning what happens if you "glance away" from something. Will someone come along and change it if you aren't paying attention? Will they tell you it didn't really happen at all? If you glance away can you see history, your family, yourself anew? Can you rewrite it, "starting over with each look?" This resonating line, "a glance away," evokes Wideman's aesthetic. You can look away from time for a moment to break its hold over you. This creates a "gap" and gives writers a chance to fill in the space with their own stories, to re-present (and represent) history on their own terms.[43] Bonnie TuSmith notes that Wideman's return to the phrase suggests that after thirty years, "a glance away" has "metamorphosed into a message of hope."[44] It certainly appears that the fear that things will change if you look away too long has evolved (or has merely been revised by Wideman and could be again) into a different type of gap, another site of revision and possibility.

Nevertheless, the phrase still contains a cautionary message. Mallory believes that the "glance" can only be momentary because if you look away for too long someone else will come along and fill in that space for you with stories that won't capture who you are. Mallory senses this danger because "they got a picture of African people locked up in their minds and nothing's gon change it."[45] His own photos are the only way to counterbalance that "picture." But focusing only on the frame, the photo directly in front of you, can cause you to miss everything else. The photo is just a single image. That's why Mallory begins to use double exposure in his photography, why he opens the shutter, over-exposing film to layer the photo—to capture all the possibilities of life and all possible stories, simultaneously. The "double exposure" also revises the image of double-consciousness that Wideman has attempted to deconstruct before. Double-consciousness is a forced reaction to confronting the singular, dominant image of African American identity by submerging another truer self. Double-exposure does not include the images that others have placed on you, but all the various identities you might possess as a reaction to the singular, dominant image of African American identity.

> And I keep pulling the trigger, snapshot after snapshot blasting holes in the world, pretending nothing changes, the ducks still sit on the water untouched, calm, waiting, until I'm ready to shoot again. My pictures are pretty postcards with the world arranged nice and neat. But I don't want to hide the damage. I want to enter the wound, cut through layer by layer like a surgeon, expose what lies beneath the skin. Go where there is no skin, no outside or inside, no body. Only traffic always moving in many directions at once. Snapshots one inside the other, notes played so they can dance away, make room for others. Free others to free themselves.[46]

While Mallory's art could shape a new image or open up the visual space for new images and stories to appear, his wish to burn the photos upon his death suggests that he believes he failed as an artist or that he never was one to begin with because, as he says earlier, he removed himself from his wife, from family, from other people. Without that love and connection he cannot be an effective voice for his people, nor can he understand himself or show others how to survive pain and suffering. Sharing his story could have been equally or even more powerful than his photography. It is in sharing stories with Kassima that he realizes his missed potential.

The single image of African American life that Mallory wants to deconstruct has operated throughout Wideman's work. The counternarratives that he has produced attempt to revise these images in much the same way that

Mallory's photographs have. This focus continues in *Hoop Roots*, a work where the basketball court figures even more prominently than it does in *Two Cities*. In 1973 Wideman told an interviewer that he was working on a book about basketball. Though that book did not immediately emerge (*Brothers and Keepers* was the next published work), Wideman ultimately found his way back to the court with both *Two Cities* and then *Hoop Roots*.[47] As a former star basketball player at the University of Pennsylvania, Wideman has written about his love of basketball in many of his memoirs and novels. He has even written essays on the sport, but *Hoop Roots* investigates the court as a site of storytelling, family, history, heroism, and love. Not only does *Hoop Roots* continue the project to dismantle negative stereotypes of African American life, it also engenders the act of storytelling with the mythic power to save the world.

The history of African American experience in *Hoop Roots* proceeds as an examination and critique of race and sports. Elsewhere Wideman has deconstructed the myth of the American Dream and its power over the imagination of whites and blacks alike. The intersection of race, sports, and the American Dream in *Hoop Roots* allows Wideman to continue to disrupt prevailing notions of African American identity, especially the concept and image of "black masculinity." The photographic work of Mallory in *Two Cities* represents the inability of mainstream America to see beyond the singular image of African Americans; the multilayered photographs are Wideman's visual version of "all stories are true."

Wideman has consistently presented readers with the stereotypes of the black male (as slave, as prisoner, as Caliban) and then subverted them through his revisionary storytelling. But in *Hoop Roots*, Wideman pays special attention to the black male athlete and the popular iconic image in America, one that seems to transcend race and trauma.[48] In Wideman's work the celebrated and successful black athlete is another false prophecy that must be revealed. As if to challenge readers with the questions, "So you think you know something about black men? About basketball players? About me?" Wideman examines these images in the context of the disparate narratives of a genealogical and communal autobiography, the history of basketball, and a blooming romantic relationship. Readers expecting the "novel about basketball" will be as disappointed as those expecting *Philadelphia Fire* to really be the novel about the MOVE bombing.

Wideman also includes the three strands of historiographic metafiction here as well. He fictionalizes basketball stories, takes ethnographic notes, and recounts historical moments in NBA and Homewood court history. And as a cultural critic, he considers the role basketball has had in the globalization process. All of this is imbricated within the emerging love story and the rise and fall of Maurice Stokes and the tragic lives of Ed Fleming; Robby Wideman's son, Omar; and a Homewood star of the past, Eldon Lawson. The love of the game helps Wideman transcend the traumatic past, and meditating on basketball's place in the world proves that the sport cannot help you defy gravity for long. Nevertheless, Wideman revises the blues hero image, the articulate survivor, and returns to his home court. While in the Homewood books he most often stands outside the works, taking notes, he is no longer "courtside" in this memoir; he is playing the game and bringing a date. The physical space of the court has changed for him. He is the wise, old man of the court, the "Doc" of "Doc's Story" in *Fever*, the articulate kinsman.

The play not only consists of the basketball game he loves so well, but also includes his verbal game and writing. The court and the page share mythic space as sites of understanding and reconciliation with the past. Basketball, like writing or music, is an expressive space that Wideman uses to play, to criticize, to celebrate, to analyze African American experience. Wideman suggests that the sport creates this space for all African Americans as well. And though basketball, or hoop—especially the playground variety—continues to grow as one of the most popular global sports, it is still popularized and dominated by African Americans. It is another sign, like African American music, of the culturally expressive traditions of African Americans, undervalued by their own nation, leaving their footprint on the world.

Paradoxically, for Wideman, basketball operates both as a celebration of African American culture and as a sign that white Americans still equate African Americans primarily with athletic ability. White, middle-class America largely supports the merchandising of basketball, but Madison Avenue still favors using African American stars as their advertising images. From Michael Jordan to LeBron James, the African American male body is displayed as something consumable. The representation of black masculinity and physicality builds on the animalistic representation of the black male body that is the source of both white male consumption and fear. Wideman argues in the work that these images continue to "cage" or frame African American identity, much like he concluded that the Moynihan Report had framed the African American family.

In *Hoop Roots*, Wideman inscribes basketball as a possible form of resistant expression that addresses and refutes black male stereotypes and reveals the spurious nature of such images. Through his own portrait in the work as a player and a writer (as well as a father, son, public intellectual, and lover), Wideman deconstructs the image—all these "stories" of Wideman are true. He further counters the stereotype of the black male body as a site of fear in the illustration of himself as a loving son, surrounded by the nurturing voices of the Wideman women, and as a romantic partner, exploring the emotional intimacy of his relationship. While these characteristics are certainly true (or could be) of any African American male who steps onto the court, it is a story that gets lost or silenced in the cacophony of television advertisements, ESPN interviews, and play-offs. It seems when the star athlete is accused of a crime—when he supposedly performs the animalistic act that the society expects of him—is the only time the cameras look further beyond the constructed advertising image.[49]

Wideman professes in *Hoop Roots* that he wants to do with writing what Michael Jordan has done with basketball: "become a standard for others to measure themselves against."[50] This linkage of writing and basketball structures the work and may ultimately disappoint readers of the book. Fans of the game expecting a work about basketball, or at least a thorough cultural analysis of the sport, will believe that Wideman has dropped the ball. Instead, Wideman proffers meditations on his personal relationships and family and an exegesis on race in America, much like he does elsewhere in his writing. And the work serves as a reminder that whether in the pulpit, in the juke joint, or on the basketball court, African Americans have always found unique, sometimes coded, avenues of self-expression in order to prove their humanity, their grace, their soul.

Wideman returns to the autobiographical narrative to counteract negative black male imagery and to reaffirm the necessity of black male subjectivity. Autobiography denies the legitimacy of narratives that construct the silent black male body—emphasizing physicality and brute animalism over creativity and intellectual prowess. In *Hoop Roots*, Wideman attempts to rewrite and redefine the popularly accepted image of the black male as a violent, inarticulate laborer. Here Wideman comes closer than he has before in displacing the "Calibanic discourse."

Drawing on his own experiences as a basketball player, Rhodes scholar, and successful novelist, Wideman aims to illustrate that the black man is more than his physical associations: he is also a father, a lover, and a writer, and scholar. Basketball is another method to regain ownership of one's individual African American identity, just as autobiography has proven to be in the past. Wideman's analysis of basketball scrutinizes the conversations of sociologists and media analysts alike over the past decade, especially in regards to "hoop dreams"—a version of the American Dream that sanctifies the game as the path out of the ghetto. These hoop dreams, redolent in the popular culture, enforce the racial paradigm of black physical prowess versus white intellectual pursuits. Wideman argues, however, that it is precisely this rhetoric of blackness and whiteness that helps maintain racial division. In writing about his own life, Wideman forges a different black male image: his own status as a writer, professor, and athlete contests the stereotypical view of black masculinity. His pursuits have been both intellectual and physical, and in all, he has consciously addressed the images and stories that others have constructed about African American life. This was what drew him to writing: "I need writing because it can extend the measure of what's possible, allow me to engage in defining standards."[51]

Another way that Wideman has contested the limited images of black masculinity is by constructing a role for himself as a public intellectual. In the past few years especially, Wideman has appeared on numerous PBS specials about race and culture. As a contributor to magazines and journals including the *New Yorker* and *Esquire*, Wideman has commented widely on the aftermath of 9-11 (September 11, 2001), politics, and race, especially on African Americans and sports. Sometimes his essays describe his love of basketball or his joy at seeing his daughter, Jamila, play, but he has also written about and/or interviewed Michael Jordan and Dennis Rodman.[52] These moments are clearly paradoxical for Wideman: in the midst of celebrating the player or the sport, he also criticizes the culture and the country for its attitudes toward race. This is apparent even in an interview Wideman conducted with actor Denzel Washington on the eve of the release of Spike Lee's film, *He Got Game*. In the interview, Wideman notes Washington's phenomenal success and celebrity, his creativity, his intelligence, *and* his ability to play basketball. As a writer and critic of the game, Wideman embraces the public intellectual role again in the interview, reflecting on sports, film, black actors, and fatherhood. More than just being the man who got the job because he used to play basketball, Wideman uses the conversation to question and to transcend stereotypical images of black male identity. Consequently, both Washington's and Wideman's voices offer a less limited picture of African American life between the pages of a mainstream magazine like *Esquire*.

Wideman breaks from the interview format several times to analyze basketball in American society:

> In the case of hoop, the game I love, the big picture includes irony, paradox, pain, poor drug-ridden communities blasted by unemployment, sudden violent death, imprisonment, the slow erosion of health and prospects, affluent communities of spenders wildly consuming, addicted to possessions, communities connected mostly by the overarching dog-eat-dog ethos reigning from top to bottom of the economic scale.[53]

Wideman takes this piece beyond the typical celebrity interview, seizing the opportunity to be heard about race and sports, which here are inseparable in Wideman's observation. In the estimation of many poor, African American youth, the promise of the NBA contract—a highly improbable dream at best—is the means of escape from poverty, drugs, and despair. As a product of American society, Wideman reiterates what many others argue elsewhere: basketball reflects the racial divide that has plagued the country for centuries. It "also functions to embody racist fantasies, to prove and perpetuate essential differences between blacks and whites, to justify the idea of white supremacy and rationalize an unfair balance of power, maintained by violence, lies, and terror, between blacks and whites."[54]

It is this racial division that Wideman endeavors to analyze in *Hoop Roots* while simultaneously honoring the sport that he loves so much. He describes the book as an attempt to "explain to myself the power of playground basketball, its hold on me, on African American men, the entire culture."[55] For Wideman, basketball also furnishes a space to create an identity of one's own, apart from the identity that others have constructed for you. This is especially true of African American males, whose lives have been the subject of stories forced on them by the white hegemony.

Still, much of the work is devoted to a specific critique of the black male athlete in the white mainstream. Possibly the most difficult balancing act in the book, Wideman negotiates this analysis at the same time that he both professes his love of the game in his own life and praises it as an African American art form. At times it reads as though two different men were writing the book. Wideman's own "double-consciousness" regarding the sport may stem not from *his* own feelings, but rather from the culture's ambivalence regarding sports and race in America. Despite the abundance of African American sports figures—heroes in the eyes of even middle-class white America—African American males continue to be primarily defined in a negative manner. Even Wideman's creation of his own identity as a writer is foregrounded by the revelations about his family's violent past and accounts of the violence that has marred the African American community, including the lives of basketball players.

The tale of basketball is obviously also the tale of racism in America. Wideman, in this vein, equates the marketing and managing of basketball metaphorically with slavery. The game, for example, used to be played behind metal cages—hence players are called "cagers"—and today, he argues, the African American athlete is "caged" by the appropriation of his body for sport and for advertising. He cautions players: "Don't allow anyone to steal your body or rent, buy, disembody, tame, virtualize, shrink, organize, defang it."[56] At the same time, Wideman projects into the text positive images of the black body and self to counteract the stereotypical images of male blackness. Those images, Wideman realizes, are the burden of Western history. The black male body became a depository of the West's "darkest places," a "walking palimpsest of the fears and fascinations possessing our cultural imagination."[57] Frantz Fanon realized this phenomena most clearly when he worked with psychiatric patients who could be described as suffering from a "despair" that troubles a psyche that has had to endure such trauma after colonization. These descriptions also echo W.E.B. DuBois's definition of double-consciousness, which cannot be accidental in a book dedicated to him and his work, *The Souls of Black Folk*.

The image of blackness as ugly, animal, sexually violent, and illiterate can be found in the earliest cultural representations of colonization and New World slavery. The character of Caliban from William Shakespeare's play *The Tempest* is a forefather of such representations, as we saw in the last chapter. Wideman uses the Prospero/Caliban relationship from *The Tempest* occasionally in this work as well. Wideman uses Caliban's problem with learning and speaking Prospero's language to critique white attitudes toward race and difference. Control of the body, as well as the rhetoric or the "story" of African American life, illustrates the cultural construction of African American identity that Wideman so urgently wants to dismantle. Since Caliban can only express himself through Prospero's tongue, he exists only through Prospero's voice. The white ownership of the African American image, especially of black males, continues to impact African American identity today—especially in the arena of sports, media, and advertising.

In both *Hoop Roots* and a *New Yorker* article on Dennis Rodman, Wideman uses the Prospero/Caliban trope to install the images of master/slave relationships and silent black male bodies that he sees operating in the NBA. Players are silent performers that are condemned when they speak up, act out, or talk back. In the essay on Rodman, Wideman compares the player's battles with NBA commissioner David Stern to the Prospero/Caliban conflict. Rodman's body was clearly on display—tattooed, dyed, and pierced—during the years he played in the league. Wideman argues that Rodman wrestled for control of his body, reacting against its silencing by the NBA, namely, by Stern.[58] Stern, because of Rodman's popularity and talent, needed the silent, black body to "rule his island."[59] Wideman asks what seems to be a rhetorical question: "Why does Rodman's refusal to allow his identity to be totally subsumed by a game offend people?"[60] The answer is clearly that America is more comfortable with, more historically accustomed to, a silent, unadorned, physical black self.

In *Hoop Roots*, Wideman cautions playground hoopsters not to let the NBA "kidnap" and "whitewash" them.[61] The rhetorical allusions to slavery and colonization here indicate Wideman's cautionary motive. What may be at stake for young players is ownership of their self-expression. Their skill and creativity belongs to the white consciousness, and their bodies will become material for someone else's story as Caliban has been in Prospero's tale—a relationship that Prospero notes in the play's last scene: "This thing of darkness I acknowledge mine."[62]

The use of blackness, particularly the employment of black male bodies, to symbolize the exotic, the Other, has enslaved African Americans in a silent melodrama. This "racial gaze" has promoted America's negative attitudes toward urban African American existence, turning men and women into the statistics recorded in the media and social programs as evidence that "black life" is bankrupt. Welfare, drug use, unemployment, crime, punishment, even teenage, single motherhood become associated with this stereotype of African American life. As Greg Tate suggests in the introduction to *Everything but the Burden: What White People Are Taking from Black Culture*, the influence of such cultural constructions has had a sweeping impact on the real lives of African Americans:

> The African-American presence in this country has produced a fearsome, seductive, and circumspect body of myths about Black intellectual capacity, athletic ability, sexual appetite, work ethic, family values, and propensity for violence and drug addiction. From these myths have evolved much of the paranoia, pathology, absurdity, awkwardness, alienation, and anomie which continue to define the American racial scene.[63]

White America's popular culture, its modes of expression, and its style are indebted to the African American tradition even though the lives behind such production are invisible to the mainstream.

While the stars of the NBA receive wealth, fame, and accolades almost beyond measure, the majority of the young men that pin their futures to basketball will fall short of their dreams of success. In *Hoop Roots*, Wideman juxtaposes an analysis of a superstar like Michael Jordan with the lives of young men whose lives are lost to the streets, including his own nephew, Omar. Omar, the son of the imprisoned Robby, was shot to death—execution style—by three men following a barroom fight in 1993. Omar's death highlights Wideman's personal pain found throughout the book, but the loss also signals those silent, invisible black bodies used and then neglected in the American consciousness, becoming a social scientist's statistic. While at the funeral of Omar, Wideman runs into Ed Fleming, a hometown boy who had a fairly successful career in the NBA in the 1950s. Nevertheless, Wideman reminds us that Fleming's success did not shield him from the effects of racism on the individual life. He carries "visible scars or the invisible ones" with him, particularly because Fleming belonged to an era when his dark skin clearly represented a threat. Wideman argues that Fleming's

> body type and color [were] a stigma, a danger to the bearer for five hundred years in racist America. Convict body, field hand body, too

unadulterated African, too raw, too black, too powerful and quick and assertive for most whites and most colored folks to feel comfortable around until Michael Jordan arrived and legitimated Ed Fleming's complexion and physique, mainstreaming them, blunting the threatening edge, commodifying the Jordan look, as if the physical, sexual potency of a dark, streamlined, muscular body could be purchased, as if anybody, everybody—Swede, Korean, Peruvian, Croat, New Englander—could be like Mike.[64]

Seeing the former NBA player in the funeral home reminds Wideman of recent stories he has heard about Fleming, especially an altercation at the school where he coached—one that left him severely beaten. In this instance, Fleming's physical presence, his "body," could not protect him from the violence of the urban neighborhood. Nor did Fleming's fame or success remove him from such a situation.

The association between Wideman's dead nephew and the beaten athlete resonate in Wideman's critique of race and sports in America. Both men, residents of the neighborhood, are unable to escape its violence and its perpetual lack of opportunity—even in the case of Fleming. Omar and his "crew" sought marginalized and violent ways to define their manhood. Unable to find an identity as a young black man beyond the limited choices prescribed for him in America, Omar took to the streets—following a path not unlike his father's and ultimately paying for his decision with his life. Fleming's flight from the ghetto, through sports, and his later decision to return as an educator and coach did not shield him from physical violence. Even if he stayed away from Homewood, his identity in racist America would always threaten his safety. Both men's blackness condemned them despite the different paths they took in life. Seemingly, only a star like Jordan seems to negate such racial constructions.

But even Wideman begins to question whether or not Jordan can "defy gravity" when it comes to race in America. While Jordan is imminently popular throughout America, his iconographic status might actually re-inscribe attitudes in the culture toward the black male body. Even though black and white kids alike might want to "be like Mike," few African American boys will ever come close to achieving his level of success, while white Americans will be content to engage in a cultural, racial masquerade, satisfied to act "like Mike" or popular rap stars without having to live their racial realities in America. As Wideman states: "Buy Jordan or be Jordan. Very different messages."[65] Wideman compares the "commerce in images of blackness" to American slavery, suggesting that "black bodies still occupy the auction block."[66] Michael Eric Dyson has made similar pronouncements about Jordan and the "desire" to own his image in America. His body has become a "cultural text" meant to entertain society, available for purchase.[67] Consequently, the popularity of the sport and of its stars continues the legacy of racial commodification.

It is on the neighborhood playground, Wideman suggests, that players may be the freest from a marketplace definition of the black male body. Here strangers, families, friends, fathers, and sons can play the game in the purest sense—as a sign of individual expression and communal identity. The playground emerges as a site of communication and possibility in the silent African American world. It offers men a place to connect beyond their family in the wake of racism and urban despair. It is here that a "counterreality is dramatized. Playing hoop, African American men act out a symbolic version of who they are, who they want to be."[68] Wideman romanticizes this urban space in *Hoop Roots* almost to the point of nostalgia, much like he did with Homewood in the books of the Homewood trilogy. It appears that it is only here that the black male body is free from the definitions that others have given it. When Wideman brings his lover, Catherine, to a game, she neglects to see this association. He believes that the failure results from differences in culture (she's European) or gender, or that he hasn't had proper time to explain the game to her. It is more likely that the game does not have the symbolic importance for her that it has for Wideman. Here men choose their names, their court titles. They define their identity.

This section of the book, titled "The Village," offers the most mixed of Wideman's responses to basketball. What begins as a desire to share a beloved pastime with Catherine and a celebration of the game ends as an indictment of America and its attitudes toward race. Interwoven in the history of the sport is the history of slavery and racism. As he does in his novels, Wideman interrogates in this chapter the ways in which history has codified racial construction. However, he has a more difficult time negotiating his examination here. His meditations move back and forth between his neighborhood, history, Carnivale, the dress of NBA players, the game he's currently watching, minstrelsy, and the beginnings of basketball in Springfield, Massachusetts.

This also happens to a lesser degree whenever Wideman talks about his family. As a young man, Wideman begins to escape his trying family situations by running to the courts. He finds solace there during the time that he cares for his ill grandmother. Though Wideman has said elsewhere that the playground has operated as a space to bring the community together, in this case, his relationships with his family seem fragmented further by his trips to the court. He even admits that he left behind the women in his family in order to find connections to other men, fathers, brothers on the playground. His own emerging identity as an adult is dependent on this separation. Yet this action echoes stereotypical representations of African American males and their absence from the household. This is, by Wideman's account, one reason why he has sought male connection on the courts in the first place. Here he seeks to find a masculine self, modeled on the men that are playing basketball. It also seems noteworthy that he brings Catherine back to his home playground as a means to explain his past, his identity, to her. Bringing a woman to the court (like Robert brings Kassima in *Two Cities*) seems to violate the masculine space it signifies. But as a revised blues hero, Wideman's position in the text requires him to return from the places where the hero and the individualistic "self-made" man of the American tradition escape to—away from home, away from women. His experiences on and off the court enable him to be the articulate kinsmen. He is able to explain the significance of the sport in terms of relationships; it helps him "set down his own roots."[69]

The creative expressions that Wideman has seen elsewhere in his culture—at church, in music—are also illustrated in the games taking place. The solo flights and team unity embody young Wideman's need to develop his voice and find companionship outside of his home life—to discover what it means to be a man in the midst of a household of women. Everywhere on the court Wideman encounters the ways basketball provides men with their sense of self in a world that seems intent on stripping them of their masculine identity. The dress, the walk, the trash-talking, all connote a ritual drama of manhood. Even slam-dunking rises beyond a test of physical prowess and "showboating" skills to represent a masculine symbol.[70]

As a budding writer, the young Wideman believed that the unique game-playing styles of the hoopsters were examples of individual creative expression. In *Hoop Roots* he often digresses from the description of a particular game or player to a story about his family or an acquaintance. Playground ball and storytelling are synonymous for Wideman as ways to combat the negative and limited portraits of African American life. One of the most prevalent and damaging images of African American masculinity, as discussed earlier, has been the association between the black male body and sexual violence. Often portrayed in history and in the American consciousness as the sexual predator, black men have borne the burden of American preoccupation with blackness as a sign of animalism. Black men have rarely been portrayed outside of their own community as loving husbands and partners. They have suffered such characterizations, in some cases, with their lives, as the history of lynching illustrates.

Basketball has served elsewhere in the book as a means to tell positive stories about the African American family—Wideman also uses the game to fashion an image of the African American male in a healthy and loving sexual relationship. His love of the game is something he wants to share with Catherine, but it also serves as a way to share stories of his past with his lover. It helps them bridge between physical and emotional intimacy. Basketball frames his youth, his relationships with his mother and grandparents. All of these autobiographical moments are essential to understanding his character, but he is unable to simply relate them to his partner. To share his inner life, Wideman has to speak through the game, showing again that he believes that basketball is a form of artistic expression.

He considers their intimate interaction a "verbal ball game." He admits the metaphor doesn't quite work, but reveals that when he went to the courts as a young man he was seeking love and acceptance. He explains to Catherine:

> Homewood boys and men running to the court to find our missing fathers. Playing the game of basketball is our way of telling stories, listening to stories, piecing a father together from them. Practicing bittersweet survival whether we find fathers or not. Recalling your stories, telling mine. I'm practicing survival again. Remembering what's lost. Remembering my stories can't save you.[71]

The image of the vulnerable, loving man emerges here as a refutation of the black sexual brute. He is searching for a mature and intimate relationship with this woman. We have already seen that basketball and love are intertwined in *Two Cities*. Like Robert with Kassima, Wideman brings Catherine to the "court" as a "courtship" ritual. Wideman revels in the wordplay when he notes that this is a "rebound" relationship. In many ways the novel is a fictional mirror of "The Village" section of *Hoop Roots* and also uses the playground as a site of connection and reconciliation. In both works, racism's impact on African American manhood complicates and even destroys love relationships—Kassima has lost sons and a husband to the streets—reminding us again that Wideman's personal life is the lens by which he examines the culture and history of America. And the focus on women and on love in the text alters the original text of the basketball court. He reclaims and revises its meaning in even more powerful ways. The basketball court's mythical space echoes the closing lines of the story of the preacher and Katherine (another double) in *The Cattle Killing* when Wideman equates stories with basketball and storytelling with survival and the impossible desire to "save" Katherine/Catherine with his stories.[72] This revision of the court as a shared space between man and woman as opposed to the space where young men flee home to prove their physical prowess inverts the tropes of alienation and flight that are found in other works by Wideman. This reflects a character, a writer, a blues hero more intimately connected to family and to another individual.

The identity of the African American community might be most secure in those spaces where cultural expression can take place. The neighborhood playground court is, in Wideman's estimation, such a space. As he tells us in *Hoop Roots*, the court in Homewood, where he grew up, was named Westinghouse, after one of the European founders of the city. Wideman argues that the space should be renamed after one of the neighborhood's inhabitants—men who played on its blacktop. This naming process is a crucial aspect of the maintenance of communal identity, as it has been in forging individual African American identities. Thinking about the players that have helped shape the neighborhood court, Wideman offers the name "The Maurice Big Mo Stokes/Eldon L. D. Lawson Memorial Playground" as an alternative to Westinghouse. The name marks the contributions of both the celebrated and the unknown players from the community—all the stories of the court. The career of NBA star Maurice Stokes is juxtaposed in the text with stories of the nearly anonymous L. D. Lawson. Though their successes might seem completely opposite of one another, both men met similar fates.

Telling these stories of the players of the game, those known and unknown, Wideman enacts a ritual designed to illustrate basketball's artistic expression and to celebrate the past. Notably, he returns to his neighborhood court to achieve this at the same time he returns to mothers and grandmothers and builds loving relationships with other women. Basketball helps frame African American experience in this country: both in the ways that it reflects the problems of racism and in the ways it helps its artists name their experience. In one of the sections of the book called "Who Invented the Jump Shot?" Wideman worries that the academic panel that has been assembled to answer this question will rewrite history, excluding the unique contributions that African American culture has made to the sport and, by extension, to America. Unless African Americans can find a space—whether a court or a blank page—to tell their story, in their own voice, their identities will continue to be owned and appropriated by someone else. Basketball, like the blues, must counter the hegemonic vision in ways that will help sustain African American life and culture.

Throughout *Hoop Roots* Wideman layers discussions about race, the history of the game, his family history, and his new love interest. Each story is like one of the beads strung together in the descriptions of African beads and beading that open several sections of the book. The circularity of the beads harkens to other circles and circular narratives in Wideman's collection of works, as do the hoop and the basketball itself. There are also passages describing the African ring shot, and we see once again the soap bubble image from the oft-repeated tale of Wideman's grandmother, Freeda, and how she got her scar. The images reflect Wideman's continued imbrications or palimpsestic style, but they also link all the seemingly disparate parts of the work.[73] Wideman is the basketball court; he is Africa; he is Freeda—they all exist within him. There is a seamless relationship between these narratives. His return to them is a return to himself. The circle also implies that these journeys are continuous—they do not end somewhere as much as they return again. If Wideman had not returned to the court (as a man now far more wise than the alter ego, Doot) and had not brought Catherine to see the game, he would not have been able to adequately reclaim the space for African American expression and storytelling and take his place as the articulate kinsmen or elder.

Wideman reclaims the court in *Hoop Roots* and continues this practice of reclaiming in his next work, *The Island*. Once more, Wideman is not an isolated figure in this text. He is not taking a solitary journey. Traveling to Martinique for an assignment for National Geographic, Wideman brings Catherine, who in the course of the work becomes Katrine and Chantal (and has been Kate in *The Cattle Killing*). Catherine is developing a league of alter egos as well in Wideman's canon, but in each case her presence emblemizes the power of love and the necessity of sharing stories as an intimate act as well as a method of surviving personal and historical trauma. The work also inverts other Wideman stories, especially *Philadelphia Fire*, which begins with Cudjoe leaving an island he's exiled himself to, alone. Wideman has chosen Martinique to better understand its history and the life of Fanon, and as "someplace beautiful where the labor of writing could be performed in pleasant surroundings."[74]

Nevertheless, the excursion to Martinique proves to be fraught with personal tragedy and reminders of the racialized past embedded in Martinique's history. And Wideman typically layers stories on top of stories here, creating narratives of John and Katrine, Paul and Chantal, Fanon, and Pere Labat alongside histories of the island and his ethnographic notes. One wonders if this is what National Geographic had in mind. Once again readers of Wideman's work are presented with a nonlinear narrative (even the genre of travelogue does not escape Wideman's palimpsestic style), three-voiced structures, doubles, and historiographic metafiction (especially in the "fictionalized" spaces of the work). He also makes it clear that there are many versions of Martinique: "The places where we meet are Martiniques of one sort or another. Your Martinique is no more or less *the* Martinique than mine."[75] All these versions exist in the text as true pictures of the island, even John and Katrine carry different versions of the island in their imaginations.

While the pervasive use of journey or quest motifs found in works by African American authors represents a search for an identity and is an allusion to paths taken by escaped slaves, how can a writer's trip with a romantic partner to a beautiful island repeat and revise such a motif? Other Wideman works are constructed upon a journey: *A Glance Away, Hurry Home, Brothers and Keepers, Philadelphia Fire, The Cattle Killing, Hoop Roots,* and *Fatheralong* each follow such an pattern. But *The Island* provides Wideman with a space that isolates him and his partner from others without alienating him, even as an artist: "The island called Katrine. The island called John. The island called John. The island called Katrine. Called John. Called Katrine. John/Katrine. Katrine/John. Calling. Being called. Separate islands. Floating. Merging."[76] The account of John (and Katrine) soon takes over the text as a metafictional voice. It is difficult to know where John and Catherine end and John and Katrine begin. But the dual couples allow for other possible lives and encounters between the two. And Wideman admits that Paul and Chantal are further doubles of these couples. John and Katrine inhabit the first part of the text, leaving on "Air Caraibes," where the writer, John, notes the layers of irony and history in the name. Reminiscent of George Wolfe's *The Colored Museum*, the scene describes passengers "packed" in "middle passage spoon fashion" and further inverts the tropes of African American movement.[77] John notices the "ghosts moaning in the machinery of the island" and the "invisible" dark bodies.[78] Nevertheless, he is determined to learn something on this journey and bask in the sun with the woman whom he has "fallen deeper in love with."[79]

Breaking the couple's solace with one another is the possibility that Katrine has become pregnant. The surprise, joy, and befuddlement at being new parents again at their age is shattered when Katrine either miscarries or discovers she was never pregnant to begin with. Whether this is a real child lost or a fictitious one is not clear, but the child represents yet another traumatic episode and repeats the image of lost children found throughout Wideman's work:

> No new life starting on this island. You're learning its long history of refusal. No union, no unity, no amalgamation. The island's persistent either/or, black or white, work or die, forsake all hope messages to slaves. Its postslavery denial of dreams. Promises broken. Promise crushed in African-descended natives. Its encouragement and scorn of daydreams.[80]

The Island begins with Wideman mourning the death of his father, his recollection of 9-11, and continuing occurrences of right-wing global politics and racism. While going to Martinique may have originated as a desire to escape the traumas of the world outside, the loss of the child reminds the characters that you cannot hide from pain. You must find ways, instead, to survive it. The loss appears to bring John and Katrine even closer, though initially Katrine wishes to be given some time alone to deal with the regret and loss. Their relationship, juxtaposed with Paul and Chantal's, offers an affirming response to grief as a condition of love and intimacy. Paul and Chantal also operate, Wideman tells us, as a "negative talisman to ward off my ancient fear of losing what's most precious and partly from the visceral, visual presence of loss and waste, the haunted, deadly past alive in Martinique's music, dance, arts, speech, faces."[81] These words, as the text later illustrates, suggest that *The Island* has little to do with Martinique and is more about his own losses and newfound love.[82]

The moment of loss brings John and Katrine to sharing stories about their initial meeting, one marked for John by the end of his thirty-year marriage and the guilt and remorse accompanying its end. As it does for the characters from *Two Cities*, the pain of further loss initially impedes the progress of this relationship, until John realizes Katrine "fit exactly my idea of the person with whom I'd want to share lots of moments like the one we'd stumbled upon."[83] His intimacy with Katrine and his support during their loss (a double of Kassima and Robert's relationship) is a redemptive narrative—especially as an inversion of Cudjoe in *Philadelphia Fire*, who runs away from family responsibilities and traumatic loss or becomes distant, isolated, and silent. John's imagination flows from remembering their initial meeting and their two different "true" versions of the event and comparing them with Columbus's first sight of Martinique. Though it didn't offer Columbus the promised gold, he nevertheless pushed onward, following a journey that changed the course of history. John equates Columbus's single-mindedness with the tenacity needed to survive, to be in love, and to hold on through grief.

Wideman uses the genre of the travel journal to reflect on race and history, but he also promotes a critique of travel itself, as a new form of exploration and colonization in the global age. Disturbed by his role as tourist, John wonders if the locals know they are performing in a historical, racialized pageant, selling their culture and themselves for entertainment:

> Passing the stage, we'd stopped a minute to checkout the action. A group of graceful, athletic brown dancers ... a quick glimpse enough to tell me I certainly didn't want to stick around. Pulling Katrine by the arm, I didn't simply leave, I fled. No way could I enjoy the skill of the dancers without also feeling sorry for them, sorry for myself. Sorrow mixed with anger and frustration.[84]

John worries that these images, like others he sees around the island, continue the legacy of commodification of the black body, advertising easy-living and lust, onto "dolls, souvenir calendars, posters—public proof of who owns the native body and can bare it with impunity."[85]

But he is also playing the role of the ethnographer, wanting to hear Martinican voices, learn customs, learn their methods of "taming grief," without appearing like an "unconnected outsider."[86] He muses that the writer may be a "special case of tourist" and questions, "Isn't the writer as troubadour, wandering minstrel, clown, blues singer, itinerant preacher, etc. a necessary and welcome exception or counterweight to assertions of ownership."[87] These questions are similar to ones he posed before in *Brothers and Keepers* when he tried to navigate telling Robby's stories without his voice controlling the narrative. The multiple narratives and voices appearing in *The Island* negotiate similar obstacles and spaces, ultimately allowing Wideman to inhabit multiple discourses in order to tell all the true stories of Martinique, even those that are uniquely personal to him. He also invokes the image of the wandering blues hero, a character in narratives we have seen before. This wandering and movement are different; the trope is revised by Katrine's continued, and connected, presence on the journey and in this book.

The history of the island is a discourse layered within the text. Wideman/John details the process of slavery and colonization, its development as a tourist destination, and its creolization. He also compares Frantz Fanon's image of Martinique with Pere Labat's image of the island and its inhabitants. Many of the characteristics of the island reveal a Manichean duality, an oppositional record of the "text" of the island. The "island" as an image and icon in colonization and New World stories is the text to be deconstructed in post-colonial literatures. Representing paradise, Eden, "a virgin land," a "brave new world," the island promises European writers a chance of redemption, a new start. It becomes a "meta-narrative," and the Caribbean, specifically, a "meta-archipelago."[88] The true history of the New World islands is anything but Edenic, however. The island, in the post-colonial imagination, is an image "whose flux, whose noise, whose presence covers the map of world history's contingencies, through the great changes in economic discourse to the vast collisions of races and cultures that humankind has seen."[89] John imagines himself as a recently kidnapped African brought to the shores of Martinique, confronted with an image of both beauty and terror.

Wideman attributes this same vision of the island to Fanon, illustrated by the epigraphs that open some of the sections of the work. Fanon's writings operate as another layer embedded in the text, a source for much of Wideman's revisioning of the island and as well as his philosophy. Notably, most of the Fanon discourse appears in the Paul and Chantal section. Fanon's words comment on the construction of Africa and Europe, and black and white, as ideas; but his comments also reflect the tension in the relationship of these lovers. Even without Wideman's prefatory notes, readers would realize that Paul and

Chantal are likely doomed as a couple because they operate under the historical weight of culture clash, colonization, and black-white relations that Fanon attempts to reveal—unless they can find ways to deconstruct these images and engage each other on intimate, human terms.

Another text layered within *The Island* is one that Fanon knew all too well, *The Tempest*. Shakespeare's play appears once again as an imbricated narrative in Wideman's work. John imagines that Katrine is Ariel, calming people's fears, telling them that John (the "fabulator") is just a writer, he "means no harm."[90] John also calls Thomas Jefferson "Prospero-like" in his ability to make history see him as an idol. But it is the play itself that is echoed once more in these pages as the meta-narrative of racial identity in America. The play is "a prison narrative, a melancholy reminder of how long the European colonial project has lasted, imprisoning first the colonized and then the colonizer."[91] Even Prospero is locked up on this island. Unlike its position in *Philadelphia Fire*,[92] Wideman uses the play to transcend issues of race and privilege in *The Island* to reveal how in our current global society we are all incarcerated: "Shakespeare's miraculous creation forecasts the modern imprisonment of all of us in somebody else's self-serving story, each lonely, distinct one of us trapped, enraptured, a performer in a globalized, virtual, administered show."[93] Like the tourists that he critiques earlier, we are all guilty of a "sentimental wish for experience without the risk of acting, for nostalgia without suffering a past."[94]

As the blues hero, Wideman returns to the text of the play written upon the colonization of the island to walk in Caliban's shoes, to see through the eyes of the natives, to inform the reader of the past and present connections between ourselves and both the colonizer and the colonized. It is an act of reclaiming the island as a text. Caliban, a reoccurring character in Wideman's pantheon, finally has a voice. It is only in this way that the text of *The Tempest* can finally be rewritten. Wideman forces his readers, no matter what their background or experience, to see themselves reflected in the history of slavery and colonization in the New World. John has earlier felt uncomfortable as a tourist, eavesdropping on the lives and the culture of the islanders, aware that he is performing a task of colonization as a writer. This moment reconciles him to the character of Prospero as well, as another "fabulator." John realizes and accepts that storytellers and historians are often forced to choose one version of an event. Wideman's work, of course, has tried to counter that dilemma all along.

Wideman has to remind himself to remain silent, to turn off his writer's imagination in *Brothers and Keepers* so that Robby's voice can inhabit and even control the text, his story. During his visit to the Habitation Anse Latouche, Wideman is forced to try to be silent again. He sees

> Africans whose muteness, tonguelessness overcomes me, sits me down on a stone beach and keeps me still, still so I can listen, interrogate the silence with my own, attend the muted spirits, summon them, beg them to forgive me for appalling distance, appalling ignorance, forgive me for not avenging their captivity, their immolation in *beke* ovens whose fires they tended and fed with the fuel of their own dark bodies, my body, my brethren I summon you, beg you to summon me.[95]

In the moments when Martinique speaks for itself, Wideman frees the textual space of the island to counter its image in the Western world. Like the court in *Hoop Roots*, Martinique is transformed by the narrative, wresting its self-image, its self-ownership from those people that have named it, appropriated it for their own profit. Wideman's silent observation and mediation allow the gap to appear for the historical voices to emerge to tell their story. As an articulate kinsmen he is able call forth these ancestral voices in the space of "Great Time."

This heroic rescue is re-enacted in the transformative relationship with Catherine/Katrine. In *Hoop Roots*, Wideman, while sharing the court with Catherine, like a personal story, had wanted to "save" her.[96] Similar language appears in the scenes of the miscarriage, where John is attempting to console her. Robert Jones in *Two Cities* wishes to "save" Kassima. But in both instances Wideman and his alter ego, Robert, understand that there is a limit to what they can offer, what their role can be. It is only when they step away from the traditional romantic hero figure that they fulfill the image of the supportive partner. This is true of *Hoop Roots* as well. In *The Island*, Wideman uses the relationships of Paul and Chantal and of John and Katrine to revise the role of male heroic savior. Paul grows increasingly jealous of Chantal's former lovers, of her past. When other men see her body, Paul covets her image. This element of their relationship ultimately dooms its survival.

John and Katrine's relationship negotiates their pasts more ably, inverting the image of male possession evident in Paul and Chantal's relationship. Watching Katrine swim, John muses, "Once I believed I required even deserved by some sort of male divine right, a woman no other man had touched."[97] The description is layered within an earlier characterization of Martinique as "virgin land." Using the common rhetoric of Old World/New World colonization, Wideman equates Katrine with island possession only to deconstruct the association and thus the image: "I realize I haven't quite shed such embarrassingly macho expectations, preoccupations, and double standards ... [and] for a moment I'm free from the need to possess Katrine's fiery otherness—free to stop asking myself *who was she* or *who was I* each time we had let go and dived into pleasure."[98] The section closes with John "watching Katrine clamber out of the smashing, grinding waves, her dash to a towel, collapsing on it, laughing, shivering, shutting her eyes, then baking in the sun.... I'm suddenly self-conscious, overwhelmed almost by the need not to possess but to share the plentitude, share my fullness because there is so much.[99] These are nearly the closing lines of the text, indicating that John has been altered by his experience on the island, by his time spent with Katrine there. Throughout the text we have seen the relationship between John and Katrine mirror John's relationship with the island itself. When he earlier gives Katrine time to be alone to "sit quiet for a minute" and wrap "her arms around herself,"[100] it echoes John listening to the island, letting it possess itself. He lets go of his image of the island and of Katrine. They should be able to tell their own stories. He successfully fulfills his blues hero role by sharing and creating stories of the traumatic past, but also by, most importantly, creating and reclaiming spaces to let these other voices be heard without feeling that he *must* fill the gap.

Earlier in the text, John contends with the images of black and white embedded in this island and in his relationship with Katrine. These conflicts are not necessarily resolved by the end of the work, but John clearly reconciles himself to the differences between Katrine and himself: "the oppositions of Europe and Africa, white and black, male and female," and between individuals discovering new roles as intimate partners.[101] The work, despite its traumas and reflections on the troubled past of the island, illustrates a "hoped-for personal and social renewal."[102]

Catherine's presence and voice foster Wideman's storytelling in *The Island*. In moments of traumatic reflection, the narrative waits to clarify that she is listening, as if it cannot continue without verifying her presence. Even though she is often silent in the text, her existence nurtures the creation of the story. We have seen this relationship between the preacher and Katherine in *The Cattle Killing* and in *Hoop Roots*, and it appears as a metafictional moment in the novel *Fanon*. While Wideman has for some time taken this position in the narrative structure of his works, the now persistent inclusion of Catherine presents readers with a metafictional couple (and a double couple) who together seem stronger than their painful situations.

The dedication of the short-story collection *God's Gym* thanks Catherine for "helping" Wideman "make these stories." The listener/reader as co-creator of the story, suggested in *The Cattle Killing* between the writer and his son and father and between the fictional preacher and Kate, is reiterated here in the framing of the collection. In the opening story, "Weight," this relationship is noted as well. After the first section of the story about his mother, the writer interrupts with a metafictional reflection on the story that he has read to his ailing mother:

> Since I was reading this story over the phone (I called it a story but Mom knew better), I stopped at the end of the paragraph above that you just completed, if you read that far, stopped because the call was long distance, daytime rates, and also because the rest had yet to be written. I could tell by her silence she was not pleased.[103]

Wideman goes on further to say that his mother has "always been [his] best critic," and when she doesn't respond to his latest effort with her usual "sunshine," he feels alone: "Don't leave me drowning like Willie Boy in the deep blue sea. Smile, Mom. Laugh. Send that healing warmth through the wire and save poor me."[104]

His strong connection to his mother and their shared history of storytelling seems more important than ever before. A consistent voice in Wideman's repertoire, as Lizabeth or Bette, she has been a major influence on the architecture of Wideman's stories. She was a structural narrative voice in *Brothers and Keepers*, and she has appeared in most of Wideman's novels, short-story collections, and memoirs, even in the most minute ways. But even when her voice is in the margins or hidden underneath a fictional creation, her presence has been immeasurable. The image of "weight" in this story tries to capture her pervasiveness in Wideman's opus, as well as the tremendous burdens she has had to bear throughout her life.

Weight is also used to cast her physical shape in contrast to what she has had to lift, especially now, frail and in poor health. The writer is struck by her small frame compared to his large stature. Yet she seems the stronger, more "flesh and bones" compared to his "wimpy shadow." Her body, her love, has given the writer his substance, his storytelling voice:

> I'd lost track of my mother's size, and mine relative to hers. Maybe because she was beyond size. If someone had asked me my mother's height or weight, I would have replied, *Huh, Ubiquitous*, I might say now. A tiny skin-and-bone woman way too huge for size to pin down.[105]

And the other image of weight in the story is realized in these moments when the writer acknowledges her inevitable and imminent absence. This is weight he will not be able to bear, to lift. Afraid he is like the man who "won't survive his mother's passing,"[106] the writer attempts to express his mother's significance in his life and what her death will mean. But the narrative wanders off, unable to pin down the words any more effectively than he was able to pin down her size. Words begin to fail in the process of understanding.

The writer also does not have her faith in God to help manage his grief. Slowly, as the writer imagines lifting his mother's casket at the funeral that will some day come, he remembers her stories, the ways she has suffered and survived. It is the memory of these stories that will help him lift the weight to come. A torch of sorts is passed from mother to son as he reflects on her "weightlifting" capabilities. Her lifelong love and the stories that she has shared with him will reconcile him to loss. What she has taught him about "weight" he can now experience and share with other listeners. Of course, if the reader considers this work within the context of so many other examples of Wideman's writing, it is clear that this instruction and illustration about creating a life out of grief and suffering, about embracing love and hope, has always been as present in Wideman's work as his mother has been.

Other works in the collection emphasize storytelling and healing as well. The story called "Sharing" is what you might expect from Wideman in a collection with this focus. Two neighbors, both separated from their spouses, discuss their broken homes. It is their first conversation, though the African American man who has stopped by for mayonnaise has lived in the neighborhood for four years. Though the man and the white woman whose door he's knocked on are strangers, the moment of needing to speak to someone transcends their difference and their isolation. It is a human connection that will not last past this event, perhaps, but it reminds the reader again of these impulses and the bridges they can build to understanding and empathy.

Silence and speaking and the tension between the two that the writer must wrestle with every time he or she fills the page are yet other thematic constants in the collection. The multiple meanings of silence in Wideman's work have changed as often as his visual manifestation of silence and empty space—the glance away. Silence, while waiting for his mother's reply to the story in "Weight," is not a silence of comfort or peace. The silence between father and son during a phone conversation in *Philadelphia Fire* is a painful reminder of loss and absence. It is also a tragic gap in the historical consciousness of African American lives whose stories have been silenced.

But silence is also the space that Wideman can fill with his fiction and his storytelling voice. Even in "In Praise of Silence" Wideman seems compelled to fill the gaps when silence or breaks occur as in a jazz composition. He states that "silence is a dreaming space where what's awaited is imagined, and when it doesn't come, the space where dreams are dismantled."[107] In the same essay he celebrates the silence of the music of Thelonious Monk. Monk's silence is counternarrative, reclaiming silence as an act of defiance, an act of creative force rather than submission or fear. The silence here takes yet another direction, and Monk's "space between the notes" both opens up textual possibilities and dismantles hegemonic discourse. This is how the allusion to Monk's "space between the notes" is used in *The Lynchers* and in the short story included in *God's Gym*, "The Silence of Thelonious Monk." The silences in Monk's music and speech remind the narrator of past encounters with a woman. The digressions are heightened at every place in the page where the writer reflects on Monk and his art. While meditating on Monk's history, the narrative connects to the narrator's past love affair. The story often addresses the lover after the narrator realizes that he is "still in love" with the woman.[108]

The work itself replicates the sound of a Monk composition; just when you think you know where the story is going, it pauses and takes off in another direction. The story jumps around, riffing on every digressive path that appears, from French poetry to love to Paris to Monk. In those silences or pauses of Monk's music, the writer creates an alternate path for the love story. The writer muses in another address to the lover, "He'll play the note that we've been waiting for. The note we thought was lost in silence."[109] The idea of silence here returns to a position of loss and absence at the same time that it operates as a space of possibility.

This is not a narrative about sharing stories as much as it is about how stories can begin in the imagination. It opens up the rest of the collection to other places where silence can be addressed by the imagination, as is the case in almost every other work included. "Who Invented the Jump Shot" (also published in *Hoop Roots*) attempts to deconstruct the popular history of the sport's birth at the same time it claims its own space to construct a history of its invention from Wideman's own mix of imagination and fact. In "What We Cannot Speak about We Must Pass Over in Silence," Wideman continues the twofold definition of silence. The silence allows him the space to revise a historical/autobiographical event that has been a source of trauma—the incarceration of his son. In *Philadelphia Fire*, the silences between father and son were tragic, but the writer has transformed that "blank space" between them into a story, where other characters and alternate realities can shape the narrative and history.

Here the narrator knows a friend whose son is in jail in Arizona. When the man dies, the narrator worries about the effect it will have on the son in jail. Wideman kills off one of his fictional alter egos in this story—and replaces the father figure with a childless, lonely man who attempts a heroic act of emotional recovery for the son of a man he barely considered a friend. The imaginative return to stories and situations we have seen in previous texts does not alter the endings of these stories, especially since the narrator is not a very different man then previous incarnations of Wideman's male protagonist. After all, he considers himself a man who prefers "to see nothing."[110] And there is still the prison system as an antagonist. Though, in this version, the new guard is technology, which keeps stalling the narrator in his attempt to find the son. Humans are almost removed completely in the discussions with the prison system. It is the "computer" that "says" the son is not in the facility that the narrator travels to. But no matter how much the story details change, the narrator and the writer cannot rescue the son from prison anymore than Thomas/the writer is able to rescue Robby from prison in *Fanon*. The silence of the title provides the comfort of the imagination, but it also reflects the post-traumatic return to suffering, to stories that keep being told.

So while several of the works in the collection return to places of healing, just as many return to places of trauma. In "Are Dreams Faster than the Speed of Light?" our narrator, clearly another fictional double, is dying, suffering from a fatal illness. One of the items on his "things-to-do-list before I die" is to take care of his father, who is in a rest home. The two men have never been close, until the son needed to take care of him. They are brought even closer by the narrator's own illness and sense of mortality. As his own body falls apart, he reflects on his father's losses, including his wife, the narrator's mother, in childbirth. Their shared loss never connected them emotionally, but he wonders, "Wouldn't his daddy know all the answers now, the whole truth and nothing but the truth?"[111]

Thinking about his illness and his father's decline in the nursing home, he hears a story about Chinese scientists attempting to prove that we could one day move faster than the speed of light. The narrator ponders the possibility of being in "two places at once" as a way to escape suffering or understand one another. He decides he must kill his father before he dies himself, to ensure that his father will not be ill-treated and alone after the narrator dies. The narrator's choice illustrates his compassion for his father as well as his own fear of loss and absence. In his imagination, his own impending death weaves with the Middle Passage and the Holocaust. The metafictional voice enters late in the text to comment on the story: "Why not believe in a different life possible, joining the other lives I daydreamed daily. Lives not in my father's house nor my mother's bosom nor God's bosom nor the streets of Homewood. Made up lives like this one I try to save holding open my father's mouth."[112] In trying to force feed his father after he began to refuse food, the narrator realizes his love for his father and that "nothing, nothing else matters."[113] The emptiness and the blanks in the "father stories" have been places of pain in previous works, but this space allows this story to fill the silence with love and empathy.

There is quite a bit of dying in the works in this collection. The mother, the father, the writer—in some ways this reflects Wideman's stage in life and the losses that he is now facing. These are all painful moments, but unlike many stories of suffering that we have seen before, these at least follow a natural order. These are not deaths from gun violence or war, nor do they involve the loss of children. These are losses that the writer has been prepared for all his life, even if he wonders how he will survive them. But the deaths in "Sightings" do come from violence, from suicide. "Sightings" also returns us to the story "Rock River," published in *All Stories Are True*. The suicides are nearly identical in both works, and they both occur in Laramie, Wyoming. The narrator of the first account, "Rock River," finds only silence when trying to fathom his friend's suicide. But in the version here, the writer is confronted with a "blank space" he needs "to fill."[114]

The narrator remembers another suicide as well. Molly, the daughter of a friend, took her own life after a traumatic event. Even though she had confided the nature of her suffering to the narrator, he was unprepared for her choice. The writing allows him to remember these friendships, to touch his friends again, to see them once more. Coming back to these moments in his past filled with memories of pain reconciles him to these losses. He may continue to have post-traumatic "sightings" of these people and such events, but it also enables the writer to manage his grief: "The *touching* are fictions, imaginary accidents that produce consequences a survivor of the collision might call *change* or *loss* or *birth* or *death*."[115]

The basketball story in the collection, "Who Weeps When One of Us Goes Down Blues?" offers another version of the interplay between storytelling and music and basketball in Wideman's work. The narrator, a basketball player and blues voice, notes the communal power of the team, the African circle they signify when they surround a player who has gone "down" and hit the floor. The "blank space" that opens up "till play resumes" is the basketball equivalent of a Monk piece. In that space, the narrator/player appears to enter "the Great Time," where he has a vision of the court as a "secret gathering of slaves in the woods."[116] This "space belongs to someone older, smarter. Maybe the ancient, crippled-up grandfather of my grandfather."[117] The team circle and the ancient voices surround the player on the ground, chanting, but "down's not out, the African's say."[118] Like the stories of flying Africans, the circle saves the player, Archie, and sends him home across an ocean. This mythic space, like the court in *Hoop Roots*, allows alternate realities and multiple possibilities through the past and through shared stories.

The stories in *God's Gym* celebrate love and possibility and second chances—especially through the power of the imagination. But the works are also populated by dead and dying people, spirits, and disease—all signs of the end of the world. This characterizes *The Cattle Killing* as well, and Wideman continues this narrative in *Fanon*. The narrator/writer's mother says in *Fanon*, "These are the last days."[119]

In the pages preceding this moment in the text, we have been confronted with images and information that might lead readers to agree. Wideman opens the novel with Thomas, a writer and Wideman's alter ego, receiving a severed head in a box, not unlike a scene out of the film *Seven*, another story with a character dwelling on the end of days.[120] After reflecting on global disease, the war on terror, 9-11, avian flu, the Southeast Asian tsunami, and every other manner of bad news, the apocalypse might seem imminent. Confronted with the choice of what to do in the event of "the end," one may choose murder and mayhem like the character in *Seven* or in any other of a number of apocalyptic films,[121] or suicide (as the case with the Xhosa in *The Cattle Killing*). Or, in the case Giovanni Boccaccio's *The Decameron* and the characters in Wim Wenders's film *Until the End of the World*, they may choose to "tell stories."[122] This is the choice made by Katherine and the preacher in *The Cattle Killing* and in Wideman's subsequent work. Storytelling as a method of survival in a hostile world or as means to transcend trauma has been ever-present in Wideman's work, but never more than it is now. And even though *Fanon* suggests things are getting worse out there, the work also argues that by sharing lives and sharing stories and embracing love, we can begin to heal and even find some peace amidst the chaos.

Thomas is reading the David Macey biography of Fanon when the Twin Towers fall on September 11, 2001. Immediately preceding this moment in the novel, Thomas has just remembered a wedding ceremony he had recently attended where the vows had included a line from a Rilke poem about "love being when two people appoint themselves guardians forever of each other's solitude."[123] Fanon, the apocalypse, and love announce themselves here as Wideman's layered texts, the sermons about surviving the fire and the fever that he will be weaving together in the novel. The events of 9-11 and its aftermath, especially in New York City, where Thomas (as well as Wideman) lives, frame the historical and personal trauma found throughout the text.

Fanon knew a "way out of this mess," but dies too soon. While Macey's biography is imbricated within the text, it is Fanon's works, *Black Skin, White Masks* and *The Wretched of the Earth*, and their appearance in the novel that reveal the most about the Fanon that Wideman wants us to see. Events from Fanon's life and the biography are repeated here, but usually with a comment that suggests we cannot really know what Fanon was really thinking or feeling at a particular biographical moment. His notes on patients and the characterization of what we would consider post-traumatic stress are connected by

Wideman to metaphorically reveal the connection between individual and collective trauma. In the novel, this trauma and terrorism are linked as symptoms of the same disease. Colonialism was an act of terror, and its victims are still suffering from that initial trauma.

But the novel does not further our knowledge of Fanon as much as it illustrates the impact his writing and his life had on Wideman. Even Wideman's use of doubles is attributed to Fanon: "When Thomas writes his Fanon book he'll borrow many voices to disguise his voice, speak from behind masks the way Fanon composed *Black Skin, White Masks.*"[124] Wideman remarks several times in the work about his "masking." And Thomas remembers going out west to teach and the masks he wore to hide while he was there, separating himself from his family and from his identity. This retelling of images from *Brothers and Keepers* and the Homewood books reinforces the gap between the young Wideman (and Thomas) and the Wideman who is closer to achieving the blues voice of his mother, and even Freeda and John French. Wideman/Thomas's dilemma as a younger man is not unlike that of the patients that Fanon treated in the psychiatric clinic: *"Dr. Fanon, Please free me. Release me from angers and fears that consume me. Heal the divisions within me my enemies exploit to keep me in a place I despise. Myself cut up, separated into bloody pieces, doctor. Like you. Fractured, dispersed, in death, as in life."*[125] Fanon is inspired to revolution and cultural deconstruction following his time helping traumatized patients. His observance of post-traumatic suffering and Wideman's emphasis throughout his work on re-imagining the painful stories of the past connect the two men. Wideman confesses, "Since I couldn't live Fanon's life, maybe I could write it."[126]

Wideman describes images of trauma and terror in the novel as well. He spends a considerable amount of time describing news footage of 9-11 and the war on terror. In several scenes Thomas refers to helicopters dotting the sky whenever he is outside, and he hears their "racket" always overhead. Wideman further comments on the use of images in advertising and in Hollywood and reflects on the craft of image-making. At one point in the novel the French filmmaker Jean-Luc Godard comes to Homewood to make a movie about the writer's mother and her time with Frantz Fanon in the hospital before he died. Wideman contemplates Godard's style, a man who may have "believed that images had lost their tongues." He is a filmmaker who realizes that images

> instead of being alive, instead of, you know, possessing agency and unscripted unpredictable possibilities, images are slaves, prisoners. Images kidnapped, copyrighted, archived, cloned. Property. Images

serving power, speaking the master's language, saying and doing what the master orders.[127]

Thomas wonders why he chooses to write about a filmmaker who is as "betrayed" by images as he has been by words. Godard joins the list of other iconoclastic artists that Wideman alludes to in his previous works—whose art he has layered within his own: Muybridge, Bearden, Giacometti, Hieronymus Bosch—all innovators of the visual arts that Wideman has celebrated in his writing and that his alter egos and characters have hailed as artist heroes and inspirations.

In an analysis of *Reuben* and *Philadelphia Fire*, Madhu Dubey contends that Wideman's use of photographic and cinematic metaphors "describes the estrangement of characters from themselves."[128] The gap between the image and the person is often responsible for the character's suffering. In *Fanon*, however, Wideman suggests that while most images inevitably fail at understanding their subjects or help perpetuate stereotypes, thus diminishing the humanity of the subjects, Godard, and artists like him, deconstruct images to break the hold they have over us. The artists' nonconformity allows for the possibility to clear a space for new images to appear and new stories to be told. Wideman's description of Godard's attempt at depicting love on film and Thomas's own imaginative re-creation of his lover's history are compared as equally unsuccessful but, nonetheless, a necessary task for artists. In the end Thomas confesses that Godard's films are "kind of a pain in the ass to watch and make sense of."[129] But making sense may not be the film's purpose or intent.

The failure of language to capture trauma or terror or love also courses through the novel. Several works of Wideman's are imbricated in the text, and the metafictional or autobiographical voice comments on their failures as art and as ways to save lives: "Almost thirty years ago I tried to write a book I hoped might free my brother from a life sentence in the penitentiary. It didn't work. Everything written after that book worked even less."[130] Besides this allusion to *Brothers and Keepers*, Wideman returns to other works as well, such as "Damballah," seemingly in an attempt to right earlier wrongs or to offer yet another alternate possibility of story.

Thomas/Wideman, while attending an academic conference, despairs over his or language's inability to create anything "new under the sun."[131] At first, he is excited by the scholar's "interdisciplinary rap" on the history and cultural significance of beheading. She is "generating a buzz about the novel" he is writing about the head by emphasizing what is his "central trope." But soon the "weight of her learning" oppresses him, stealing his enthusiasm for his story, for all stories."[132] The speaker "outed my new fiction as old fact. *Me whispering to her, Look at the beautiful star, the incredible snowflake.* Ho-hum, she replies. The sky's full of them."[133] The event compels him to drop the head story and start over with Fanon. Fanon saves the book, allowing Thomas to "wear the mask of him" and get a fresh start. It also gives Wideman a chance to bring something else into the story: "I decided the morning after Fanon saved my life that Thomas needed love."[134]

The love story that takes center stage may or may not be based on the "real one" that the writer does not want to jinx. But Thomas's love will be "autumnal" like the writer's—mature, "mellow and wise."[135] It is a love story that creates a separate peace from the apocalyptic times outside the front door. This "metafictional couple," which we have already seen in several incarnations, is the call-and-response in the novel—a relationship that operates on "give and take" and "choose and choose not." They move in this section of the text in circular patterns, silently tethered:

> Soon, I'll go up the stairs, find a woman waiting for me and not waiting, not locked up by my expectations, in sync rather with a mutual, unspoken rhythm, the woman I've always hoped I'd find and now she's here, for no particular reason, every possible reason required to unfold this piece of the world.[136]

While this is the only major appearance of Catherine (the woman described here) in the text, her description fits that of the Katrine in *The Island*, yet another double in Wideman's work. This section is also included in *God's Gym*. Here Catherine continues to act as a necessary presence, listening to Wideman's stories in a manner that allows them to grow and develop. During this interlude, he discusses the new book he is writing on *Fanon*, he ponders his mother's love of God and how writing for him is like a musician listening for the space between the notes, and he wonders aloud what this digression has to do with finishing the book on *Fanon*. The elements that give his life substance—his family, his love—are inseparable from his writing. As the dedication to *God's Gym* suggests, the partner becomes the audience, the co-creator in the call-and-response dialogue that these scenes imply—even though there is no dialogue. They are each other's "guardians of solitude."

Not only is the relationship the one that he has waited a lifetime for, but it has the power to heal and transform. He describes it as a "peace" that "seems everlasting, invincibly secure, a full stomach, a bed to sleep in, someone to talk with and share the bed, no agonized screams, no bombs exploding or fires crackling, no collapses or shutdowns or excruciating pain inside my body."[137]

Fanon is also a culmination—a work he has been writing for a lifetime—of a writing career spent reflecting on the connections between storytelling and history and love and race that we have seen throughout his work.

At one point in *Fanon*, Thomas wonders about the elements of the plot and decides the protagonist will be a newlywed and a teacher of creative writing. This is yet another one of several instances where Wideman's biography is alluded to as being the subject of the novel. Going back in time, the changes in the plot suggest a revision of Wideman's life, a second chance. Only in the imagination can Thomas's history be rewritten. The writer considers the story of Thomas and his love the "Paris romance (or Paris *Romance*)."[138] Going on to define the difference between novel and romance outlined by Nathaniel Hawthorne in "The Custom House" section of *The Scarlet Letter*, Wideman layers multiple meanings of romance at once in the text. *Fanon* is a love story, but it is also the heroic romance that the blue hero embarks on—attempting to recover Fanon and historical and literary texts to bring back to the community. And it is Hawthorne's romance where the "Actual and the Imaginary may meet."[139] The reference to *The Scarlet Letter* reiterates the need for imaginative re-creation of the past as this is a novel that also attempts to resolve the burden and pain of history by rewriting it through a story of love and redemption.

Wideman continues to return to his own literary and biographical past in *Fanon* through other allusions to works and images he has written or used before. He refers to Prospero and *The Tempest* several times in the novel. We have seen Wideman signify on *The Tempest* before, especially in *Philadelphia Fire*. In his later years, however, Wideman seems to be identifying as much with Prospero's waning reign as the magician, as the "fabulator" of texts, as he has in previous texts with Caliban. The palimpsestic technique continues with his own texts as well as others that he has played with before, including *Tristram Shandy*, a work that recalls Wideman's time at Oxford and its impact on his style (and its vision of history that goes "backwards"). *The Souls of Black Folk*, the writings of James Baldwin and Freud, and *Uncle Tom's Cabin* are all woven within the novel as well. Thomas/Wideman calls Godard's work a bricolage—a style and technique that could describe the structure of this novel as well. Bricolage, yet another incarnation of terms like imbrication, layering, mosaic, weaving, and palimpsestic, continues to define Wideman's narrative style.

Fanon also layers within its narrative specific passages and images from *Brothers and Keepers* and the short story "Damballah." The story reappears as the "conclusion" of an earlier narrative begun in the book about the severed head in a box that Thomas receives. Wideman's inability to wrap up this strand of the Thomas story pops up occasionally in the work, needling him and us with the promise of an answer to that mystery. But like all detective stories in

Wideman's work, there are no easy solutions, just as there is no easy path to composing a portrait of Fanon (or Wideman's work). And readers anxious to read a novel about Fanon's life will be as disappointed as they have been when they expected *Philadelphia Fire* to be about MOVE. This work presents Wideman's imaginative re-creation of Fanon, his struggle with trying to capture the spirit of Fanon's work and his legacy.

When "Damballah" appears as a layered text, we are directed to recall the story and the gap between the time of that text and the one we are reading. The linking between the two requires readers to know the stories within the grander vision of Wideman's writing so that we can re-contextualize "Damballah" as an antecedent to *Fanon*. This moment is harder to successfully achieve if the reader has not been engaged with Wideman's stories all along. Indeed, when Wideman addresses the reader directly in this section as "my reader" and "fellow traveler," we should infer that the journey he is referring to is not just the path we are currently taking with *Fanon*, but all the paths (stories) that have brought us to this point. It also reminds us that as the blues hero, he has been on a journey leading him to his role as artist and elder.

In this version of "Damballah" Thomas is the creator (Tommy was, however, the brother's name in the collection *Damballah*). Wideman tells us that Thomas can do what he wants with the story and its severed head since these are his creations: "Why not recycle a good thing. Thomas had invented the ending, the boy, the head. They belonged to him. Couldn't he do with them as he pleased. Off with the head."[140] Wideman returns to "Damballah" and to the severed head as a revision of the blues hero. Orion's head in "Damballah," cut off and tossed in the river, has been traveling across time and space to arrive at this moment. Cycling back to this story brings the reader back to its themes and its ideas—the image of the African slave, Orion, and the unnamed boy disconnected from his traditions and stories because of southern slavery. The boy in "Damballah" has always been an alter ego of Wideman (and now by extension an alter ego of the alter ego, Thomas).

In the story, the boy throws Orion's head into the river and watches the ripples, the circles stretching out. It is one of Wideman's most memorable "circular" images, repeated again and again in his work. This image is repeated and reversed here—with Wideman signifying on his own work—when he writes:

> No halo of ripples spreading as far as Africa, no shivering crown like he'd imagined around the old African's head after the boy had heaved it as far as he could, farther than he'd guessed he'd be able, out into a lazy southern river, a river broad, as cloaked in mist at daybreak as the reach of Joseph Conrad's fabled Thames.[141]

Thomas recalls this fiction he has created one morning when he is running alongside the East River. And even though he cautions that "no ripples [are] spreading as far as Africa" now, the allusion to *Heart of Darkness* and the linking of the East River to the Thames and, by association, to the Congo in Conrad's work, signal a return to Africa, to the past. The connection also indicts America's continuing role as a colonial power. Thomas receives the box and its severed head to remind him and us of something. Orion represents the ancestral voice in "Damballah," and in *Fanon* his severed head is the figurative dismemberment that occurs when we do not or cannot "remember" the past.

Wideman wrestles with memory and the past in the novel as an older, wiser, and more settled man. The severed head could have another possible, concurrent meaning. The head might be a reminder that sometimes in order to move past trauma, memories must be placed aside, put in the past. The severing of the head and its delivery is a sign of a past coming back to haunt you in a post-traumatic moment, but Wideman's unwillingness to pursue the mystery of the head suggests a decision to put the past behind him, at least for now. There are new relationships to nurture, the future must be considered, and not everything in his past is a stable character or narrative. The lives of his family are also changing.

This is evidenced to some degree by the earlier description of the relationship with Catherine, but it is also illustrated in his conversations with his mother and with Robby. Not unlike the same type of exchanges in *Brothers and Keepers* and in the short story "All Stories Are True," these moments have transformed over time:

> Rob twenty-four years old, twenty-eight years ago when the cops picked him up and never let him go. When Mom and Rob get together, sooner or later they go back to this beginning, or end you might say, almost thirty years ago, when they last lived in the same house, Robby just barely maintaining himself on the civilian side of prison walls.[142]

Wideman's mother later falls asleep during this visit. And Robby admits to Wideman that family visits have kept him alive all these years. Sharing stories helped him survive, but lately he has wanted to cancel family time because waiting for the visits and the visits themselves make him "weak." They draw him away from the real life behind bars. Wideman feels the failure of thirty years of trying to write Robby "out of these walls." But Robby has not remained the same man that went to prison as he is now—his identity, his character, is not frozen in time. He is no longer even the Robby of *Brothers and Keepers*.

Wideman returns to the stories of Robby and his mother to reflect this shift and the revisions that must occur in the narratives.

While regret and hopelessness set the tone for most of this section, Wideman confesses that his brother's experience—and Fanon's—revealed to him the pitfalls of being black in America. Before in *Brothers and Keepers*, Wideman responded to these lessons with anger and self-recrimination. Here those moments of enlightenment are remarked upon, but in this return to the prison, Wideman finds more in common with his mother's position. He describes her here and elsewhere as a woman who never gives up, who "says *question* and says *keep pushing*."[143] Robby notes this same quality in his brother: "Always fussing cause you say nobody reads them, but you keep writing them. I dig it."[144] Wideman also emphasizes here that his mother is the real storyteller in the family (a quality he has also noted before). Clearly, Wideman fills the same position in the family—especially for Robby, who appreciates his brother's talent and waits anxiously for the new book on Fanon (or the "one about the head").

Despite Wideman's belief that he has failed Robby—that his writing has failed Robby—his stories, his blues voice, reaches beyond the walls to Robby. The alienated figure he presented in *Brothers and Keepers* is inverted in this narrative in the return to the prison—even the prison is being rebuilt—to Robby, to the text. Wideman is more deeply connected to his brother now than when he first wrote the work. The connection has been strengthened through the writing, but it also has been deepened through shared traumas and losses. Both men worry about the inevitable loss of their mother; both have shared the loss of their father; and both have shared grief over the losses of their sons.

Wideman's mother and the dichotomy between her precarious body and her indomitable spirit remind us of earlier portraits of Freeda French, Wideman's maternal grandmother. The two women share a strength of character and a storytelling talent, and it was Freeda's death that sent Wideman back to his roots and to Homewood, eventually writing *Damballah*. Since both *Brothers and Keepers* and *Damballah*—twin texts in Wideman's canon—are imbricated in *Fanon*, it is clear that Wideman needs to and wants us to return "home" once more.

Wideman's mother, with her declining health, also appears in the short story "Weight." In "Weight" Wideman juxtaposes the physical image of his mother as weak with her faith and survival instinct. The "weight" she carries is not a physical burden; she walks with the burden of trauma, of her losses: "Would you have breathed easier after releasing the heaviness of silent words hoarded so unbearably, unspeakably long. Let go, Mom. Shed the weight once more."[145] Wideman admits to his fear of losing his mother, of her strength, and of her reassuring words: "Everything's gonna be all right."[146] Wideman's mother and her voice, her message about life, permeate this text, giving even Fanon hope, even in the darkest of times, the "end of times."

A similar confession appears in *Fanon*. Wideman/Thomas says several times in the text that he needs his mother's voice. Their storytelling call-and-response structures the narratives Wideman writes; it constructs reality. Much like Catherine's voice, Wideman's mother's voice has been a consistent and necessary presence in his work. He also needs her strength and her faith in God: "Her belief generates an appetite for love, a flickering presence around her and an abundant radiance within her she shines on me, and who needs, who comprehends more reality than that."[147] Wideman/Thomas addresses his mother later when he admits he could not have written this novel without her "voice." Wideman/Thomas's mother binds him to others and connects to him through love and shared loss: both are now parents of sons in prison. But her love—her "gentleness"—in the face of pain, suffering, and even violence and anger, imbues Wideman with an imaginative power to address his own tragedies; her "gentleness [is] the good news."[148]

Her ability to transcend trauma and pain and still proffer to people "the benefit of the doubt" inspires Wideman and Fanon. In the sections of the book where the mother and Fanon meet in a hospital ward recovering from their illnesses, we are reminded of the closing scenes of *The Cattle Killing*, where the preacher soothes Katherine's fever with stories. Wideman/Thomas imagines this anachronistic meeting to re-emphasize love and storytelling as anathemas to the collapse of the world. In the short story "Fanon" (which appeared in *The Island* and in *God's Gym*) Wideman opens the work by quoting Fanon as saying, "Today I believe in the possibility of love."[149] This love is realized in *The Island* as the relationship between John and Katrine (and Paul and Chantal), and it appears in the final moments of Fanon's life as he is nursed by the mother. Wideman/Thomas envisions his mother "mopping [Fanon's] brow like she used to mop mine when I had a fever."[150] Though Fanon is dead by this time in history, Wideman's re-imagining of his life vis-à-vis his mother's conversations permits him to reclaim Fanon's voice as a necessary touchstone in this period of conflict, terror, and death. Fanon's vision of change and his mother's vision of love blend as the only possible story to combat this current madness. The story "Fanon" appearing in three consecutive works may just be a publishing device, but it more significantly connotes the primacy of love that the writer/narrator has been searching for and has finally found. The love, the connection it illustrates, finally dispels the alienated figure found in almost every work. The return to previously published works, especially to stories about his mother and his brother, the mother's failing health, the reclaiming of the heroic Fanon through the imagination, and the maturity and intimacy of the romantic love relationship, indicates that it is the writer/Thomas/Wideman's time to enter the ancestral storytelling space of Aunt May and John French, the articulate kinsmen, and share his wisdom with the community.

And though the blues hero must sometimes be apart from the community to better understand it, he cannot divorce himself from its humanity. This human connection is clearly visible in the stories of mother and home, but those connections develop even further when Wideman/Thomas inhabits Fanon's consciousness as he cares for his patients and as the scenes between "Mrs. Wyman" and Fanon are reconstructed. The deeper, more intimate, and empathetic connections are drawn in the earlier descriptions of the writer and the woman he loves. The allusion to the Rilke quote on love and solitude and the writer's characterization of the day the two spend together—apart and independent, yet accommodating each other's rhythms and needs—reveal the deeper bonds. The writer and his lover let each other be themselves without the need to control each other's lives.

The details of this relationship echo back in *The Island* when the writer sits quietly and lets the ancestral voices of the past on the island speak. He sits and listens rather than trying to mold their stories, connecting to them, becoming a vessel of their stories. Thomas/Wideman senses this as a change in his writing when he comments on the difficulties of telling Robby's story years before or his mother's, and how often he felt compelled to direct their stories rather than let their voices speak on their own.

The concluding lines of the novel suggest that Wideman/Thomas sees Fanon as accomplishing this as a philosopher and thinker—letting his patients and the colonized tell their own stories rather than have someone else control their narratives, their consciousness, and their histories. Colonization and its traumatic aftermath can only be negotiated in this act of healing and storytelling. The controlling of images is an act of terrorism, and historically this has destroyed cultures and personal lives—and as Wideman indicates earlier in the novel, this continues to happen today. Fanon understood how to heal this trauma, as all blues heroes do: "Unless the map, as Fanon understands it, the map that erases him by erasing itself by erasing him, can be flipped over to its unwritten side and then perhaps you could begin a fresh drawing of the world. Speak."[151] The need to make new maps is reminiscent of Wideman's description of maps and Promised Land, South Carolina, in *Fatheralong*. The invitation to "speak," the final, stand-alone word of the novel, asks everyone to tell their story and let others tell theirs—this is the revolution that will end terror by connecting us through our shared stories and humanity.

By "creating alternative lives" in his fiction and by reclaiming Fanon as hero and as desperately needed historical and philosophical voice, Wideman actualizes his own position as a committed blues hero.[152] And by balancing Fanon's revolutionary rhetoric with his mother's love and ability to offer the "benefit of the doubt," Wideman reinvents the blues hero image as one reintegrated into the community, connected to family, to lovers. The reconstruction of images occurs throughout the work in the scenes with Jean Luc-Goddard and the allusions to the Lumiere brothers. Like the references to Giacometti, Bearden, and Mallory's photography, these moments emphasize the need to reinvent the stories others tell about us; and by re-imagining Fanon and his last days, where Wideman's own mother nourished him with love and stories, Wideman re-imagines himself and history and seeks ways to "combat the madness" of the present in order to preserve the future.

Conclusion

> To be in someone's thoughts or stories keeps the dead alive, the Igbo say.
> —JOHN EDGAR WIDEMAN, *Fanon*

In concluding a study about the work of John Edgar Wideman, it makes perfect sense to end where you began. How better to capture the recursive nature of the writer's work? Charles Johnson's characterization of Wideman as an archaeologist who uncovers the past for "the sake of" of future generations in many ways helped frame this study. Wideman's oft-repeated evocation, "all stories are true," also inspired the course of this exploration. But another inducement has been to provide some answers to a question I am almost always asked by students, colleagues, and even other scholars after they have read a couple of Wideman's works, "Why this story again?" I was infinitely pleased when a student, after having three different courses with me—with three different Wideman texts for reading—announced that not only was she "finally getting Wideman" but that listening to yet another version of a Damballah tale was "like going home and hearing your family tell their old stories. You've heard them a hundred times, but each time there's a little new detail. And it makes you comfortable; it makes you feel like you are home."

Wideman's own characterization of Thomas's writing in *Fanon* echoes these three strands in this study. When acknowledging the repetition and revisiting of stories, he notes that it is "a playing out of remembering and forgetting, a cover up and recovery of old stories, a kind of perpetual archaeological dig."[1] It is not enough to describe Wideman's writing as palimpsestic unless we recall that term's full definition. It is not just that there are layers of images and texts written upon again and again; some of those overwritten texts are still visible *through* the layers of new material. Like shadows and afterimages of double-exposed photos, we can still see the ghosts of something or someone that came before. Like an archaeologist, Wideman's search for the remains, for the stories of the dead, reveals something of the past as well as the present—but the search also allows those voices to speak to us:

> I cite the Igbo to acknowledge my unanticipated good fortune, my gratitude for the presence of what might be called ancestors (like you) waiting to be discovered. Ancestors who speak, not on demand, but if and when they choose. The simultaneous loss and discovery of their presence defines a space I might inhabit if I learn how, a vast solitude, a space less alone, less silent perhaps because others once occupied it and I've been expected."[2]

The silence of the past is less deafening in the world that Wideman imagines. The repetition and layering of stories creates a collective document with the feeling and force of history. The stories feel true because we have heard them before; they confirm one another—which, one could argue, gives history its feeling of veracity. If you repeat a story enough, there will be some who will accept it as authoritative. The scope of Wideman's work—its weight—balances itself against the weight of the historical record. When asked in 2002 if he views his writing as many critics do—that the early work is more European and the latter more influenced by African American culture—Wideman responded:

> I don't buy that kind of bifurcation. I think throughout my writing life I've been looking at the people and experiences closest to me and trying to find a way to talk about them. What has happened over time is a natural growth, or change or sophistication of technique and different modes of representation, which I have played around with and moved on with. But the subject matter remains essentially the same. If you look a little more closely, I think the same people keep coming up again and again in my writing.[3]

Wideman goes on to say that his substance and style are inseparable. The layering and cyclic nature of his storytelling is demanded by the stories he tells. The literary doubles, the fictional doubles, not only remind us that all stories are true, but also reflect the writer's imagination, the creative exploration of possible selves and scenarios. At the same time, those doubles are signs of the need to return to sites of suffering to gain some control and understanding, even to attempt healing.

Even in Wideman's latest publication, *Briefs*, these considerations are visible. By now, it should not seem remarkable that Wideman returns again to some of the same stories, themes, and characters. What is noteworthy about their reappearance in *Briefs* is the form that these new versions take. *Briefs* is a collection of "microstories" or "flash fiction," snapshot stories that give us a "brief" glimpse into a moment in a character's life or an event in time. The experience of reading the stories in *Briefs* is strikingly similar to flipping through a photo album, a collection of images that I've seen before, representing the life of Wideman' stories. Some of the returning sketches include Cudjoe and the fire, shooting deaths of teenage boys, a passage (in the story "Ghetto") from *Hurry Home*, Ralph Ellison, a Paris romance, basketball, Emmett Till, family stories, prisons, the Holocaust, the deaths of mothers and fathers, the writer contemplating writing—the list could go on. It also includes new stories of grandchildren, Madonna and Barry Bonds, and allusions to Emily Dickinson and Tim O'Brien. Some of these newer members of the Wideman symphony are humorous and hopeful; some are somber and openly critical of the recent American political scene.

The descriptions of writing found in *Briefs* continue Wideman's legacy, the characteristic contemplation of cyclic and repeating narratives, blank spaces, doubles, nonlinear time. The writer returns with "copies of himself from Kinkos."[4] He wrestles with the dictionary and the definition of "brief."[5] His palimpsestic style continues: "his story, his words following on after another, erasing, consuming each other ending like these."[6] Included is even a primer on how to write a review of a collection of stories like *Briefs* (I guess I should have read that one first). What is most surprising is the compression of styles and techniques in *Briefs* that are endemic of other writing by Wideman. The use of actual blank space on the pages—even in a tale that is only a page in length to begin with—reaffirms Wideman's interest in both the silence and the possibility the break signifies. He characterizes the work in *Briefs*, in a Lulu.com blog interview, as a meditation on "holes, spaces, reminders, mirrors, the unheard pattern of silences that organizes a composition's meaning and moves its audience."[7]

Wideman always appears to be interested in looking for any way possible to tell a story. And while it is clear that Wideman is still intent on exploring these spaces, *Briefs* represents a creative revolution in the way that he creates space. In previous works, gaps and spaces appeared in the narrative through Wideman's use of layering, his loose narrative structuring, his jazz-like passages.

Here, gaps and spaces and fissures in the text do not erupt; they materialize in the brevity; they are the gap that is formed by the "glance away."

Of course, the "glance away" has been a repeated image and thematic emblem from the very beginning of Wideman's career; and as yet another sign of his recursive style, the image returns in *Briefs* as the foundation of the collection. Like the stories in the collection, we only get a glimpse of these characters and their lives; as we move on to the end and then on to the next work, we have no idea what will happen next or what happened before. We are left with a gap that we may or may not fill, but we are nonetheless left wondering, "Where's anyone go the moment you take your eyes of them?"[8]

"Going backward to go forward" for a moment, the "glance away" appearing throughout the breadth of Wideman's writing further crystallizes his concern with history and with discovering all the possibilities of self and story that occur in that space. The description of Freeda French's "glance away" illustrates this most clearly when she contemplates the bubble in the kitchen sink, one of Wideman's most repeated images and stories: "She couldn't remember what had pulled her away, but it continued pulling, drawing her past the edges of herself. Since that day, whenever she looked away from something, she was never sure it would be there when she looked back."[9] The last line echoes the title *A Glance Away* and the story "First Love Suite: II" in *Briefs*. The bubble is an image that evokes both the circular version of history that Wideman represents elsewhere and the rainbow image of the god Damballah.[10] The bubble also symbolizes Homewood itself, a beautiful, perfectly shaped "bubble" protecting the neighborhood.[11]

Wideman states in an interview given over thirty-five years ago: "The way time passes sometimes makes time seem like no more than a 'glance' and a 'glance away.' When you look away from somebody you open up this immensity of time, this gap that is almost impossible to talk about in terms of years or days or seconds.... This has to do with history, it has to do with the relationship of the two people, and some strange thing about time."[12] There is some hopefulness in the use of gaps and "looking away" in *Briefs*, but these moments are contextual. While these places do allow for the writer's imagination to counter silence, to combat the trauma of history, they can also represent absence and loss, as they do in the story "Bones." This tension in Wideman is all-encompassing and unresolved. There is not one version of Wideman, the artist, any more than there is only one version of a story or one reading of silences, gaps, and glances away in his work.

Perhaps this is the failure of language, its inability to offer a singular reading or interpretation, its inability to capture completely a character or a moment in time. Wideman's writing alter egos often complain about language's ineffectiveness, often resulting in the chasms of silence. But just as often, the writer expresses relief that language allows for malleable images, for multiple versions of reading and interpretation. This is why we can read a work of Wideman and concurrently feel the weight of post-traumatic silences in history as well as the elations of uncovering new possibilities and healing in the discovery of unknown stories. That both of these can happen simultaneously in the same space reminds us of the magic and the power of the imagination. Wideman allows the "pain of being two" to be equally as true as the possibility of "being two places at once." Sometimes one character can inhabit both of these descriptions. A character can be both a victim of and a victor over pain and suffering. One can be both Caliban and Prospero. The blues mind balances these types of tensions; the blues hero employs a type of "negative capability" in order to transform trauma and survival and love into art. It is what Wideman thinks is most powerful in African American music when we listen to it:

> Something connects us so that the past is alive again. The past and the present merge, and you merge with the blues singer, and the blues signer merges with other blues singers, and ultimately with the drums and Africa, and with something that transcends time and place that is more about the human capacity to turn experience into metaphor, into language, into music, into a particular way of holding and touching someone else. So that is the ultimate project for me—figuring out how language can perform this same kind of trick that music does.[13]

This condition in Wideman is why I can never dutifully answer yet another question I am often asked: "If you had to suggest one Wideman book to read, which would it be?" My response, "You can't read just one," seems to be usually taken as the words of an enthusiastic fan or an addict. But what is missed in the exchange is my argument that Wideman requires a long-term commitment by a reader. If you want a relationship with a Wideman novel, you have to agree to be in for the long haul. It is a rocky road as well, and one you are likely to get lost on (Wideman especially has a distrust of maps). In attempting to help anyone navigate this journey, students, fellow readers, well-meaning friends, I have tried to draw from any source available to me, any theory, any reading, any signpost. But as Wideman reminds us of the maxim "all stories are true," while it suggests a kind of ultimate democracy, it also suggests a kind of chaos.[14]

While we may want resolutions, a singular path to emerge, more and more I find getting lost can be more enlightening. The idea that "all stories are true" was once an intellectual conundrum for me, especially as I began this study. But in the interim, I became a mother—a mother of a curious and precocious child who asked me just a few weeks after entering kindergarten why her teacher kept telling her certain stories were not true, that they were myths or "fairy stories." At first my scholarly bells and whistles went off, alerting me to all sorts of ideas for the study at hand. What surprised me out of my academic reverie was my daughter's visible sadness at being forced to choose which stories to believe in, being *told* which ones to believe in. In that moment, I realized more clearly than I had before why the Igbo have the saying "all stories are true." Embodied in my daughter's distress was the loss of a sense of wonder, a loss of a sense of the magic of stories. But her despair about being forced to choose revealed that the notion that "all stories are true" connects us to one another, to each other's stories of ourselves and our world. When we begin saying that this story is more accurate and that one is mythology, we enforce a hierarchy; we judge one another against our beliefs; we break our connections to the rest of the world around us. While my daughter thus far steadfastly refuses to choose (celebrating all holidays as well), I wait in angst for the teacher who will try to demolish her because of it. Her empathy for these stories she believes and for their characters and for the people that tell them serves as a daily reminder of the transformative power of storytelling.

This digression hopefully illustrates the method of storytelling that Wideman's work embodies. Drawing on all cultures, places, times, structures, all ways of seeing the world, Wideman reveres the power of the story to connect us. He expresses in his last works, as he has in all of his writings, that how we imagine ourselves and our own stories is crucial to surviving the trauma of the past. To create new stories out of the fabric of history is a goal of many African American writers. It is a recovery of the self and of the community, a "process" of making a fiction that is not "merely a lie or a fabrication. Rather it is a way of grasping the totality of human existence when that totality is hidden from view."[15] Wideman admits that the other side of the maxim "all stories are true" is that all stories are lies or that "none of them are true."[16] A lie, of course, in fiction is nothing new, and as we have seen it is nothing new to autobiography either. The stories are lies that reveal truth. Ralph Ellison analyzes the paradoxical relationship even further in his 1981 introduction to *Invisible Man*: "I knew that I was composing a work of fiction, a work of literary art and one that would allow me to take advantage of the novel's capacity for telling the truth while actually telling a 'lie,' which is the Afro-American folk term for an improvised story."[17] This is what Wideman has done all along in his work. Like a jazz musician, he improvised on the literary tradition of his family and personal history and of communal and recorded history. He is a trickster figure—wearing multiple masks, speaking in tongues, parodying the audience, telling us lies. As a trickster figure, he echoes the blues hero and this character's trickster qualities. But like all trickster figures, there is an ultimate message to be imparted.

Our understanding of that message comes from the realization that in every work—fiction and nonfiction—a child or children have been lost, either literally or figuratively: Eugene Lawson in *A Glance Away*; Cecil Braithwaite's son, Simon, in *Hurry Home*; Wilkerson's pupils; the newborn and Tommy in *Damballah*; Bess's son and Shirley's daughter in *Hiding Place*; Junebug in *Sent for You Yesterday*; Cudjoe in *Reuben*; Simba and Wideman's son in *Philadelphia Fire*; orphans burned to death, the dead baby held by the African woman, and the children that Liam and his wife can never have in *The Cattle Killing*; Garth and Robby (and even the possible loss of the premature Jamila) in *Brothers and Keepers*; Wideman's son in *Fatheralong*; Omar Wideman and Kassima's sons in *Two Cities*; the miscarriage in *The Island*. All lost. Notably, *Fanon* closes with a letter to his mother about Romeo, Catherine's son (we are told in *The Island*), and his decision to grow dreadlocks. Dan's marriage at the end of *Fatheralong* is an equally significant scene, as is the inclusion of a story addressed to a grandchild in *Briefs*. These images of a child alive and thriving stand in stark contrast to those others we have seen before. They offer readers the brightest glimmers of hope in the works of Wideman's epic vision.

Wideman has called history a "cage, a conundrum we must escape or resolve before our art can go freely about our business."[18] Wideman repeats images and stories, layering them throughout the texts, to illuminate those hidden and silent lives, to illustrate the possibilities of new stories if we can just imagine them for ourselves. He expresses all of our stories—the stories of our loss, of our suffering, of anger, of devastation, of warmth and joy through the celebration of family and love—the sacred and the profane. The storyteller is "working hard, taking chances, having fun, failing, suffering, ... [and] through the tales [he] makes us aware of a larger, unfinished story, the collective, collaborative utterance never completed because there's always another voice worth hearing."[19] These stories connect us to each other, to our past, and to our future. Wideman believes, unflinchingly, in the power of the story to save us, himself, his family, the world—to gather each piece in a world fragmented by the paradigms of race and devastating loss. His achievement is marked by his accomplishments in revising genres and storytelling techniques, in "dismantling masterplots," in imagining an epic vision of African American life, and in reminding us that our stories are also true. His work is also a testament of the redemptive blues spirit that, despite its revelation of traumatic history, soars.

Notes

Introduction

1. Keith Byerman, "Wideman's Career and Literary Reception," in *Critical Essays on John Edgar Wideman*, ed. Bonnie TuSmith and Keith Byerman (Knoxville: University of Tennessee Press, 2006), x.

2. Ishmael Reed, *Airing Dirty Laundry* (Reading, MA: Addison, 1993), 144.

3. See also Keith Byerman's study of Wideman's short stories: *A Study of the Short Fiction* (New York: Twayne Pub., 1998).

4. See chapter 2, this volume, for a more thorough discussion of Wideman's relationship to T. S. Eliot.

5. James Coleman, *Blackness and Modernism: The Literary Career of John Edgar Wideman* (Jackson: University Press of Mississippi, 1989), 137.

6. Ibid., 4.

7. Ibid., 138. There is some debate as to what book is the first in the trilogy. However, when the books were published together as *The Homewood Books*, *Damballah* was first.

8. J. Coleman, *Blackness and Modernism*, 6.

9. Ibid., 44.

10. Bernard Bell, *The Afro-American Novel and Its Traditions* (Amherst: University of Massachusetts Press, 1987), 311–312.

11. Ibid., 315. Bonnie TuSmith focuses on the Homewood trilogy as well in her study, *All My Relatives: Community in Contemporary Ethnic American Literatures*. TuSmith examines Wideman's return to the community and the importance of the family to Wideman's aesthetic, as seen in *Sent for You Yesterday*. The reimmersion into the community connects Wideman to his roots, to his family, and to the importance of the folk stories that sustain the family. Some of this had already been discussed by James Coleman, but TuSmith sees this as essential to understanding Wideman's work. She calls the "fragmented" voices of *Sent for You Yesterday* a "typical modernist technique," yet Coleman had suggested that by this time Wideman was moving toward a postmodernist voicing of African American experience. Bonnie TuSmith, *All My Relatives: Community in Contemporary Ethnic American Literatures* (Ann Arbor: University of Michigan Press, 1993), 90; J. Coleman, *Blackness and Modernism*, 97.

12. J. Coleman, *Blackness and Modernism*, 137–138; Dorothea Mbalia, *John Edgar Wideman: Reclaiming the African Personality* (London: Susquehanna University Press, 1995), 16.

13. Mbalia, *John Edgar Wideman*, 46, 110.

14. See Mbalia, *John Edgar Wideman*, 17, 69–70, 74–75, 80–82. The impression one is left with after reading the study is that Mbalia believes that every African American intellectual in each novel is Wideman and every European woman represents his now ex-wife, Judy. She notes that "significantly, there are no European female characters in the new stories, contrasted with his earlier works, from *A Glance Away* to *Sent for You Yesterday*; this omission is quite a useful gauge of Wideman's new thinking." Mbalia, *John Edgar Wideman*, 128. Since Mbalia's study, at least three other works of Wideman's, *Hoop Roots*, *The Island*, and *Fanon*, do feature a prominent white, European woman.

15. Mbalia, *John Edgar Wideman*, 35.

16. Ibid., 108–109.

17. J. Coleman, *Blackness and Modernism*, 16.

18. See, for example, Kathryn Hume's "'Dimensions' and John Edgar Wideman's Mental Cosmology," *Contemporary Literature* 44, no. 4 (Winter 2003): 697–726; Kimberly Ruffin, "Mourning in the 'Second Middle Passage': Visual and Verbal Praxis in John Edgar Wideman's *Two Cities*," *CLA Journal* 48, no. 4 (2005): 415–439.

19. John Edgar Wideman, *Brothers and Keepers* (New York: Holt, 1984), 76.

20. See especially James Coleman's analysis of Wideman after the trip to Homewood. He states that Wideman, in *The Lynchers*, "does not achieve the full, mature black voice that we find in the Homewood trilogy, however . . . when he wrote *Lynchers*, Wideman was not knowledgeable enough about the workings of black tradition to achieve this full, mature black voice. Later, when Wideman had informed himself about the richness and substance of black culture, had distanced the mainstream modernist concept of the alienated artist-intellectual, and had himself moved closer to the black community, he strengthened his black voice, made it dominant over the mainstream modernist voice, and integrated the black intellectual into the substantive black culture and community of which he had become aware." J. Coleman, *Blackness and Modernism*, 44.

21. John Edgar Wideman, preface to *The Homewood Trilogy* (New York: Avon, 1985), vii.

22. J. Coleman, *Blackness and Modernism*, 44.

23. She contends further that his reimmersion in the works of African American writers in 1968 affects his writing style: "It frees him from the constraints of the Western literary tradition and centers him within the African tradition, a tradition which has its own standards that are always being creatively renamed and revised. In preparing for teaching this class, but most important, in preparing for the transition from the aping of post-modernists European writers such as T. S. Eliot to the creative, self-assured African writer he becomes beginning with the Homewood trilogy, Wideman begins to appreciate his race, his culture, himself." Mbalia, *John Edgar Wideman*, 28–29.

24. Charles Johnson, *Being and Race: Black Writing since 1970* (Bloomington: Indiana University Press, 1988), 74–75.

25. Notable exceptions are Trudier Harris's reading of *The Lynchers* and Aldon Nielsen's consideration of Wideman and his use of history in his brief discussion of *Hurry Home* in *Writing between the Lines: Race and Intertextuality* (Athens: University of Georgia Press, 1994). See Trudier Harris, *Exorcising Blackness: Historical and Literary Lynching and Burning Rituals* (Bloomington: Indiana University Press, 1984), 129–147.

26. J. Coleman, *Blackness and Modernism*, 158.

27. Quoted in Laura Miller, "Interview with John Edgar Wideman," *Salon Magazine*, November 11, 1997, http://www.salon.com/nov96/interview961111.html (accessed April 2, 1998).

28. Patricia Smith, "Getting under Our Skin," in *Conversations with John Edgar Wideman*, ed. Bonnie TuSmith (Jackson: University Press of Mississippi, 1998), 141.

29. Kay Bonetti, "Interview with John Edgar Wideman," in *Conversations with John Edgar Wideman*, ed. TuSmith, 52.

30. See J. Coleman, *Blackness and Modernism*, 158; Ishmael Reed, "Interview with John Edgar Wideman," in *Conversations with John Edgar Wideman*, ed. TuSmith, 126; and Miller, "Interview with John Edgar Wideman."

31. Originally this collection was published in *The Stories of John Edgar Wideman*. Later the collection was published on its own under the title *All Stories Are True*.

32. John Edgar Wideman, *Fatheralong* (New York: Pantheon, 1994), 62.

33. John Edgar Wideman, *The Cattle Killing* (Boston: Houghton Mifflin, 1996), 53.

34. Bonnie TuSmith, "Benefit of the Doubt: A Conversation with John Edgar Wideman," in *Conversations with John Edgar Wideman*, ed. TuSmith, 198.

35. J. Coleman, *Blackness and Modernism*, 152.

36. Charles Rowell, "An Interview with John Edgar Wideman," *Callaloo* 13, no. 1 (Winter 1990): 54.

37. John Edgar Wideman, *Fatheralong* (New York: Pantheon, 1994), 95.

Chapter One

1. Jean-Pierre Richard refers to Wideman's work as the "thirty-year palimpsest" in his article, "From Slavers to Drunken Boats: A Thirty-Year Palimpsest in John Edgar Wideman's Fiction," *Callaloo* 22, no. 3 (1999): 656–664. Jacqueline Berben-Masi writes, "Wideman's entire opus is a palimpsest: thematically, the past lives on in the present" in "Mother Goose and Brother Loon: The Fairy-Tale-in-the-Tale as Vehicle of Displacement," *Callaloo* 22, no. 3 (1999): 594–602.

2. Ashraf Rushdy considers the palimpsestic narrative as a conversation between traditions and African American writers' attempts to write against the "culture of slavery." See Rushdy's *Remembering Generations: Race and Family in Contemporary African American Fiction* (Chapel Hill: University of North Carolina Press, 2000). He does not, however, mention Wideman's work in this volume, though he has written extensively on Wideman elsewhere.

3. Rushdy, *Remembering Generations*, 27.

4. Kathyrn Hume outlines a study of Wideman's work based on this layering structure in "'Dimensions' and John Edgar Wideman's Mental Cosmology," *Contemporary Literature* 44, no. 4 (Winter 2003): 697–726. She explains that "to understand fully the nature of his overarching enterprise, one must look at the whole corpus of his work and how it has evolved, not just at single works. This vision manifests itself in metaphors for human experience expressed in terms of 'layers' or 'dimensions'" (698). Hume's call is an important one, but her brief study does not fully examine the use of layering—especially in terms of history, which, she argues, does not really occur until works after *Philadelphia Fire*. She further suggests that he does not "focus upon history in an analytic or personal fashion until his story, 'Fever' and his memoir, *Fatheralong*" (707). I disagree with this particular

assessment. As I will argue throughout this study, Wideman has been analyzing and layering fiction, autobiography, and history throughout his work.

5. John Edgar Wideman, *Two Cities* (New York: Houghton Mifflin, 1998), 91.

6. Ibid., 83.

7. Arnold E. Sabatelli, "John Edgar Wideman," in *Conversations with John Edgar Wideman*, ed. Bonnie TuSmith (Jackson: University Press of Mississippi, 1998), 149–150.

8. Ibid., 150.

9. Ishmael Reed, *Airing Dirty Laundry* (Reading, MA: Addison, 1993), 144.

10. Charles Rowell, "An Interview with John Edgar Wideman," *Callaloo* 13, no. 1 (Winter 1990): 60.

11. Albert Murray, *Stomping the Blues* (New York: Da Capo Press, 1976), 63; Stanley Crouch, "Jazz Criticism and Its Effect on the Art Form," *New Perspectives on Jazz*, ed. David Baker (Washington, DC: Smithsonian Institute Press, 1990), 76; Ted Gioia, *The Imperfect Art: Reflections on Jazz and Modern Culture* (New York: Oxford University Press, 1988), 33; David Perry, *Jazz Greats* (London: Phaidon Press, 1996), 13.

12. Ihab Hassan, "Toward a Concept of Postmodernism," in *The Postmodern Reader*, ed. Joseph Natoli and Linda Hutcheon (Albany: SUNY Press, 1993), 280–281.

13. M. M. Bakhtin, *The Dialogic Imagination: Four Essays*, ed. Michael Holquist, trans. Caryl Emerson and Michael Holquist (Austin: University of Texas Press, 1981), 358.

14. Bernard Bell, "Introduction: Clarence Major's Double Consciousness as a Black Postmodernist Artist," *African American Review* 28, no. 1 (1994): 8.

15. Wideman, quoted in John O'Brien, *Interviews with Black Writers* (New York: Liveright Press, 1973), 217.

16. Wideman, quoted in James Coleman, *Black Male Fiction and the Legacy of Caliban* (Lexington: University Press of Kentucky, 2001), 149. See also Phillip Howlett, "Letter from the Publisher," in *Conversations with John Edgar Wideman*, ed. Bonnie TuSmith (Jackson: University Press of Mississippi, 1998), 33.

17. Mark Anthony Neal, *Soul Babies* (New York: Routledge, 2002), 2–3.

18. Hayden White, *Metahistory: The Historical Imagination in Nineteenth-Century Europe* (Baltimore: Johns Hopkins University Press, 1973), 2.

19. Lynn Hunt, *The New Cultural History* (Berkeley: University of California Press, 1989), 8; Frederic Jameson, *Postmodernism, or the Cultural Logic of Late Capitalism* (Durham: Duke University Press, 1991), 367.

20. Dominick LaCapra, *History and Criticism* (Ithaca, NY: Cornell University Press, 1985), 116.

21. Dominick LaCapra, *Writing History, Writing Trauma* (Baltimore: John Hopkins University Press, 2001), 14.

22. Hayden White, *Tropics of Discourse: Essays in Cultural Criticism* (Baltimore: Johns Hopkins University Press, 1978), 40.

23. David Cowart, *History and the Contemporary Novel* (Carbondale: Southern Illinois University Press, 1989), 6.

24. Several critics have noted Wideman's work as an example of "historiographic metafiction." See Katie Birat, "'All Stories Are True': Prophecy, History, and Story in *The Cattle Killing*," *Callaloo* 22, no. 3 (1999): 629–643.

25. Linda Hutcheon, "Beginning to Theorize Postmodernism," in *The Postmodern Reader*, ed. Linda Hutcheon and Joseph Natoli (Albany: SUNY Press, 1993), 246, 250.

26. Linda Hutcheon, *A Poetics of Postmodernism* (New York: Routledge, 1988), 114–118.

27. Ibid., 109.

28. John Edgar Wideman, *The Cattle Killing* (Boston: Houghton Mifflin, 1996), 1–4.

29. Hutcheon, *The Poetics* 10, 126–130.

30. Bakhtin, *Dialogic Imagination*, 6–7.

31. Madelyn Jablon, *Black Metafiction: Self-Consciousness in African American Literature* (Iowa City: University of Iowa Press, 1997), 10.

32. Samuel Floyd Jr., *The Power of Black Music* (New York: Oxford University Press, 1995), 141.

33. Henry Louis Gates Jr., *The Signifying Monkey* (New York: Oxford University Press, 1988), 110–113. Several other critics of African American literature have connected the multivocality of African American texts, past and present, with the theories of M. M. Bakhtin. Albert Stone implies that the experimental nature of African American autobiography and its inclusion of varied and various forms and modes, especially fiction, fit "the broad historical development that Bakhtin claims for Western narrative discourse: the novelization of all genres." William Andrews notes this in his study of the slave narratives as well. Mae Gwendolyn Henderson finds in African American women's fiction a "discursive diversity, or simultaneity of discourse," which she calls "speaking in tongues," a phrasing that she argues resonates in Bakhtin's theories of dialogism, heteroglossia, and polyphonic texts but is also intimately connected with the African American religious and linguistic traditions in the form of sermons, testimonials, testifying, witnessing, and the "call and response" between the minister and the congregation. Albert Stone, "After *Black Boy* and *Dusk of Dawn*: Patterns in Recent Black Autobiography," in *African-American Autobiography*, ed. William Andrews (Englewood Cliffs, NJ: Prentice Hall: 1993), 188; William Andrews, "Toward a Poetics of Afro-American Autobiography," in *Afro-American Literary Study in the 1990s*, ed. Houston Baker and Patricia Redmond (Chicago: University of Chicago Press, 1989), 85; and Mae Gwendolyn Henderson, "Speaking in Tongues: Dialogics, Dialectics, and the Black Woman Writer's Literary Tradition," in *Reading Black, Reading Feminist*, ed. Henry Louis Gates Jr. (New York: Viking Penguin, 1990), 122–124.

34. Bernard Bell, "*Beloved*: A Womanist Neo-Slave Narrative; or Multivocal Remembrances of Things Past," *African American Review* 26.1 (1992): 12.

35. Houston Baker, *Blues, Ideology, and Afro-American Literature* (Chicago: University of Chicago Press, 1984), 176.

36. While Bakhtin doesn't mention which discourses have specifically become novelized, it appears from our study thus far that many critics in the fields of literature, history, autobiography, and anthropology contend that there is a trend in all academic discourses toward fictionalization. For anthropology's response to Bakhtin and the "fictionalization" of all discourses, see James Clifford's introduction in *Writing Culture: The Poetics and Politics of Ethnography*, ed. James Clifford and George Marcus (Berkeley: University of California Press, 1986), 6.

37. Bakhtin, *Dialogic Imagination*, 429.

38. Ibid., 87.

39. John Edgar Wideman, "The Black Writer and the Magic of the Word," *New York Times Book Review*, January 24, 1988, 28.

40. Hutcheon, *A Poetics*, 9, 134.

41. Albert Stone, "Identity and Art in Frederick Douglass's Narrative," *CLA Journal* 17, no. 2 (December 1973): 194.

42. William Andrews, introduction to *African-American Autobiography*, ed. William Andrews (Englewood Cliffs, NJ: Prentice Hall, 1993), 5; Roger Rosenblatt, "Black Autobiography: Life as Death Weapon," *Autobiography: Essays Theoretical and Critical*, ed. James Olney (Princeton: Princeton University Press, 1980), 170. Other novels and autobiographies also blur genre distinctions (such as *The Autobiography of Martin Luther King*, Ernest Gaines's *The Autobiography of Miss Jane Pittman*, and Jamaica Kincaid's *The Autobiography of My Mother*). The most notable example may be Audre Lorde's *Zami*, described by the writer as a "biomythography," voicing the discourses of myth, history, poetry, and biography. The number of works that bridge these distinctions in the African American tradition are nearly too numerous to note here.

43. Albert Stone, "After *Black Boy* and *Dusk of Dawn*: Patterns in Recent Black Autobiography," in *African-American Autobiography*, ed. William Andrews (Englewood Cliffs, NJ: Prentice Hall: 1993), 188.

44. Michael Cooke, *Afro-American Literature in the Twentieth Century: The Achievement of Intimacy* (New Haven: Yale University Press, 1984), 208.

45. Jane Campbell, *Mythic Black Fiction: The Transformation of History* (Knoxville: University of Tennessee Press, 1986), 155.

46. Darwin Turner, "Black Fiction: History and Myth," *Studies in American Fiction* 5, no. 1 (1977): 110.

47. "Reinterpretations of history or contemporary reality for the purpose of racial retrieval" is also a concern of much African literature. Turner, "Black Fiction," 105. Also see Wole Soyinka's *Myth, Literature, and the African World* (Cambridge: Cambridge University Press, 1976), 97–135. A further description of these types of narratives, and the reason for their critical success is in chapter 2.

48. Malcolm X and Alex Haley, *The Autobiography of Malcolm X* (New York: Ballantine Books, 1964), 178–190.

49. John Edgar Wideman, "Malcolm X: The Art of Autobiography," in *Malcolm X: In Our Own Image*, ed. Joe Wood (New York: St. Martin's Press, 1992), 101–116.

50. Wideman studied at Oxford from 1963 to 1966. In an interview with Charles Rowell, Wideman said not only that he was not involved with the Black Arts Movement because of his studies at Oxford, which took him away from the country, but that he was also suspicious of "groups." Charles Rowell, "An Interview with John Edgar Wideman," *Callaloo* 13, no. 1 (Winter 1990): 50. For a further illustration of Wideman's position on the Black Arts Movement, see his introduction to *Live from Death Row*, by Mumia Abu-Jamal (New York: Avon, 1995), xxiii–xxxiv.

51. Wideman, quoted in Rowell, "An Interview with John Edgar Wideman," 50.

52. Joe Weixlmann, "The Uses and Meaning of History in Modern Black American Fiction," *Black American Literature Forum* 11, no. 4 (Winter 1977): 123.

53. Georg Lukas, *The Historical Novel*, trans. Hannah Mitchell and Stanley Mitchell (1962; reprint, Lincoln: University of Nebraska Press, 1983), 232.

54. John Edgar Wideman, "The Architectonics of Fiction," *Callaloo* 13, no. 1 (Winter 1990): 43.

55. See chapter 2 for more discussion of the relationship between Wideman and Eliot.

56. We should also reflect here on the difficulty of defining terms like "modern" and "postmodern." Much of the disparity regarding the categorizing of Wideman's work may be due to the fluidity of these terms. Some techniques that TuSmith calls modernist Coleman argues are the beginning of his postmodernism. Mbalia calls Eliot a "post-modernist,"

Coleman calls him a modernist, yet both agree Wideman is influenced by T. S. Eliot in the first books. Clearly, there is some difficulty in defining these labels. As some critics suggest, "no clear consensus about its meaning exists among scholars," and there "is already some evidence that postmodernism, and modernism even more, are beginning to slip and slide in time, threatening to make any diacritical distinction between them desperate." Ihab Hassan, "Toward a Concept of Postmodernism," in *The Postmodern Reader*, ed. Joseph Natoli and Linda Hutcheon (Albany: SUNY Press, 1993), 277.

57. Cornell West, "The Dilemma of the Black Intellectual," in *Breaking Bread: Insurgent Black Intellectual Life*, ed. bell hooks and Cornel West (Boston: South End Press, 1991), 143–144.

58. Craig Hansen Werner, *Playing the Changes: From Afro-Modernism to the Jazz Impulse* (Urbana: University of Illinois Press, 1994), xvii.

59. Bernard Bell, "Introduction: Clarence Major's Double Consciousness as a Black Postmodernist Artist," *African American Review* 28, no. 1 (1994): 8; Bernard Bell, *The Afro-American Novel and Its Traditions* (Amherst: University of Massachusetts Press, 1987), 284.

60. Craig Werner coins multicultural postmodernism "the Jazz impulse," which is even more self-referential. Werner, *Playing the Changes*, xx.

61. Madelyn Jablon, *Black Metafiction: Self-Consciousness in African American Literature* (Iowa City: University of Iowa Press, 1997), 59. Notably, there are few studies on the links between African American culture and postmodernism. While hooks and West have represented the need to realize and explore those links in the sources noted above (as well as in West's "Black Culture and Postmodernism"), little scholarly work has been done to address those connections. Some exceptions are those referred to above by Bell and Hogue. Other works include Madelyn Jablon's *Black Metafiction*, Craig Hansen Werner's *Playing the Changes*, and individual studies such as Robert Fox's *Conscientious Sorcerers: The Black Postmodernist Fiction of Amiri Baraka, Ishmael Reed, and Samuel Delaney*. Both Gates, in *The Signifying Monkey*, and Houston Baker, in *Blues, Ideology, and Afro-American Literature*, while not specifically using the word "postmodern," describe the influences of Bakhtin, Jameson, and White on their work. Bakhtin is also an influence on Mae Gwendolyn Henderson's "Speaking in Tongues: Dialogics, Dialectics, and the Black Woman's Literary Tradition."

62. Kathyrn Hume suggests that Wideman layers these different influences across the scope of his work; I believe that from the beginning of his career he layered these influences, even *within* works. See Kathyrn Hume, "'Dimensions' and John Edgar Wideman's Mental Cosmology," *Contemporary Literature* 44, no. 4 (Winter 2003): 697–726.

63. John Edgar Wideman, preface to *The Homewood Trilogy* (New York: Avon, 1985), vii.

64. Wideman, quoted in Judith Rosen, "John Edgar Wideman," *Publisher's Weekly*, November 17, 1989, 37.

65. Michael Silverblatt, "John Edgar Wideman," in *Conversations with John Edgar Wideman*, ed. Bonnie TuSmith (Jackson: University Press of Mississippi, 1998), 120.

66. Wideman, quoted in James Coleman, *Blackness and Modernism: The Literary Career of John Edgar Wideman* (Jackson: University Press of Mississippi, 1989), 159.

67. See Michael North, "The Dialect of Modernism: Pound and Eliot's Racial Masquerade," *American Literary History* 4, no. 1 (Spring 1992): 56–76.

68. Jablon, *Black Metafiction*, 170; Gene Seymour, "Dream Surgeon," review of *The Cattle Killing*, by John Edgar Wideman, *Nation*, October 28, 1996, 58.

69. John Edgar Wideman, "Stomping the Blues: Ritual in Black Music and Speech," *American Poetry Review* 7 (1978): 44.

70. Jonny King, *What Jazz Is* (New York: Walker and Co., 1997), 6–33. This characteristic is the very essence of jazz improvisation. Musicians in the act of improvisation "display their mastery over the language and tradition of jazz by flaunting its conventions"—a kind of "musical signifying" (Paul Berliner, *Thinking in Jazz: The Infinite Art of Improvisation* [Chicago: University of Chicago Press, 1994], 257). These rephrasings or acts of signifying can be responses within the jazz tradition itself: a jazz musician's rerecording and revision of one of his or her previous works, or one artist's revoicing of a previous artist's standards (i.e., Thelonious Monk's version of Duke Ellington's "Black and Tan Fantasy"). Revoicings can occur cross-culturally, as in the case of John Coltrane's now legendary response to the song "My Favorite Things" (popularized by Julie Andrews) or Duke Ellington's revision of Chopin's "Funeral March" in "Black and Tan Fantasy" (making Monk's version a revoicing of a revoicing, illustrating very clearly the transparent layers of a "story"). Rephrasings can also take place between discourses. Branford Marsalis's response to the African writer Ayi Kwei Armah and his novel *The Beautiful Ones Are Not Yet Born* is such an example.

71. Henry Louis Gates Jr., "On Bearing Witness," in *Bearing Witness*, ed. Henry Louis Gates Jr. (New York: Pantheon Books, 1991), 63–64.

72. John Edgar Wideman, *All Stories Are True* (New York: Vintage, 1993), 71–72.

73. Henry Louis Gates Jr., *The Signifying Monkey* (New York: Oxford University Press, 1988), 105.

74. Wideman's "stream-of-consciousness" is incredibly musical, more like scatting. If he was merely mimicking Eliot's style, I would concur with Michael North that it was Eliot who was mimicking African American music. See Michael North, *The Dialect of Modernism: Race, Language, and Twentieth-Century Literature* (New York: Oxford University Press, 1994) and chapter 2, this volume.

75. Murray, *Stomping*, 99.

76. Ted Gioia, *The Imperfect Art: Reflections on Jazz and Modern Culture* (New York: Oxford University Press, 1988), 76.

77. John Edgar Wideman, *The Lynchers* (New York: Holt, 1973), 54.

78. John Edgar Wideman, *Sent for You Yesterday* (New York: Holt, 1981), 55.

79. In a conversation circa 1998, E. Ethelbert Miller suggested to me another reason for these gaps. They might be considered places of "highly concentrated blackness" or points of "saturation" or "black holes" in which the "black experience has its roots."

80. King, *What Jazz Is*, 55. Mbalia argues that this passage describes Wilkes's isolation from the community. Bonnie TuSmith similarly reads Wilkes in this manner in *All My Relatives: Community in Contemporary Ethnic American Literatures* (Ann Arbor: University of Michigan Press, 1993), 77.

81. Ralph Ellison, *Shadow and Act* (1953; reprint New York: Random House, 1995), 234.

82. Wideman, preface to *The Homewood Trilogy*, v.

83. John Edgar Wideman, "The Architectonics of Fiction," *Callaloo* 13, no. 1 (Winter 1990): 45.

84. John Edgar Wideman, *Fatheralong* (New York: Pantheon, 1994), 21.

85. Both Ishmael Reed and Charles Johnson found *Philadelphia Fire* disappointing and problematic. See interview with Rebekah Presson, "John Edgar Wideman," in *Conversations*

with John Edgar Wideman, ed. Bonnie TuSmith (Jackson: University Press of Mississippi, 1998), 109.

86. Eleanor Traylor, "Response: The First Person in Afro-American Literature," in *Afro-American Literary Study in the 1990s*, ed. Houston Baker and Patricia Redmond (Chicago: University of Chicago Press, 1992), 133. We may also consider these gaps where marginalized writers can speak, or clear space, as an example of a "chronotope." Mikhail Bakhtin defines a "chronotope" as restructured or reinvented space where writers or voices usually not accommodated by the dominant discourses can be heard. Bakhtin, *Dialogic Imagination*, 84–85, 295. Wideman creates spaces or chronotopes by the purposeful disruption of narrative time and space in almost every text (including the nonfiction). His hybrid or mosaic texts that allow other, multiple voices to speak recreate genre as well. The blurring of genre types in Wideman's fiction—the mixing of fiction, history, autobiography—gives him new places, new blanks on which to write. The voices, discourses, and texts imbricated in Wideman's work are equally a form of jazz signifying as well as the hybridization, heteroglossia, and polyglossia described by Bakhtin as the mode of the dialogic novel.

87. Karla F. C. Holloway, *Moorings and Metaphors: Figures of Culture and Gender in Black Women's Literature* (New Brunswick, NJ: Rutgers University Press, 1992), 10. Kimberly Benston calls this genealogical revisionism "a reformation of self and familial past where both notions of identity, communal and individual are interwoven. African-American literature is seen then as one genealogical poem that attempts to restore continuity to the ruptures or discontinuities imposed by the history of black presence in America." "'I Yam What I Am': The Topos of (Un)naming," in *Black Literature and Literary Theory*, ed. Henry Louis Gates Jr. (New York: Rutledge University Press, 1984), 152.

88. Houston Baker, *Blues, Ideology, and Afro-American Literature* (Chicago: University of Chicago Press, 1984), 7.

89. Bonnie TuSmith refers to Wideman's work as "shapeshifting" or "tricksterism." See TuSmith, "Optical Tricksterism: Dissolving and Shapeshifting in Wideman's Work," in *Critical Essays on John Edgar Wideman*, ed. Bonnie TuSmith and Keith Byerman (Knoxville: University of Tennessee Press, 2006), 243–258.

90. Gates, *The Signifying Monkey*, 49.

91. Maya Deren, *Divine Horsemen: The Living Gods of Haiti* (New York: McPherson and Co., 1983), 305.

92. Wideman, *Fatheralong*, 62.

93. Renee Olander, "An Interview with John Edgar Wideman," in *Conversations with John Edgar Wideman*, ed. Bonnie TuSmith (Jackson: University Press of Mississippi, 1998), 167.

94. Ishmael Reed, "Interview with John Edgar Wideman," in *Conversations with John Edgar Wideman*, ed. Bonnie TuSmith (Jackson: University Press of Mississippi, 1998), 127.

95. Michael Fischer, "Ethnicity and the Post-Modern Arts of Memory," in *Writing Culture: The Poetics and Politics of Ethnography*, ed. James Clifford and George Marcus (Berkeley: University of California Press, 1986), 213.

96. James Berger, *After the End: Representations of Post-Apocalypse* (Minneapolis: University of Minnesota Press, 1999), 50.

97. Michael Fischer, "Ethnicity and the Post-Modern Arts of Memory," in *Writing Culture: The Poetics and Politics of Ethnography*, ed. James Clifford and George Marcus (Berkeley: University of California Press, 1986), 213.

98. Wideman, preface to *The Homewood Trilogy*, vii.
99. John Edgar Wideman, *Fanon* (Boston: Houghton Mifflin Co., 2008), 19.
100. See chapters 2 and 3 for a further examination of this relationship.
101. John Edgar Wideman, *Reuben* (New York: Viking Penguin, 1987), 170.
102. I will track Wideman's double throughout the following chapters in this study.
103. Gates, *The Signifying Monkey*, 131.
104. Robert Farris Thompson, *Flash of the Spirit: African and Afro-American Art and Philosophy* (New York: Random House, 1983), 18; Gates, *The Signifying Monkey*, 34; and Maya Deren's *Divine Horseman*.
105. Berger, *After the End*, 50. Early slave narrators often played another role, not only to hide their true identity, but also to outsmart the master or the society at large. Ellison's unnamed protagonist is confused with the character Rinehart, who is known for his ability to shift between roles. And contemporary novelists such as Charles Johnson, Samuel Delaney, Ishmael Reed, and Clarence Major use doubles and double imagery in their work to highlight possible other selves. This is especially true in Johnson's novel *Dreamer*, which follows the life of a man who is Martin Luther King's double.
106. Gordon Slethaug, *The Play of the Double in Postmodern American Fiction* (Carbondale: Southern Illinois University Press, 1993), 5. I agree with Yves-Charles Grandjeat's assessment of the doubles as Wideman uses them in *Reuben*. They symbolize creation, rather than "cultivating a pathetic sense of mourning and nostalgia." Yves-Charles Grandjeat, "'These Strange Dizzy Pauses': Silence as Common Ground in John Edgar Wideman's Texts," *Callaloo* 22, no. 3 (1999): 617. I do think, however, that doubles in Wideman's work do not always represent the same idea.
107. Ishmael Reed, "Of One Blood, Two Men," Review of *Brothers and Keepers*, by John Edgar Wideman, *New York Times Book Review*, November 4, 1984, 33.
108. Wideman, quoted in Silverblatt, "John Edgar Wideman," 121.
109. Ashraf Rushdy, "Fraternal Blues: John Edgar Wideman's *Homewood Trilogy*," *Contemporary Literature* 32, no. 3 (Fall 1991): 313.
110. Mbalia notes the three-part structure in *Philadelphia Fire*, viewing it as Wideman's new "Africanness," and James Coleman points out the three-part structure in *A Glance Away*, arguing that this is evidence of Wideman's voicing of European modernism.
111. Other critics of African American writing have examined three-part structures inherent in the literature. Michael Fischer suggests that the three voices/selves in jazz musician Charles Mingus's autobiography, *Beneath the Underdog*, "appear throughout the text as alternating, interbraided voices—like the call-and-response of a jazz session." Michael Fischer, "Ethnicity and the Post-Modern Arts of Memory," in *Writing Culture: The Poetics and Politics of Ethnography*, ed. James Clifford and George Marcus (Berkeley: University of California Press, 1986), 213. Fischer's work with other ethnic autobiographies also establishes that three-voiced structures appear as "triangulations" of identity. The first-person narrative or voice is concerned with individual identity, the second-person voice is cross-cultural or cross-historical and "resonate" with "double-voicings," and the third-person voice represents "a collective voice or identity." Michael Fischer, "Autobiographical Voices (1, 2, 3) and Mosaic Memory: Experimental Sondages in the (Post)modern World," in *Autobiography and Postmodernism*, ed. Kathleen Ashley and Leigh Gilmore (Amherst: University of Massachusetts Press, 1994), 79. Fischer's theory of autobiographical writing has numerous implications for our study of Wideman's writing. Not only do the three-part structures and three voices in Wideman's work connote the jazz and the blues, they

also parallel developments of other postmodern autobiographers—who are interested in communal as well as personal identity and the multiple positions that people living in the margins must maintain.

112. Hutcheon, *A Poetics*, 61.

113. David Cowart, *History and the Contemporary Novel* (Carbondale: Southern Illinois University Press, 1989), 28.

114. Matthew Wilson uses the circle as a metaphor for Wideman's construction of history in the Homewood trilogy, and John Bennion sees the circle as the shape of Wideman's memory in *Sent for You Yesterday*. Matthew Wilson, "The Circles of History in John Edgar Wideman's *The Homewood Trilogy*," *CLA Journal* 33, no. 3 (1990): 239–259; John Bennion, "The Shape of Memory in John Edgar Wideman's *Sent For You Yesterday*," *Black American Literature Forum* 20, no. 2 (1986): 149.

115. Jablon, *Black Metafiction*, 12.

116. Silverblatt, "John Edgar Wideman," 123.

117. Samuel A. Floyd Jr., *The Power of Black Music* (New York: Oxford University Press, 1995), 43.

118. This characterization of trauma and re-memory is outlined by J. Brooks Bouson in her study, *Quiet as It's Kept: Shame, Trauma, and Race in the Novels of Toni Morrison* (Albany: SUNY Press, 2000).

119. John Edgar Wideman, "The Color of Fiction," *Mother Jones* 15 (November/December 1990): 64.

120. Andreas Huyssen, *Present Pasts: Urban Palimpsests and the Politics of Memory* (Stanford: Stanford University Press, 2003), 14.

121. See Eric Sundquist, *To Wake the Nations* (Cambridge: Harvard University Press, 1993).

122. Bouson, *Quiet as It's Kept*, 6.

123. Dominick LaCapra, *Writing History, Writing Trauma* (Baltimore: John Hopkins University Press, 2001), xxi.

124. Ann E. Kaplan, *Trauma Culture: The Politics of Terror and Loss in Media and Literature* (New Brunswick, NJ: Rutgers University Press, 2005), 2.

125. Berger, *After the End*, 41.

126. Shoshama Felman, and Dori Laub, *Testimony: Crisis of Witnessing in Literature, Psychoanalysis, and History* (New York: Routledge, 1992), xiv.

127. Anne Whitehead, *Trauma Fiction* (Edinburgh: Edinburgh University Press, 2004), 12.

128. Kirby Farrell, *Post-Traumatic Culture: Injury and Interpretation in the Nineties* (Baltimore: Johns Hopkins University Press, 1998), 2.

129. It is perhaps one reason why, I believe, the work of Toni Morrison has gained such popular prominence with the audiences devoted to talk shows like Oprah Winfrey's. Morrison's work—which often focuses on childhood pain, abuse, and loss—resonates with a crowd that has heard a litany of daytime trauma. This is not to take anything away from Morrison's masterful work; it is meant to merely suggest why her work, more than any other African American artist's, has been embraced by the white middle class, which by its own admission and actions is attracted to the post-traumatic narrative. Morrison's work is one of the few ever mentioned within the framework of post-traumatic studies, but almost always as a psychoanalytic reading of the texts. I think a more revealing analysis would look more broadly at trauma and post-trauma as cultural narrative reflected not only in

her work but also in its reception. Wideman and Morrison share a devotion to history and memory in the African American experience.

130. Cathy Caruth, *Unclaimed Experience: Trauma, Narrative, and History* (Baltimore: Johns Hopkins University Press, 1996), 8.

131. Laurie Vickroy, *Trauma and Survival in Contemporary Fiction* (Charlottesville: University of Virginia Press, 2002), 29. See also Lawrence Langer, *Holocaust Testimonies: The Ruins of Memory* (New Haven: Yale University Press, 1991); and Whitehead, *Trauma Fiction*.

132. Wideman, *Fatheralong*, xxiii.

133. Ibid., 61.

134. John Edgar Wideman, *Fever* (New York: Penguin, 1989), 60.

135. Ibid., 68.

136. Ibid., 66.

137. John Edgar Wideman, *Hoop Roots* (Boston: Houghton Mifflin, 2001), 2.

138. Ibid., 10.

139. Ibid., 11.

140. Wideman, *Fever*, 78.

141. John Edgar Wideman, *Fanon* (Boston: Houghton Mifflin Co., 2008), 15.

142. Wideman, *Fever*, 82.

143. Ibid., 90.

144. Ibid., 95.

145. Ibid., 92.

146. Ibid., 97.

147. Ibid., 99.

148. Ibid., 105.

149. Ibid., 101.

150. See Linda Dahl, *Stormy Weather: The Music and Lives of a Century of Jazzwomen* (New York: Pantheon Books, 1984).

151. She is "variously said to have been placed under house arrest in Sweden or in Denmark, to have been confined in a concentration camp for one, two, or three years, and to have lost so much weight that she was down to sixty-eight pounds at the time of her release (escape). As a black, she was undoubtedly the target of Nazi abuse, but I have been unable to establish the facts about her European tribulations during the second World War." Dahl, *Stormy Weather*, 82.

152. Wideman, *Fever*, 40.

153. The complex relationship between the trauma of slavery and its continued impact on African Americans and the trauma of the Holocaust and the impact on its victims played out most recently during Barack Obama's campaign for presidency. Concerns from both the African American community and the Jewish community about Obama's commitment to Israel and his associations with Reverend Jeremiah Wright ignited controversy prior to Obama's election.

154. The Lamed-Vovnik are thirty-six men in Hasidic literature who are chosen to be the role models for the rest of humanity. They are deeply religious, just, and compassionate, but are also likely to suffer tremendously because of these characteristics.

155. Wideman, *Fever*, 154.

156. Ibid., 53.

157. Ibid., 56.

158. Keith Byerman, *John Edgar Wideman: A Study of the Short Fiction* (New York: Twayne Publishers, 1998), 54.

159. Anne Cheng, *The Melancholy of Race: Psychoanalysis, Assimilation, and Hidden Grief* (New York: Oxford University Press, 2001), 7.

160. Berger, *After the End*, 53.

161. Ellison, *Shadow and Act*, 78.

Chapter Two

1. A version of this chapter appeared in the collection *Critical Essays on John Edgar Wideman*. "'All My Father's Texts': John Edgar Wideman's Historical Vision in *Philadelphia Fire, The Cattle Killing*, and *Fatheralong*, in *Critical Essays on John Edgar Wideman*, ed. Bonnie TuSmith and Keith Byerman (Knoxville: University Press of Tennessee, 2006), 175–190.

2. John Edgar Wideman, *Fatheralong* (New York: Pantheon, 1994), 63.

3. Michael Silverblatt, "Interview with John Edgar Wideman," in *Conversations with John Edgar Wideman*, ed. Bonnie TuSmith (Jackson: University Press of Mississippi, 1998), 162. See also Jacqueline Berben-Masi, "Prodigal and Prodigy: Fathers and Sons in Wideman's Work," *Callaloo* 22, no. 3 (Summer 1999): 677–684.

4. See John Edgar Wideman, introduction to *Live from Death Row*, by Mumia Abu-Jamal (New York: Avon, 1995), xxiii–xxxiv; and John Edgar Wideman, "Charles Chesnutt and the WPA Narratives: The Oral and Literate Roots of Afro-American Literature," *American Scholar* 42, no. 1 (1973): 128–134.

5. Henry Louis Gates Jr., *The Signifying Monkey* (New York: Oxford University Press, 1988), xxv.

6. James Olney, "The Founding Fathers—Frederick Douglass and Booker T. Washington," in *Slavery and the Literary Imagination*, ed. Deborah McDowell and Arnold Rampersad (Baltimore: John Hopkins University Press, 1989), 20.

7. Hazel Carby, "Ideologies of Black Folk: The Historical Novel of Slavery," in *Slavery and the Literary Imagination*, ed. McDowell and Rampersad, 125. Carby and Olney are not alone in their assessment of the connections between African American literature and the slave narrative. Many prominent critics of African American literature and culture, such as Henry Louis Gates Jr., William Andrews, Robert Stepto, Houston Baker, Bernard Bell, Sidonie Smith, and Valerie Smith, to name just a few, have suggested, to different degrees, that the slave narrative is the progenitor of the African American literary tradition.

8. Ishmael Reed, quoted in Calvin Hernton, *The Sexual Mountain and Black Women Writers* (New York: Anchor Books, 1987), 4.

9. They are perhaps also a response to the 1968 publication of William Styron's controversial *The Confessions of Nat Turner*. Ashraf Rushdy, "The Phenomenology of the Allmuseri: Charles Johnson and the Subject of Narrativity," *African American Review* 26.3 (1992): 375; and Ashraf Rushdy, "Reading Black, White, and Gray in 1968: The Origins of the Contemporary Narrativity of Slavery," in *Criticism and the Color Line*, ed. Henry B. Wonham (New Brunswick, NJ: Rutgers University Press, 1996), 66. At a time when Malcolm X was urging people to "know their history," the neo-slave narratives reflected a pressing need to address the burden of the past and revisit it in a critical and artistic manner.

10. Arnold Rampersad, "Slavery and the Literary Imagination: DuBois' *The Souls of Black Folk*," in *Slavery and the Literary Imagination*, ed. Deborah McDowell and Arnold Rampersad (Baltimore: Johns Hopkins University Press, 1989), 123.

11. Timothy A. Spaulding, *Reforming the Past: History, the Fantastic, and the Postmodern Slave Narrative* (Columbus: Ohio State University Press, 2005), 3–4.

12. Rushdy, "Phenomenology," 375.

13. For example, consider the relationship between Tommy, Lawson's brother, and Sybela Owens, the former slave who is the family ancestor.

14. Rushdy describes the first category as types of writing that focuses on a slave or former slave retelling slave stories (or stories that are set in the antebellum South). One of his examples of this type of narrative is Morrison's *Beloved*. The fourth category is circumscribed by texts that imitate the forms and conventions of the slave narrative, such as Ishmael Reed's *Flight to Canada* and Charles Johnson's *Middle Passage*. I would further suggest that the story "Damballah" and the novel *The Cattle Killing* reflect and combine the characteristics of his first and fourth categories. *Damballah* (the work as a whole), Rushdy points out, is a "genealogical narrative," his third type of "narrativity of slavery," where texts "represent the slave experience in the process of tracing the history of a family through the broad outlines of the Black experience." Rushdy, "Phenomenology," 375.

15. Rushdy, "Phenomenology," 375.

16. Robert Stepto, *From behind the Veil: A Study of African-American Narrative* (Chicago: University of Illinois Press, 1991), xx.

17. See Gates, *The Signifying Monkey*. Wideman wrote a review of this work for the *New York Times Book Review* in 1988.

18. Houston Baker Jr., *The Journey Back: Issues in Black Literature and Criticism* (Chicago: University of Chicago Press, 1980), 57. The number of critics and scholars who have illustrated these connections are too numerous to mention in this study. Some notable studies, including the modern and contemporary fiction writers that Valerie Smith examines, are drawn to the strategies of nonfiction employed by the slave narrators as well as to their concern with identity, authority, and selfhood. Valerie Smith, *Self-Discovery and Authority in Afro-American Narrative* (Cambridge: Harvard University Press, 1987), 153. And Charles Nichols finds the archetypes for modern black voices (including Wright's *Black Boy*, Malcolm X, Ishmael Reed, and Clarence Major) in the eighteenth-century slave narratives, written, for example, by Olaudah Equiano and Briton Hammon, that emphasized picaresque adventures and conversion stories. Charles Nichols, "The Slave Narrators and the Picaresque Mode: Archetypes for Modern Black Personae," in *The Slave's Narrative*, ed. Charles T. Davis and Henry Louis Gates Jr. (New York: Oxford University Press, 1985), 298. Not only critics argue that the relationship between the slave narrative and the African American literary tradition exists; Alice Walker remarks most emphatically and succinctly that "our literary tradition is based on slave narratives." Walker, quoted in John Sekora, "Is the Slave Narrative a Species of Autobiography?" *Studies in Autobiography*, ed. James Olney (New York: Oxford University Press, 1988), 100.

19. Deborah McDowell, "In the First Place: Making Frederick Douglass and the Afro-American Tradition," in *African-American Autobiography*, ed. William Andrews (Englewood Cliffs, NJ: Prentice Hall, 1993), 36. Charles Davis and Henry Louis Gates (in *The Slave's Narrative*) argue that *Up from Slavery* is the antecedent of *The Autobiography of Malcolm X*, *Their Eyes Were Watching God*, *Black Boy*, *Invisible Man*, and *Flight to Canada*. Andrews draws this line of descent even further. He also traces the connections

between Frederick Douglass and Booker T. Washington, as well as James Weldon Johnson's *The Autobiography of an Ex-Coloured Man*, to *Invisible Man*, *Black Boy*, *The Autobiography of Miss Jane Pittman*, and *The Color Purple*. Along the same course as the cultural and linguistic theories of intertextuality projected by Gates and Robert Stepto, Andrews characterizes the history of African American narrative as being "informed by a call-and-response relationship between autobiography and its successor, the novel." William Andrews, introduction to *African-American Autobiography*, ed. William Andrews (Englewood Cliffs, NJ: Prentice Hall, 1993), 1. Andrews further believes that the narratives of Frederick Douglass and Harriet Jacobs read like novels, stressing themes of identity and freedom that reoccur in the twentieth century. William Andrews, *To Tell a Free Story: The First Century of Afro-American Autobiography, 1760–1865* (Urbana: University of Illinois Press, 1986), 272. Andrews's list of intertexts is remarkably similar to Stepto's and Davis and Gates's.

20. Wideman, introduction to *Live from Death Row*, xxx.

21. James Olney, "'I Was Born': Slave Narratives, Their Status as Autobiography and Literature," in *The Slave's Narrative*, ed. Davis and Gates, 158.

22. James Olney has compiled a list of slave narrative conventions in his article "'I Was Born.'"

23. Wideman, introduction to *Live from Death Row*, xxxi.

24. R.W.B. Lewis, *The American Adam* (Chicago: University of Chicago Press, 1955), 5. As Nina Baym argues, the tradition of American literature is based on the movement away from society into nature; and then, "in order to represent some kind of believable flight into the wilderness, one must select a protagonist with a certain believable mobility, and mobility has until recently been a male prerogative." Nina Baym, "Melodramas of Beset Manhood," in *The New Feminist Criticism: Essays on Women, Literature, and Theory*, ed. Elaine Showalter (New York: Pantheon, 1985), 72. I would further add a white male prerogative.

25. Valerie Smith, introduction to *Incidents in the Life of a Slave Girl* (New York: Oxford University Press, 1988), xxix.

26. Raymond Hedin, "The American Slave Narrative: The Justification of the Picaro," *American Literature* 53, no. 4 (1982): 642. Even though Frederick Douglass's 1845 *Narrative* "might easily be read as a black contribution to the literature of romantic individualism and anti-institutionalism," after his escape he devoted himself to the abolition of slavery and to helping "his brethren." William Andrews, "The Representation of Slavery and the Rise of African-American Realism," in *African-American Autobiography*, ed. William Andrews (Englewood, NJ: Prentice Hall, 1993), 78.

27. William Nichols, "Individualism and Autobiographical Art: Frederick Douglass and Henry David Thoreau," *CLA Journal* 16, no. 2 (1972): 155.

28. Wideman, introduction to *Live from Death Row*, xxx.

29. Wideman, quoted in Patricia Smith, "Getting under Our Skin," in *Conversations with John Edgar Wideman*, ed. Bonnie TuSmith (Jackson: University Press of Mississippi, 1998), 141.

30. Wideman has explained the importance of the novels of Wright and Ellison on his work, as well as slave narratives and African American folklore. See O'Brien, *Interviews with Black Writers*.

31. James Baldwin, *Notes of a Native Son* (Boston: Beacon Press, 1957), 7.

32. John Edgar Wideman, introduction to *The Souls of Black Folk*, by W.E.B. DuBois (New York: Library of America, 1990), xii.

33. Gene Shalit, "The Astonishing John Wideman," *Look*, May 21, 1963, 33.

34. Cornell West, "The Dilemma of the Black Intellectual," in *Breaking Bread: Insurgent Black Intellectual Life*, ed. bell hooks and Cornel West (Boston: South End Press, 1991), 131.

35. Albert Murray describes these selves in *The Omni-Americans*. Albert Murray, *The Omni-Americans: New Perspectives on Black Experience and American Culture* (New York: Outerbridge and Dienstfrey, 1970), 451. The tension between these selves is one of the "crises" of Harold Cruse's 1967 work, *The Crisis of the Negro Intellectual*. Even earlier, Carter Woodson's seminal work *The Mis-education of the Negro* (published in 1933) asserted that "one of the most striking evidences of the failure of higher education among Negroes is their estrangement from the masses." Carter Woodson, *The Mis-education of the Negro* (1933; reprint, Trenton, NJ: Africa World Press, 1990), 52.

36. Wideman reveals that *Sent for You Yesterday* is a prolonged mediation on the characters and themes of *A Glance Away*. Kay Bonetti, "Interview with John Edgar Wideman," in *Conversations with John Edgar Wideman*, ed. Bonnie TuSmith (Jackson: University Press of Mississippi, 1998), 46. Even as early as the James Coleman interview, Wideman argued that his early work connects to the Homewood trilogy: "But even in the first three books, as I look back on them now, I was very much concerned with family and community and the people I grew up with, and I thought, in my own way, that I was addressing that audience quite directly." James Coleman, *Blackness and Modernism: The Literary Career of John Edgar Wideman* (Jackson: University Press of Mississippi, 1989), 146.

37. John Edgar Wideman, *A Glance Away* (New York: Holt, 1967), 3.

38. Wideman, *A Glance Away*, 3.

39. Dorothea Mbalia argues that free indirect discourse first appears in *Philadelphia Fire*. Dorothea Mbalia, *John Edgar Wideman: Reclaiming the African Personality* (London: Susquehanna University Press, 1995), 108. Gates describes free indirect discourse as a voice that "is not the voice of both a character and a narrator; rather it is a bivocal utterance, containing elements of both direct and indirect speech. It is an utterance that no one could have spoken, yet which we recognize because of its characteristic 'speakerliness,' its paradoxically written manifestation of the aspiration to the oral." Gates, *The Signifying Monkey*, 208, and see descriptions of free indirect discourse on 209–210.

40. See John O'Brien, *Interviews with Black Writers* (New York: Liveright Press, 1973), 216.

41. Linda Hutcheon, *A Poetics of Postmodernism* (New York: Routledge, 1988), 11.

42. Ibid., 19.

43. Michael North argues that Eliot (and Pound) "used the language of race to strike down the restrictive linguistic boundaries and social conventions and simultaneously to solidify boundaries whose loss both Eliot and Pound deeply feared. Dialect, which was to signify the subversive freedom of the modernist, also marks the language of modernism with this fear." North also points out that Eliot sent Pound letters signed "Tar Baby." It is in these letters that North contends the two poets re-imagined themselves as "Others." Michael North, "The Dialect of Modernism: Pound and Eliot's Racial Masquerade," *American Literary History* 4, no. 1 (Spring 1992): 63–64.

44. North reminds us that Gates considered Sweeney a model for African American writing. North, "Dialect of Modernism," 68. Also see Gates, *The Signifying Monkey*.

45. Mbalia, *John Edgar Wideman*, 35; J. Coleman, *Blackness and Modernism*, 12. Mbalia also criticizes Wideman for his use of "beat generation" themes (34). This relationship is also a form of cultural dialogue and revision. Amiri Baraka points to the

relationship between the Beats and African American writers. The Beats were attracted to African American culture because they felt the same alienation and isolation that they perceived African Americans felt. Amiri Baraka, *Blues People* (New York: William Morrow, 1963), 231.

46. Stein, Faulkner, and O'Neil use African Americans as subjects—characters that are isolated in their society (see *Melanchtha*, *Light in August*, and *Emperor Jones*). See also North's book *The Dialect of Modernism: Race, Language, and Twentieth- Century Literature* (New York: Oxford University Press, 1994), which traces the influences of African and African American art on these and other modernist writers.

47. Interestingly, while Wideman has been criticized for doing this, the same criticisms have not been leveled against Morrison. The writers of the Black Arts Movement did criticize Ellison, however. He was accused of "mimicking" the style of white writers. Madelyn Jablon, *Black Metafiction: Self-Consciousness in African American Literature* (Iowa City: University of Iowa Press, 1997), 16–18.

48. Gates, *The Signifying Monkey*, 122.

49. Wilfred Samuels, "Going Home: A Conversation with John Edgar Wideman," *Callaloo* 6, no. 1 (1983): 46.

50. J. Coleman, *Blackness and Modernism*, 158. While they may not be the exact same characters, both men are albino, both men are linked to music, and both men are storytellers. Both men are also linked to trains, an African American cultural trope; Brother in *A Glance Away* always thinks about trains (67), and *Sent for You Yesterday* opens with Brother's dream about trains. John Edgar Wideman, *Sent for You Yesterday* (New York: Holt, 1981), 10.

51. Wideman, *A Glance Away*, 23.

52. Ibid., 27.

53. The scene is reminiscent of Claude Brown's portrait of the aftereffects of the great migrations and the description of life in the northern ghettos: "To add to their misery, they had little hope of deliverance. For where does one run to when he's already in the Promised Land"? Claude Brown, *Manchild in the Promised Land* (New York: MacMillan Co., 1965), 8.

54. Wideman, *A Glance Away*, 24. Such an image appears in *Fatheralong* as well, when Wideman recalls that as a young man he did not want to go South, where they lynched boys like Emmett Till.

55. Melvin Dixon, *Ride Out the Wilderness: Geography and Identity in Afro-American Literature* (Urbana: University of Illinois Press, 1987), 34.

56. Wideman, *A Glance Away*, 27.

57. Ibid., 27.

58. Ibid., 170.

59. J. Coleman, *Blackness and Modernism*, 11.

60. Wideman, *A Glance Away*, 116.

61. Ibid., 137.

62. Ibid., 92.

63. Ibid., 92.

64. This is another indication that Martha is a double of another of Wideman's characters, Mother Bess in *Hiding Place*.

65. Wideman, *A Glance Away*, 104.

66. Ibid., 125.

67. Ibid., 127.

68. Ibid., 129. I do not believe that Eddie "murdered" his mother, as one critic has suggested. Mbalia, *John Edgar Wideman*, 85.

69. Wideman, *A Glance Away*, 162.

70. Ibid., 35.

71. J. Coleman, *Blackness and Modernism*, 11.

72. Wideman, *A Glance Away*, 71.

73. Ibid., 41.

74. Ibid., 138.

75. This blending of voices is an example of modernist and postmodernist style, but it is also a characteristic that Wideman notes in African American writing, especially Charles Chesnutt's work. In *The Conjure Woman* (1899), Wideman asserts, Chesnutt "blends the literary and oral traditions without implying that the black storyteller's mode of perceiving and creating reality is any less valid than the written word." John Edgar Wideman, "Charles Chesnutt and the WPA Narratives: The Oral and Literate Roots of Afro-American Literature," in *The Slave's Narrative*, ed. Charles T. Davis and Henry Louis Gates Jr. (New York: Oxford University Press, 1985), 60. The stories of "Eliot" are as "true" and as essential as the stories of the African American tradition (embodied by Brother).

76. Bernard Bell, *The Afro-American Novel and Its Traditions* (Amherst: University of Massachusetts Press, 1987), 308.

77. Houston Baker, *Blues, Ideology, and Afro-American Literature* (Chicago: University of Chicago Press, 1984), 200.

78. Samuel A. Floyd Jr., *The Power of Black Music* (New York: Oxford University Press, 1995), 214.

79. John Edgar Wideman, "The Language of Home," *New York Times Book Review*, January 13, 1985, BR1.

80. John O'Brien, *Interviews with Black Writers* (New York: Liveright Press, 1973), 223.

81. Elizabeth Schultz, "The Heirs of Ralph Ellison: Patterns of Individualism in the Contemporary Afro-American Novel," *CLA Journal* 22, no. 1 (December 1978): 105.

82. Ashraf Rushdy, "Fraternal Blues: John Edgar Wideman's *Homewood Trilogy*," *Contemporary Literature* 32, no. 3 (Fall 1991): 317–318. Braithwaite fails to achieve the blues mind in this work, but his path is one traversed by many African American artists, including James Baldwin, Richard Wright, W.E.B. DuBois, and Langston Hughes. Each of these artists had to leave his society to establish fully his blues mind that could speak to the communal self and the personal self.

83. Wideman, quoted in O'Brien, *Interviews with Black Writers*, 219.

84. Ibid.

85. John Edgar Wideman, *Hurry Home* (New York: Holt, 1970), 50.

86. Ibid., 15.

87. Ibid., 167.

88. Ibid., 28.

89. Ibid., 44.

90. John Edgar Wideman, "Stomping the Blues: Ritual in Black Music and Speech," *American Poetry Review* 7 (1978): 45.

91. Wideman, *Hurry Home*, 46.

92. Ibid., 46.

93. Webb also has an implied double in the character of Robert Thurley in *A Glance Away*. Both men are white, middle-aged men who represent, in their respective works, the European past and artistic tradition. They are "father figures" in the texts as well.

94. Wideman, *Hurry Home*, 109.
95. Ibid., 150.
96. Ibid., 113.
97. Ibid., 114.
98. Aldon Nielsen argues that the "Middle Passage may be the great repressed signifier of American historical consciousness." Aldon Nielsen, *Writing between the Lines: Race and Intertextuality* (Athens: University of Georgia Press, 1994), 101. Nielsen goes on to suggest that African American writers have reinscribed the text of the Middle Passage (and he includes *Hurry Home* as a novel that attempts to do this [ibid., 114]).
99. Wideman, *Hurry Home*, 148. Robert Hayden's "Middle Passage," Nielsen points out, was informed by African American texts and the European modernists, both discourses that Hayden realized shared a similar style. Hayden noticed a "certain resonance between the palimpsestic styles of Eliot, Pound, H. D., and other modernists and the earlier prose texts of African American literary traditions with their embedded layers of actual and fictive documents." Nielsen, *Writing between the Lines*, 118.
100. Wideman, *Hurry Home*, 112.
101. Nielsen, *Writing between the Lines*, 125.
102. Hutcheon, *A Poetics*, 16.
103. Wideman, *Hurry Home*, 130.
104. Ibid., 170.
105. Ibid., 145.
106. Ibid., 185.
107. James Coleman asserts that Braithwaite's job at the beauty parlor isolates Braithwaite further. He compares the novel to *Portrait of the Artist as a Young Man* and argues that "Cecil is isolating himself from the black community because he thinks he must, but he should [be moving] outside of himself and connect[ing] to others, because his surrealistic fantasy indicates that he is moving further into an intellectual world where he loses touch with everyone." J. Coleman, *Blackness and Modernism*, 38.
108. Wideman, *Hurry Home*, 201. Mbalia goes further in her criticism of the novel and proclaims that the novel, including its depiction of African women, "reflects Wideman's own self-hatred" and shows a lack of concern for the African community. Mbalia, *John Edgar Wideman*, 71–72. Charles Johnson has a completely different reading of the novel than either Mbalia or Coleman (as does Nielsen). He characterizes the work as the story of a "black lawyer's journey through European and African culture—in other words, his past—and back to a deeper involvement in the black American community." Charles Johnson, *Being and Race: Black Writing since 1970* (Bloomington: Indiana University Press, 1988), 74. This interpretation is in opposition to Coleman's view that Braithwaite is still isolated at the end of the work. Bernard Bell, even though he considers the work Eurocentric, believes that as Braithwaite "actually and imaginatively travels back in the past for answers, his personal experience is conflated into the collective history of his race." Bernard Bell, *The Afro-American Novel and Its Traditions* (Amherst: University of Massachusetts Press, 1987), 308.
109. Wideman, quoted in O'Brien, *Interviews with Black Writers*, 221.
110. Bonetti, "Interview with John Edgar Wideman," 45.
111. Wideman, quoted in O'Brien, *Interviews with Black Writers*, 220.
112. John Edgar Wideman, *The Lynchers* (New York: Holt, 1973), 219.
113. Ibid., 198.
114. Ibid., 118.

115. The "problem with the plan, Wideman seems to suggest, is that Littleman too consistently uses whites as the model for change." Trudier Harris, *Exorcising Blackness: Historical and Literary Lynching and Burning Rituals* (Bloomington: Indiana University Press, 1984), 134.

116. Wideman, *The Lynchers*, 213.

117. Ibid., 73.

118. Ibid., 84.

119. Ibid., 83.

120. Ibid., 116.

121. I disagree with Mbalia's assessment of this section. She states that Littleman (Wideman) "seems unaware of his history." Mbalia, *John Edgar Wideman*, 46. Littleman may be ignorant, but the association between Wideman and his character seems misplaced. There is nothing to indicate that Wideman was ignorant of these moments. As well, she seems to contradict herself on the following page: "Following his own advice in *The Lynchers*, Wideman's message in this novel is that an African must confront and accept his history, his identity." Mbalia, *John Edgar Wideman*, 47. We know that by the time of the publication of this novel, Wideman had already taught African American literature courses; there are references in the book to Equiano, and he was developing the Afro-American studies program at University of Pennsylvania. So he knew the "history" that Littleman seems to be unaware of.

122. Wideman, *The Lynchers*, 167.

123. Bell, *The Afro-American*, 311. Mbalia argues that Littleman is Wideman's voice in the novel. Mbalia, *John Edgar Wideman*, 46.

124. Wideman, *The Lynchers*, 116.

125. Ibid., 49.

126. Keith Byerman, "Queering Blackness: Race and Sexual Identity in *A Glance Away* and *Hurry Home*," in *Critical Essays on John Edgar Wideman*, ed. Bonnie TuSmith and Keith Byerman (Knoxville: University of Tennessee Press, 2006), 94.

127. They believe their plan is a "symbolic action that will reverse black and white realities and change history. It will reverse, or at least stop, the oppressive historical pattern documented in the early pages of the novel." J. Coleman, *Blackness and Modernism*, 48.

128. David Coward, *History and the Contemporary Novel* (Carbondale: Southern Illinois University Press, 1989), 1.

129. Harris, *Exorcising Blackness*, 129.

130. Wideman, *The Lynchers*, 172–173.

131. Ibid., 179.

132. Anne Cheng, *The Melancholy of Race: Psychoanalysis, Assimilation, and Hidden Grief* (New York: Oxford University Press, 2001), x.

133. Harris, *Exorcising Blackness*, 147.

134. Wideman, *The Lynchers*, 175–176.

135. Harris, *Exorcising Blackness*, 141–142.

136. Ashraf Rushdy, "'A Lynching in Blackface': John Edgar Wideman's Reflections on the Race Question," in *Critical Essays on John Edgar Wideman*, ed. Bonnie TuSmith and Keith Byerman (Knoxville: University of Tennessee Press, 2006), 115.

137. Wideman, *The Lynchers*, 223.

138. Wilkerson stands in direct refutation of Mbalia's argument that Wideman believes that the entire "black community is impotent and bent on self-destruction." Mbalia, *John Edgar Wideman*, 58.

139. Wideman, *The Lynchers*, 224.

140. James Berger, *After the End: Representations of Post-apocalypse* (Minneapolis: University of Minnesota Press, 1999), 50.

141. Wideman, *The Lynchers*, 216; John Edgar Wideman, *The Cattle Killing* (Boston: Houghton Mifflin, 1996), 4.

142. Yves-Charles Grandjeat traces the doubles and brothers in *Reuben* and *Sent for You Yesterday* as examples of creative possibilities meant to transform loss into the "very principle of fictional creation." Yves-Charles Grandjeat, "Brother Figures: The Rift and Riff in John E. Wideman's Fiction," *Callaloo* 22, no. 3 (1999): 616. The double can be read as a site of creative re-imagining of possible lives.

143. With the publication of *The Homewood Trilogy*, Dorothea Mbalia asserts that Wideman had resolved the problem of the African American intellectual in his work. Mbalia, *John Edgar Wideman*, 34.

144. John Edgar Wideman, "The Beginning of Homewood," in *Damballah* (New York: Vintage, 1981), 195.

145. Ibid., 200.

146. Ibid., 205.

147. For analyses of the circular repetition and movement in the trilogy, especially as markers of history and memory, see John Bennion, "The Shape of Memory in John Edgar Wideman's *Sent for You Yesterday*," *Black American Literature Forum* 20, no. 2 (1986): 143–150; and Matthew Wilson, "The Circles of History in John Edgar Wideman's *The Homewood Trilogy*," *CLA Journal* 33, no. 3 (1990): 239–259.

148. John Edgar Wideman, *Sent for You Yesterday* (New York: Holt, 1981), 179.

149. All three works of the Homewood trilogy will be discussed further in chapter 3.

150. John Edgar Wideman, *Brothers and Keepers* (New York: Holt, 1984), 33.

151. Ishmael Reed, "Of One Blood, Two Men," review of *Brothers and Keepers* by John Edgar Wideman, *New York Times Book Review*, November 4, 1984, 32.

152. Wideman, *Brothers and Keepers*, 27.

153. Ibid., 26.

154. Ibid., 24.

155. Of course, the two are linked historically; the very amendment that abolished slavery in this country made legal much of our current prison system. H. Bruce Franklin goes so far as to suggest that "America itself is a prison, and the main lines of American literature can be traced from the plantation to the penitentiary." H. Bruce Franklin, *Prison Literature in the United States: The Victim as Criminal and Artist* (New York: Oxford University Press, 1989), xxii.

156. Wideman, *Brothers and Keepers*, 25.

157. John Edgar Wideman, *Reuben* (New York: Viking Penguin, 1987), 117.

158. Ibid., 202.

159. The collection *Fever* appears between *Reuben* and *All Stories Are True*. It was discussed in chapter 1.

160. John Edgar Wideman, "All Stories Are True," in *All Stories Are True* (New York: Vintage, 1993), 4.

161. Ibid., 5.

162. Ibid., 17.

163. Ibid., 136.

164. Ibid., 136.

165. Ibid., 140.

166. Ibid., 140.
167. Ibid., 141.
168. Ibid., 31.
169. Ibid., 32.
170. Ibid., 39.
171. Ibid., 43.
172. Jacquie Berben-Masi analyzes Foster's schizophrenic personality in "Mother Goose and Brother Loon: The Fairy-Tale-within-a-Tale as Vehicle of Displacement," *Callaloo* 22, no. 3 (1999): 594–602.
173. Wideman, *All Stories Are True*, 127.
174. This is especially direct in the opening section of *Fatheralong*.
175. Wideman, *All Stories Are True*, 124.
176. I could not help noticing the similarity between this story published in 1992 and the Rebecca Gilman play *Spinning into Butter*, which debuted in 1999. The basics of the plot are too close not to think about the connections. The play has met with a great deal of controversy as well as acclaim. But the primary difference is point of view. "Signs" is told from the point of view of the victim of the alienation and trauma—a far more emotional and psychological narrative. Gilman's play focuses on the reactions of the white, liberal dean of students whose own experiences as a confused and angry white woman take precedence over the acute racism, self-loathing, and post-traumatic suffering of its African American victim.
177. Wideman, *All Stories Are True*, 79.
178. Ibid., 79.
179. Ibid., 80.
180. Ibid., 81.
181. Ibid., 82.
182. Ibid., 92.
183. Ibid., 90.
184. Ibid., 94.
185. Ibid., 94.
186. Ibid., 94.
187. Ibid., 20.
188. Ibid., 20.
189. Ibid., 21.
190. Ibid., 21.
191. John Edgar Wideman, *Philadelphia Fire* (New York: Vintage, 1990), 182.
192. Ibid., 9–10.
193. Ibid., 199.
194. An analysis of *Philadelphia Fire* and *The Cattle Killing* is developed more fully in chapter 4.
195. John Edgar Wideman, *Fatheralong* (New York: Pantheon, 1994), 15.
196. Ibid., 103.
197. Ibid., 50.
198. Wideman relates this description in both *Fatheralong* and in *Hoop Roots* (Boston: Houghton Mifflin, 2001).
199. Wideman, *Fatheralong*, 24
200. Ibid., 73, 74.

201. See Anne Cheng's *The Melancholy of Race* and Paul Gilroy's *Postcolonial Melancholia* (New York: Columbia University Press, 2005) for further discussions of this phenomena. This psychological response to such racial trauma is also the double-consciousness defined by W.E.B. DuBois and the basis of much of the work of Frantz Fanon.

202. Marion Wilson Starling, *The Slave Narrative* (Boston: G. K. Hall, 1981), 50, 54. The picaresque emphasizes the growth of a young man or woman as he or she discovers his or her origins. The hero of these tales, most often an orphan, usually turns out to be a missing child of a wealthy or important family. That a slave's story would be based on such a form is bitterly ironic. The slave would be forever orphaned from his country and his culture, and the only identity that he would uncover would be the one that he was forced to create. The picaro is a character type that has been repeated throughout the African American tradition from Olaudah Equiano to Richard Wright. The "black picaroon" leaves his community (either willingly or forcibly) in search of freedom and identity; the story is a version of the "rake's progress."

203. Charles Nichols, "The Slave Narrators and the Picaresque Mode: Archetypes for Modern Black Personae," in *The Slave's Narrative*, ed. Charles T. Davis and Henry Louis Gates Jr. (New York: Oxford University Press, 1985), 288.

204. Wideman, *The Cattle Killing*, 33.

205. *The Cattle Killing* is analyzed further in chapters 4 and 5.

206. John Edgar Wideman, *Two Cities* (New York: Houghton Mifflin, 1998), 107.

Chapter Three

1. Wideman, quoted in Charles Rowell, "An Interview with John Edgar Wideman," *Callaloo* 13, no. 1 (Winter 1990): 54.

2. Wideman, quoted in Laura Miller, "Interview with John Edgar Wideman," *Salon*, November 11, 1997, http://www.salon.com/nov96/interview961111.html (November 11, 1997).

3. If we try doing such an experiment, we might find how difficult the path of connections becomes. One example of this occurs in the novel *A Glance Away*. Eddie Lawson is the main character of the novel. Lawson is Wideman's paternal grandmother's maiden name. Her son is named Edgar, and she had a son named Eugene who died in the war. Wideman's grandmother's name is Martha. On the surface this looks like the mother of the book, and it would seem that the work is a fairly straightforward autobiographical novel. But Wideman's grandmother did not lock herself in her room, as Martha Lawson does in this work, nor did she fall down the stairs, nor did her son think that he killed her. Nor is her daughter named Bette; Bette is Wideman's mother's name. And in the book, Martha's parents are Eugene and Freeda, but Freeda is Wideman's maternal grandmother's name. Martha Lawson appears in the story "Backseat" as well. To add to the layers of identity here, Wideman has said that Martha in *A Glance Away* is the same grandmother we see in *Sent for You Yesterday*, who is named Freeda, which is the name of Martha's mother in the book and who was actually married to John French, not Harry Wideman; we are successfully lost in the attempt to find the "true" Martha Lawson. See James Coleman, *Black Male Fiction and the Legacy of Caliban* (Lexington: University Press of Kentucky, 2001), 146.

4. We have seen this already in the studies done by James Coleman and Dorothea Mbalia. It is echoed in Bell's reading of Wideman and in Raymond Janifer's "Looking

Homewood: The Evolution of John Edgar Wideman's Folk Imagination," *Contemporary Black Men's Fiction and Drama*, ed. Keith Clark. (Champaign: University of Illinois Press, 2001), 54–70.

5. John Edgar Wideman, preface to *The Homewood Trilogy* (New York: Avon, 1985), vii.

6. Many of the stories in the short-story collections, *All Stories Are True* especially, are also set in Homewood.

7. Michael Gorra, "The Choral Voices of Homewood," review of *The Short Stories of John Edgar Wideman*, by John Edgar Wideman, *New York Times Book Review*, June 14, 1992, 13.

8. John O'Brien, *Interviews with Black Writers* (New York: Liveright Press, 1973), 220.

9. John Edgar Wideman, *Brothers and Keepers* (New York: Holt, 1984), 98.

10. Ted L. Clontz, *Wilderness City: The Post–World War II American Urban Novel from Algren to Wideman* (New York: Routledge, 2005), 140.

11. J. Coleman, *Black Male Fiction*, 79.

12. This is the reading of the Homewood books embraced by James Coleman as well as Dorothea Mbalia, Bernard Bell, Raymond Janifer, and Bonnie TuSmith. Coleman writes that "during his career as a writer-intellectual, John Edgar Wideman in his personal life has overcome feelings of alienation from the black community and re-oriented himself as a participant in black culture." J. Coleman, *Blackness and Modernism*, 3. TuSmith notes that "Wideman's experience as an upwardly mobile individual who became an unwitting assimilationist had direct bearing on his art." Bonnie TuSmith, *All My Relatives: Community in Contemporary Ethnic American Literature* (Ann Arbor: University of Michigan Press, 1993), 86. Bell suggests that "the Homewood trilogy marks the culmination of Wideman's move from a Eurocentric to a fundamentally Afrocentric tradition, his coming home as it were in the form and style of an extended meditation on history." Bernard Bell, *The Afro-American Novel and Its Traditions* (Amherst: University of Massachusetts Press, 1987), 311–312. And Raymond Janifer's "Looking Homewood: The Evolution of John Edgar Wideman's Folk Imagination," in *Contemporary Black Men's Fiction and Drama*, ed. Keith Clark (Champaign: University of Illinois Press, 2001), 54–70, outlines the changes in Wideman's writing as a result of his return home and his introduction to Afrocentric philosophy, which brought him to a greater understanding of African American vernacular culture. Janifer suggests that Wideman "discovered that scores of black American writers invoke the blues as metaphoric language" (55). The idea that Wideman "discovered" the blues language only after preparing to teach an Afro-American studies course is problematic. Throughout his writing Wideman comments on how important the music of his culture has been to him; he, no doubt, understood the blues growing up. He did not need to discover its meaning. He may have needed the blues more once he left home and had to face more direct racism outside of the warmth and safety of his home.

13. Keith Byerman, *Remembering the Past in Contemporary African-American Fiction* (Chapel Hill: University of North Carolina Press, 2008), 160.

14. Wideman, *Brothers and Keepers*, 30–31.

15. Jessica Lustig, "Home: An Interview with John Edgar Wideman," *Conversations with John Edgar Wideman*, ed. Bonnie TuSmith (Jackson: University Press of Mississippi, 1998), 115.

16. Wideman, quoted in Lustig, "Home: An Interview with John Edgar Wideman," 114.

17. Maya Deren, *Divine Horsemen: The Living Gods of Haiti* (New York: McPherson and Co., 1983), 116.

18. Wideman, preface to *The Homewood Trilogy*, v.

19. Wideman's connection to the African *griot* has been noted by many critics of his work as well. His attention to cultural preservation, especially, places him in the tradition: "Like the African *griot* who preserves and propagates the myths of his tribal history, Wideman deals in private, family myths that serve as shibboleth and rallying cry, talisman and initiation, resistance and solidarity for the Happy Few." Jacqueline Berben, "Towards a Black Realization of the Hegelian Ideal: John Edgar Wideman's 'Homewood,'" *Cycnos* 4 (1988): 45.

20. Wideman, *Brothers and Keepers*, xi.

21. James Clifford, "Introduction: Partial Truths," in *Writing Culture: The Poetics and Politics of Ethnography*, ed. James Clifford and George Marcus (Berkeley: University of California Press, 1986), 6, 9.

22. Mary Louise Pratt, *Imperial Eyes: Studies in Travel Writing and Transculturation* (New York: Routledge, 1992), 45.

23. The form of autoethnography exists only in those places where cultures come into contact with one another, what Pratt calls a "contact zone." In this social space, cultures speak to one another. Most artifacts of the contact zone are used to define the Other. It is usually the dominant culture that does the defining. The autoethnography is the response.

24. John Edgar Wideman, "Malcolm X: The Art of Autobiography," in *Malcolm X: In Our Own Image*, ed. Joe Wood (New York: St. Martin's Press, 1992), 101.

25. Francois Lionnet, *Autobiographical Voices: Race, Gender, and Self-Portraiture* (Ithaca, NY: Cornell University Press, 1989), 119.

26. Ibid., 99, 112. Examining the work of Native American authors, Arnold Krupat discovers tendencies of representation similar to those found in autoethnographies. Krupat does not use the term "autoethnography," but he does describe a form wherein "any narration of personal history is more clearly marked by the individual's sense of himself in relation to collective social units or groupings." He calls this form "a synecdochic sense of self." Arnold Krupat, *Ethnocriticism: Ethnography, History, and Literature* (Berkeley: University of California Press, 1992), 212.

27. Frantz Fanon, *Black Skin, White Masks* (New York: Grove Press, 1967), 35, 111.

28. James Coleman's *Black Male Fiction and the Legacy of Caliban* addresses the connection between Caliban and contemporary writers, including Wideman. See chapter 4 for further discussion.

29. See chapter 4 for further examples of these types of pamphlets.

30. Consider, for example, the somewhat recent controversy surrounding Henry Louis Gates's arrest and President Barack Obama's remarks about the Cambridge, Massachusetts, police officer's actions. The "criminal" body of the African American male is still a pervasive image in the American consciousness. Not even the most preeminent African American intellectuals are immune from the practice and the trauma it produces.

31. In October 2005, William Bennett responded to a call-in listener of his morning radio program on the topic of abortion. In the discussion Bennett used the example of forcing African American mothers to get abortions as a means to alleviate crime. It was apparently meant as an example of an "immoral" argument in the tradition of Jonathan Swift's "A Modest Proposal." However, his remarks were not read satirically, and in the months following the incident waves of pundits and journalists analyzed the image of the African American family in the American consciousness.

32. E. Franklin Frazier, quoted in Joanne Martin and Elmer Martin, *The Helping Tradition in Black Family and Community* (Silver Springs, MD: National Association of Social Workers, 1985), 2.

33. Albert Murray, *The Omni-Americans: New Perspectives on Black Experience and American Culture* (New York: Outerbridge and Dienstfrey, 1970), 36, 41.

34. Quoted in Martin and Martin, *Helping Tradition*, 1.

35. The study includes graphs, tables, and charts that illustrate unemployment statistics, the number of African American unwed mothers, and family households run by a single female. Lee Rainwater's *The Moynihan Report and the Politics of Controversy* (Cambridge, MA: MIT Press, 1967) includes the entire report, as well as responses from other sociologists and leaders in the African American community who criticized Moynihan's findings. Moynihan made connections between male unemployment rates and illegitimate births, for example, arguing that this was an example of the strong matriarchal dominance in the household: "The husbands have unusually low power" (67), and "white children without fathers at least perceive all about them the pattern of men working. Negro children without fathers flounder—and fail" (81).In "essence, the Negro community has been forced into a matriarchal structure which, because it is so out of line with the rest of society, seriously retards the progress of the group as a whole, and imposes a crushing burden on the Negro male and, in consequence, on a great many Negro women as well" (75).

36. The mainstream press seems to mention Moynihan whenever they talk about African American families. For example, see the cover story of the August 30, 1993, issue of *Newsweek*: "A World without Fathers: The Struggle to Save the Black Family." The article reiterates Moynihan's assumptions that the "fatherless" homes were the reason for the economic difficulties suffered by African American families. The article also interviews families and leaders in the African American community who suggest that the report has some validity. One wonders if the report has influenced people's perceptions so much that they have accepted its conclusions.

37. "Moynihan's work took the form of testing the accuracy of and then restating Frazier's predictions about the intertwining effects of socioeconomic deprivation and family disorganization on the situation of Negro Americans as they migrated to the cities." Rainwater, *The Moynihan Report*, 7.

38. Albert Murray, *The Omni-Americans: New Perspectives on Black Experience and American Culture* (New York: Outerbridge and Dienstfrey, 1970), 108. In his review of Albert Murray's *Train Whistle Guitar*, Wideman emphasizes the influence of Murray's vision of musical tradition and family on his own work.

39. Wideman, quoted in John O'Brien, *Interviews with Black Writers* (New York: Liveright Press, 1973), 217–218.

40. Wideman, preface to *The Homewood Trilogy*, vi.

41. Kay Bonetti, "Interview with John Edgar Wideman," in *Conversations with John Edgar Wideman*, ed. Bonnie TuSmith (Jackson: University Press of Mississippi, 1998), 57.

42. John Edgar Wideman, "The Divisible Man," *Life* 11 (Spring 1988): 116.

43. Ishmael Reed, "Interview with John Edgar Wideman," *Conversations with John Edgar Wideman*, ed. Bonnie TuSmith (Jackson: University Press of Mississippi, 1998), 127.

44. John Edgar Wideman, "Doing Time, Marking Race," *Nation* 261 (1995): 504.

45. This is evidenced even in criticism of rap music in the 1990s. Its growing popularity in white suburban communities was seen as a violent threat, encouraging

parents' organizations and school districts to try to ban the music and to censor its physical style of dress and mannerisms being imitated by teenage males.

46. Robert Sayre, "Autobiography and the Making of America," *Autobiography: Essays Theoretical and Critical*, ed. James Olney (Princeton: Princeton University Press, 1980), 165.

47. Leroi Jones (Amiri Baraka), *Black Music* (New York: William Morrow, 1968), 190.

48. Wilfred Samuels, "Going Home: A Conversation with John Edgar Wideman," *Callaloo* 6, no. 1 (1983): 41.

49. John Edgar Wideman, *Damballah* (New York: Vintage, 1981), 41.

50. John Edgar Wideman, *Sent for You Yesterday* (New York: Holt, 1981), 198.

51. John Edgar Wideman, *A Glance Away* (New York: Holt, 1967), 92. The works set outside of Homewood also include family names and some family stories. Cecil Braithwaite's uncle in *Hurry Home* is named Otis, as is Wideman's real uncle, as we are told in *Brothers and Keepers*. Later in *Fatheralong* we discover that Sweetman was a friend of his father. Sweetman is the nickname of Orin Wilkerson in *The Lynchers*. And *Philadelphia Fire* relates the story of Wideman's son to the reader.

52. John Edgar Wideman, *The Lynchers* (New York: Holt, 1973), 148.

53. Ibid., 224.

54. James Coleman, *Blackness and Modernism: The Literary Career of John Edgar Wideman* (Jackson: University Press of Mississippi, 1989), 156.

55. The order of the books in the trilogy is often debated. For the purpose of this study I have chosen to consider *Damballah* the opening chapter.

56. Wideman, *Damballah*, 5.

57. Ibid., 5.

58. Ralph Ellison, *Invisible Man* (New York: Random House, 1980), 266.

59. Melvin Dixon, "The Black Writer's Use of Memory," in *History and Memory in African-American Culture*, ed. Genevieve Fabre and Robert O'Meally (New York: Oxford University Press, 1994), 21.

60. Wideman, *Damballah*, 7.

61. Robert Farris Thompson, *Flash of the Spirit: African and Afro-American Art and Philosophy* (New York: Random House, 1983), 176-177.

62. Madelyn Jablon, *Black Metafiction: Self-Consciousness in African American Literature* (Iowa City: University of Iowa Press, 1997), 11.

63. While Mbalia argues that Wideman does not use free indirect discourse until *Philadelphia Fire*, Ashraf Rushdy contends that it is clearly evident in *Damballah*. Dorothea Mbalia, *John Edgar Wideman: Reclaiming the African Personality* (London: Susquehanna University Press, 1995), 108; Ashraf Rushdy, "Fraternal Blues: John Edgar Wideman's Homewood Trilogy," *Contemporary Literature* 32, no. 3 (Fall 1991): 326.

64. Other scholars have noted the collection of texts and discourses in Wideman. Bernard Bell argues that in *Damballah* "the generic distinctions between history and fiction, novel and romance, orality and literariness collapse as Wideman blends epistle, legend, myth, fable, biography, and autobiography in a series of interdependent fictive constructs." Bernard Bell, *The Afro-American Novel and Its Traditions* (Amherst: University of Massachusetts Press, 1987), 312.

65. See Wideman's analysis of Chesnutt's writing in the *Conjure Woman* and *The Marrow of Tradition*, as well as Chesnutt's connection to the WPA slave narratives. See John Edgar Wideman, "Charles Chesnutt and the WPA Narratives: The Oral and Literate Roots

of Afro-American Literature," in *The Slave's Narrative*, ed. Charles T. Davis and Henry Louis Gates Jr. (New York: Oxford University Press, 1985), 59–78.

66. Wideman, *Damballah*, 18.
67. Ibid., 21.
68. Maya Deren, *Divine Horsemen: The Living Gods of Haiti* (New York: McPherson and Co., 1983), 84.
69. Deren, *Divine Horsemen*, 35.
70. Wideman, *Damballah*, 21.
71. Ibid., 26.
72. Ibid., 59.
73. Ibid., 106.
74. Ibid., 123.
75. Ibid., 83.
76. Ibid., 85.
77. Ibid., 91.
78. Ibid., 93.
79. Ibid., 95.
80. Keesha is a surviving daughter in the short story "Welcome."
81. Wideman, *Damballah*, 154.
82. Ibid., 195.
83. See, for example, Frances Harper's post-Reconstruction novel, *Iola Leroy*.
84. Wideman, *Damballah*, 199
85. Ibid., 202.
86. Ibid., 205.
87. His voice is reminiscent of Benjy's in *The Sound and the Fury*.
88. Melvin Dixon, *Ride Out the Wilderness: Geography and Identity in Afro-American Literature* (Urbana: University of Illinois Press, 1987), 5.
89. Wideman, *Hiding Place*, 22.
90. Ibid., 49.
91. Ibid., 51.
92. Bonnie TuSmith concludes that "Tommy is killed by the police" at the end of *Hiding Place*. Bonnie TuSmith, *All My Relatives: Community in Contemporary Ethnic American Literatures* (Ann Arbor: University of Michigan Press, 1993), 85.
93. Wideman, *Damballah*, 200. The different readings of the book's final events certainly challenges Mbalia's characterization of Wideman's writing in this work, however. She states that in *Hiding Place* "Wideman examines his own family history, an examination that is straightforward, unclouded by a contortionist structure or by heavy symbolism. Wideman's clear, unencumbered writing suggests that the knowledge he learned so impacted upon him that he wanted to record it clearly as a historian would relate the facts of the event." Mbalia, *John Edgar Wideman*, 48. The novel shifts in time, jumps from speaker to speaker with only a little warning, and is open-ended enough to solicit two different interpretations of events. It must not be as clear as Mbalia suggests. She also argues that *Hiding Place* is the beginning of his African centeredness, which the writing style reflects in its rejection of Eliot's "post-modernism." I am not sure that many critics would agree that Wideman's writing style after *Hiding Place* continues in the vein that she describes here. Certainly, a work like *Philadelphia Fire* is contortionist and defies the linear narrative presented by historians, a type of narrative that Wideman argues against throughout his work and in his interviews.

94. Jacqueline Berben, "Beyond Discourse: The Unspoken versus Words in the Fiction of John Edgar Wideman," *Callaloo* 8, no. 3 (Fall 1985): 529.

95. Wideman, *Hiding Place*, 79–78.

96. Ibid., 95.

97. Ibid., 97.

98. Ibid., 132.

99. Ibid., 147.

100. Ibid., 150.

101. Ibid., 151.

102. Ibid., 158.

103. The "reader's struggle to apprehend the familiar and foreign elements of the novel approximates the characters' struggle to apprehend their own world through perception, memory and metaphorical reconstruction of perception and memory." Madelyn Jablon, "The Shape of Memory in John Edgar Wideman's *Sent for You Yesterday*," *Black American Literature Forum* 20, no. 2 (1986): 143. Matthew Wilson also comments on the circular structure of history and memory in the trilogy as a counternarrative of Western historical discourse. Matthew Wilson, "The Circles of History in John Edgar Wideman's *The Homewood Trilogy*," *CLA Journal* 33, no. 3 (1990): 239–259. Jacquie Berben also notes the circular patterns of narrative, emblemized by the soap bubble, in her essay "Towards a Black Realization of the Hegelian Ideal: John Edgar Wideman's Homewood," *Cycnos* 4 (1988): 43–48.

104. Samuel A. Floyd Jr., *The Power of Black Music* (New York: Oxford, 1995), 235–216.

105. John Edgar Wideman, *Sent for You Yesterday* (New York: Holt, 1981), 163. We can see this relationship between memory and re-membering in *Reuben* in the Osiris myth and in the description of the spirit that draws the children together, the "beloved," in the quote that opens this chapter.

106. See earlier discussion on *A Glance Away*.

107. Wideman, *Sent for You Yesterday*, 27.

108. Ibid., 38.

109. In "Backseat" the writer says that he is nicknamed Doot by his grandmother, Martha Lawson.

110. Wideman, *Sent for You Yesterday*, 17.

111. Ibid., 17.

112. Ibid., 20.

113. Ibid., 26.

114. Ibid., 31-32.

115. Wideman states: "The way time passes sometimes makes time seem like no more than a 'glance' and a 'glance away.' When you look away from somebody you open up this immensity of time, this gap that is almost impossible to talk about in terms of years or days or seconds.... This has to do with history, it has to do with the relationship of the two people, and some strange thing about time." Wideman, quoted in O'Brien, *Interviews with Black Writers*, 221.

116. See Matthew Wilson, "The Circles of History," 239–259.

117. Jacquie Berben notes a similar reading of the bubble: "My premise is that Wideman's fictional Homewood is the modern American transposition of Hegel's ideal city of antiquity: happy, beautiful, and free in the wholeness of its past, but pitiful, ugly, and in bondage to the external forces that are disintegrating it today. By an effort of the imagination, Wideman sustains the relative utopia that was Homewood in the 1920s; he

projects its fated demise onto the soap bubble crystal ball that Grandmother Freeda catches between her fingers at the kitchen sink." Berben, "Towards a Black Realization of the Hegelian Ideal," 43.

118. Wideman, *Sent for You Yesterday*, 55.

119. Ibid., 68. TuSmith reads Wilkes's music and position in the text differently. She contends that when "Albert returns to Homewood ... he behaves like the isolated individualist he had always been." He is "alienated," which Wideman conveys "through the analogy with his music. While people in the community hear affirmation in Albert's notes, Albert himself is fixated on the silence in between the notes." TuSmith, *All My Relatives*, 91. As we have seen in the works of Houston Baker and Albert Murray, noted earlier, the blues hero is an individualist by the nature of his position in the community.

120. Wideman, *Sent for You Yesterday*, 189.

121. Ibid., 17.

122. Ibid., 58, 60.

123. Wideman, preface to *The Homewood Trilogy*, vi.

124. See Albert Murray, *The Hero and the Blues* (New York: Random House, 1973).

125. Wideman, *Sent for You Yesterday*, 80.

126. Ibid., 93.

127. Ibid., 118.

128. Yet Mbalia argues that she is only "partly drawn. The reader rarely gets her side of the story." Mbalia, *John Edgar Wideman*, 78.

129. Wideman, *Sent for You Yesterday*, 207.

130. Ibid., 170.

131. Ibid., 171.

132. Ibid., 182.

133. Wideman, quoted in Kay Bonetti, "Interview with John Edgar Wideman," *Conversations with John Edgar Wideman*, ed. Bonnie TuSmith (Jackson: University Press of Mississippi, 1998), 56–57.

134. Denise Rodriguez makes a strong case for Doot as a revision of Ralph Ellison's *Invisible Man*. And in "bringing the Invisible Man out of hibernation, Wideman seeks to reintroduce the isolated artist to his community and thereby explores his social function." Denise Rodriguez, "Homewood 'Music of Invisibility,' John Edgar Wideman's *Sent for You Yesterday* and the Black Urban Tradition," in *Critical Essays on John Edgar Wideman*, ed. Bonnie TuSmith and Keith Byerman (Knoxville: University of Tennessee Press, 2006), 131.

135. Donald Petesch, *A Spy in the Enemy's Country: The Emergence of Modern Black Literature* (Iowa City: University of Iowa Press, 1989), 42.

136. Philip Page notes this characteristic as well, suggesting that it is another example of one of Wideman's "central tenets" of storytelling—that all "versions are equally true." Philip Page, "'Familiar Strangers': The Quest for Connection and Self-Knowledge in *Brothers and Keepers*," in *Critical Essays on John Edgar Wideman*, ed. Bonnie TuSmith and Keith Byerman (Knoxville: University of Tennessee Press, 2006), 8.

137. John Edgar Wideman, *Brothers and Keepers* (New York: Holt, 1984), 27.

138. Ibid., 194.

139. Ibid., 237.

140. Daniel Challener, *Stories of Resilience in Childhood: The Narratives of Maya Angelou, Maxine Hong Kingston, Richard Rodrigues, John Edgar Wideman, and Tobias Wolf* (New York: Garland Pub., 1997), 153.

141. Margot Hennessy, "Listening to the Secret Mother: Reading John Edgar Wideman's *Brothers and Keepers*," in *American Women's Autobiography: Feasts of Memory*, ed. Margaret Culley (Madison: University of Wisconsin Press, 1992), 307.

142. Wideman, *Brothers and Keepers*, 26.

143. Ibid., 27–28.

144. This is discussed more fully in chapter 2. See also Wideman's introduction to Mumia Abu-Jamal's *Live from Death Row*.

145. Yves-Charles Grandjeat, "'These Strange Dizzy Pauses': Silence as Common Ground in John Edgar Wideman's Texts," *Callaloo* 22, no. 3 (1999): 689.

146. Michael Moreno, "The Last Iron Gate: Negotiating the Incarceral Spaces of John Edgar Wideman's *Brothers and Keepers*," *Journal X* 9, no. 1 (2004), 60.

147. Wideman, *Brothers and Keepers*, 6.

148. Ibid., 24.

149. Ibid., 21.

150. Ibid., 79.

151. Ibid., 79.

152. Jerry Bryant, "*Born in a Mighty Bad Land*": *The Violent Man in African-American Folklore and Fiction* (Bloomington: Indiana University Press, 2003), 177.

153. Wideman, *Brothers and Keepers*, 14.

154. Ibid., 44.

155. John Edgar Wideman, *Fatheralong* (New York: Pantheon, 1994), 52.

156. Even his paternal grandmother remembers few stories. In the short story "Backseat" we do learn that she is the one who named him "Doot." Her maiden name is also Lawson, which we see in *A Glance Away* and in the trilogy. His grandmother has not yet told her story. And she never does really, at least not to him. She dies before she is able. All that he knows about her story is that no one could "usurp" it: "In her own good time, in words or deeds or fiery silence, the truth of her witness would be heard. Oh yes. Their side was on the record, it was the record according to their books, laws, customs, schools, and laboratories." John Edgar Wideman, *All Stories Are True* (New York: Vintage, 1993), 28–30.

157. This is focus of chapter 2 of this study.

158. Wideman, *Fatheralong*, 80.

159. Ishmael Reed, "Interview with John Edgar Wideman," *Conversations with John Edgar Wideman*, ed. Bonnie TuSmith (Jackson: University Press of Mississippi, 1998), 127.

160. John Edgar Wideman, *Reuben* (New York: Viking Penguin, 1987), 67.

161. Ashraf Rushdy notes this relationship between remembering and "re-membering" in his discussion of *Sent for You Yesterday*: "Gathering one's body together is an act, literally, of *re-membering* one's self and one's racial history." Ashraf Rushdy, "Fraternal Blues: John Edgar Wideman's Homewood Trilogy," *Contemporary Literature* 32.3 (1991): 337. Rushdy writes about this act in an analysis of Toni Morrison's *Beloved*. Notably, Wideman, in "Malcolm X: The Art of Autobiography," describes the "beloved" as a woman or spirit engaged in such an act of "re-membering."

162. Wideman, *Reuben*, 16.

163. Ibid., 18.

164. Ibid., 61. The "flash of the spirit" also alludes to the title of Robert Farris Thompson's study of African and African-American art and philosophy, *Flash of the Spirit: African and Afro-American Art and Philosophy*.

165. Wideman, *Reuben*, 63.

166. Ibid., 19. Yves Grandjeat details the doubling in *Reuben* in far more depth in his essay, "Brother Figures: The Rift and Riff in John E. Wideman's Fiction," *Callaloo* 22, no. 3 (1999): 615–622.

167. Wideman, *Reuben*, 63.

168. Ibid., 62.

169. Ibid., 44.

170. Klaus Schmidt, "Reading Black Postmodernism: John Edgar Wideman's *Reuben*," in *Flip Sides: New Critical Essays in American Literature*, ed. Klaus Schmidt (Frankfurt: Peter Lang, 1995), 84.

171. Wideman, *Reuben*, 5, 47.

172. Ibid., 36.

173. Ibid., 196–197.

174. Schmidt, "Reading Black Postmodernism, 95.

175. Wideman, *Reuben*, 64.

176. Ibid., 66–67.

177. Wideman, quoted in James Coleman, "Interview," in *Blackness and Modernism: The Literary Career of John Edgar Wideman* (Jackson: University Press of Mississippi, 1989), 154.

178. Robert Farris Thompson, *Flash of the Spirit: African and Afro-American Art and Philosophy* (New York: Random House, 1983), xv.

179. Thompson, *Flash of the Spirit*, 18. Also see Gates, *The Signifying Monkey*; and Deren's *Divine Horseman*.

180. Wideman, *Reuben*, 140.

181. Ibid., 102.

182. Ibid., 208.

Chapter Four

1. A version of this chapter appears in *Critical Essays on John Edgar Wideman*, ed. Bonnie TuSmith and Keith Byerman (Knoxville: University Press of Tennessee, 2006), 175–190.

2. See Wideman's essay "Charles Chesnutt and the WPA Narratives: The Oral and Literate Roots of Afro-American Literature," in *The Slave's Narrative*, ed. Charles T. Davis and Henry Louis Gates Jr. (New York: Oxford University Press, 1985), 59–78.

3. John Edgar Wideman, *Fatheralong* (New York: Pantheon, 1994), 115.

4. Brian McHale, *Postmodernist Fiction* (New York: Methuen, 1987), 90.

5. As Kathie Birat points out, *The Cattle Killing* is a "textbook example" of Linda Hutcheon's genre. Kathie Birat, "'All Stories Are True': Prophecy, History, and Story in *The Cattle Killing*," *Callaloo* 22, no. 3 (1999): 630. Sheri Hoem, likewise, considers the novel a reflection of this form. Sheri Hoem, "'Shifting Spirits': Ancestral Constructs in the Postmodern Writing of John Edgar Wideman," *African American Review* 34, no. 2 (Summer 2000): 249–262.

6. McHale, *Postmodernist Fiction*, 96.

7. Wideman, quoted in Laura Miller, "Interview with John Edgar Wideman," *Salon*, November 11, 1997, http://www.salon.com/nov96/interview961111.html (February 2, 1999).

8. John Edgar Wideman, "The Color of Fiction," *Mother Jones* 15 (November/December 1990): 64.

9. Wideman, quoted in Charles Rowell, "An Interview with John Edgar Wideman," *Callaloo* 13, no. 1 (Winter 1990): 57.

10. John Edgar Wideman, *Brothers and Keepers* (New York: Holt, 1984), 19.

11. Ibid., 33.

12. Ibid., 23.

13. Ibid., 74.

14. Ibid., 39.

15. Ibid., 74.

16. Ibid., 42.

17. In *Fatheralong*, Wideman is struck by the "cartridge-like boxes" of documents about slaves found in the Abbeville records. Even all these years later, their lives are hidden away and contained (113).

18. Wideman, *Brothers and Keepers*, 42.

19. John Edgar Wideman, "Ascent by Balloon from the Walnut Street Jail," *Callaloo* 19, no. 1 (Winter 1996): 2.

20. Ibid., 2.

21. Ibid., 2.

22. Ibid., 1.

23. Ibid., 5.

24. Of all of Wideman's late works, *The Cattle Killing* has been the most analyzed. A significant portion of my work on Wideman was devoted to a new historicist/postmodern reading of the novel, especially as an example of "historiographic metafiction." Several essays in the John Edgar Wideman issue of *Callaloo* (1999) were also focused on *The Cattle Killing*. These include essays by Katie Birat, Fritz Gysin, and Yves Grandjeat. Other critics soon thereafter analyzed the novel, especially in terms similar to those of the *Callaloo* contributors. These include Sheri Hoem, Lisa Lynch, and Kathryn Hume. Noted among many of these interpretations was *The Cattle Killing*'s designation as an example of historiographic metafiction, Linda Hutcheon's term. Lisa Lynch also analyzed the language of disease in the novel in her essay, and James Coleman returned to scholarship on Wideman with his investigation of "Calibanic" discourse in *Black Male Fiction: The Legacy of Caliban*. His reading is also largely postmodern and historical. Stephen Casmier and Jennifer Douglas have both written analyses about *The Cattle Killing* that go beyond the scope of postmodernist versions of historiography. While I agree with a great deal that has already appeared on the novel, I think that it plays a much more significant role in Wideman's overall vision. And rather than being the only, or the strongest, example of his response to historiography, stands as one of many ways that Wideman attempts to deconstruct historiography through his narrative style and his focus on contested sites of the past.

25. Miller, "Interview with John Edgar Wideman."

26. Rowell, "An Interview with John Edgar Wideman," 58.

27. Miller, "Interview with John Edgar Wideman."

28. Gene Seymour, "Dream Surgeon," review of *The Cattle Killing*, by John Edgar Wideman, *Nation*, October 28, 1996, 58–60.

29. Renee Olander, "An Interview with John Edgar Wideman," in *Conversations with John Edgar Wideman*, ed. Bonnie TuSmith (Jackson: University Press of Mississippi, 1998), 167.

30. Wideman has stated before that *Tristram Shandy* was a very influential work on his development as a writer. See John O'Brien, *Interviews with Black Writers* (New York: Liveright Press, 1973).

31. See chapter 2 for a further discussion of the picaresque.

32. Linda Hutcheon, *A Poetics of Postmodernism* (New York: Routledge, 1988), 118.

33. Keith Byerman has said that the novel illustrates that "the achievements of the Enlightenment are inextricably linked to its 'madness.'" Keith Byerman, *Remembering the Past in Contemporary African-American Fiction* (Chapel Hill: University of North Carolina Press, 2008), 185.

34. Anne Cheng, *The Melancholy of Race: Psychoanalysis, Assimilation, and Hidden Grief* (New York: Oxford University Press, 2001), 13.

35. Bonnie TuSmith, "Benefit of the Doubt: A Conversation with John Edgar Wideman," in *Conversations with John Edgar Wideman*, ed. Bonnie TuSmith (Jackson: University Press of Mississippi, 1998), 208.

36. John Edgar Wideman, *The Cattle Killing* (Boston: Houghton Mifflin, 1996), 8.

37. Ibid., 13.

38. Ibid., 54.

39. Derek McGinty, "John Edgar Wideman," in *Conversations with John Edgar Wideman*, ed. Bonnie TuSmith (Jackson: University Press of Mississippi, 1998), 182.

40. Of the 20,000 citizens that fled the city, only 209 were African American. Within the month of November, when the fever claimed the least victims, 4,000 inhabitants died from the disease. See J. H. Powell, *Bring out Your Dead: The Great Plague of Yellow Fever in Philadelphia in 1793* (New York: Time Inc., 1970); and Gary Nash, *Forging Freedom: The Formation of Philadelphia's Black Community: 1720–1840* (Cambridge, MA: Harvard University Press, 1988).

41. Powell, *Bring out Your Dead*, 101.

42. Later, of course, city officials and doctors would claim that the epidemic was brought to American shores by Haitian refugees. See Powell's *Bring out Your Dead*.

43. Nash, *Forging Freedom*, 123.

44. Powell, *Bring out Your Dead*, 100.

45. Nash, *Forging Freedom*, 124.

46. Jones and Allen describe numerous stories of African American Good Samaritan practices in Richard Allen and Absalom Jones, *Narrative of the Proceedings of the Black People, During the Late Awful Calamity in Philadelphia, in the Year 1793: A Refutation* (Philadelphia, 1794). Jones and Allen tell the stories of men and women like "the poor, black man Sampson," who worked without pay and died from the fever, leaving no one to take care of his family (11–12). The list includes Sarah Bass and Caesar Cranchal; both nursed the sick without pay and later died from the epidemic. Numerous "angels" are unknown or unnamed in the account, but Jones and Allen tell their anonymous stories to refute publicly the picture Carey drew of the community.

47. Rowell, "An Interview with John Edgar Wideman," 57.

48. As critic Lisa Lynch suggests, the "trauma of the epidemic, linked in its tragic effects to the trauma of the Xhosa's cattle killing, also serves as a metonym for the larger trauma of the enslavement and mistreatment of African Americans." Lisa Lynch. "The Fever Next Time: The Race of Disease and the Disease of Racism in John Edgar Wideman," *American Literary History* 14, no. 4 (2002): 791. Lynch also notes the "looping" quality of the novel, a style endemic to literary trauma. Tuire Valkeakari likewise connects the novel to trauma theory.

49. The moment of "rebirth or transformation was a central event in the slave's life. In this way it gave individuals an outline of personal history and made them aware of their

part in the larger history of the racial group." Melvin Dixon, "Singing Swords: The Literary Legacy of Slavery," In *The Slave's Narrative*, ed. Charles T. Davis and Henry Louis Gates Jr. (New York: Oxford University Press, 1985), 302.

50. Wideman, *The Cattle Killing*, 131.
51. Ibid., 68.
52. Ibid., 76.
53. Ibid., 69.
54. Jennifer D. Douglas, "Ill Seen Ill Said": Tropes of Vision and the Articulation of Race Relations in *The Cattle Killing*," in *Critical Essays on John Edgar Wideman*, ed. TuSmith and Byerman, 209.
55. See Maya Deren's *Divine Horsemen: The Living Gods of Haiti* (New York: McPherson and Co., 1983), 305. Hoem connects "Damballah" and *The Cattle Killing* in her essay "'Shifting Spirits.'"
56. Heather Andrade considers the "Great Sea of Time" as Wideman's creative, "alternative discursive space." Heather Andrade, "Race, Representation, and Intersubjectivity in the Works of John Edgar Wideman," in *Critical Essays on John Edgar Wideman*, ed. TuSmith and Byerman, 50.
57. Wideman, *The Cattle Killing*, 55.
58. Ibid., 44.
59. Ibid., 53.
60. Ibid., 147.
61. Ibid., 7.
62. Miller, "Interview with John Edgar Wideman."
63. Noel Mostert, *Frontiers: The Epic of the Creation of South Africa and the Tragedy of the Xhosa People* (New York: Alfred Knopf, 1992), 1187.
64. John Edgar Wideman, introduction to *Live from Death Row*, by Mumia Abu-Jamal (New York: Avon, 1995), xxiii.
65. Fritz Gysin points out that the episode remains one of the most controversial and debated moments in South African history. Fritz Gysin, "'Do not fall asleep in your enemy's dream': John Edgar Wideman and the Predicaments of Prophecy," *Callaloo* 22, no. 3 (1999): 623.
66. Wideman, *The Cattle Killing*, 144.
67. Noel Mostert, *Frontiers: The Epic of the Creation of South Africa and the Tragedy of the Xhosa People* (New York: Alfred Knopf, 1992), 1187.
68. See Mostert's *Frontiers*.
69. James Berger, *After the End: Representations of Post-Apocalypse* (Minneapolis: University of Minnesota Press, 1999), 34–35.
70. Wideman, *The Cattle Killing*, 7 (italics added).
71. Wideman, *The Cattle Killing*, 7.
72. Ibid., 161.
73. Nash, *Forging Freedom*, 213.
74. Though, in *Philadelphia Fire*, Wideman portrays this event occurring in 1805.
75. Wideman, *The Cattle Killing*, 141.
76. Ibid., 211.
77. Ibid., 207.
78. I do not agree with Lisa Lynch's reading of this scene. Kate does not appear to be committing suicide or "willing" her own death. She is likely a victim of the fever, and the

narrator is trying to save her life. Lisa Lynch, "The Fever Next Time: The Race of Disease and the Disease of Racism in John Edgar Wideman," *American Literary History* 14, no. 4 (2002): 776–804.

79. Wideman, *The Cattle Killing*, 49.
80. Judith Rosen, "John Edgar Wideman," *Publisher's Weekly*, November 17, 1989, 37.
81. John Edgar Wideman, "Fever," in *Fever* (New York: Penguin, 1989), 127.
82. Ibid., 141.
83. Ibid., 132.
84. Ibid., 133.
85. See Dominick LaCapra, *Writing History, Writing Trauma* (Baltimore: John Hopkins University Press, 2001).
86. Wideman, "Fever," 160–161.
87. Ibid., 155.
88. John Edgar Wideman, *Philadelphia Fire* (New York: Vintage, 1990), 7.
89. Ibid., 22.
90. Rosemanry L. Bray, review of *Philadelphia Fire*, by John Edgar Wideman, *New York Times Book Review*, September 30, 1990, 7.
91. Ishmael Reed, *Airing Dirty Laundry* (Reading, MA: Addison, 1993), 144. Wideman tells us that Charles Johnson had problems with the work as well. See Rebekah Presson, "John Edgar Wideman," in *Conversations with John Edgar Wideman*, ed. Bonnie TuSmith (Jackson: University Press of Mississippi, 1998), 109. See Johnson's review of the work in *Washington Post Book World*, September 30, 1990. While impressed with Wideman's prose, he was disappointed that the book didn't tell us anything about the MOVE bombing that we didn't already know. Jan Clausen describes the structure of the novel as a "series of strategic disruptions beginning about halfway through (that) pries the narrative open, creating a layering of voices that represents not an organic community, rooted in the past, but a community of strangers, transfixed by a common despair and outrage." Jan Clausen, "Native Fathers," *Kenyon Review* 14, no. 2 (Spring 1992): 50.
92. R. Z. Sheppard, "Lion among the Ruins," *Time*, October 1, 1990, 90.
93. I think it was Keith Byerman who first used this phrase.
94. Wideman, *Philadelphia Fire*, 125.
95. Rudi Blesch, quoted in Amiri Baraka (Leroi Jones), *Blues People* (New York: William Morrow, 1963), 190.
96. Cornell West, "Black Postmodernism: An Interview with Anders Stephanson," in *Modernism/Postmodernism*, ed. Peter Brooker (London: Longman, 1992), 219–220.
97. Arnold E. Sabatelli, "John Edgar Wideman," in *Conversations with John Edgar Wideman*, ed. Bonnie TuSmith (Jackson: University Press of Mississippi, 1998), 150.
98. Mae Gwendolyn Henderson, "Speaking in Tongues: Dialogics, Dialectics, and the Black Woman Writer's Literary Tradition," in *Reading Black, Reading Feminist*, ed. Henry Louis Gates Jr.(New York: Viking Penguin, 1990), 116–142. She connects this call-and-response image to Mikhail Bakhtin's heteroglossia.
99. Linda Hutcheon, "Beginning to Theorize Postmodernism," in *The Postmodern Reader*, ed. Linda Hutcheon and Joseph Natoli (Albany: SUNY Press, 1993), 250.
100. Dorothea Mbalia calls this technique the "triple-voiced narrator," and indicates that these voices speak to each other in the text. Dorothea Mbalia, *John Edgar Wideman: Reclaiming the African Personality* (London: Susquehanna University Press, 1995). See the introduction of this study to see Mbalia's description of this narrative structure. This

contrapuntal relationship also reverberates in Bakhtin's theories of dialogism. Craig Werner notes that it is in works like *Philadelphia Fire* that the jazz impulse is evident. Craig Werner, *Playing the Changes: Afro-Modernism to the Jazz Impulse* (Urbana: University of Illinois Press, 1994), 62.

101. Mbalia, *John Edgar Wideman*, 15.

102. Wideman, *Philadelphia Fire*, 115.

103. Ibid., 122.

104. Bray, review of *Philadelphia Fire*, 7.

105. Miller, "Interview with John Edgar Wideman."

106. Cudjoe even leaves a Greek island in allusions to both the exiled Oedipus, found elsewhere in the novel, and Odysseus.

107. Madelyn Jablon, *Black Metafiction: Self-Consciousness in African American Literature* (Iowa City: University of Iowa Press, 1997), 141.

108. Albert Murray, *The Hero and the Blues* (New York: Random House, 1973), 101.

109. Houston Baker, *Blues, Ideology, and Afro-American Literature* (Chicago: University of Chicago Press, 1984), 122.

110. Wideman, *Philadelphia Fire*, 16.

111. Ibid., 94.

112. Ibid., 19.

113. Wideman, quoted in Presson, "John Edgar Wideman," 109.

114. Wideman, *Philadelphia Fire*, 103.

115. John Edgar Wideman, "In Praise of Silence," *Callaloo* 22, no. 3 (1999): 547–549.

116. Wideman, *Philadelphia Fire*, 97–98.

117. Ibid., 127.

118. A term coined by Paul Gilroy, *Postcolonial Melancholia* (New York: Columbia University Press, 2005).

119. Steven Greenblatt continues: "Shakespeare does not shrink from the darkest European fantasies about the Wild Man; indeed he exaggerates them.... According to Prospero he is not even human. *The Tempest* utterly rejects the uniformitarian view of the human race, the view that would later triumph in the Enlightenment and prevail in the West to this day. All men, the play seems to suggest, are not alike. Strip away the adornments of culture and you will not reach a single human existence." Steven Greenblatt, "*The Tempest* and the New World," in *Bedford Introduction to Drama*, ed. Lee Jacobus. 2nd ed. (Boston: Bedfords/St. Martin's Press, 1993), 381.

120. Wideman, *Philadelphia Fire*, 128.

121. James Coleman, "Clarence Major's *All-Night Visitors*: Calibanic Discourse and Black Male Expression," *African American Review* 28, no. 1 (1994): 95–119.

122. Wideman, *Philadelphia Fire*, 145.

123. Ibid., 132.

124. Ibid., 132.

125. Wideman, *The Cattle Killing*, 147.

126. Jerry Varsava's insightful article notes that the novel is a "textbook illustration" of Bakhtin's heteroglossia. Jerry Varsava, "Woven of Many Strands: Multiple Subjectivity in John Edgar Wideman's *Philadelphia Fire*," *Critique* 41, no. 4 (2000): 438.

127. Mary Carden, "If the City Is a Man: Founders and Fathers, Cities and Sons in John Edgar Wideman's *Philadelphia Fire*," *Contemporary Literature* 44, no. 3 (Fall 2003): 473.

128. Wideman, *Philadelphia Fire*, 105.

129. Wideman, *Philadelphia Fire*, 132.

130. Leslie Lewis points out that Wideman plays with puns between tail and tale in the work: "And thereby hangs a tale." And the point of producing the play is to "unteach" the tale by removing "de tail." Lewis agrees that such lines illustrate that Wideman is addressing and deconstructing "dehumanizing myths." Leslie Lewis, "*Philadelphia Fire* and *The Fire Next Time*: Wideman Responds to Baldwin," in *Critical Essays on John Edgar Wideman*, ed. TuSmith and Byerman, 153.

131. This production of *The Tempest* began its run as a "Shakespeare in the Park" performance in the summer of 1995. The New York Public Theater then performed the play in the fall of 1995. Patrick Stewart and Teagle Bougere played Prospero and Caliban, respectively. The *New York Times* reviewer, Margo Jefferson, noted that "the master denounces vengeful bestiality in his slave, then, having done so, must acknowledge and reluctantly renounce it in himself." Margo Jefferson, "No Age Can Trap Shakespeare the Chameleon," *New York Times*, July 16, 1995, 5.

132. Wideman, *Philadelphia Fire*, 106.

133. Ibid., 119.

134. *Time* magazine reported "suddenly a naked child dashed from the flaming wreckage near the MOVE headquarters. A team of policeman charged in pursuit. 'They grabbed him by the shoulders and just carried him off.'" "After the Bomb," *Time*, October, 1985, 16. The bombing made front-page news on May 16, 1985. Already, as the *New York Times* reported, there were conflicting reports about the cause of the fire. *Time*, *Newsweek*, and *U.S. News and World Report* devoted significant coverage to the bombing in their May 27, 1985, issues. In each of the early reports, the incident was only referred to as "a fire." In the June 24 issue of the same year, *Jet* offered a brief follow-up on Birdie Africa, the boy seen running through the flames. "Philly Boy Who Escaped MOVE Fire, Lives with Dad," *Jet*, June 24, 1985, 25. The only other major story covering the bombing appeared in October. The media used the word "bomb" this time around, but the story only mentions the rebuilding efforts (briefly) and the investigation of the officials' actions during the incident.

135. Wideman, quoted in Jules Chametzky, ed., *Black Writers Redefine the Struggle: A Tribute to James Baldwin* (Amherst: Institute for Advanced Studies, 1989), 55.

136. Wideman, *Philadelphia Fire*, 91.

137. Ibid., 74.

138. Ibid., 107.

139. Charles Chesnutt, *The Marrow of Tradition* (New York: Viking Penguin, 1993), 329.

140. John Edgar Wideman, "Charles W. Chesnutt: *The Marrow of Tradition*," *American Scholar* 42, no. 1 (1973): 132.

141. Wideman, *Philadelphia Fire*, 199.

142. See James Coleman's *Black Male Fiction and the Legacy of Calibanism* (Lexington: University Press of Kentucky, 2001) for a reading of "calibanistic discourse" in both *The Cattle Killing* and *Philadelphia Fire*. Philip Auger argues that Cudjoe's attempts at rewriting the Caliban story ultimately fail, but there is a hope that "black men have the potential, however much unrealized, to 'rewrite' their lives ... [and] that tales can be told in more than one way." Philip Auger, *Native Sons in No Man's Land: Rewriting Afro-American Manhood in the Novels of Baldwin, Walker, Wideman, and Gaines* (New York: Garland Pub., 2000), 55.

143. John Edgar Wideman, *The Lynchers* (New York: Holt, 1973), 72.

144. Ibid., 110–111.

145. Ibid., 111.

146. Ibid., 172–173.

147. John Edgar Wideman, introduction to *Live from Death Row*, by Mumia Abu-Jamal (New York: Avon, 1995), xxix.

148. Wideman, *Fatheralong* (New York: Pantheon, 1994), 34.

149. Darryl Pinchney, review of *Fatheralong*, by John Edgar Wideman, *New York Review of Books*, May 11, 1995, 31.

150. Wideman, *Fatheralong*, 97.

151. Jackie Berben-Masi, "Prodigal and Prodigy: Fathers and Sons in Wideman's Work," *Callaloo* 22, no. 3 (Summer, 1999): 680.

152. Wideman, *Fatheralong*, 101.

153. Ibid., 17.

154. Ibid., 17.

155. Ibid., 31.

156. Ibid., 94.

157. The image of the promised land and of the town itself is inscribed as pastoral and Edenic in African American history and tradition. Wideman extends that image into Greenwood and even into the camp in Maine once owned by his father-in-law. See Claude Julien, "Figures of Life in *Fatheralong*," in *Critical Essays on John Edgar Wideman*, ed. TuSmith and Byerman, 22. These descriptions suggest false promises and lost innocence. Eric Sundquist notes this as well about Promised Land, South Carolina, in the text: "For Wideman, however, what counts is not Promised Land the historic black community but Promised Land the metaphor of black modernity. . . . Wideman's Promised Land is principally an emblem of freedom's betrayal in the long aftermath of Jim Crow." Eric Sundquist, "Fly Away Home: John Edgar Wideman's *Fatheralong*," *Triquarterly* 126 (2006): 14–15.

158. Wideman, *Fatheralong*, 94–95.

159. This act, according to Sherri Hoem, is reminiscent of Michel Foucault. By constructing "a 'counter-memory,'" Wideman "transforms traditional 'history' into what Nietzsche called 'effective' history.'" Sherri Hoem, "Recontextualizing Fathers: Wideman, Foucault, and African American Genealogy," *Textual Practice* 14, no. 2 (2000): 237.

160. Wideman, *Fatheralong*, 106.

161. Ibid., 107.

162. Ibid., 71.

163. Ibid., 107.

Chapter Five

1. Wideman, quoted in Chris Okonkwo, "It Was Like Meeting an Old Friend: An Interview with John Edgar Wideman," *Callaloo* 29, no. 2 (2006): 354.

2. John Edgar Wideman, *The Cattle Killing* (Boston: Houghton Mifflin, 1996), 49.

3. Robert Stepto, *From behind the Veil: A Study of African-American Narrative* (Chicago: University of Illinois Press, 1991), 167.

4. John Edgar Wideman, *A Glance Away* (New York: Holt, 1967), 93.

5. Ashraf Rushdy, "Fraternal Blues: John Edgar Wideman's *Homewood Trilogy*," *Contemporary Literature* 32, no. 3 (Fall 1991): 319.

6. Ibid., 317.

7. Ibid., 319.

8. See especially Albert Murray, *The Hero and the Blues* (New York: Random House, 1973); and Houston Baker, *Blues, Ideology, and Afro-American Literature* (Chicago: University of Chicago Press, 1984).

9. John Edgar Wideman, *Philadelphia Fire* (New York: Vintage, 1990), 105.

10. Ibid., 7–8.

11. John Edgar Wideman, *Fatheralong* (New York: Pantheon, 1994), 49.

12. Eric Sundquist, "Fly Away Home: John Edgar Wideman's *Fatheralong*," *Triquarterly* 126 (2006): 11.

13. Sundquist also notes the relationship between the work and Stepto's description of "tribal literacy." Sundquist, "Fly Away Home," 13–14.

14. Keith Byerman, *Remembering the Past in Contemporary African-American Fiction* (Chapel Hill: University of North Carolina Press, 2008), iii.

15. Wideman, *Fatheralong*, 194.

16. This comes from the *Truth and Reconciliation Commission of South Africa Report of 2003*, vol. 6, with a foreword by Archbishop Desmond Tutu, http://www.info.gov.za/otherdocs/2003/trc/foreword.pdf (August 12, 2009).

17. John Edgar Wideman, *Two Cities* (New York: Houghton Mifflin, 1998), 11.

18. Ibid., 13.

19. Ibid., 13.

20. Ibid., 120.

21. Ibid., 40.

22. Ibid., 47.

23. Kimberly Ruffin notes that the use of "lamentations" as a narrative model reconnects the work to the relationship between the Bible and the African American literary tradition. Especially significant in this relationship is the Bible's influence on "self-affirmation and communal liberation" in African American narrative as a way to combat suffering. Wideman has often discussed his mother's strength deriving from her faith. Kimberly Ruffin, "Mourning in the 'Second Middle Passage': Visual and Verbal Praxis in John Edgar Wideman's *Two Cities*," *CLA Journal* 48, no. 4 (2005): 422.

24. Wideman, *Two Cities*, 51.

25. Ibid., 55.

26. Wideman admits that trying to "figure out someone like Kassima, who is visited by all the tragedies she is visited by, [and] maintains dignity and strength and creates a life"—she was a character he had been trying to write for sometime. Wideman, quoted in Lisa Baker, "Storytelling and Democracy (in the Radical Sense): A Conversation with John Edgar Wideman," *African American Review* 34, no. 2 (2000): 272.

27. Wideman, *Two Cities*, 61.

28. Ibid., 114.

29. Ibid., 117.

30. Ibid., 91.

31. Ibid., 117.

32. Ibid., 119.

33. Ibid., 120.

34. Ibid., 128.

35. Ibid., 128.

36. Ibid., 216.

37. Tyrone R. Simpson II, "'And the Arc of His Witness Explained Nothing': Black

Flanerie and Traumatic Photorealism in Wideman's *Two Cities*," in *Critical Essays on John Edgar Wideman*, ed. Bonnie TuSmith and Keith Byerman (Knoxville: University of Tennessee Press, 2006), 229.

38. Wideman, *Two Cities*, 82.

39. Ibid., 107.

40. Ibid., 192–195.

41. Ibid., 91.

42. Ibid., 146.

43. John O'Brien, *Interviews with Black Writers* (New York: Liveright Press, 1973), 221.

44. Bonnie TuSmith, "Optical Tricksterism: Dissolving and Shapeshifting in the Works of John Edgar Wideman," in *Critical Essays on John Edgar Wideman*, ed. TuSmith and Byerman, 225.

45. Wideman, *Two Cities*, 229.

46. Ibid., 118–119.

47. Wideman also tells interviewer Lisa Baker that *Hoop Roots* will "be about basketball in the same way that C.L.R. James's *Beyond the Boundary* is about cricket. Really a study of race and culture." Baker, "Storytelling and Democracy," 272.

48. See Madhu Dubey's *Signs and Cities: Black Literary Postmodernism* (Chicago: University of Illinois Press, 2003) for an extensive study of African American writers' interest in demystifying black images: "given that black bodies represent both the exotic fetish and the taboo object of postmodern urbanism," it is apparent that writers like Wideman and Toni Morrison would be interested in visual images that continue African American "commodification and containment" (108).

49. This image even infiltrated the iconic picture of Tiger Woods. Once Woods's scandal broke in the press, *Vanity Fair* magazine released photos taken by celebrated photographer Annie Leibowitz. The photos had been taken previous to the stories of Woods's sexual escapades being revealed. The images of Woods in *Vanity Fair* are not the polo-clad golfer who had been promoted elsewhere. Woods is shirtless, lifting weights, and wearing a black knit cap. He appears as a far more masculine image with a black, physical, athletic body. The timing of the photos seems to be coincidental, but their popular exposure during the media frenzy helped to change Woods's status from All-American nice guy to something more dangerous and suspect.

50. John Edgar Wideman, *Hoop Roots* (Boston: Houghton Mifflin, 2001), 13.

51. Ibid., 13.

52. See, for example, John Edgar Wideman, "Playing Dennis Rodman," *New Yorker*, April 29, 1996; John Edgar Wideman, "My Daughter the Hoopster," *Essence*, November 1996; John Edgar Wideman, "Michael Jordan Leaps the Great Divide," *Esquire*, November 1990.

53. John Edgar Wideman, "This Man Can Play," *Esquire*, May 1998, 71.

54. Wideman, *Hoop Roots*, 167.

55. Ibid., 163.

56. Ibid., 180.

57. Maurice O. Wallace, *Constructing the Black Masculine* (Durham: Duke University Press, 2002), 2.

58. David Stern condemned Rodman for his on-court antics and flagrant fouls, levying numerous fines and suspensions against the player during his very celebrated years as a Chicago Bull. At the same time, Stern kept Rodman in the news, thus ensuring that the viewing public would tune in to see what Rodman might do (or tattoo) next.

59. Wideman, "Playing Dennis Rodman," 95.

60. Ibid.
61. Wideman, *Hoop Roots*, 189.
62. In Wideman, "Playing Dennis Rodman," 95.
63. Greg Tate, *Everything but the Burden: What White People Are Taking from Black Culture* (New York: Broadway, 2003), 4.
64. Wideman, *Hoop Roots*, 40.
65. Wideman, "Michael Jordan," 389.
66. Wideman, *Hoop Roots*, 41–42.
67. Michael Eric Dyson, "Be like Mike: The Pedagogy of Desire," in *Signifyin, Sanctifyin, and Slamdunking: A Reader in African-American Expressive Culture*," ed. Gena Caponi (Amherst: University of Massachusetts Press, 1999), 408.
68. Wideman, *Hoop Roots*, 164.
69. Jacqueline Berben-Masi, "Of Basketball and Beads: Following the Thread of One's Origin," in *Critical Essays on John Edgar Wideman*, ed. TuSmith and Byerman, 36.
70. Wideman, *Hoop Roots*, 246.
71. Ibid., 134.
72. Ibid., 134.
73. Karen Jahn analyzes the images of circles, rings, and bubbles in *Hoop Roots* in her essay, "Will the Circle Be Unbroken? Jazzing Story in *Hoop Roots*," in *Critical Essays on John Edgar Wideman*, ed. TuSmith and Byerman, 57–70. She connects these images to the epigraphs on beading that open the chapters and to how the disparate sections of the book are "strung together" as if Wideman is beading a story.
74. John Edgar Wideman, *The Island* (Washington, DC: National Geographic Society, 2003), xx.
75. Ibid., xxv.
76. Ibid., 13.
77. Ibid., 6.
78. Ibid., 7.
79. Ibid., xx.
80. Ibid., 12.
81. Ibid., xxviii.
82. I remember finding *The Island* in the travel section of the bookstore and wondering what an unsuspecting reader would think of the book. As a typical "travel" book, it has as much to do with Martinique as *Philadelphia Fire* has to do with the MOVE bombing and *Hoop Roots* has to do with basketball.
83. Wideman, *The Island*, 15.
84. Ibid., 35.
85. Ibid., 37.
86. Ibid., 26.
87. Martinican 29.
88. Antonio Benitez-Rojo, *The Repeating Island: The Caribbean and the Postmodern Perspective* (Durham: Duke University Press, 1996), 5.
89. Ibid.
90. Wideman, *The Island*, 30.
91. Ibid., 76.
92. W. Lawrence Hogue's description of class and privilege in *Philadelphia Fire* is important to note in comparison to *The Island*. Hogue states that *Philadelphia Fire*

"gives the reader a radically democratic text where African Americans from different socioeconomic, educational, and cultural levels represent the same event/social reality, the bombing of the MOVE row house. It shows how each station in life, along with its own individuality, affects the construction/perception of reality." W. Lawrence Hogue, "Radical Democracy, African American (Male) Subjectivity, and John Edgar Wideman's *Philadelphia Fire*," MELUS 33, no. 3 (Fall 2008): 46. Wideman's conflation of individuals and their perception on *The Island* condemns everyone to being a victim of someone else's story.

93. Wideman, *The Island*, 77.
94. Ibid., 77.
95. Ibid., 161.
96. Ibid., 134.
97. Ibid., 161.
98. Ibid., 165.
99. Ibid., 166.
100. Ibid., 12.
101. Ibid., xxviii.
102. Gerald Bergevin, "'Traveling Here Below': *The Island: Martinique* and the Strategy of Melancholy," in *Critical Essays on John Edgar Wideman*, ed. TuSmith and Byerman, 73.
103. John Edgar Wideman, *God's Gym* (Boston: Houghton Mifflin, 2005), 4–5.
104. Ibid., 5.
105. Ibid., 4.
106. Ibid., 13.
107. John Edgar Wideman, "In Praise of Silence," *Callaloo* 22, no. 3 (1999): 548.
108. Wideman, *God's Gym*, 44.
109. Ibid., 52.
110. Ibid., 109.
111. Ibid., 59.
112. Ibid., 70.
113. Ibid.
114. Ibid., 158.
115. Ibid., 172.
116. Ibid., 148.
117. Ibid., 145.
118. Ibid., 149.
119. John Edgar Wideman, *Fanon* (Boston: Houghton Mifflin, 2008), 71.
120. The novel makes a reference to another serial killer film, *The Silence of the Lambs*, which also includes a severed head.
121. Or these characters in apocalyptic stories may be symbols of the victims of the coming of the end as well. The recent popularity of the zombie signals the murder, mayhem, and cannibalism that apocalyptic novels and films use to suggest the loss of our common humanity. The novel's reference to *The Silence of the Lambs*—a study of a man who eats others—suggests this as well. James Berger's study of apocalyptic and post-apocalyptic fiction and film, *After the End*, was invaluable in framing Wideman's apocalypse novels in this broader cultural context.
122. James Berger, *After the End: Representations of Post-Apocalypse* (Minneapolis: University of Minnesota Press, 1999), 34.
123. Wideman, *Fanon*, 18.

124. Ibid., 36.
125. Ibid., 47.
126. Ibid., 4.
127. Ibid., 80.
128. Madhu Dubey, *Signs and Cities: Black Literary Postmodernism* (Chicago: University of Illinois Press, 2003), 114.
129. Wideman, *Fanon*, 106.
130. Ibid., 52.
131. Ibid., 85.
132. Ibid., 84.
133. Ibid., 85.
134. Ibid., 86.
135. Ibid., 86.
136. Ibid., 141.
137. Ibid., 144.
138. Ibid., 91.
139. Nathaniel Hawthorne, *The Scarlet Letter*, Modern Library Edition (New York: Random House, 2000), 32.
140. Wideman, *Fanon*, 184.
141. Ibid., 185.
142. Ibid., 58.
143. Ibid., 227.
144. Ibid., 64.
145. Wideman, *God's Gym*, 15.
146. Ibid., 16.
147. Wideman, *Fanon*, 143.
148. Ibid., 77.
149. Wideman, *God's Gym*, 120.
150. Wideman, *Fanon*, 76.
151. Ibid., 222.
152. Ibid., 5.

Conclusion

1. John Edgar Wideman, *Fanon* (Boston: Houghton Mifflin, 2008), 105.
2. Ibid., 108.
3. Wideman, quoted in Steven Beeber, "Interview," *Paris Review* 44, no. 161 (2002): 148.
4. John Edgar Wideman, *Briefs: Stories for the Palm of the Mind* (Raleigh, NC: Lulu Press, 2010), 104.
5. Ibid., 1.
6. Ibid., 118.
7. John Edgar Wideman, "Guest Author Blog: John Edgar Wideman," March 14, 2010, http://lulublog.com/2010/03/14/john-edgar-wideman/ (accessed May 19, 2010).
8. Wideman, *Briefs*, 113.
9. John Edgar Wideman, *Sent for You Yesterday* (New York: Holt, 1981), 31–32.

10. See Matthew Wilson, "The Circles of History in John Edgar Wideman's *The Homewood Trilogy*," *CLA Journal* 33, no. 3 (1990): 239–259.

11. Jacquie Berben notes a similar reading of the bubble: "My premise is that Wideman's fictional Homewood is the modern American transposition of Hegel's ideal city of antiquity: happy, beautiful, and free in the wholeness of its past, but pitiful, ugly, and in bondage to the external forces that are disintegrating it today. By an effort of the imagination, Wideman sustains the relative utopia that was Homewood in the 1920s; he projects its fated demise onto the soap bubble crystal ball that Grandmother Freeda catches between her fingers at the kitchen sink." Jacquie Berben, "Towards a Black Realization of the Hegelian Ideal: John Edgar Wideman's 'Homewood,'" *Cycnos* 4 (1988): 43.

12. Wideman, quoted in John O'Brien, *Interviews with Black Writers* (New York: Liveright Press, 1973), 221.

13. Wideman, quoted in Beeber, "Interview," 151.

14. Ibid., 149–150.

15. James H. Evans, *Spiritual Empowerment in Afro-American Literature* (Lewiston: Edwin Mellen Press, 1987), 13.

16. Ishmael Reed, "Interview with John Edgar Wideman," in *Conversations with John Edgar Wideman*, ed. Bonnie TuSmith (Jackson: University Press of Mississippi, 1998), 127.

17. Ralph Ellison, *Invisible Man* (1947; reprint, New York: Random House, 1980), xxii.

18. John Edgar Wideman, "The Color of Fiction," *Mother Jones* 15 (November/December 1990): 59.

19. John Edgar Wideman, introduction to *The Best American Short Stories: 1996*, ed. John Edgar Wideman (Boston: Houghton Mifflin, 1996), xx.

Bibliography

Adams, Timothy Dow. *Telling Lies in Modern American Autobiography.* Chapel Hill: University of North Carolina Press, 1990.

"After the Bomb." *Time*, October 28, 1985, 13.

Andrade, Heather Russell. "Race, Representation, and Intersubjectivity in the Works of John Edgar Wideman." In *Critical Essays on John Edgar Wideman.* Ed. Bonnie TuSmith and Keith Byerman. Knoxville: University of Tennessee Press, 2006. 43–55.

Andrews, William. "African-American Autobiography Criticism: Retrospect and Prospect." In *American Autobiography.* Ed. Paul John Eakin. Madison: University of Wisconsin Press, 1991. 195–215.

———. Introduction. In *African-American Autobiography.* Ed. William Andrews. Englewood Cliffs, NJ: Prentice Hall, 1993. 1–7.

———. "The Representation of Slavery and the Rise of African-American Realism." In *African-American Autobiography.* Ed. William Andrews. Englewood, NJ: Prentice Hall, 1993. 77–89.

———. *To Tell a Free Story: The First Century of Afro-American Autobiography: 1760–1865.* Urbana: University of Illinois Press, 1986.

———. "Toward a Poetics of Afro-American Autobiography." In *Afro-American Literary Study in the 1990s.* Ed. Houston Baker and Patricia Redmond. Chicago: University of Chicago Press, 1989. 78–91.

Auger, Philip. *Native Sons in No Man's Land: Rewriting Afro-American Manhood in the Novels of Baldwin, Walker, Wideman, and Gaines.* New York: Garland Pub., 2000.

Awkward, Michael. "Boundaries: Or Distant Relations and Close Kin." In *Afro-American Literary Study in the 1990s.* Ed. Houston Baker and Patricia Redmond. Chicago: University of Chicago Press, 1989. 73–77.

Baker, Houston. *Blues, Ideology, and Afro-American Literature.* Chicago: University of Chicago Press, 1984.

———. *The Journey Back: Issues in Black Literature and Criticism.* Chicago: University of Chicago Press, 1980.

———. *The Long Black Song.* Charlottesville: University Press of Virginia, 1972.

———. "Meditation on Tuskegee: Black Studies Stories and Their Imbrications." *Journal of Blacks in Higher Education* 9 (Autumn 1995): 51–59.

———. *Workings of the Spirit: The Poetics of Afro-American Women's Writing*. Chicago: University of Chicago Press, 1991.
Baker, Lisa. "Storytelling and Democracy (in the Radical Sense): A Conversation with John Edgar Wideman." *African American Review* 34, no. 2 (2000): 263–272.
Bakhtin, M. M. *The Dialogic Imagination: Four Essays*. Ed. Michael Holquist. Trans. Caryl Emerson and Michael Holquist. Austin: University of Texas Press, 1981.
Baldwin, James. *Notes of a Native Son*. Boston: Beacon Press, 1957.
Baraka, Amiri (Leroi Jones). *Black Music*. New York: William Morrow, 1968.
———. *Blues People*. New York: William Morrow, 1963.
Baym, Nina. "Melodramas of Beset Manhood." In *The New Feminist Criticism: Essays on Women, Literature, and Theory*. Ed. Elaine Showalter. New York: Pantheon, 1985. 63–80.
Bechet, Sidney. *Treat It Gentle*. New York: Hill and Wang, 1960.
Beeber, Steven. "Interview." *Paris Review* 44, no. 161 (2002): 137–160.
Bell, Bernard. *The Afro-American Novel and Its Traditions*. Amherst: University of Massachusetts Press, 1987.
———. "*Beloved*: A Womanist Neo-Slave Narrative; or Multivocal Remembrances of Things Past." *African American Review* 26, no. 1 (1992): 7–15.
———. "Introduction: Clarence Major's Double Consciousness as a Black Postmodernist Artist." *African American Review* 28, no. 1 (1994): 5–9.
Benitez-Rojo, Antonio. *The Repeating Island: The Caribbean and the Postmodern Perspective*. Durham: Duke University Press, 1996.
Bennion, John. "The Shape of Memory in John Edgar Wideman's *Sent for You Yesterday*." *Black American Literature Forum* 20, no. 2 (1986): 143–150.
Benston, Kimberly. "'I Yam What I Am': The Topos of (Un)naming." In *Black Literature and Literary Theory*. Ed. Henry Louis Gates Jr. New York: Rutledge University Press, 1984. 151–172.
Berben-Masi, Jacqueline. "Beyond Discourse: The Unspoken versus Words in the Fiction of John Edgar Wideman." *Callaloo* 8, no. 3 (Fall 1985): 525–534.
———. "Mother Goose and Brother Loon: The Fairy-Tale-in-the-Tale as Vehicle of Displacement." *Callaloo* 22, no. 3 (1999): 594–602.
———. "Of Basketball and Beads: Following the Thread of One's Origin." In *Critical Essays on John Edgar Wideman*. Ed. Bonnie TuSmith and Keith Byerman. Knoxville: University of Tennessee Press, 2006. 31–41.
———. "Prodigal and Prodigy: Fathers and Sons in Wideman's Work." *Callaloo* 22, no. 3 (Summer 1999): 677–684.
———. "Towards a Black Realization of the Hegelian Ideal: John Edgar Wideman's 'Homewood.'" *Cycnos* 4 (1988): 43–48.
Berger, James. *After the End: Representations of Post-Apocalypse*. Minneapolis: University of Minnesota Press, 1999.
Bergevin, Gerald. "'Traveling Here Below': *The Island: Martinque* and the Strategy of Melancholy." In *Critical Essays on John Edgar Wideman*. Ed. Bonnie TuSmith and Keith Byerman. Knoxville: University of Tennessee Press, 2006: 71–89.
Bergland, Betty. "Postmodernism and the Autobiographical Subject: Reconstructing the 'Other.'" In *Autobiography and Postmodernism*. Ed. Kathleen Ashley and Leigh Gilmore. Amherst: University of Massachusetts Press, 1994. 130–159.
Berliner, Paul. *Thinking in Jazz: The Infinite Art of Improvisation*. Chicago: University of Chicago Press, 1994.

Bigsby, C.W.E. *The Second Black Renaissance: Essays in Black Literature*. Westport, CN: Greenwood Press, 1980.
Birat, Kathie. "'All Stories Are True': Prophecy, History, and Story in *The Cattle Killing*." *Callaloo* 22, no. 3 (1999): 629–643.
Blassingame, John. "Black Autobiography as History and Literature." *Black Scholar* 5, no. 4 (Winter 1973–1974): 2–9.
Bonetti, Kay. "Interview with John Edgar Wideman." In *Conversations with John Edgar Wideman*. Ed. Bonnie TuSmith. Jackson: University Press of Mississippi, 1998. 42–61.
Bouson, J. Brooks. *Quiet as It's Kept: Shame, Trauma, and Race in the Novels of Toni Morrison*. Albany: SUNY Press, 2000.
Bray, Rosemary L. Rev. of *Philadelphia Fire*, by John Edgar Wideman. *New York Times Book Review*, September 30, 1990, 7.
Brown, Claude. *Manchild in the Promised Land*. New York: MacMillan Co., 1965.
Bryant, Jerry. *"Born in a Mighty Bad Land": The Violent Man in African-American Folklore and Fiction*. Bloomington: Indiana University Press, 2003.
Burke, Kenneth H., and David Kirby. *Individual and Community: Variations on a Theme in American Fiction*. Durham, NC: Duke University Press, 1975.
Butterfield, Stephen. "Black Autobiography." PhD diss. University of Massachusetts, 1972.
Byerman, Keith. *John Edgar Wideman: A Study of the Short Fiction*. New York: Twayne Publishers, 1998.
———. "Queering Blackness: Race and Sexual Identity in *A Glance Away* and *Hurry Home*. In *Critical Essays on John Edgar Wideman*. Ed. Bonnie TuSmith and Keith Byerman. Knoxville: University of Tennessee Press, 2006. 93–105.
———. *Remembering the Past in Contemporary African-American Fiction*. Chapel Hill: University of North Carolina Press, 2008.
———. "Wideman's Career and Literary Reception." In *Critical Essays on John Edgar Wideman*. Ed. Bonnie TuSmith and Keith Byerman. Knoxville: University of Tennessee Press, 2006. x–xi.
Callahan, John. *In the African-American Grain: Call-and-Response in Twentieth-Century Black Fiction*. Urbana: University of Illinois Press, 1988.
Campbell, Jane. *Mythic Black Fiction: The Transformation of History*. Knoxville: University of Tennessee Press, 1986.
Carby, Hazel. "Ideologies of Black Folk: The Historical Novel of Slavery." In *Slavery and the Literary Imagination*. Ed. Deborah McDowell and Arnold Rampersad. Baltimore: Johns Hopkins University Press, 1989. 125–143.
Carden, Mary. "If the City Is a Man: Founders and Fathers, Cities and Sons in John Edgar Wideman's *Philadelphia Fire*." *Contemporary Literature* 44, no. 3 (Fall 2003): 472–500.
Caruth, Cathy. *Unclaimed Experience: Trauma, Narrative, and History*. Baltimore: Johns Hopkins University Press, 1996.
Casmier, Stephen. "The Funky Novels of John Edgar Wideman: Odor and Ideology in *Reuben*, *Philadelphia Fire*, and *The Cattle Killing*." In *Critical Essays on John Edgar Wideman*. Ed. Bonnie TuSmith and Keith Byerman. Knoxville: University of Tennessee Press, 2006: 191–204.
Challener, Daniel. *Stories of Resilience in Childhood: The Narratives of Maya Angelou, Maxine Hong Kingston, Richard Rodriguez, John Edgar Wideman, and Tobias Wolff*. New York: Garland Publishing, 1997.

Chametzky, Jules, ed. *Black Writers Redefine the Struggle: A Tribute to James Baldwin*. Amherst: Institute for Advanced Studies, 1989.
Cheng, Anne. *The Melancholy of Race: Psychoanalysis, Assimilation, and Hidden Grief*. New York: Oxford University Press, 2001.
Chesnutt, Charles Waddell. *The Conjure Woman*. 1899. Durham: Duke University Press, 1996.
———. *The Marrow of Tradition*. 1901. New York: Viking Penguin, 1993.
Clausen, Jan. "Native Fathers." *The Kenyon Review* 14, no. 2 (Spring 1992): 44–55.
Clifford, James. "Introduction: Partial Truths." In *Writing Culture: The Poetics and Politics of Ethnography*. Ed. James Clifford and George Marcus. Berkeley: University of California Press, 1986. 1–26.
Clontz, Ted. L. *Wilderness City: The Post–World War II American Urban Novel from Algren to Wideman*. New York: Routledge, 2005.
Coleman, James. *Black Male Fiction and the Legacy of Caliban*. Lexington: University Press of Kentucky, 2001.
———. *Blackness and Modernism: The Literary Career of John Edgar Wideman*. Jackson: University Press of Mississippi, 1989.
———. "Clarence Major's *All-Night Visitors*: Calabanic Discourse and Black Male Expression." *African American Review* 28, no. 1 (1994): 95–119.
———. "Going Back Home: The Literary Development of John Edgar Wideman." *CLA Journal* 28, no. 3 (1985): 326–343.
Coleman, Wanda. "On Theloniousism." *Caliban* 4 (1988): 67–79.
Cooke, Michael. *Afro-American Literature in the Twentieth Century: The Achievement of Intimacy*. New Haven: Yale University Press, 1984.
———. "Modern Black Autobiography in the Tradition." In *Romanticism, Vistas, Instances, and Continuities*. Ed. David Thorburn and Geoffrey Hartman. Ithaca, NY: Cornell University Press, 1973. 255–280.
Cowart, David. *History and the Contemporary Novel*. Carbondale: Southern Illinois University Press, 1989.
Crouch, Stanley. "Jazz Criticism and Its Effect on the Art Form." In *New Perspectives on Jazz*. Ed. David Baker. Washington D.C.: Smithsonian Institute Press, 1990. 71–87.
Dahl, Linda. *Stormy Weather: The Music and Lives of a Century of Jazzwomen*. New York: Pantheon Books, 1984.
Davis, Charles T. *Black Is the Color of Cosmos: Essays on Black Literature and Culture, 1942–1981*. New York: Garland, 1982.
Davis, Charles T., and Henry Louis Gates Jr. "Introduction: The Language of Slavery." In *The Slave's Narrative*. Ed. Charles T. Davis and Henry Louis Gates Jr. New York: Oxford University Press, 1985. xi–xxxiv.
Deren, Maya. *Divine Horsemen: The Living Gods of Haiti*. 1953. New York: McPherson and Co., 1983.
"Did It Have to Happen?" *Newsweek*, May 27, 1985, 22–25.
Dixon, Melvin. "The Black Writer's Use of Memory." In *History and Memory in African-American Culture*. Ed. Genevieve Fabre and Robert O'Meally. New York: Oxford University Press, 1994. 18–27.
———. *Ride Out the Wilderness: Geography and Identity in Afro-American Literature*. Urbana: University of Illinois Press, 1987.

———. "Singing Swords: The Literary Legacy of Slavery." In *The Slave's Narrative*. Ed. Charles T. Davis and Henry Louis Gates Jr. New York: Oxford University Press, 1985. 298–317.

Douglas, Jennifer D. "'Ill Seen Ill Said': Tropes of Vision and the Articulation of Race Relations in *The Cattle Killing*." In *Critical Essays on John Edgar Wideman*. Ed. Bonnie TuSmith and Keith Byerman. Knoxville: University of Tennessee Press, 2006. 205–219.

Douglass, Frederick. *The Narrative of the Life of Frederick Douglass*. In *The Classic Slave Narratives*. Ed. Henry Louis Gates Jr. New York: Viking Penguin, 1987. 243–331.

Dubey, Madhu. *Signs and Cities: Black Literary Postmodernism*. Chicago: University of Illinois Press, 2003.

DuBois, W.E.B. *On Sociology and the Black Community*. Ed. Dan S. Green and Edwin D. Driver. Chicago: University of Chicago Press, 1978.

———. *The Souls of Black Folk*. Library of America edition. New York: Vintage, 1990.

Dyson, Michael Eric. "Be Like Mike: The Pedagogy of Desire." In *Signifyin, Sanctifyin, and Slamdunking: A Reader in African-American Expressive Culture*." Ed. Gena Caponi. Amherst: University of Massachusetts Press, 1999.

Eakin, Paul John. "Malcolm X and the Limits of Autobiography." In *African-American Autobiography*. Ed. William Andrews. Englewood Cliffs, NJ: Prentice Hall, 1993. 151–161.

Ellison, Ralph. *Invisible Man*. 1947. New York: Random House, 1980.

———. *Shadow and Act*. 1953. New York: Random House, 1995.

"Endangered Family." *Time*, August 30, 1993, 16–29.

Evans, James H. *Spiritual Empowerment in Afro-American Literature*. Lewiston: Edwin Mellen Press, 1987.

Fanon, Frantz. *Black Skin/White Masks*. New York: Grove Press, 1967.

Farrell, Kirby. *Post-Traumatic Culture: Injury and Interpretation in the Nineties*. Baltimore: Johns Hopkins University Press, 1998.

Felman, Shoshana, and Dori Laub. *Testimony: Crisis of Witnessing in Literature, Psychoanalysis, and History*. New York: Routledge, 1992.

Fischer, Michael. "Autobiographical Voices (1, 2, 3) and Mosaic Memory: Experimental Sondages in the (Post)modern World." In *Autobiography and Postmodernism*. Ed. Kathleen Ashley and Leigh Gilmore. Amherst: University of Massachusetts Press, 1994. 79–129.

———. "Ethnicity and the Post-Modern Arts of Memory." In *Writing Culture: The Poetics and Politics of Ethnography*. Ed. James Clifford and George Marcus. Berkeley: University of California Press, 1986. 194–233.

Floyd, Samuel A., Jr. *The Power of Black Music*. New York: Oxford University Press, 1995.

Fox, Robert. *Conscientious Sorcerers: The Black Postmodernist Fiction of Amiri Baraka, Ishmael Reed, and Samuel Delaney*. New York: Greenwood Press, 1987.

Franklin, H. Bruce. *Prison Literature in the United States: The Victim as Criminal and Artist*. New York: Oxford University Press, 1989.

Frazier, Kermit. "The Novels of John Edgar Wideman." *Black World* 24 (1975): 18–35.

Gates, Henry Louis, Jr. "On Bearing Witness." In *Bearing Witness*. Ed. Henry Louis Gates Jr. New York: Pantheon Books, 1991. 3–9.

———. *The Signifying Monkey*. New York: Oxford University Press, 1988.

Gibson, Donald B. "Individualism and Community in Black History and Fiction." *Black American Literature Forum* 11, no. 3 (1977): 123–129.

———. "Reconciling Public and Private in Frederick Douglass' Narrative." *American Literature* 58 (December 1985): 549–569.
Gilmore, Leigh. "The Mark of Autobiography: Postmodernism, Autobiography, and Genre." In *Autobiography and Postmodernism*. Ed. Kathleen Ashley and Leigh Gilmore. Amherst: University of Massachusetts Press, 1994. 3–20.
Gilroy, Paul. *Postcolonial Melancholia*. New York: Columbia University Press, 2005.
Gioia, Ted. *The Imperfect Art: Reflections on Jazz and Modern Culture*. New York: Oxford University Press, 1988.
Gorra, Michael. "The Choral Voices of Homewood." Rev. of *The Short Stories of John Edgar Wideman*, by John Edgar Wideman. *New York Times Book Review*, June 14, 1992, 13.
Grandjeat, Yves-Charles. "Brother Figures: The Rift and Riff in John E. Wideman's Fiction." *Callaloo* 22, no. 3 (1999): 615–622.
———. "'These Strange Dizzy Pauses': Silence as Common Ground in John Edgar Wideman's Texts." *Callaloo* 22, no. 3 (1999): 685–694.
Greenblatt, Steven. "*The Tempest* and the New World." In *Bedford Introduction to Drama*. Ed. Lee Jacobus. 2nd ed. Boston: Bedfords/St. Martin's Press, 1993. 380–382.
Guzzio, Tracie Church. "'All My Father's Texts': John Edgar Wideman's Historical Vision in *Philadelphia Fire*, *The Cattle Killing*, and *Fatheralong*." In *Critical Essays on John Edgar Wideman*. Ed. Bonnie TuSmith and Keith Byerman. Knoxville: University Press of Tennessee, 2006. 175–190.
———. "All Stories Are True: John Edgar Wideman's Responses to History." PhD diss., Ohio University, 1999.
———. "Courtside: Race and Basketball in the Works of John Edgar Wideman." In *In the Game*. Ed. Amy Bass. New York: Palgrave Macmillan, 2005. 221–236.
Gysin, Fritz. "'Do Not Fall Asleep in Your Enemy's Dream:' John Edgar Wideman and the Predicaments of Prophecy." *Callaloo* 22,. no. 3 (1999): 623–628.
———. "John Edgar Wideman's 'Fever.'" *Callaloo* 22, no. 3 (1999): 715–726.
Hanley, Robert. "Philadelphia Officials Debate Fire Cause." *New York Times*, May 16, 1985, A1.
Harris, Trudier. *Exorcising Blackness: Historical and Literary Lynching and Burning Rituals*. Bloomington: Indiana University Press, 1984. 129–147.
Hassan, Ihab. "Toward a Concept of Postmodernism." In *The Postmodern Reader*. Ed. Joseph Natoli and Linda Hutcheon. Albany: SUNY Press, 1993. 273–286.
Hawes, Clement. "Leading History by the Nose: The Turn to the Eighteenth Century in *Midnight's Children*." *Modern Fiction Studies* 39, no. 1 (1993): 147–168.
Hawthorne, Nathaniel. *The Scarlet Letter*. Modern Library Edition. New York: Random House, 2000.
Hedin, Raymond. "The American Slave Narrative: The Justification of the Picaro." *American Literature* 53, no. 4 (1982): 630–645.
Henderson, Mae Gwendolyn. "Speaking in Tongues: Dialogics, Dialectics, and the Black Woman Writer's Literary Tradition." In *Reading Black, Reading Feminist*. Ed. Henry Louis Gates Jr. New York: Viking Penguin, 1990. 116–142.
Hennessy, C. Margot. "Listening to the Secret Mother: Reading John Edgar Wideman's *Brothers and Keepers*." In *American Women's Autobiography: Feasts of Memory*. Ed. Margaret Culley. Madison: University of Wisconsin Press, 1992. 295–321.
Hentoff, Nat. "John Coltrane." In *Reading Jazz: A Gathering of Autobiography, Reportage, and Criticism from 1919 to Now*. Ed. Robert Gottlieb. New York: Pantheon, 1996. 620–628.

Hernton, Calvin. *The Sexual Mountain and Black Women Writers.* New York: Anchor Books, 1987.
Hoem, Sheri I. "Recontextualizing Fathers: Wideman, Foucault, and African American Genealogy." *Textual Practice* 14, no. 2 (2000): 235–251.
———. "'Shifting Spirits': Ancestral Constructs in the Postmodern Writing of John Edgar Wideman." *African American Review* 34, no. 2 (Summer 2000): 249–262.
Hogue, W. Lawrence. *Discourse and the Other: The Production of the African-American Text.* Durham: Duke University Press, 1986.
———. *Race, Modernity, and Postmodernity.* Albany: SUNY Press, 1996.
———. "Radical Democracy, African American (Male) Subjectivity, and John Edgar Wideman's *Philadelphia Fire*. MELUS 33, no. 3 (Fall 2008): 45–69.
Holloway, Karla F. C. *Moorings and Metaphors: Figures of Culture and Gender in Black Women's Literature.* New Brunswick, NJ: Rutgers University Press, 1992.
hooks, bell. *Yearning: Race, Gender, and Cultural Politics.* Boston: South End Press, 1990.
Howlett, Phillip. "Letter from the Publisher." In *Conversations with John Edgar Wideman.* Ed. Bonnie TuSmith. Jackson: University Press of Mississippi, 1998. 32–33.
Hume, Kathryn. "'Dimensions' and John Edgar Wideman's Mental Cosmology." *Contemporary Literature* 44, no. 4 (2003): 697–726.
Hunt, Lynn, ed. *The New Cultural History.* Berkeley: University of California Press, 1989.
Hutcheon, Linda. "Beginning to Theorize Postmodernism." In *The Postmodern Reader.* Ed. Linda Hutcheon and Joseph Natoli. Albany: SUNY Press, 1993. 243–272.
———. *A Poetics of Postmodernism.* New York: Routledge, 1988.
Huyssen, Andreas. *Present Pasts: Urban Palimpsests and the Politics of Memory.* Stanford: Stanford University Press, 2003.
Iser, Wolfgang. *The Act of Reading.* Baltimore: Johns Hopkins University Press, 1978.
"It Looks Just Like a War Zone." *Time*, May 27, 1985, 16–22.
Jablon, Madelyn. *Black Metafiction: Self-Consciousness in African American Literature.* Iowa City: University of Iowa Press, 1997.
Jahn, Karen. "Will the Circle Be Unbroken? Jazzing Story in *Hoop Roots*." In *Critical Essays on John Edgar Wideman.* Ed. Bonnie TuSmith and Keith Byerman. Knoxville: University of Tennessee Press, 2006. 57–70.
Jameson, Frederic. *The Political Unconsciousness: Narrative as a Socially Symbolic Act.* Ithaca, NY: Cornell University Press, 1981.
———. *Postmodernism, or the Cultural Logic of Late Capitalism.* Durham: Duke University Press, 1991.
Janifer, Raymond. "Looking Homewood: The Evolution of John Edgar Wideman's Folk Imagination." In *Contemporary Black Men's Fiction and Drama.* Ed. Keith Clark. Champaign: University of Illinois Press, 2001. 54–70.
Jefferson, Margo. "No Age Can Trap Shakespeare the Chameleon." *New York Times*, July 16, 1995, late ed., sec. H:1+.
"John Wideman." *In Black and White: Six Profiles of African-American Authors.* Writ. Barbara Christian. Vol. 5. RTSI Swiss TV/California Newsreel, 1992.
Johnson, Charles. *Being and Race: Black Writing since 1970.* Bloomington: Indiana University Press, 1988.
Jones, Absalom, and Richard Allen. "A Narrative of the Proceedings of the Black People, During the Late Awful Calamity in Philadelphia, in the Year of 1793." Philadelphia: William W. Woodward at Franklin Head, 1794.

Julien, Claude. "Figures of Life in *Fatheralong*." In *Critical Essays on John Edgar Wideman*. Ed. Bonnie TuSmith and Keith Byerman. Knoxville: University of Tennessee Press, 2006. 17-29.

Kaplan, E. Ann. *Trauma Culture: The Politics of Terror and Loss in Media and Literature*. New Brunswick, NJ: Rutgers University Press, 2005.

Karrer, Wolfgang. "The Novel as Blues: Albert Murray's *Train Whistle Guitar*." In *Afro-American Novel since 1960*. Ed. Peter Bruck and Wolfgang Karrer. Amsterdam: B. R. Gruner Pub., 1982. 237-261.

King, Jonny. *What Jazz Is*. New York: Walker and Co., 1997.

Krupat, Arnold. *Ethnocriticism: Ethnography, History, and Literature*. Berkeley: University of California Press, 1992.

LaCapra, Dominick. *History and Criticism*. Ithaca, NY: Cornell University Press, 1985.

———. *History, Politics, and the Novel*. Ithaca, NY: Cornell University Press, 1987.

———. *Writing History, Writing Trauma*. Baltimore: Johns Hopkins University Press, 2001.

Langer, Lawrence. *Holocaust Testimonies: The Ruins of Memory*. New Haven: Yale University Press, 1991.

Levine, Lawrence. *Black Culture and Black Consciousness*. New York: Oxford University Press, 1977.

Lewis, Leslie. "*Philadelphia Fire* and *The Fire Next Time*: Wideman Responds to Baldwin." In *Critical Essays on John Edgar Wideman*. Ed. Bonnie TuSmith and Keith Byerman. Knoxville: University of Tennessee Press, 2006: 311-334.

Lewis, R.W.B. *The American Adam*. Chicago: University of Chicago Press, 1955.

Lionnet, Francois. *Autobiographical Voices: Race, Gender, and Self-Portraiture*. Ithaca, NY: Cornell University Press, 1989.

Lukacs, Georg. *The Historical Novel*. Trans. Hannah and Stanley Mitchell. 1962. Lincoln: University of Nebraska Press, 1983.

Lustig, Jessica. "Home: An Interview with John Edgar Wideman." In *Conversations with John Edgar Wideman*. Ed. Bonnie TuSmith. Jackson: University Press of Mississippi, 1998. 113-118.

Lynch, Lisa. "The Fever Next Time: The Race of Disease and the Disease of Racism in John Edgar Wideman." *American Literary History* 14, no. 4 (2002): 776-804.

Macey, David. *Frantz Fanon: A Biography*. New York: Picador, 2000.

Major, Clarence. "Journey through Grief." Rev. of *Two Cities*, by John Edgar Wideman. *Washington Post*, October 4, 1998, Sunday ed.: X05.

Malcolm X and Alex Haley. *The Autobiography of Malcolm X*. New York: Ballantine Books, 1964.

Martin, Joanne, and Elmer Martin. *The Helping Tradition in Black Family and Community*. Silver Springs, MD: National Association of Social Workers, 1985.

Mbalia, Dorothea. *John Edgar Wideman: Reclaiming the African Personality*. London: Susquehanna University Press, 1995.

McBride, Dwight. *Impossible Witnesses: Truth, Abolitionism, and Slave Testimony*. New York: New York University Press, 2001.

McDowell, Deborah. "In the First Place: Making Frederick Douglass and the Afro-American Tradition." In *African-American Autobiography*. Ed. William Andrews. Englewood Cliffs, NJ: Prentice Hall, 1993. 36-58.

McDowell, Deborah, and Arnold Rampersad, eds. *Slavery and the Literary Imagination.* Baltimore: Johns Hopkins University Press, 1989.
McGinty, Derek. "John Edgar Wideman." In *Conversations with John Edgar Wideman.* Ed. Bonnie TuSmith. Jackson: University Press of Mississippi, 1998. 180–194.
McHale, Brian. *Postmodernist Fiction.* New York: Methuen, 1987.
Miller, Laura. "Interview with John Edgar Wideman." *Salon*, November 11, 1997, http://www.salon.com/nov96/interview961111.html (February 2, 1999).
Moglen, Helene. "(W)holes and Noses: The Indeterminacies of *Tristram Shandy*." *Literature and Psychology* 41, no. 3 (1995): 44–79.
Moreno, Michael. "The Last Iron Gate: Negotiating the Incarceral Spaces of John Edgar Wideman's *Brothers and Keepers*." *Journal X* 9, no. 1 (2004): 53–70.
Mosley, Walter. "Love among the Ruins." Rev. of *Two Cities*, by John Edgar Wideman. *New York Times Book Review*, October 4, 1998, 12–13.
Mostert, Noel. *Frontiers: The Epic of South Africa's Creation and the Tragedy of the Xhosa People.* New York: Alfred Knopf, 1992.
Murray, Albert. *The Hero and the Blues.* New York: Random House, 1973.
———. *The Omni-Americans: New Perspectives on Black Experience and American Culture.* New York: Outerbridge and Dienstfrey, 1970.
———. *Stomping the Blues.* New York: Da Capo Press, 1976.
———. *Train Whistle Guitar.* 1974. Boston: Northeastern University Press, 1989.
Murray, Roland. *Our Living Manhood: Literature, Black Power, and Masculine Ideology.* Philadelphia: University of Pennsylvania Press, 2007.
Nash, Gary. *Forging Freedom: The Formation of Philadelphia's Black Community: 1720–1840.* Cambridge: Harvard University Press, 1988.
Neal, Mark Anthony. *New Black Man.* New York: Routledge, 2006.
———. *Soul Babies: Black Popular Culture and the Post-Soul Aesthetic.* New York: Routledge, 2002.
———. *What the Music Said: Black Popular Music and Black Popular Culture.* New York: Routledge, 1999.
Nichols, Charles. "The Slave Narrators and the Picaresque Mode: Archetypes for Modern Black Personae." In *The Slave's Narrative.* Ed. Charles T. Davis and Henry Louis Gates Jr. New York: Oxford University Press, 1985. 283–297.
Nichols, William. "Individualism and Autobiographical Art: Frederick Douglass and Henry David Thoreau." *CLA Journal* 16, no. 2 (1972): 145–158.
Nielsen, Aldon. *Writing between the Lines: Race and Intertextuality.* Athens: University of Georgia Press, 1994.
Niemtzow, Annette. "The Problematic of Self in Autobiography: The Example of Slave Narrative." In *The Art of the Slave Narrative.* Ed. John Sekora and Darwin T. Turner. Macomb: Western Illinois University Press, 1982. 96–109.
"Nightmare in Philadelphia." *US News and World Report*, May 27, 1985, 20–21.
Nisenson, Eric. *Ascension: John Coltrane and His Quest.* New York: St. Martin's Press, 1993.
North, Michael. "The Dialect of Modernism: Pound and Eliot's Racial Masquerade." *American Literary History* 4, no. 1 (Spring 1992): 56–76.
———. *Dialect of Modernism: Race, Language, and Twentieth-Century Literature.* New York: Oxford University Press, 1994.
O'Brien, John. *Interviews with Black Writers.* New York: Liveright Press, 1973.

Ohmann, Carol. "*The Autobiography of Malcolm X*: A Revolutionary Use of the Franklin Tradition." *American Quarterly* 22, no. 2 (1970): 131–149.

Okonkwo, Chris. "It Was like Meeting an Old Friend: An Interview with John Edgar Wideman." *Callaloo* 29, no. 2 (2006): 347–360.

Olander, Renee. "An Interview with John Edgar Wideman." In *Conversations with John Edgar Wideman*. Ed. Bonnie TuSmith. Jackson: University Press of Mississippi, 1998. 165–179.

Olney, James. "The Founding Fathers—Frederick Douglass and Booker T. Washington." In *Slavery and the Literary Imagination*. Ed. Deborah McDowell and Arnold Rampersad. Baltimore: Johns Hopkins University Press, 1989. 1–24.

———. "'I Was Born': Slave Narratives, Their Status as Autobiography and Literature." In *The Slave's Narrative*. Ed. Charles T. Davis and Henry Louis Gates Jr. New York: Oxford University Press, 1985. 147–175.

Page, Eugene Phillip. "'Familiar Strangers': The Quest for Connection and Self-Knowledge in *Brothers and Keepers*." In *Critical Essays on John Edgar Wideman*. Ed. Bonnie TuSmith and Keith Byerman. Knoxville: University of Tennessee Press, 2006. 3–15.

———. *Reclaiming Community in Contemporary African-American Literature*. Jackson: University of Mississippi, 1999.

Perry, David. *Jazz Greats*. London: Phaidon Press, 1996.

Petesch, Donald. *A Spy in the Enemy's Country: The Emergence of Modern Black Literature*. Iowa City: University of Iowa Press, 1989.

"Philly Boy Who Escaped MOVE Fire, Lives with Dad." *Jet*, June 24, 1985, 25.

Pinckney, Darryl. Rev. of *Fatheralong*, by John Edgar Wideman. *New York Review of Books*, May 11, 1995, 27–34.

Powell, J. H. *Bring out Your Dead: The Great Plague of Yellow Fever in Philadelphia in 1793*. New York: Time Inc., 1970.

Pratt, Mary Louise. *Imperial Eyes: Studies in Travel Writing and Transculturation*. New York: Routledge, 1992.

Presson, Rebekah. "John Edgar Wideman." In *Conversations with John Edgar Wideman*. Ed. Bonnie TuSmith. Jackson: University Press of Mississippi, 1998. 105–112.

Rainwater, Lee. *The Moynihan Report and the Politics of Controversy*. Cambridge, MA: MIT Press, 1967.

Rampersad, Arnold. "Slavery and the Literary Imagination: DuBois' *The Souls of Black Folk*." In *Slavery and the Literary Imagination*. Ed. Deborah McDowell and Arnold Rampersad. Baltimore: Johns Hopkins University Press, 1989. 104–124.

Ramsey, Priscilla. "John Edgar Wideman's First Fiction: Voice and the Modernist Narrative." *CLA Journal* 41, no. 1 (Fall 1997): 1–23.

Reed, Ishmael. *Airing Dirty Laundry*. Reading, MA: Addison, 1993.

———. "Interview with John Edgar Wideman." In *Conversations with John Edgar Wideman*. Ed. Bonnie TuSmith. Jackson: University Press of Mississippi, 1998. 126–138.

———. "Of One Blood, Two Men." Rev. of *Brothers and Keepers*, by John Edgar Wideman. *New York Times Book Review*, November 4, 1984, 1, 32–33.

Richard, Jean-Pierre. "From Slavers to Drunken Boats: A Thirty-Year Palimpsest in John Edgar Wideman's Fiction." *Callaloo* 22, no. 3 (1999): 656–664.

Rodriguez, Denise. "Homewood 'Music of Invisibility': John Edgar Wideman's *Sent for You Yesterday* and the Black Urban Tradition." In *Critical Essays on John Edgar Wideman*. Ed.

Bonnie TuSmith and Keith Byerman. Knoxville: University of Tennessee Press, 2006. 127–143.

Rosen, Judith. "John Edgar Wideman." *Publisher's Weekly*, November 17, 1989: 37–38.

Rosenblatt, Roger. "Black Autobiography: Life as Death Weapon." In *Autobiography: Essays Theoretical and Critical*. Ed. James Olney. Princeton: Princeton University Press, 1980. 169–180.

Rowell, Charles. "An Interview with John Edgar Wideman." *Callaloo* 13, no. 1 (Winter 1990): 47–61.

Ruffin, Kimberly. "Mourning in the 'Second Middle Passage': Visual and Verbal Praxis in John Edgar Wideman's *Two Cities*." *CLA Journal* 48, no. 4 (2005): 415–439.

Rushdy, Ashraf. "Fraternal Blues: John Edgar Wideman's *Homewood Trilogy*." *Contemporary Literature* 32, no. 3 (Fall 1991): 312–345.

———. "A Lynching in Blackface: John Edgar Wideman's Reflections on the Race Question." In *Critical Essays on John Edgar Wideman*. Ed. Bonnie TuSmith and Keith Byerman. Knoxville: University of Tennessee Press, 2006. 107–125.

———. *Neo-Slave Narratives: Studies in the Social Logic of a Literary Form*. New York: Oxford University Press, 1999.

———. "The Phenomenology of the Allmuseri: Charles Johnson and the Subject of Narrativity." *African American Review* 26, no. 3 (1992): 373–394.

———. "Reading Black, White, and Gray in 1968: The Origins of the Contemporary Narrativity of Slavery." In *Criticism and the Color Line*. Ed. Henry B. Wonham. New Brunswick, NJ: Rutgers University Press, 1996. 63–94.

———. *Remembering Generations: Race and Family in Contemporary African American Fiction*. Chapel Hill: University of North Carolina Press, 2000.

Sabatelli, Arnold. E. "John Edgar Wideman." In *Conversations with John Edgar Wideman*. Ed. Bonnie TuSmith. Jackson: University Press of Mississippi, 1998. 145–157.

Samuels, Wilfred. "Going Home: A Conversation with John Edgar Wideman." *Callaloo* 6, no. 1 (1983): 40–59.

Sanders, Charles. "*The Waste Land*: The Last Minstrel Show." *Journal of Modern Literature* 8, no. 1 (1980): 23–38.

Sayre, Robert F. "Autobiography and the Making of America." In *Autobiography: Essays Theoretical and Critical*. Ed. James Olney. Princeton: Princeton University Press, 1980. 146–168.

Schmidt, Klaus. "Reading Black Postmodernism: John Edgar Wideman's *Reuben*." In *Flip Sides: New Critical Essays in American Literature*. Ed. Klaus Schmidt. Frankfurt: Peter Lang, 1995. 81–102.

Schultz, Elizabeth. "The Heirs of Ralph Ellison: Patterns of Individualism in the Contemporary Afro-American Novel." *CLA Journal* 22, no. 1 (December 1978): 101–122.

———. "The Insistence upon Community in the Contemporary Afro-American Novel." *College English* 41, no. 2 (October 1979): 170–184.

———. "To Be Black and Blue: The Blues Genre in Black American Autobiography." *Kansas Quarterly* 7, no. 3 (1975): 81–96.

Sekora, John. "Is the Slave Narrative a Species of Autobiography?" In *Studies in Autobiography*. Ed. James Olney. New York: Oxford University Press, 1988. 99–111.

Seymour, Gene. "Dream Surgeon." Rev. of *The Cattle Killing*, by John Edgar Wideman. *Nation*, October 28, 1996, 58–60.

Shalit, Gene. "The Astonishing John Wideman." *Look*, May 21, 1963, 30–36.
Sheppard, R. Z. "Lion among the Ruins." *Time*, October 1, 1990, 90.
Silverblatt, Michael. "Interview with John Edgar Wideman." In *Conversations with John Edgar Wideman*. Ed. Bonnie TuSmith. Jackson: University Press of Mississippi, 1998. 158–164.
———. "John Edgar Wideman." In *Conversations with John Edgar Wideman*. Ed. Bonnie TuSmith. Jackson: University Press of Mississippi, 1998. 119–125.
Simpson, Tyrone R., II. "'And the Arc of His Witness Explained Nothing': Black Flanerie and Traumatic Photorealism in Wideman's *Two Cities*." In *Critical Essays on John Edgar Wideman*. Ed. Bonnie TuSmith and Keith Byerman. Knoxville: University of Tennessee Press, 2006. 221–239.
Slethaug, Gordon. The *Play of the Double in Postmodern American Fiction*. Carbondale: Southern Illinois University Press, 1993.
Smith, Patricia. "Getting under Our Skin." In *Conversations with John Edgar Wideman*. Ed. Bonnie TuSmith. Jackson: University Press of Mississippi, 1998. 139–144.
Smith, Sidonie. *Where I'm Bound: Patterns of Slavery and Freedom in Black American Autobiography*. Westport, CN: Greenwood Press, 1974.
Smith, Valerie. Introduction to *Incidents in the Life of a Slave Girl*, by Harriet Jacobs. New York: Oxford University Press, 1988.
———. *Self-Discovery and Authority in Afro-American Narrative*. Cambridge: Harvard University Press, 1987.
Smitherman, Geneva. *Talkin' and Testifin': The Language of Black America*. Boston: Houghton Mifflin, 1977.
Soyinka, Wole. *Myth, Literature, and the African World*. Cambridge: Cambridge University Press, 1976.
Spaulding, A. Timothy. *Reforming the Past: History, the Fantastic, and the Postmodern Slave Narrative*. Columbus: Ohio State University Press, 2005.
Sprinker, Michael. "Fictions of the Self: The End of Autobiography." In *Autobiography: Essays Theoretical and Critical*. Ed. James Olney. Princeton: Princeton University Press, 1980. 321–342.
Starling, Marion Wilson. *The Slave Narrative*. Boston: G. K. Hall, 1981.
Stepto, Robert. *From behind the Veil: A Study of African-American Narrative*. Chicago: University of Illinois Press, 1991.
Stone, Albert. "After *Black Boy* and *Dusk of Dawn*: Patterns in Recent Black Autobiography." In *African-American Autobiography*. Ed. William Andrews. Englewood Cliffs, NJ: Prentice Hall, 1993. 171–195
———. *Autobiographical Occasions and Original Acts*. Philadelphia: University of Pennsylvania Press, 1982.
———. "Identity and Art in Frederick Douglass's Narrative." *CLA Journal* 17, no. 2 (December 1973): 192–213.
Sundquist, Eric. "Fly Away Home: John Edgar Wideman's *Fatheralong*." *Triquarterly* 126 (2006): 9–28.
———. *To Wake the Nations*. Cambridge: Harvard University Press, 1993.
Tate, Greg. *Everything but the Burden: What White People Are Taking from Black Culture*. New York: Broadway, 2003.
Thompson, Robert Farris. *Flash of the Spirit: African and Afro-American Art and Philosophy*. New York: Random House, 1983.

Traylor, Eleanor. "Response: The First Person in Afro-American Literature." In *Afro-American Literary Study in the 1990s*. Ed. Houston Baker and Patricia Redmond. Chicago: University of Chicago Press, 1992. 128–134.
Turner, Darwin. "Black Fiction: History and Myth." *Studies in American Fiction* 5, no. 1 (1977): 109–126.
TuSmith, Bonnie. *All My Relatives: Community in Contemporary Ethnic American Literatures*. Ann Arbor: University of Michigan Press, 1993. 84–102.
———. "Benefit of the Doubt: A Conversation with John Edgar Wideman. In *Conversations with John Edgar Wideman*. Ed. Bonnie TuSmith. Jackson: University Press of Mississippi, 1998. 195–219.
———. "Optical Tricksterism: Dissolving and Shapeshifting in the Works of John Edgar Wideman." In *Critical Essays on John Edgar Wideman*. Ed. Bonnie TuSmith and Keith Byerman. Knoxville: University of Tennessee Press, 2006. 243–258.
Varsava, Jerry. "'Woven of Many Strands': Multiple Subjectivity in John Edgar Wideman's *Philadelphia Fire*." *Critique* 41, no. 4 (2000): 425–444.
Vickroy, Laurie. *Trauma and Survival in Contemporary Fiction*. Charlottesville: University of Virginia Press, 2002.
Wallace, Maurice O. *Constructing the Black Masculine*. Durham: Duke University Press, 2002.
Weixlmann, Joe. "Culture Clash, Survival, and Transformation: A Study of Some Innovative Afro-American Novels of Detection." *Mississippi Quarterly* 38, no. 1 (Winter 1984–1985): 21–31.
———. "The Uses and Meaning of History in Modern Black American Fiction." *Black American Literature Forum* 11, no. 4 (Winter 1977): 1–23.
Werner, Craig Hansen. *Playing the Changes: From Afro-Modernism to the Jazz Impulse*. Urbana: University of Illinois Press, 1994.
West, Cornell. "Black Culture and Postmodernism." In *The Postmodern Reader*. Ed. Joseph Natoli and Linda Hutcheon. Albany: SUNY Press, 1993. 390–397.
———. "Black Postmodernism: An Interview with Anders Stephanson." In *Modernism/Postmodernism*. Ed. Peter Brooker. London: Longman, 1992. 272–282.
———. "The Dilemma of the Black Intellectual." In *Breaking Bread: Insurgent Black Intellectual Life*. Ed. bell hooks and Cornel West. Boston: South End Press, 1991. 131–146.
White, Hayden. *The Content of the Form*. Baltimore: Johns Hopkins University Press, 1987.
———. *Metahistory: The Historical Imagination in Nineteenth-Century Europe*. Baltimore: Johns Hopkins University Press, 1973.
———. *Tropics of Discourse: Essays in Cultural Criticism*. Baltimore: Johns Hopkins University Press, 1978.
Whitehead, Anne. *Trauma Fiction*. Edinburgh: Edinburgh University Press, 2004.
Wideman, John Edgar. *All Stories Are True*. New York: Vintage, 1993.
———. "The Architectonics of Fiction." *Callaloo* 13, no. 1 (Winter 1990): 42–46.
———. "Ascent by Balloon from the Walnut Street Jail." *Callaloo* 19, no. 1 (Winter 1996): 1–5.
———. "The Black Writer and the Magic of the Word." *New York Times Book Review*, January 24, 1988, 3, 26, 28.
———. *Briefs: Stories for the Palm of the Mind*. Raleigh, NC: Lulu Press, 2010.
———. *Brothers and Keepers*. New York: Holt, 1984.
———. *The Cattle Killing*. Boston: Houghton Mifflin, 1996.

———. "Charles Chesnutt and the WPA Narratives: The Oral and Literate Roots of Afro-American Literature." In *The Slave's Narrative*. Ed. Charles T. Davis and Henry Louis Gates Jr. New York: Oxford University Press, 1985. 59–78.
———. "Charles W. Chesnutt: *The Marrow of Tradition*." *American Scholar* 42, no. 1 (1973): 128–134.
———. "The Color of Fiction." *Mother Jones* 15 (November/December 1990): 59–60, 64.
———. *Damballah*. New York: Vintage, 1981.
———. "Defining the Black Voice in Fiction." *Black American Literature Forum* 11, no. 3 (1977): 79–82.
———. "The Divisible Man." *Life* 11 (Spring 1988): 116.
———. "Doing Time, Marking Race." *Nation* 261 (1995): 503–505.
———. *Fanon*. Boston: Houghton Mifflin Co., 2008.
———. *Fatheralong*. New York: Pantheon, 1994.
———. *Fever*. New York: Penguin, 1989.
———. *A Glance Away*. New York: Holt, 1967.
———. *God's Gym*. Boston: Houghton Mifflin, 2005.
———. *Hiding Place*. New York: Holt, 1981.
———. *Hoop Roots*. Boston: Houghton Mifflin, 2001.
———. *Hurry Home*. New York: Holt, 1970.
———. "In Praise of Silence." *Callaloo* 22, no. 3 (1999): 547–549.
———. Introduction to *The Best American Short Stories: 1996*. Ed. John Edgar Wideman. Boston: Houghton Mifflin, 1996. xv–xx.
———. Introduction to *Live from Death Row*. By Mumia Abu-Jamal. New York: Avon, 1995. xxiii–xxxiv.
———. Introduction to *The Souls of Black Folk*. By W.E.B. DuBois. New York: Library of America, 1990, xi–xvi.
———. *The Island*. Washington, DC: National Geographic Society, 2003.
———. "The Language of Home." *New York Times Book Review*, January 13, 1985, BR1, 35.
———. *The Lynchers*. New York: Holt, 1973.
———. "Malcolm X: The Art of Autobiography." In *Malcolm X: In Our Own Image*. Ed. Joe Wood. New York: St. Martin's Press, 1992. 101–116.
———. "Michael Jordan Leaps the Great Divide." *Esquire*, November 1990, 138–145, 210–216.
———. "My Daughter the Hoopster." *Essence*, November 1996, 79–80, 190.
———. *Philadelphia Fire*. New York: Vintage, 1990.
———. "Playing Dennis Rodman." *New Yorker*, April 29, 1996.
———. "Playing, Not Joking, with Language." Rev. of *The Signifying Monkey*, by Henry Louis Gates Jr. *New York Times Book Review*, August 14, 1988, 3.
———. Preface to *The Homewood Trilogy*. New York: Avon, 1985. v–vii.
———. *Reuben*. New York: Viking Penguin, 1987.
———. Rev. of *Train Whistle Guitar*. *New York Times Book Review*, May 12, 1974, 7.
———. *Sent for You Yesterday*. New York: Holt, 1981.
———. "Stomping the Blues: Ritual in Black Music and Speech." *American Poetry Review* 7 (1978): 42–45.
———. *The Stories of John Edgar Wideman*. New York: Pantheon, 1992.
———. "This Man Can Play." *Esquire*, May 1998, 67–73.
———. *Two Cities*. New York: Houghton Mifflin, 1998.

Wilson, Matthew. "The Circles of History in John Edgar Wideman's *The Homewood Trilogy*." *CLA Journal* 33, no. 3 (1990): 239–259.

Woodson, Carter. *The Mis-education of the Negro*. 1933. Trenton, NJ: Africa World Press, 1990.

Index

Abu-Jamal, Mumia, 164, 166
Achebe, Chinua, 30
Africa, 30, 34, 64–69, 73, 112, 137, 153–58, 163, 165, 190–91, 220, 228, 235
Africa, Birdie, 179–81
Africa, John, 31, 170, 197, 198
African American athlete, 205–15, 219. *See also* Black male body and/or masculinity
African American community, 103, 106–7, 121, 124, 127–32, 172, 180, 216
African art, 26, 33
African cosmology, 102, 142, 160
African spirits, 139, 153, 155, 159–60, 161, 163, 191
African storytelling, 103, 151
Afrocentric, 6–7, 17, 24
Alienation (isolation)
  in *All Stories Are True*, 84–92
  and blues hero, 79–81, 92
  in *Brothers and Keepers*, 81–82
  in *The Cattle Killing*, 95–96
  in early works, 6, 8, 11, 13
  in *Fanon*, 236–37
  between fathers and sons, 93–95, 103, 128, 132–34, 138, 191–94
  in *A Glance Away*, 57–60
  in *Hiding Place*, 80, 121–22
  in *Hoop Roots*, 202, 215
  in *Hurry Home*, 64, 68–71
  in *The Island*, 219–20

  in *The Lynchers*, 71–79
  and modernism, 58
  in *Philadelphia Fire*, 92–93
  in *Sent for You Yesterday*, 79–80
  in slave narratives, 52–54, 79–80
  trope in American romantic individualism, 53–54
  trope of alienated artist and/or intellectual, 48–50, 54–56, 78–79
  in *Two Cities*, 96
"All stories are true" (phrase), 11, 15–18, 26–27, 30, 33, 49, 108, 134, 141, 161, 205, 246
"All Stories Are True" (story), 83–85, 123
All Stories Are True (story collection), 11, 83–92, 94, 115, 235
Allen, Richard, 46, 152, 156, 168–70
A.M.E. Zion, 156, 168
American individualism (American romanticism), 47, 53
Anderson, Sherwood, 113
Apocalypse, 47, 164, 190, 196, 228–29, 232
"Are Dreams Faster Than the Speed of Light?," 227–28
Articulate kinsmen or survivor, 44, 103, 126, 192–93, 199, 206. *See also* Stepto, Robert
"Ascent by Balloon from Walnut Street Jail," 149–51, 156, 165
Ashe, 142
Aunt May, 117, 119–20, 124, 238

Autobiography
  and autoethnography, 103–4
  and historiographic metafiction, 21–22
  mix of fact and fiction, 23, 26
  and postmodernism, 23, 26, 133–34
  relationship to African American literature, 51–53
  and slave narratives, 50–54
Autoethnography, 21, 98, 103–5, 108–11, 115, 132–35, 142

"Backseat," 30, 56, 80, 86–87, 93
Bakhtin, Mikhail, 17, 21, 22, 32, 141, 192, 201
Baldwin, James, 54, 71, 167, 233
Baraka, Amiri, 108
Basketball, 33, 40–41, 195, 198–200, 205–17, 228, 243
Bearden, Romare, 113, 201, 231, 239
"Beginning of Homewood," 99, 119–20, 123–24, 147
Berger, James, 164, 229
Black Arts Movement, 24
Black male body and/or masculinity
  in *Brothers and Keepers*, 134–38
  in *The Cattle Killing*, 155
  as doubles for white Americans, 107–8, 138
  Fanon's description of, 105, 209–10
  in *Fatheralong*, 184;
  in *Hoop Roots*, 205–15
  in *The Island*, 219
  in *Philadelphia Fire*, 176–78
Black Skin, White Masks, 229–30
Blues
  and basketball, 216
  and Brother in *A Glance Away*, 64
  crossroads image, 29, 114
  in *Damballah*, 117–22
  and heroic romance, 190–96
  and historical trauma, 147
  influence of the blues, 17
  and Mallory in *Two Cities*, 202–3
  and post-traumatic narratives, 34, 40–44, 190–96
  writing style, 27–30, 103–8
Blues hero
  characters: in *All Stories Are True*, 42–47;
  in *The Cattle Killing*, 196; in *Fanon*, 233–34, 238–39; in *A Glance Away*, 64; in *Hoop Roots*, 206, 214–15; in *Hurry Home*, 65, 70; in *The Island*, 221, 223; in *The Lynchers*, 75; in *Sent for You Yesterday*, 125–32; in *Two Cities*, 199–203
  and detective story, 173–75
  and Doot (in the Homewood books), 101–3, 132
  failure of, 70, 81, 88, 143
  French, John, 96
  and the return home, 193–95
  and romance, 190–96
  Wideman as, 101–4, 223, 245
Bosch, Hieronymus, 107, 231
Braithewaite, Cecil, 31, 37, 64–71, 79, 82–83, 91, 174, 177, 193–94, 247
Breaks. *See* Silence
Briefs, 243–45
Brother, in *A Glance Away*, 56–64
Brother Tate, in *Sent for You Yesterday*, 80–81, 125–32, 143, 193–94
Brothers and Keepers. *See also* Wideman, Robby
  alienation in, 80–82, 86
  analysis of, 132–38
  connection to *Damballah*, 81, 97–98, 101–3, 112–19, 137, 168, 230, 236
  double-consciousness in, 31–32
  in *Fanon*, 230–31, 233, 235–36
  flight from community in, 54, 81
  history in, 147–49
  in *The Island*, 218, 220–21
  reception of, 10–13
  and the slave narratives, 51–54, 81–82
  structure of, 33, 132, 133–34

Caliban, 92, 170, 176–83, 205, 207, 210, 221, 233, 245
Call-and-response
  in *Fanon*, 232, 237
  in *God's Gym*, 232
  in heroic romance, 193
  in *Hurry Home*, 70
  in *Philadelphia Fire*, 175
  in *Sent for You Yesterday*, 125, 128

between slave narratives and literature, 51
structure, 23, 26–29
"Casa Grande," 91–92
Catherine (Katherine),
  character doubles: Chantal in *The Island*, 232, 237; Kassima in *Two Cities*, 219; Kate (Katherine) in *The Cattle Killing*, 152, 159–61, 166–68, 191, 215, 237; Katrine in *The Island*, 217–23
  in *Fanon*, 232, 234
  in *God's Gym*, 223
  in *Hoop Roots*, 214–15, 217
Cattle Killing, The
  analysis of, 152–68
  apocalypse in, 153–55, 228–29
  and "Ascent from Walnut Street Jail," 149–51
  blues hero in, 173, 196–98
  crossroads in, 95–96, 159–60
  detective, 173
  doubles in, 31–33
  father stories, 143, 196
  and "Fever," 45, 156–57
  and historical trauma, 146–47, 182–83
  and *The Island*, 217–18, 223
  Kate/Katherine in, 216–17, 223
  and romance, 143, 191–96
  and slave narratives, 51, 53, 58
  Xhosa prophecy, 78, 153–55, 228–29
Cesaire, Aime, 178
Chesnutt, Charles, 39, 113, 116, 145, 177, 180–81
Circles, and circular narrative,
  in *The Cattle Killing*, 162–63, 166–67
  in *Damballah*, 115–17, 120
  in *Fanon*, 234
  in *Fatheralong*, 138
  in *God's Gym*, 228
  in the Homewood books, 99
  in *Hoop Roots*, 216–17
  image of, 10–12
  in *Reuben*, 141
  in *Sent for You Yesterday*, 125–27, 130
  and structure, 10, 12, 31–34
  in *Two Cities*, 198
"Concert," 42–43

Conrad, Joseph, 234–35
Conversion narratives, 157–58
Crossroads, 29–32, 64, 95, 113–14, 142, 159–60, 187–88
Cudjoe
  as alienated artist/intellectual character, 82, 92–93
  doubles of, 30–31
  as failed blues hero, 192–94
  Kwansa's son in *Reuben*, 243
  in *Philadelphia Fire*, 170–81, 217, 219

"Daddy Garbage," 88–89, 107, 114–15, 118
Damballah (deity), 30, 94–95, 102, 110–15, 120, 127, 131, 138–39, 142, 160, 244
"Damballah" (short story), 113–14, 234–35
Damballah (story collection)
  analysis of, 110–22
  and *Brothers and Keepers*, 97–99, 101–3
  and *Fanon*, 231–36
  post-traumatic narrative, 79
  prefatory material, 110–11
  structure of, 31–33
Decameron, The, 229
Detective story, 129, 152, 161, 173–75, 233
Dialogism, 16, 20–22, 26, 49, 57, 147, 150, 192
"Doc's Story," 39–41, 200, 206
Doot, in the Homewood books, 30, 79–81, 87–90, 114–16, 125–32, 143, 192–94
Double-consciousness
  in *All Stories Are True*, 86–91
  in *Brothers and Keepers*, 56, 101
  in *Fanon*, 56
  in *Fatheralong*, 138
  in *A Glance Away*, 60, 65
  in *Hoop Roots*, 209–10
  in *Hurry Home*, 64–67, 69
  in *Philadelphia Fire*, 56
  in *Reuben*, 56, 83
  revision of, 50, 55, 65, 81, 171, 204
  Wideman's, 101, 133
Doubles. *See also* Wideman's doubles
  in *Brothers and Keepers*, 78–81
  in *The Cattle Killing*, 160, 168
  in *Damballah*, 112, 115, 122
  examples of in Wideman's work, 31
  in *Fanon*, 229–30, 236

Fanon's description of, 105, 108
in *A Glance Away*, 58, 60–61
in *Hurry Home*, 66–68
in *The Island*, 215–19
in *The Lynchers*, 73, 78
in Mallory's photography, 31, 200–204
meaning of, 20, 30–32
in *Reuben*, 138–43
Wideman's use of, 78–79
Douglass, Frederick, 50, 55, 94, 193
DuBois, W. E. B., 11, 32, 50, 54–55, 100, 133, 210, 233

Eighteenth-century literature, 20, 150–54, 158
Eliot, T. S.
African American influences on, 57–58
African American writers' use of, 58
in *All Stories Are True*, 89
in *A Glance Away*, 57, 60, 63, 69
in *Hurry Home*, 57, 67, 69
Thurley as Eliot's Prufrock, 60, 63
Wideman's use of, 6–7, 17, 25–26, 57–58, 69
Ellison, Ralph, 17, 28, 51, 54–55, 58, 60, 94, 108, 111, 187, 243
Enlightenment, The, 20, 146, 154, 182, 192
Equiano, Olaudah, 153, 158
Eurocentric (Western) tradition, 17, 21, 24, 26–27, 48–49, 62–64, 69, 89, 102, 145, 170
"Everybody Knew Bubba Riff," 27, 87–88

Family stories, 9, 13, 21, 27, 37–38, 42, 97–143, 147, 168, 184, 243
Fanon, 14, 29–33, 40, 49, 96, 227–39
Fanon, Frantz, 97, 105, 133, 209, 217, 220–21, 229–32, 234, 236
Father stories, 49–50, 68, 72, 93–94, 143, 183–89, 194–96, 227
Fatheralong
alienation in, 93–95
"all stories are true" in, 11
analysis of, 183–89
blues hero in, 193–96, 218
crossroads in, 160, 187–88
father stories, 93–96

history in, 145, 186–89
and slave narrative, 53–54
trauma, 173
Faulkner, William, 17, 58, 100
Fever. *See* Yellow Fever epidemic
Fever (short story collection), 39, 45, 168, 206
"Fever" (story), 39–40, 45–47, 151, 168–72, 195, 202
Fielding, Henry, 153
"Flash of the spirit," 139
Fleming, Ed, 206, 211–12
Foucault, Michel, 19, 25
French, Freeda (grandmother)
in "The Chinaman's Story" in *Damballah*, 56, 117, 118, 198
funeral of, 34, 101, 117–18, 236
in *A Glance Away*, 56, 244
and "Homewood ear" story, 8, 11, 55, 100
and soap bubble image, 33, 115, 127, 216–17, 236, 244
story of scar, 31, 115, 201, 216
French, John (grandfather)
in *All Stories Are True*, 88–89
as blues hero, 135, 230, 238
in "Daddy Garbage," 114–15
as Daddy Gene in *A Glance Away*, 56–57, 109
in *Damballah*, 114–15, 124
in *Sent for You Yesterday*, 109, 128, 130–31
Freud, Sigmund, 32, 233

Gaines, Ernest, 50
Gaps in narrative. *See* Silence
Gates, Henry Louis, Jr., 18–22, 32–49, 51–52, 142
Genocide, 197
Giacometti, Alberto, 16, 200–203, 231, 239
"Glance away" (phrase), 203–4
Glance Away, A
alienation in, 49–53
analysis of, 56–64
double-consciousness in, 101
doubles in, 79, 81, 83
Eliot in, 57, 60, 63, 69
family in, 72, 97, 109
and *Hiding Place*, 124–26
and Homewood, 99

postmodernism in, 31–33
structure of, 26–28, 31–33, 38
in *Two Cities*, 203–4
Godard, Jean-Luc, 230–31, 233
God's Gym, 14, 41, 85, 199, 223–28, 232, 237

Hawthorne, Nathaniel, 233
Heart of Darkness, 234–35
Heteroglossia, 21–22
Hiding Place, 5–6, 13, 31–33, 56, 80, 86–88, 116, 120–25, 134, 143
Historiographic metafiction, 20–21, 40, 145, 170, 205, 217
History
    African American, 23–26, 29, 61, 65, 71, 136, 145, 166, 205, 214
    in "Ascent by Balloon from Walnut Street Jail," 147–51
    in *Brothers and Keepers*, 135–36, 147–49
    in *The Cattle Killing*, 147, 152–68, 196
    and family, 10, 13, 15, 21, 31, 34, 37, 82, 97–137, 147, 186
    in *Fanon*, 237
    in *Fatheralong*, 93–95, 145, 147, 183–89, 194–96
    in "Fever," 168–69
    and Homewood, 57, 99, 148–49
    in *Hurry Home*, 65–70
    in *The Island*, 217–22
    and literature, 10–11, 18–20, 49–50, 111, 145, 170
    in *The Lynchers*, 71–78, 182–83
    in *Philadelphia Fire*, 147, 169–81
    and postmodernism, 15, 18–26, 29–35, 76, 145, 182–83
    in *Reuben*, 138–41
    and trauma, 9–13, 15, 32–37, 48–53, 68, 75–78, 96, 98–103, 112, 138, 169, 187–88, 195
    Wideman's writing as counternarrative to, 4, 9–14, 18–23, 26–29, 64, 71, 107, 120, 144–51, 233, 242–47
    writing of, 10, 15, 18–20, 26, 144–47
Holocaust, The, 36, 39, 45–46, 187–88, 195, 227
Homewood
    in *All Stories Are True*, 83–92
    in *Brothers and Keepers*, 147–48
    community of, 84, 87–88, 99–104, 107, 138
    in *Damballah*, 110–22
    in *Fanon*, 230
    in *Fever*, 40–42
    in *A Glance Away*, 56–57, 99
    in *Hiding Place*, 120–25
    history of, 57, 79, 126–27, 132, 136, 148
    in *Hoop Roots*, 205–6, 213, 215–16
    as mythic text, 81, 100–102, 104–5, 109, 120, 127–28, 132, 147, 160, 213, 236, 244
    as place, 13, 27–28, 79, 97–105, 127–29, 134–36, 205
    in *Reuben*, 138–43
    in *Sent for You Yesterday*, 125–32
    in *Two Cities*, 197–201
    works outside of, 99
"Homewood Ear, The," 8, 11, 55, 100–101, 133
Homewood Trilogy, The (Homewood books), 4–8, 31, 51, 56, 64, 79–81, 97–112, 120–32, 160, 172, 201, 213. *See also individual works*
Hoop Roots
    analysis of, 205–17
    autobiography, 98
    connection to "Doc's Story," 40–41
    Freeda's story in, 115, 118
    and *God's Gym*, 226, 228
    in *The Island*, 222–23
    in *Two Cities*, 195–98, 201
"Hostages," 46–47, 195
Hurry Home
    Africa, 64–69
    alienation in, 51, 53, 55, 57, 83, 101
    analysis of, 64–71
    detective story in, 174
    doubles in, 66–68
    Eliot in, 57, 67, 69
    history in, 65–68
    journey in, 55, 64–69, 218
    structure of, 28, 31, 33
Hurston, Zora Neale, 104–5, 113
Hutcheon, Linda, 19–22, 40, 145, 170

Igbo, 3, 241–42, 246
Imbrications. *See* Palimpsestic style

"In Praise of Silence," 225–26
Intertextuality, 10, 16–17, 20, 27. *See also* Palimpsestic style
Invisible Man, 111, 170–71, 174, 187, 193, 246
Irving, Washington, 100
Island, The, 14, 30, 33, 217–23, 232, 237–38

Jazz, 17, 21–29, 32, 42–44, 56–58, 118, 126, 134, 168, 171, 174, 225
Jet, 179
Johnson, Charles, 9–10, 23, 50, 241
Jones, Absalom, 46, 156
Jones, Robert, 197–202, 215, 219, 222
Jordan, Michael, 206–8, 211–12
Joyce, James, 113
Junebug, 27, 130–31

Kassima, 197–202, 214–15, 219, 222
Kwansa, 141–42

Lacan, Jacques, 32
LaCapra, Dominick, 35
Lamed-Vovnik, 46
Lawson, Carl, 56–57, 60, 80–82, 118, 123–32, 143, 203
Lawson, Eddie, 38, 40, 56–64, 82, 94, 132, 184, 193
Lawson, Eldon, 206, 216
Lawson, John. *See* Doot
Lawson, Martha, 56, 60–62, 80, 86, 200
Lawson, Tommy, 80, 84–86, 118–25, 234
Layering. *See* Palimpsestic style
Lee, Spike, 208
Lionnet, Francois, 105, 239
"Little Brother," 39, 41
Littleman
  alienated artist/intellectual, 71–77
  double in *Fatheralong*, 185
  double of Reuben, 138
  failure as a blues hero, 182–83
  in *The Lynchers*, 71–79
Longfellow, Henry Wadsworth, 100
"Loon Man," 88
Lost children
  in *All Stories Are True*, 83, 88, 91
  in *The Cattle Killing*, 162–63, 166
  in *Damballah*, 114
  in *Fatheralong*, 95, 173, 196
  in "Fever," 170
  as image and theme, 10, 191, 196, 247
  in *The Island*, 218
  in *Philadelphia Fire*, 92–93, 175, 179–81
  in *Reuben*, 139
  in *Sent for You Yesterday*, 81, 126, 130–31
  in *Two Cities*, 197–200
Lucy (Tate), 125–31
Lumiere Brothers, 239
Lynchers, The
  alienation in, 49, 71–77
  analysis of, 71–79
  family stories, 109
  historical trauma, 71–79, 182–85
  post-traumatic narrative, 147–48
  reception of, 5–8
Lynching, 71–75, 174, 182–83, 186, 214

Macey, David, 229
Major, Clarence, 178
Malcolm X, 11, 23–24, 30, 76
Mallory, 16, 31, 37, 95–96, 113, 197–205
Marrow of Tradition, The, 180–81
Martinque, 190, 217–22
McHale, Brian, 19–20, 145
Memory, 29, 34, 36–37, 47, 93, 103, 142, 160, 186, 188, 235
Middle Passage, the, 25, 36–37, 48, 69–70, 188, 218, 227
Migration, 48, 50, 58–60, 81
Modernism, 6–7, 9, 17, 25–28, 33, 48–49, 57–58, 69
Monk, Thelonious, 28–29, 201, 225–26
Montaigne, Michel, 105
Morrison, Toni, 17, 20, 23, 34, 36, 50, 58, 81, 195
Moseley, Walter, 173
Mother Bess, 120–25, 200
MOVE, and bombing of MOVE house, 92, 107–8, 147, 155, 166, 169–79, 202, 205
Moynihan Report, The, 106–8, 206
Murray, Albert, 27–28, 106, 128, 173–74
Music, 26–29, 42–44, 128, 206, 214
Muybridge, Eadweard, 139–40, 231
Myths. *See also* Blues heroes
  ancestral, 109, 112–14, 116, 119–20, 125–26

to combat trauma, 99, 101
the crossroads, 95
and Damballah, 95, 110–15, 120, 142
failure of, 72
and heroes, 101–3, 131, 134, 138–39, 143, 196
Homewood, 79, 100–105, 127–29, 136
new, 25, 76, 177, 181–83
Osiris, 139
in western tradition, 53, 170, 173, 181

NBA (National Basketball Association), 205, 208, 210–13
Neo-slave narratives, or narrativity of slavery, 23, 50
"Newborn Thrown in Trash and Dies," 88–89, 115
9/11 (September 11, 2001), 208, 218, 229
North, Michael, 58, 63

Oedipus, 170, 194
Oedipus at Colonnus, 92–93, 102, 170–72, 178
Orion, 102, 112–14, 119–20, 143, 147, 234–35
Owens, Sybela, 79–80, 112, 119–21, 136, 143, 147
Oxford University, 20, 24, 48, 56, 99, 154, 233

Palimpsestic style
in *All Stories Are True*, 45
in *Briefs*, 243
in *Brothers and Keepers*, 103
in *The Cattle Killing*, 151–54, 196
in *Damballah*, 111, 115, 216–17
in *Fanon*, 233
in *Fatheralong*, 145, 195
in *A Glance Away*, 57
in *Hoop Roots*, 205, 209, 216–17
in *The Island*, 217
and jazz, 26–27
and narrative, 9, 12, 15–18, 34–39, 192, 241–43, 247
in *Philadelphia Fire*, 194
and polyphonic structure, 32–39
and *Two Cities*, 202, 204–5

Philadelphia, 45–46, 95, 149, 155–56, 165–66, 169, 174, 179, 191, 197
Philadelphia Fire
alienation in, 92–94
analysis of, 170–81
and blues hero, 192–96, 217–19
and family stories, 99
and *Fanon*, 233–34
and father stories, 92–94, 144, 183–84, 225–26
and heroic romance, 192–96, 217–19
and *The Island*, 219–21
reception of, 7–8, 10, 13
and silence, 175–76, 181, 225
and slave narratives, 51, 53
structure of, 29–33
trauma in, 92–94
Photography, 201–5
Picaresque (picaro), 21, 95, 153, 158, 191
Pittsburgh, 148, 197. *See also* Homewood
Polyphonic structure (polyvocal)
and African American tradition, 20–22, 26, 171
and Bakhtin, Mikhail, 21–22, 141
in *Brothers and Keepers*, 133–34
and *The Cattle Killing*, 31–33
in *Damballah*, 113
in *Hiding Place*, 123
and history, 171
and jazz, 21–22, 26
and palimpsestic style, 32–39
in *Philadelphia Fire*, 29–33, 171–72, 178
and postmodernism, 26
in *Reuben*, 141
in *Two Cities*, 201
Wideman's use of, 7, 10, 12, 20–22, 26, 32–34
Postmodernism, 6–7, 12, 15–19, 22–26, 31–34, 37, 40, 47, 50, 56–57, 103, 145
Post-trauma
in "Ascent by Balloon from Walnut Street Jail," 150
in *Brothers and Keepers*, 80–84, 132–33, 227
in *The Cattle Killing*, 154–62
in *Fanon*, 227, 235
in *God's Gym*, 228–30

and history, 31–37, 45–47, 50, 59, 154–62, 191
in the Homewood books, 79–81, 102–3, 144
in *Hurry Home*, 65–66
in *The Lynchers*, 75–79, 147–48, 182
in *Philadelphia Fire*, 93, 170–81
structure of, 31–37, 45–47, 143–47, 191, 244
in *Two Cities*, 95–96, 196–203
Pratt, Mary Louise, 104–5
"Presents," 43–44
Prison, 54, 82–85, 92–93, 108, 137, 149–51, 173, 177–78, 205, 211, 221, 226–27, 235
Promised Land, 14, 59, 81, 83, 93, 185–88, 238
Prospero, 92, 170, 177–79, 210, 221, 233, 245

Quakers, 149

Reed, Ishmael, 4, 17, 20, 23, 32, 50, 81, 138, 170–71
Reuben, 5–6, 13, 30–33, 82–83, 97–99, 138–43, 153, 231
Reuben (character), 78, 82–83, 138–43, 193
Rhodes scholar, 24, 28, 56
Richardson, Samuel, 153
Rinehart, 170–71
"Rock River," 39–41, 228
Rodman, Dennis, 208, 210
Rush, Benjamin (Benjamin Thrush), 46, 150, 152, 156, 159, 161, 165, 168
Rushdy, Ashraf, 50–51, 193

Scarlet Letter, The, 233
Sent for You Yesterday
analysis of, 125–32
blues hero in, 79–80, 192
characters: Brother Tate, 80–81, 125–32, 143, 193–94; Carl Lawson, 56–57, 60, 80–82, 118, 123–32, 143, 203; Doot Lawson, 30, 79–81, 87–90, 114–16, 125–32, 143, 192–94; Freeda French, 127 (*see also* French, Freeda); John French, 128, 130–31 (*see also* French, John); Lucy Tate, 125–31
and *Damballah*, 115–18
doubles in, 173
and *A Glance Away*, 56–60

reception of, 5–6
structure of, 31–34
trains in, 80–81
Seven (film), 229
Shakespeare, William, 55, 69, 105, 176, 178, 210, 221
"Sharing," 225
"Sightings," 228
Signifying, 18, 23, 50–52, 168, 234
"Signs," 89–91
Silence, or gaps/breaks in the narrative,
in *All Stories Are True*, 85–86, 89, 94
in *Briefs*, 243–44
in *Brothers and Keepers*, 132–35, 148–49
in *The Cattle Killing*, 152, 158
in *Damballah*, 117–18
in *Fatheralong*, 145, 187–88
in "Fever," 39
in *A Glance Away*, 62–64
in *God's Gym*, 225–26
in history, 28–29, 100, 144, 175
and "In Praise of Silence," 225–26
in *The Island*, 221
in jazz, 28–29, 225–26
in *The Lynchers*, 79
as narrative structure, 28–29, 34, 37, 225–26
in *Philadelphia Fire*, 175–76, 181, 225
in *Sent for You Yesterday*, 128–30
in *Two Cities*, 201, 203
"Silence of Thelonious Monk, The," 226
Simba, 166, 172, 174, 179–81, 194
Slave narrative, 17, 21–22, 29, 48–55, 82, 95, 104, 110–11, 119, 152, 158, 193
Stepto, Robert, 51, 103, 192–93
Stern, David, 210
Sterne, Laurence, 153–54
Stokes, Maurice, 206, 216
"Surfiction," 39–40

"Tambourine Lady, The," 42–43
Tempest, The, 92, 105, 170–80, 194–96, 210, 221, 233
Thomas, 227, 229–35, 237–38
Thomas, Bigger, 176
Thrush, Benjamin. *See* Rush, Benjamin

Till, Emmett, 93, 186, 198, 202, 214–15, 219, 222, 243
Toomer, Jean, 54, 59, 113
Trauma
  and alienated intellectual, 53–56
  in *All Stories Are True*, 83–92
  in "Ascent by Balloon from Walnut Street Jail," 150
  in *Brothers and Keepers*, 80–84, 132–33
  in *The Cattle Killing*, 95, 154, 160–62
  in *Damballah*, 103, 112, 114–17
  family trauma, 79–80, 98, 101–3
  in *Fanon*, 226–30
  in *Fatheralong*, 186–88
  in *A Glance Away*, 54–59, 109
  in *Hiding Place*, 123
  historical, 9–13, 37, 48–53, 75–78, 98–103, 112, 117, 126, 132, 147, 154, 165, 174, 187–88
  and the Holocaust, 36, 39, 45–46, 102, 187, 195, 227
  in *Hurry Home*, 65–68
  in *The Island*, 218–23
  in *The Lynchers*, 75–79
  in *Philadelphia Fire*, 92–93, 170–81
  in *Sent for You Yesterday*, 81, 125–26
  and structure, 31–37, 144–47
  in *Two Cities*, 95–96, 202–3, 205
Trauma theory, 15, 35–37
Tristram Shandy, 17, 20, 153–54, 233
Two Cities, 31, 40–41, 95–96, 99, 113–15, 197–205

Uncanny, The, 32
Uncle Otis, 41, 66, 68, 70
Uncle Tom's Cabin, 233
Until the End of the World, 229

"Valaida," 42, 44–45, 168, 195

Washington, Denzel, 208
Weaving. *See* Palimpsestic style
"Weight," 223–25, 231
"Welcome," 85, 86
West, Cornel, 25, 56, 171
"What We Cannot Speak about We Must Pass over in Silence," 226–27
"When It's Time to Go," 42–43
"Who Invented the Jump Shot?," 216, 226
"Who Weeps When One of Us Goes Down Blues?," 228
Wideman, Edgar (father), 183–89, 195
Wideman, Harry (grandfather), 148, 183, 186
Wideman, John Edgar
  and Achebe, Chinua, 30
  and African American tradition, 17–18, 26, 28
  "All Stories Are True" (story), 83–85, 123
  All Stories Are True (story collection), 11, 83–92, 94, 115
  "Are Dreams Faster Than the Speed of Light?," 227–28
  "Ascent by Balloon from Walnut Street Jail," 149–51
  "Backseat," 80, 86–87
  "Beginning of Homewood," 119–20, 123–24
  "Black Writer and the Magic of the Word," 177
  as blues hero, 101–3
  Briefs, 243–45
  Brothers and Keepers, 132–38
  "Casa Grande," 91–92
  The Cattle Killing, 152–68
  "Charles Chesnutt and the WPA Narratives," 177
  "Concert," 42–43
  critical reception of, 4–8
  "Daddy Garbage," 88–89, 107, 114–15
  "Damballah" (short story), 113–14, 234–35
  Damballah (story collection), 110–22
  "Doc's Story," 39–41, 200
  and double-consciousness, 55, 101
  and doubles (*see* Wideman's doubles)
  and W. E. B. DuBois, 55
  and T. S. Eliot, 25–26
  Ralph Ellison, 108
  Fanon, 227–39
  and Frantz Fanon, 230, 232–34
  Fatheralong, 183–96
  "Fever" (short story), 39–40, 45–47, 168–72

Fever (short story collection), 39, 45, 168, 206
A Glance Away, 56–64
God's Gym, 223–28, 232, 237
Hiding Place, 86–88, 116, 120–25
homes of, 99, 216
The Homewood Trilogy, 4–10, 79–81, 97–112, 132, 160
Hoop Roots, 205–17
"Hostages," 46–47
Hurry Home, 64–71
"In Praise of Silence," 225–26
The Island, 217–23, 232, 237–38
"Little Brother," 39, 41
"Loon Man," 88
The Lynchers, 71–79
and Malcolm X, 23–24
and Moynihan Report, 106–8
and music, 26–29, 42–44, 128
"Newborn Thrown in Trash and Dies," 88–89, 115
at Oxford, 20, 24, 28, 48, 56, 154, 233
Philadelphia Fire, 170–81
"Presents," 43–44
Reuben, 82–83, 97–99, 138–43
"Rock River," 39–41, 228
Sent for You Yesterday, 125–32
"Sharing," 225
"Sightings," 228
"Signs," 89–91
"The Silence of Thelonious Monk," 226
and slave narratives, 22, 50–52
"Surfiction," 39–40
"The Tambourine Lady," 42–43
and *Tristram Shandy*, 17
Two Cities, 197–205
at University of Pennsylvania, 203
"Valaida," 42, 44–45, 168, 195
"Weight," 223–25, 231
"Welcome," 85, 86
"What We Cannot Speak about We Must Pass over in Silence," 226–27
"When It's Time to Go," 42–43
"Who Invented the Jump Shot?," 216, 226
"Who Weeps When One of Us Goes Down Blues?," 228
in Wyoming, 137

Wideman, Lizbeth (mother)
in "All Stories Are True," 83–85
as Bette Lawson in *A Glance Away*, 33, 60–63
in *Brothers and Keepers*, 132–38, 224
in *Damballah*, 115–19
in *Fanon*, 235–37
in *Hiding Place*, 117, 122
as Mrs. Wyman in *Fanon*, 235–37
in "Weight," 223–25, 235–37
Wideman, Omar (nephew), 197, 206, 211–12
Wideman, Robby (brother)
in "All Stories Are True," 83–85
in *Brothers and Keepers*, 81–82, 132–38, 147, 220–21
in *Damballah*, 110–12, 116, 122
as double, 81–82, 137
in *Fanon*, 231, 234–35
in *God's Gym*, 227, 236
in *Philadelphia Fire*, 177–78
Wideman children, 42, 91–92, 136, 172, 175, 208, 227
Wideman's doubles, 30
in *All Stories Are True*, 87, 91, 206
Cudjoe as, 92, 172–73
Doot, 30, 87, 101, 103, 173, 217
in *God's Gym*, 226–27
in *The Island*, 217–23
Reuben as, 141–42
Robby as, 81–82, 137
Robert as, 95, 200, 206
Thomas as, 30, 96, 229
Wilkerson, Thomas, 71–79, 193
Wilkes, Albert, 28, 81, 115, 125–32, 143, 193–94
Wolfe, George, 178, 218
Wretched of the Earth, The, 229
Wright, Richard, 23, 51, 54, 60, 76, 94
Wyoming, 48, 83, 133, 137

Xhosa, 153–55, 162–64, 167, 179, 187, 229

Yeats, William Butler, 100
Yellow Fever epidemic, 45–46, 147, 151, 155–70, 181, 191, 196

www.ingramcontent.com/pod-product-compliance
Lightning Source LLC
Chambersburg PA
CBHW030334240426
43661CB00052B/1630